In Other Words: Literature by Latinas of the United States

Edited by Roberta Fernández

with Foreword by Jean Franco

Arte Público Press
Houston, Texas
1994

This book is made possible through support from the National Endowment for the Arts (a federal agency), the Lila Wallace-Reader's Digest Fund and the Andrew W. Mellon Foundation.

Recovering the past, creating the future

Arte Público Press
University of Houston
Houston, Texas 77204-2090

Cover design by Mark Piñón
Original art by Leslie Nemour
"Vestir Santos" (Dressing Saints)
Mixed Media/Paper 50" x 38"

In other words : literature by Latinas of the United States / edited by Roberta Fernández
p. cm.
English and Spanish.
Includes bibliographical references.
ISBN 1-55885-110-0
1. American literature-Hispanic American authors. 2. Hispanic American literature (Spanish)—Women authors. 3. Hispanic American women—Literary collections. 4. Hispanic Americans—Literary collections. 5. American literature—Women authors. I. Fernández, Roberta.
PS508.H57I5 1994
810.8'0868—dc20 94-9206
CIP

The paper used in this publication meets the requirements of the American National Standard for Permanence of Paper for Printed Library Materials Z39.48-1984. ∞

Roberta Fernández

is also the author of

Intaglio: A Novel in Six Stories

To the Staff at Arte Público Press—

Hilda Hinojosa, *Office Manager*; Cynthia Juárez, *Marketing Coordinator*; Rebecca Evans Lane, *Senior Typesetter;* Rita Mills, *Managing Editor;* Marina Tristán, *Assistant Director*

Unselfishly committed

to the numerous details of the production process,
to the needs and demands of our writers,
to the promotion of our literature,
to the love of words.

To the Writers
In Celebration of Ourselves

Lucha: who's shared this cycle from the beginning
Lorna: who, when the tape recorder failed, poured another cup of coffee and repeated hours worth of dialogue
Teresa: whose mother's quilt protects against a winter's chill
Rhina: bitter coffee, musty beans, caramel and guava jam
Graciela: reclamando justicia continental
Marjorie: in solidarity!
Nina: who empowered us all
Nora: bridging the Américas (con acento)
Cherríe: courageous, unbending, non-negotiable
Gloria: whose letter we have all read and taken to heart
Pat: a curandera of the soul
Cecilia: a weaver of air, wind, earth and water
Ángela: who captures hands in concrete and hearts in space
Iraida: desde la primera conversación, cariñosa y generosa
Lourdes: who introduced me to a whole new set of writers
Verónica: responding to a lightening call, rejoining us all
Anita: such drama! such flair!
Gloria: who reminds us of what should have been ours
Vangie: who offers much needed advice
Carmen: por aquí, por abril, por fin! por fin!
Elena: in due time the pleasure shall be mine

Carolina: memorias de un futuro encuentro en la feria de Miami
Mary Helen: an earthling in my favorite city
María: the quintessential explorer
Naomi: who took the risk and discovered that there's life outside of California
Helena María: who's about to do the same
Margarita: who's learned the power of songs
Judith: dancing in silence, eloquently
Sandra María: who wears shells on her hair, raises eyebrows, believes in herself
Luz María: a warrior woman
Aurora: an icicle in the desert
Olga Elena: a song so high and clear
Leslie: re-arranging *milagros*, re-arranging cultures
Marie Elise: she who embodies cultures re-arranged
Bessy: tirelessly composing arte-factos
Alicia: reclaiming our mothers's tales in gothic form
Bernice: releasing serpents
Alma Luz: surely she never stops writing!
Nicholasa: a model of self-empowerment
Rosemary: our leading arts administrator
Beatriz: reclaiming her early promise
Dolores: ¡aha! también a través de la risa se llega a la verdad
Jean: who showed us how to question—mil gracias!
Estela: nuestra abrecaminos!
Natashia and Linda: abriendo caminos for a new generation

Contents

Foreword

Jean Franco

When I received *In Other Words: Literature by Latinas of the United States* in the mail, I had just finished writing a downbeat piece with a title, "What's left of literature?" It was inspired by the sad sight of LaGuardia airport bookstores where all the books have ugly embossed covers in gilt and red with bloody daggers and corpses, by the security guards in a bookstore on Broadway, and by an unexciting *New Yorker* special issue on literature. Could it be that literature and, especially, poetry was, as Octavio Paz stated in *The New York Times* recently, an art of the catacombs, a minority pursuit?

Reading *In Other Words* makes me realize how much is going on outside the mainline circuits of publishing and distribution. "Latino" literature and the "Latina" have, it is true, become marketable categories along with "Asian American literature" and "Afro American literature," and in some bookstores they are now found in a section labeled "multiculturalism," as if this were a gesture of benevolent pluralism that had given Latinas and others "permission to speak." Yet it is enough to read the brief biographies of many of these writers to realize how difficult and even (in some cases) impossible has been this entry into the mainstream. Reading the resumes, I was struck by the vitality and ingenuity of small presses and regional poetry magazines, by the fact that Lorna Dee Cervantes "learned the craft of printing in order to publish the work of other Chicano poets," that Rosemary Catacalos is author of a "hand letter press chapbook," that so much poetry is still read aloud in public performances. I learned of poetry magazines and literary reviews named *Huehuetitlán, Caminos Magazine, Caracol, Red Dirt, Blue Mesa Review,* and *Poetry Conspiracy*. Many of the writers, it is true, have gone on to publish in major poetry and literary magazines, to win prizes and awards, and have seen their work translated into other languages. Yet as Cherríe Moraga writes in the essay in this anthology, "Art in América con Acento," Latina writers have to be especially attuned to the danger of "looking solely to the Northeast for recognition." "I fear," she writes, "that we will find ourselves writing more and more in translation through the filter of Anglo-American censors." Fear of being mainstreamed is, however, relatively new for minority writers. In the early seventies, Arturo Islas was having a hard time finding a publisher for the first volume of his Texas trilogy, and with rare exception all Latino literature was published by small presses. Nowadays, not only are Latinos and Latinas sought out by mainstream publishers, but ventures such as Arte Público Press and the "Recovering the U.S. Hispanic Literary Heritage" project offer alternatives to trade publishing and the dominant literary canon.

What impresses me about *In Other Words*, however, is the extraordinary variety of cultural experiences and backgrounds from which these women write. We learn that Marie Elise Wheatwind is half Chicana, one-quarter Swedish and one-quarter Russian Jew; that Sandra María Esteves is a Puerto Rican-Dominican Latina; that Olga Elena Mattei was born in Puerto Rico of a Colombian mother and Puerto Rican father; that there are Chilean Latinas, Mexican Latinas, Latinas born in Texas and California; and that there are Jewish Latinas, Dominicans, Puerto Ricans, and Cubans born in the islands or here in the U.S.A. This implies a vast and heterogeneous cultural repertoire, a variety of heritages reflected in this anthology.

In the essay on "The New Mestiza" from her book *Borderlands/ La Frontera*, Gloria Anzaldúa privileges the consciousness that comes from such mixing. "The new mestiza copes by developing a tolerance for contradictions, a tolerance for ambiguity. She learns to be an Indian in Mexican culture, to be Mexican from an Anglo point of view. She learns to juggle cultures. She has a plural personality, she operates in a pluralistic mode—nothing is thrust out, the good the bad and the ugly, nothing rejected, nothing abandoned. Not only does she sustain contradictions, she turns the ambivalence into something else." What Anzaldúa seems to describe is not the *aufhebung* of the Hegelian dialectic in which contradictions are resolved at a more abstract level, but rather a lateral movement into another space which Anzaldúa will call a third space or "Aztlán," and which Ana Castillo will call Sapogonia. Sylvia Molloy, writing of Latin American women writers, calls it a *dislocation in order to be*. "One is (and one writes) elsewhere, in a *different* place, a place where the female subject chooses to relocate in order to represent itself anew."[1] For Anzaldúa, the border crossing, whether real or imagined, produces in the very violence of the process a mestiza consciousness; she describes "la frontera" as an "open wound" and turns to ancestral

[1]Sara Castro-Klaren, Sylvia Molloy, Beatriz Sarlo, *Women's Writing in Latin America*, Westview Press, 1991, p. 107.

shamanism for its healing. The mestiza is the point of intersection between *lo heredado, lo adquirido, lo impuesto*, in other words, between nature, nurture, and education, between what divides and what unites. Analdúa cannot embrace a tradition that includes machismo and homophobia any more than she can cross happily into a culture where class and racial discrimination are so perversely mingled.

Anzaldúa's visionary writing contrasts with the sober political assessment of Cherríe Moraga who collaborated with Anzaldúa on the pathbreaking anthology, *A Bridge Called My Back*, which first brought together the writings of women of color and challenged the masculine hijacking of definitions of Chicano identity. Moraga is aware of the historical mutations that have profoundly altered minority culture and politics. Immigrants now come from all parts of Latin America and the Caribbean, not to mention Asia and the Phillipines. "What was once largely a Chicano/Mexicano population in California is now *guatemalteco, salvadoreño, nicaragüense*. What was largely a Puerto Rican and Dominican "Spanish Harlem" of New York is now populated with *mexicanos* playing *rancheras* and drinking *cerveza*." (And, one might add, by *brasileños* and Colombians and Central Americans). Moraga underscores the fact that "Latinos in the United States do not represent a homogeneous group. Some of us are native born, whose ancestors precede not only the arrival of the Anglo American but also of the Spaniard. Most of us are immigrants, economic refugees coming to the United States in search of work. Some of us are political refugees, fleeing death squads and imprisonment; others come fleeing revolution and loss of wealth. (...) U.S. Latinos represent the whole spectrum of color and class and political position, including those who firmly believe they can integrate into the mainstream of North American life."

The television channel Univision has its own definition of Latino identity, one that Celia Cruz endorses in her popular song, "Pasaporte latinoamericano," in which she urges her audience to make it in U.S. society without losing their "Latinidad." "Si no lo hacemos nosotros, ¿quién va a ayudarnos?" she asks. Latina writers, on the other hand are very much aware that border crossing needs more than goodwill and a song in the heart. Instead of the abstract community of "Latinidad," Cherríe Moraga emphasizes the need for a political community in order to transform "these Americas," and resist dissolution and fragmentation. "The *reto* (challenge)," she writes, "is to remain as culturally specific and as culturally complex as possible, even in the face of mainstream seduction to do otherwise."

The "we" of the Latina encompasses a great deal, therefore, but most of all it implies the privilege and the problems of being bi- and sometimes tricultural. For the passage from one place and its culture to another between conflicting ways of life and languages is always violent, like the in-between passageways of sewers, the barbed wire fence, or the Caribbean raft. Even for the Latina who is born in the United States, there is an ancestral memory of violence and loss, though the details may be different in each version. The immigrant Mexican farmworker's family, the Puerto Rican crossing the Caribbean in the airbus, the Cuban whose family left after the Revolution, the girl from Puerto Rico going to do domestic service in New York, the Tarahumara Indian living in a Catholic village all know the meaning of loss and the difficulty of having to refashion themselves in a strange place. Memory, family, longing for an ancestral homeland, therefore, recur in Latina writing. "How do I tell my children: forgetting is worse than pain," writes Pat Mora, "forgetting stories old as the moon." Rhina Espaillat, who describes herself as "one more exile with very little money and lots of old photographs," describes memory as a "filament / weaving, weaving what I am / bitter coffee, musty beans, / caramel and guava jam." The sense of loss is often activated by fleeing memories of scents, smells of objects, or landscapes, but that loss goes deeper than the merely individual.

There is another side to this story of border-crossing, in-betweenness, and the anguish of memory. Not all Latinas are immigrants. Gloria Anzaldúa reminds us that there is a past before conquest and a knowledge that is different from post-Enlightenment rationality. Not all Latinas feel themselves to be newcomers in a strange land. Pat Mora for example claims the Texas desert as her mother:

> I say comfort me.
> She invites me to lay on her firm body.
>
> I say heal me.
> She gives me *manzanillo, orégano, dormilón.*

For Lorna Dee Cervantes, California has been stolen from its native inhabitants. The sense of its loss produces the powerful cosmic sweep of "Pleiades from the Cables of Genocide" in which the poet recreates the ancestral memory of a race descended from the Seven Sisters, the Pleiades, which are at once remote, "radiant in your black light / Height, humming as you are in my memory," and at the same time, dimmed and impoverished in their earthly descendants dressed in the ragged clothes of the dispossessed. The journey of recovery takes the woman wanderer "through the Reagan Ranch her mothers owned."

She is singing
The stories of Calafia ways and means, of the nacre
Of extinct oysters and the abalone I engrave
With her leftover files. She knows the words
To the song now, what her grandmother sang
Of how they lit to this earth from the fire
Of fusion, on the touchstones of love tribes.

In quite a different version of this recovery of ancestral memory, Helena María Viramonte's story, "The Moths," evokes a womantime that precedes clocktime, worktime and church time. In the striking conclusion of the story, the young narrator nurses and bathes her dying grandmother as if she were a child. There is anguish of wanting "to return to the waters of the womb with her so that we would never be alone again," but also the knowledge that has been passed on from one generation to another, not through words but through touch.

Often in these stories and poems, it is through the maternal line that these women encounter not only the lost place but the lost past. The women ancestors are the conduit of what would otherwise be lost, even though the transition from orality to writing may be a slippery one as Roberta Fernández shows in her story, "Zulema."

The focus on family and growing up in these stories and poems is not accidental, since it is the family which often intensifies the conflict between the old and the new, tradition and modernity, rituals and school or university. Family is often a trope for community, encompassing aunts, uncles, grandparents and neighbors. It is the place where the wounds of immigration are suffered and sometimes healed. The Freudian narrative limits family to "mummy, daddy and me." In this account, becoming a women is fraught with difficulty, but the difficulty has to do with individuation rather than community. But when that rite of passage from childhood to womenhood coincides with emigration and exile, "becoming a women" can turn into tragedy. In Nicholasa Mohr's story, "Happy Birthday," a woman dying alone of tuberculosis in a hospital on Welfare Island recalls the Puerto Rican river of her childhood and the dazzling sight of translucent fish and tadpoles caught in the rays of the sun. "She had loved that part of the river. It had all been magical and wonderful, and belonged to her, until the day she began to bleed in the water." The joy and innocence of childhood are dissipated at that moment; womanhood is emigration, domestic labor and prostitution. The irony is that only at the moment of dying does Lucía recover her sense of joy as she steps once again into the river. "Slowly, and without any resistance, Lucía let the current take her downstream and she drifted with the river into a journey of quiet bliss. "Women's impossible desire for the healing of the wound seems only to be satisfied by death. There is a similar link between water and death in several of the stories and poems—in Helena María Viramontes' "The Moths," in Estela Portillo Trambley's "The Burning" in which a curandera persecuted for witchcraft has a final vision of her little gods "racing to the waterfall." On the other hand, in Alicia Gaspar de Alba's striking story, "Cimarrona," the runaway slave leaps into the sea searching for freedom only to struggle against this loss of the self.

Finding no place in official history, the Latina looks to oral tradition and legend, to La Llorona, the Indian woman who perpetually laments for her drowned children; to Marina (or La Malinche), the Indian mistress of Cortés who in Mexican official history is a traitor to the Indian race. What was for Octavio Paz the tragedy of "the sons of La Malinche" acquires a quite different significance in the literature of the Chicanas. Cherríe Moraga acknowledged, in one of her essays, her descent "from a long line of traitresses (vendidas)," thus liberating herself from misguided quests for origins and purity. For Lucha Corpi, Marina is not only the raped and abandoned mistress of the conqueror but the necessary conduit to a new future, a figure both of conquest and rebirth—"mourning shadow of an ancestral memory, / crossing the bridge at daybreak, her hands full of earth and sun."

In the constant quest for meaning and identity, the Latina draws on a wide repertoire, experimenting with language, with bilingual poetry, writing in Spanish and English, mixing poetry with prose, crossing gender and genre boundaries, but also at times reviving older forms. The anthology includes two very striking poems written in the traditional ballad or *romance* form—Lucha Corpi's "Dark Romance" with its echoes of García Lorca's gypsy ballads, and Rhina Espaillat's "The Ballad of San Isidro." Both ballad poems describe rapes; the impersonal voice of the ballad allows for understatement that is far more effective than the scream. And this understatement is an indirect comment on the heroic tradition of the *corrido* with its celebration of the outlaw and the revolutionary.

Latinas are sensitive not only to the violence of hero myths but also of the violence in Guatemala or El Salvador and other parts of the world. Being writers, however, they are above all sensitive to the violence of a language that is used to subjugate, terrorize, divide and conquer. Carmen Tafolla defies the thought police who command, "Write in one language," by mixing everything. "Por aquí, poquito and a dash all también / salsa-chacha-disco-polka / Rock that Texas cumbia / in a molcajete mezcla."

Like other groups claiming visibility in the public sphere, the Latina is concerned with problems of self-representation, and hence with the claims, often conflicting, of self and community. There is no easy resolution, for the name of the game is often sheer survival. In Sandra María Esteves's, "Autobiography of a Nuyorican," a baby is born even though "the world did not want another brown, / another slant-eyed-olive-indian-black-child." But, she is born nonetheless, "gathering weapons into her being with each breath that filled her, / growing stronger, / determined / to beat all the odds."

Jean Franco
Columbia University

Preface

Roberta Fernández

A literary "boom" among Latino writers of the United States has been gathering momentum since the mid-1960s. Accompanying this outpouring of poetry, theater, fiction and the essay has been an equally important phenomenon—the creation of an audience for our literature—as writers, critics, publishers and arts administrators sponsor numerous activities to make this literature more accessible to an ever expanding audience. Across the entire country, a vast network exists among writers who read, critique and disseminate each others' work. Yet, for the most part, the greater reading public has been unaware of this literary undercurrent. *In Other Words* seeks to ameliorate this situation.

In Other Words is aimed at both the general reader and the university student audience. It is the first anthology to bring together a broad spectrum of works by Latinas presently writing within the United States. Included herein is the work of not only the three major groups of Latina writers—Mexican-Americans or Chicanas, Puerto Ricans, and Cuban-Americans—but also the literature of writers of Argentinian, Chilean, Columbian, Dominican and Sephardic ancestry, all of whom are presently contributing to the ever-growing corpus identifiable as Latina/o literature of the United States.

In Other Words is inclusive rather than exclusive; it seeks to acknowledge the differences among and within the various national groups *and* to embrace the totality of who we are, the fastest growing ethnic group in the United States. The reader will thus find works that represent different perspectives on issues pertaining to race, ethnicity, class and gender.

As Latina writers we look to our sources on a hemispheric scale. Thus, our inspiration may come from various traditions:

1) the regional cultures of the United States;
2) the ancient *and* contemporary Amerindian cultures;
3) the Hispano-Arabic and Judeo-Western traditions;
4) the Afro-Hispanic and Afro-American traditions;

5) the multicultural discourse that has developed in the last two decades in this country;
6) the thematics of immigrant literature which emphasize the search for individual and group identity, the challenges of living in two or more cultures, and the recognition of our ability to self-express in two or more languages;
7) the contemporary post-colonial perspectives of emerging nations;
8) the ever-evolving feminist agendas to which we have added our own perspective—-that of indigenous feminism, a feminism that arises out of our particular social realities;

As Latina writers we may be influenced *both* by the thematics of marginalization in the fiction of the Mexican short-story writers and novelists Juan Rulfo and Elena Poniatowska *and* by the "womanist" discourse of the Afro-American writer Alice Walker. We are as likely to admire the magical realism of the Columbian novelist and short-story writer Gabriel García Márquez as the poetic innovations of Jewish-Americans Philip Levine and Adrienne Rich. For some of us, our subject matter might be related to the telluric themes of the (South) American continent found in the works of such writers as Chilean poet Pablo Neruda; others might find their inspiration in the thematics on gender expounded by the Black writer Barbara Smith or the late Audre Lorde. Some of us might look to the cosmopolitanism of the late Argentinian novelist Julio Cortázar, while others bring to their fiction the politics of liberation exemplified by the Mayan leader Rigoberta Menchú of Guatemala, the Chicano labor organizer César Chávez and the mothers of the Plaza de Mayo in Buenos Aires.

The language we use to create our literature may also differ. Some of us are comfortable writing either in English or in Spanish, some of us write in English only, others write mostly in Spanish. Some combine the two languages. Others add a smattering of the Amerindian Nahuatl, Mayan or Quechua, perhaps even some Yiddish, French or Greek. Black English and the cadences of the Caribbean are particularly represented in our work. We see ourselves as bilingual, even multilingual. We write—following the advice of Gloria Anzaldúa—about our particulars, about our regions, our barrios, our homes in order to add our experiences to the universal experiences. We add our voice(s) to the common chorus of humankind.

Above all, we have been influenced by each other. We read and critique each others' works, and exchange notes on our emerging or developed discourses: the politics of the family, the influence of ancestors, the ancient and the new myths, the politics of liberation in the Americas, the evolving thematics centered on community—be it the community of the barrio, of women's culture(s), of the community as oppression, of the community as liberation, of the community as *we* would want it to be.

We identify with the words of Lorna Dee Cervantes when she speaks of her identity as a poet:

> I am a poet who longs to dance on rooftops,
> to whisper delicate lines about joy
> and the blessings of human understanding.

And we understand her as she acknowledges that desire and possibility are not necessarily the same:

> Every day I am deluged with reminders
> that this is not
> my land and this is my land.
> I do not believe in the war between races
> but in this country
> there is war.

We struggle, therefore, against *racism*. In the greater culture as well as in our Latino culture. Cervantes also reminds us, succinctly:

> Racism is not intellectual.
> I can not reason these scars away.

We struggle against *classism*. In this country, as a people we are of the working class. As Latinas, our cultures of origin inculcated in us an acceptance of class differences which we now attempt to eradicate from ourselves. We imagine a different community. For ourselves and for everyone else.

We struggle against *sexism*. Sexism is perhaps our greatest monster, for it reigns everywhere, even at home. In her short story, "Growing," Helena María Viramontes aptly describes the effect that domestic sexism has on a girl child: "It was Apá who refused to trust her and she could not understand what she had done to make him so distrustful. TU ERES MUJER, he thundered like a great voice above the heavens, and that was the end of any argument, any question, because he said those words not as a truth, but as a verdict, and she could almost see the clouds parting, the thunderbolts breaking the tranquility of her sex." The conflict presented here occurs not because father/daughter are Latinos but rather because of male/female and age inequalities found in traditional family structures. Viramontes presents a specific case in a universal experience.

We struggle against *homophobia*, against *ageism*, against *consumerism* and *materialism*. Against *war*. Against *disease*. Against the *cultural imperialism* which our country exports to other countries. Against the cultural imperialism that reigns supreme within this country that privileges the culture of the Northeast, and even then privileges only certain aspects of a narrowly recognized elite. We struggle against our own internalizing of these values, so that we ourselves do not begin to believe that we must accept that same value system which recognizes only the literature published by the presses of cultural hegemony.

We struggle to believe in ourselves. To reinvent ourselves. To continue to write about the subjects that are important to us as individuals and as a people. To write in our languages. In our own words. En nuestras propias palabras. In other words.

Roberta Fernández
University of Houston

Introduction
A Mosaic of Latino Literature of the United States

Roberta Fernández

To be a contemporary Latina writer of the United States implies resistance to cultural hegemony. While it is true that the European roots of contemporary Latino literature date back to the sixteenth-century Spanish colony in what today comprises the American Southwest, Florida and California—and the Native American roots date even further back—the flowering of contemporary Latino literature is intertwined with the political repercussions of the civil rights movements of the 1960s and early 1970s. This literature has evolved out of the particular historical situations of an oppressed minority whose writers perceive themselves as socially committed to the elimination of the colonial status of their people. Thus, the content of Latino literature is closely identified with a discourse of contestation and self-definition. In addition, women writers also challenge the patriarchal traditions of their own culture and, thereby, create an even more complex literature of multiple dimensions. Crossing boundaries has become the dominant metaphor for both the content and the style of contemporary Latino literature, with its emphasis on individual and group identity.

By no means is this literature homogeneous. The Chicana writer from Los Angeles, the Puerto Rican essayist from Oakland, the Cuban-American playwright from New York, the Mexican-American short story writer from Texas, the Chilean-American poet from Boston, the Cuban-American novelist from Southern California and the Chicana-Greek poet from San Antonio all add their individual contributions to the growing body of literature identifiable as Latino literature of the United States, a literature with a long, albeit little known tradition, with roots in the Hispanic Southwest and even in the literary traditions of the countries of origin of many of these writers.

Beginning in the early nineteenth century, Spanish-language print media became an important means of creating community identity both in the Southwest and Northeast. The literary pages of the newspapers of

Santa Fe, Los Angeles, San Francisco, San Antonio, New York and Philadelphia became outlets for the dissemination of literature by Spanish, Mexican and Latin American writers at the same time that they offered local writers, particularly poets, the opportunity to get into print. In the early twentieth century, serialized novels were popular among the growing Latino population; the first and best-known novel of the Mexican Revolution, *Los de abajo,* appeared in 1915 in serialized form in the newspaper *El Paso del Norte* in El Paso prior to its being published in Mexico.

However, since most of this literature was written in Spanish at a time when the cultural expressions of the Latino people in the United States were not perceived as a vital component of the American experience, these literary creations have remained, for the most part, unknown. The task of the Rockefeller-sponsored "Recovering the U.S. Hispanic Literary Heritage Project," based at the University of Houston, is the recovery of works of literary value that have been forgotten in the archives of Latino communities throughout the United States. In the future, this research by scholars, who teach in universities throughout the United States, will challenge the canon of the literatures of the Americas. As a result of the recovery of manuscripts, books and periodicals of Latino writers of the United States and the subsequent publication of these works, it is expected that definitions of both American literature and Latin American literature will be broadened to include the work of Latino writers of the United States, written both in English and Spanish.

In the last few years, prestigious literary prizes have been awarded to the work of Latino writers: the American Book Award, the National Book Award, the Casa de las Américas Prize, the Pulitzer Prize. How their literature came to be recognized and honored is a parallel story; in addition to the writing and publishing of these works, a great effort has been made to create an audience for this literature.

Numerious reviews/*revistas* have been created, readings have been organized, book fairs and festivals have taken place, writers' workshops have been held and literary contests have been sponsored—all activities that have brought attention to new writers. Publishing houses such as Arte Público Press, the Bilingual Review Press, Third Woman Press, Pajarito Publications, Casa Editorial, Fuego de Aztlán, Linden Lane Press, White Pine Press and Broken Moon Press have all served to introduce important writers to the public. Some of these writers have gone on to be published by mainstream and university presses; others have opted to remain with the Latino presses in order to continue the movement in support of Latino literary self-determination. With so much activity supporting such an array of creative effort, it is no wonder that the Latino literary movement is projected to produce the most vital and innovative literature of the United States in the twenty-first century. While its contemporary beginnings are grounded in the Chicano movement of the 1960s and early 1970s, regional literary developments among the various Latino national groups in different parts of the country show parallel yet distinct characteristics.

Literature of the Chicano Movement

In 1965 in Delano, California, César Chávez organized a strike among the farmworkers, thus beginning what came to be known as the Chicano Movement for civil rights. That same year, as a means of raising awareness for the strike among the farmworkers, Luis Valdez founded the Teatro Campesino. Out of these two social and cultural events grew the literary movement that identified itself with the "movimiento" and served as an instrument of social struggle. In many ways, this was an *indigenista* movement that bore the characteristics of other *indigenista* movements in Latin America: it was led by *mestizos* who created a mythology around the grandeur of the Indian past as a means of claiming for themselves a place in contemporary society. The writers of the "Movimiento" issued proclamations about Aztlán, the place of origin of the Aztecs, which came to signify the Chicano homeland or the Southwest. The "Plan Espiritual de Aztlán" espoused the concept of "brotherhood" or *carnalismo*, a spirit which characterized the literature of the "Movimiento" with its heavy emphasis on male heroes as portrayed in the best known poem of the period, "I Am Joaquín." Two other important inspirations for the literature of the Chicano movement were the barrio and its hero, the Pachuco. A number of critics of this period created the canon of Chicano literature and only the works that bore the above-named characteristics came to be accepted as authentic Chicano literature. Presently, a younger generation of critics and activists have tended to deconstruct the tenets of "movement literature" in order to open up a space for their own creative efforts.

The San Francisco Bay Area Boom

In the late 1950s, Allen Ginsberg and the Beat poets introduced the drama of performance art into poetry readings in San Francisco. By the early 1970s, literary readings had achieved a highly creative level, unique to the area. Weekly announcements in *Poetry Flash* testify to the numerous readings that occur in the Bay Area every single day of the year. To this flourishing public literary activity, Latino writers have added their own rhythm and energy.

Unique also to San Francisco has been the solidarity among writers of color, one of the inherent characteristics of Third World literature of the United States. Cecil Williams's Glide Memorial Church and the Mission Cultural Center were only two of the numerous locales where Asian American, Black, Chicano/Latino and Native American writers performed together in literary readings. Through these readings an audience for their work emerged even before the works appeared in print. It was not unusual for requests for specific poems to be called out from the audience as writers began their readings. For the writers, a composite energy built up from the interaction with the audience and with each other, which in turn nurtured their imagination and their pen.

Collectivity, then, was an important characteristic of the Third World literary movement, and Latino writers, with roots in numerous Latin American countries, contributed greatly to the San Francisco Third World literary scene. The Pocho Che collective, a loose coalition of writers, began in the East Bay in the late 1960s as an off-shoot of the Third World student movement at UC, Berkeley. Led by Roberto Vargas from Nicaragua, Nina Serrano, of Colombian heritage, Alfonso Maciel from Peru and Alejandro Murguía, originally from Mexico, the Pocho Che collective published some of the first books of the contemporary Latino literary renaissance. By the early 1970s, the group joined efforts with other writers of color in San Francisco, such as Janice Mirikitani, Jessica Tarahata Hagedorn and Ntozake Shangé to form the Third World Collective which published *Third World Women* (1972),the first anthology of literature written by women of color in the United States. The Latino writers began publication of their own review *Tin Tán*. By the mid-1970s the group had established the Mission Cultural Center, which branched out into promoting all of the various aspects of the Latino arts: the visual arts, the movement arts, theater and literature.

The San Francisco East Bay and Central California

In Berkeley, Octavio Romano's Tonatiuh-Quinto Sol Publications published *El espejo* in 1967, the first anthology of modern Chicano literature. In 1970, Tonatiuh-Quinto Sol Publications began to sponsor an annual contest for the best collection of fiction, resulting in the publication of several works that are now considered classics of Chicano literature. Among them were *...y no se lo tragó la tierra/...and the earth did not part* by Tomás Rivera and *Bless Me, Ultima* by Rudolfo Anaya, winners of the 1970 and 1971 contests respectively. Two other presses were also established: Herminio Ríos's Justa Publications in Hayward and a press associated with the Chicano Studies Program at the University of California, Berkeley—Fuego de Aztlán Publications, spearheaded by the late Oscar Treviño. In San Jose, Lorna Dee Cervantes published poetry chapbooks through Mango Publications, a kitchen-table press. By the early 1980s all of these early Chicano presses had ceased their activity but other presses in other parts of the country had emerged: Arte Público Press headed by Nicolás Kanellos in Houston and Bilingual Review/Revista Bilingual Publications headed by Gary Keller and now housed at Arizona State University in Tempe.

Between 1979 and 1982, at Mills College in Oakland, Roberta Fernández coordinated *Prisma: A Multicultural, Multilingual Women's Literary Review*; and in the early 1980s, at Indiana University, Norma Alarcón founded *Third Woman*, a review also dedicated to works by women. Third Woman Publications is now housed at the University of California, Berkeley.

Margaret Shedd, director of the Centro Mexicano de Escritores in Mexico City between 1950 and 1968, helped to establish Aztlán Cultural in Berkeley in the early 1970s along with Lucha Corpi, Roberta Fernández, Eduardo Hernández and Guillermo Hernández. Aztlán Cultural promoted all of the Chicano arts. With several grants from the California Arts Council and other sources, the organization sponsored literary festivals and conferences, initiated a Bilingual Arts Program in the Oakland Schools and sponsored a photography exhibit, curated by Carolina Juárez, which traveled to Erlangen, Germany. In the early 1980s, Aztlán Cultural combined efforts with Juan Felipe Herrera and Francisco Alarcón of Poetaumanos to form Centro Chicano de Escritores. With funding from the National Endowment for the Arts, the Centro organized literary workshops and readings in Oakland as well as in mid-sized Chicano communities throughout California. Other writers, such as Ana Castillo, Barbara Brinson Curiel, Juan Pablo Gutiérrez and Cherríe Moraga, formed part of the group associated with the Centro Chicano de Escritores. Today, the Centro Chicano de Escritores continues to organize occasional programs.

Two of the progenitors of Chicano theater, which mushroomed all over the country in the early 1970s, continue their activities: Luis Valdez's Teatro Campesino, based in San Juan Bautista, and the Teatro de la Esperanza, founded in Santa Barbara by Jorge Huerta and later directed by Rodrigo Duarte. Teatro Campesino events are social as well as artistic phenomena. Its celebration of *Día de los Muertos* (November 2) packs the little mission town with visitors from all over California who come to participate in a procession through the cemetery and to enjoy the traditional theatrical production of "El fin del mundo." The annual "La Pastorela," held in the mission church attracts an even larger crowd over several week-ends. In Santa Barbara, the Teatro de la Esperanza collaborated with Francisco González and Yolanda Broyles González's Christmas pageant, "La aparición de la Virgen del Tepeyac," which in 1985 initiated the newly renovated Presidio Chapel. Since then, the Teatro de la Esperanza has moved to San Francisco, but the Santa Barbara plays have become an annual event. Mobility continues to characterize the actions of Latino artists in California as they travel up and down the state in mutually beneficial interaction.

Southern California Writers

Today, the number of people of Mexican descent in Los Angeles is greater than the population of Guadalajara, the second largest city in Mexico. With its ever-increasing numbers of Latinos from every country in Central and South America, the City of Angels ranks as one of the great urban centers of the Americas, and is home to many of the best writers of Latino heritage in the United States. La Plaza de la Raza and the Instituto Cultural Mexicano in Los Angeles and the Centro Cultural Chicano of San Diego are cultural centers of great vitality in Southern California. The Chicano Studies Centers at the University of California in Los Angeles, Irvine, Riverside and San Diego have nurtured and published Latino writers. UC, Irvine, in particular, through its literary contest, now in its nineteenth year, has encouraged Latino literary creativity.

In the late 1960s, a group of writers in San Diego flourished around the poet Alurista, who is credited with the re-creation of the modern-day myth of Aztlán. Alurista's *indigenista* writers produced the literary review *Maize* which promoted the values then perceived as inherent to Chicano literature: bilingualism, homages to the barrio and to *carnalismo* (brotherhood), and a committment to bettering the social conditions of *la gente* (the people).

Other literary activities in Southern California revolved around the Chicana activist and scholar Rosaura Sánchez and her circle which published the work of women writers in *Requisa treinta y dos*. Graduate students of the Spanish Dept at UC, Irvine, initiated the review *Melquiades*, and in Los Angeles, *ChismeArte* y served as an important publishing outlet for local writers. Luis Valdez's "Zoot Suit" had its debut at the Mark Taper Forum in 1978 and, until recently, other Latino plays had their first runs at the Los Angeles Theater Center. Many Latino writers have participated in the reading series offered by Beyond Baroque in Venice. Throughout Southern California numerous Latino literary activities take place on a continuous basis.

Literary Activities in the Hispanic Southwest

The centuries-old cultures of Native American peoples have produced the oldest living examples of creative expressions in the Americas. Hispanic culture in New Mexico, dating back to the late sixteenth century, is the next oldest continuous culture in the United States. Santa Fe, one of the administrative centers of the extensive Spanish colonies in the New World, developed its own unique culture and literature, as can be seen in such works as Gaspar Pérez de Villagra's *Historia de la Nueva México* (1610), the colonial plays *Los Comanches* (1777?) and *Los Tejanos* (1850?) and numerous *pastorelas* (shepherd plays.) Oral traditions and Spanish-language newspapers such as *El Crepúsculo de la Libertad*, dating back to 1834, have served as vehicles of cultural transmission in the area.

With the Treaty of Guadalupe Hidalgo of 1848, New Mexicans, like other Spanish-speaking people who were annexed as part of the former Mexican territory, became the colonized subjects of the United States. As such, in the latter part of the nineteenth century and the early part of the twentieth century, they underwent the indignities that are common experiences to colonized people, for in order to complete the mandates of Manifest Destiny, Anglo-American society propagated a vision of New Mexicans as barbarian, lazy, dark-skinned people whose culture had to be substituted by the hard-working, visonary newcomers before the territory could achieve a level worthy of statehood. [See Cecil Robinson's *With the Ears of Strangers* for a description of the image of the Mexican in American literature. See also David J. Weber's *Foreigners in Their Native Land*.] Thus, ironically, in 1912 the territory with the oldest living cultures in the United States became the last state within the mainland to enter the union.

The literature of New Mexico bears witness to the anguish of a people who were cognizant of the disappearance of an ancestral way of life. As such, New Mexican writers of the late nineteenth century and the early twentieth century tended to take a defensive stance in their work; they wrote typically romantic *costumbrista* literature (literature of customs) as a way of documenting a life-style that they knew would be disappearing soon. Even though they defended the use of Spanish and the continuation of their life-style, writers such as Fabiola Cabeza de Baca, Nina Otero Warren and Cleofas Jaramillo became problematic later for the critics associated with the Chicano movement who viewed their work primarily as a defense of upper-class values.

Having grown up in a society where a large percentage of the population is of Mexican descent, contemporary New Mexican writers have a unique perspective in their work. Their constant contact with Native American cultures has given them a great respect for the land; thus, a mytho-poetics stemming from this concern for the land can be seen in the work of the poet Jimmy Santiago Baca and in Rudolfo Anaya's *Bless Me, Ultima*, to date the most widely read novel written by a Latino in the United States. Ana Castillo in *So Far from God* has attempted to re-create this same *ambiente*.

Legacies and the Tejano Writer

Texas has produced more Chicano writers than any other state in the country. Even when the writers live away from their native land, the subject of their work tends to be linked to the centuries-old heritage of *mexicano* culture in Texas, particularly to that of South Texas. The United States-Mexican border is longer in Texas than in any other state, and as a general rule, Tejanos are close to their Mexican roots. Their communities have a higher percentage of *mexicanos* than those of other states, and a unique Tejano culture has evolved in many cultural spheres: in music, in literature, in the visual and culinary arts.

As a whole, Tejano writers are closely identified with the area of the state in which they spent their youth. Thus, many writers are closely linked to particular communities, even though they may no longer reside there:

El Paso: Aristeo Brito, José Antonio Burciaga, Carlos Nicolás Flores, Ray González, the late Arturo Islas, Pat Mora, Estela Portillo Trambley, John Rechy, Ricardo Sánchez

The Río Grande Valley: Gloria Anzaldúa, Irene Beltrán Hernández, Lionel García, Genaro González, Rolando Hinojosa, Américo Paredes

Laredo: Norma Cantú, Roberta Fernández, Cecilio González Camarillo, Ellie Hernández

San Antonio: Ángela de Hoyos, Max Martínez, the late Tomás Rivera, Carmen Tafolla, Evangelina Vigil-Piñón, Xelina, and more recently, Sandra Cisneros

Austin area: Juan Rodríguez, Raul Salinas, Tino Villanueva

Houston: Inés Hernández Avila, Emma Pérez

Due to the important role that Arte Público Press of the University of Houston, headed by Nicolás Kanellos, plays in the national and international literary world, Houston draws many Latino writers to readings, book fairs and conferences, and a good number of writers now call Houston home, including the Spanish poet Revueltas Gutiérrez, the Costa Rican novelist Rima Vallbona as well as Lionel García, Evangelina Vigil and Roberta Fernández, and in the near future, the Chicana poet Lorna Dee Cervantes. *The Americas Review*, formerly *Revista Chicano Riqueña*, published through Arte Público Press and edited by Julián Olivares, celebrated its twentieth anniversary in 1992 and now has the longest life of any literary review devoted to US Latino literature.

Other important reviews that have played an important role in disseminating works by Tejano writers are *Caracol*, *Mictlán*, *Revista Río Bravo*, *Tejidos*, *Tonantzín*, and more recently, *The Guadalupe Review*. The literary contest at the University of Texas, El Paso, has supported the work of writers from both sides of the border. And the Annual Book Fair sponsored by the Guadalupe Center in San Antonio has become one of the most important book fairs in the country.

East Coast Writers

The East Coast literary establishment of the United States has long considered recognition by the New York publishing world to be the maximum honor a writer can receive. Latino writers who view themselves and their work as contestory challenge this type of cultural hegemony, and produce literature, which in the view of novelist Isabel Allende, is the most exciting work being produced in the United States at the moment, precisely because these writers are opening new paths, stylistically and in content, within the international literary scene.

Puerto Ricans, the largest Latino group in the northeastern coast of the United States, tend to be committed to the elimination of their colonial status both in the mainland and in the island. Their perspective is ironic, their linguistic expression is bilingual in English and Spanish, and their content at times is linked to the themes of immigrant literature, that is, to the question of finding one's identity in a new homeland.

The first contemporary work of a mainland Puerto Ricans to receive acclaim was Piri Thomas's *Down These Mean Streets* (1967), with its close links to the urban crisis of Black youth as exemplied in Claude Brown's best-selling *Manchild in the Promised Land.* The New York publishing world thought it had found its female counterpart in Nicholasa Mohr, who instead opened up new paths for Latina writers by insisting on representing the sensibilities of adolescent women in the barrio. Her book, *Nilda*, became a best-seller on its own terms.

Latino writers from other national groups are quite active in the East Coast; many of them are actively engaged with the Institute of Latin American Writers. Some of the best known are Marjorie Agosín (Chilean-American), Julia Alvarez (Dominican-American), Elena Castedo (Chilean-American), Oscar Hijuelos (Cuban-American) and the recently published Cuban-American writer Cristina García whose 1992 novel, *Dreaming in Cuban*, was a finalist for the National Book Award.

The literature of Latino writers in the East Coast is supported by the Nuyorican Poets Cafe in the Lower East Side with its numerous literary readings. The New York Latino artistic community is linked through the newsletter of *AHA*!—The Association of Hispanic Arts. The review *Brújula/Compass* includes interviews with Latino writers as well as their work. Kitchen Table Women of Color Press in Albany publishes work by women from different parts of the country, and the many campuses of the East Coast sponsor numerous conferences and literary readings. Many writers from throughout the country, but particularly East Coast writers, are awarded residencies in artists' colonies at the MacDowell Colony in Peterborough, New Hampshire, Yaddo in Saratoga, New York, and the Millay Colony for the Arts in Austerlitz, New York.

Cuban American Literature

Silvia Burunat and Ofelia García, the editors of *Veinte años de literatura cubanoamericana* (1988), give emphasis to the fact that Cuban-American literature differs from that of Mexican-Americans and Nuyoricans. While the literature of the two main Latino groups in the United States is generally one of resistance to the majority culture, Cuban-American literature tends to focus on a nostalgia for Cuban culture and history, a characteristic which, Burunat and García believe, connects their literature more to the American ethnic and immigrant experience.

Burunat and García attribute the distinction between their literature and that of the other Latino groups mainly to class differences: unlike the great majority of Mexican and Puerto Rican immigrants, the first waves of Cubans to arrive in this country (1959-1962 and 1965-1968) came from the middle class and/or the professional class. Thus, the writers associated with these groups received a traditional Hispanic education in Cuba. Their literature, written in Spanish, upholds the traditional values of their class and focuses on the historical reason for their exile—the Cuban Revolution. While this wave of immigrants has refrained from assimilating linguistically and culturally to mainstream America, they nonetheless have had the skills to experience a high degree of economic success in this country. Thus, they have no reason to feel confrontational towards Anglo-Saxon culture and their literature lacks an activist tone.

Burunat and García point out that a large percentage of the next wave of Cuban immigrants (1980), the Marielitos, were non-white and poor. As a less elite group of Cubans, the Marielitos have experienced racial and class prejudice and, generally, have more in common with other Latino groups in the United States than they do with the elite Cubans who arrived in the 1960s. Burunat and García project that by the year 2000 the literature stemming from this second group will be written in English and will have a tone similar to that of the literature of Latino activism. A third component of the Cuban-American community is the children of the immigrants who do not share their parents' enthusiasm for a literature written in a purist's Spanish. They have no memories of the Cuban natural setting nor do they experience nostalgia for the Cuba of their parents' youth. Yet, their parents have carefully nurtured in them an appreciation for their Cuban heritage.

Thematically, the literature of this group tends towards the American assimilationist experience common to the literature of other first-generation ethnic Americans. The best known example of this perspective is Oscar Hijuelo's Pulitzer Prize winning novel, *The Mambo Kings Play Songs of Love* (1989). Yet, thematically the Cuban-American novel is in flux, for Cuban-born Cristina García's *Dreaming in Cuban*—a finalist for the 1992 National Book award—is steeped in memories of Cuba and centers on the effect of the revolution on several generations of exiles. Thulani Davis, in the *New York Times Book Review* November 17, 1992, describes García's book as "the latest sign that American literature has its own hybrid off-spring of the Latin American school." Margarita Engle's *Singing to Cuba* (1993) further substantiates Davis's statement.

Opening New Directions

Innovation must be situated within a temporal context. In the 1960s, Chicano writers opened up new directions for self-definition by insisting that bilingualism and the perspective of the working class be considered legitimate characteristics of their literature. By the mid-1970s, women writers began to introduce a new dimension to the concept of resistance that had become another characteristic of the literature. Portraying the negative as well as the positive roles for women in Latino culture, women writers introduced themes of intracultural resistance into their literature. By speaking about oppression from class, race and gender perspectives, women writers broadened the thematic space of Latino literature. In 1981, the release of *This Bridge Called My Back: Writings by Radical Women of Color*, edited by Cherríe Moraga and Gloria Anzaldúa, marked an important literary and cultural milestone not only in Latino literature but also in American women's literature.

A younger generation of writers has insisted on writing about the political importance of gender issues and questions of sexuality. With the publication of the anthology, *Chicana Lesbians: We Are the Girls Your Mother Warned Us About*, Third Woman Press opened up new literary paths although an earlier and smaller book with a gay perspective had included the work of Francisco Alarcón, Juan Pablo Gutiérrez and Rodrigo Reyes. *Pa'delante, Carnal*, however, had not reached a wide audience.

Two writers, born and educated in this country's educational system, Marta Cotera and Erlinda Gonzales-Berry, have each published novels in Spanish, *Puppet* and *Paletitas de guayaba*. Unlike writers born and educated in Latin America who continue to use their native Spanish in their works which are then published in their country of origin, few Latino writers born in this country have insisted on an entirely different sort of resistance—the acquisition of advanced language skills in Spanish. It is no coincidence that Cotera is from Texas and Gonzales-Berry from New Mexico, where a strong resistance to the disappearance of

Mexican culture has always been maintained. They offer a challenge to other writers, for the colonializing linguistic effects on the continual use of Spanish have been almost totalizing. Few presses in this country offer an outlet for Latino authors who write in Spanish.

In Other Words has attempted to address this issue by including in bilingual form the work of several poets who write in Spanish. Lucha Corpi, originally from Mexico, writes poetry in Spanish which is translated by Catherine Rodríguez-Nieto. The poetry of Chilean-Americans Marjorie Agosín and Cecilia Vicuña has been translated into English by Naomi Lindstrom, and Suzanne Jill Levine and Eliot Weinberger, respectively. Anita Vélez-Mitchell, a Puerto Rican poet and playwright, has rendered her poetry collection, *Primavida,* in both English and Spanish versions. While this anthology is primarily a collection of works written in English or bilingually, a few poems written primarily in Spanish have also been included. For practical pedagogical purposes, *In Other Words* has been conceptualized as a compilation of works in English or in English/Spanish bilingual versions. A future sister volume will consist of works written in Spanish; and a third volume will include the work of authors from Latin America who live in this country but publish in Spanish in Latin American or Spanish presses.

Foreign Reception to Latino Literature of the United States

The literature of the Latino populations of the United States has gained not only attention in Europe and in some Latin American countries—primarily in Mexico—, but also a substantial academic following. A number of international conferences have brought together European and American scholars or Mexican and Chicana authors to discuss and celebrate the literary contributions of Mexican Americans, Puerto Ricans, Cubans and other Latinos in the United States. Wolfgang Binder, Heiner Bus, Jean Cazemajou, Genviever Fabre, Marcienne Roncard, Hub Hermans and Franca Bacchiega are but some of the European scholars of Latino literature of the United States who have published extensively on this subject. Measured by the number of graduate students from Europe who come to do dissertation research in archives in this country, one can see that there is a growing interest in European universities in Latino literature.

The Mexican government is presently expressing a great interest in the cultural creations of Mexican Americans and individual Mexican authors and critics, such as Gustavo Sainz, Elena Poniatowska, Carlos Monsiváis, María Luisa Puga, Elena Urrutia and Claire Joysmith have been dialoguing with Chicano writers for a long time. Various literary conferences have been held along the border which attest to this exchange. *Mujer y literatura mexicana y chicana; culturas en contacto,* published by El Colegio de la Frontera Norte, is a collection of essays read at the *encuentros* (exchanges) held in Tijuana by women writers from Mexico and from the United States. Publishers from Spain and Mexico have expressed great interest in the joint publications of the works associated with the "Recovering the U.S. Hispanic Literary Heritage Project" and some of the work of individual writers has been translated into numerous languages.

Clearly, a Latino literary renaissance has been taking place in the world of letters in the final decades of the twentiethth century. Best-selling writers of the Latin American literary boom have helped to create an interest in the Latino world. To a degree, Latino writers have benefited from this ready-made readership which nonetheless has to be educated to the differences in outlooks espoused by the Latin American writers and the ones held by Latino writers in this country who live their reality on the margins. As more and more writers move into the mainstream and yet hold on to a cultural intergrity, Latino literature promises to become the most exciting and innovative literature of the twenty-first century in the United States.

This collection of works by forty-five Latina authors reflects the multidimensional aspect of our literature. *In Other Words* has been conceptualized as a reader for university classes. Writers whose works are easily available through mainstream presses may be added to the core text. In this way, the reader will have access to most of what is presently being written in every region of the United States.

Roberta Fernández
University of Houston

In Other Words: Literature by Latinas of the United States

Part One: Poetry

Teresa Palomo Acosta

Teresa Palomo Acosta grew up in McGregor, Texas, a town in Central Texas to which her parents and their immediate families migrated during the Great Depression. She writes about herself, her family and her people as a means to re-envision and retell Chicana and Tejano history. Acosta received a B.A. in Ethnic Studies from the University of Texas in Austin and a M.S. in Journalism from Columbia University. She has written for Latino theatrical productions, and has done extensive research and critical studies on Mexican Americans for the Texas State Historical Association. She teaches at the University of Texas in Austin. Her poetry has appeared in literary journals such as *Tejidos*, *Saguaro*, *Riversedge* and *Descant* as well as in various anthologies, including *Festival de flor y canto: An Anthology of Chicano Literature* (1976); *New Texas'92: An Anthology of Texas Writing*; *Houghton Mifflin English* (a high school reader); and *Infinite Divisions: An Anthology of Chicana Literature* (1993). In 1984 she published her own chapbook, *Passing Time*. More recently, she has published another collection of poems, *Nile and Other Poems: A 1985-1994 Notebook* (1994), a compilation of poetry from four manuscripts completed over nine years. The editors of *New Texas '93* selected her work for its Voertman's Poetry Award.

My Mother Pieced Quilts

Teresa Palomo Acosta

they were just meant as covers
in winters
as weapons
against pounding january winds

but it was just that every morning I awoke to these
october ripened canvases
passed my hands across their cloth faces
and began to wonder how you pieced
all these together
these strips of gentle communion cotton and flannel
nightgowns
wedding organdies
dime store velvets

how you shaped patterns square and oblong and round
positioned
balanced
then cemented them
with your thread
a steel needle
a thimble

how the thread darted in and out
galloping along the frayed edges, tucking them in
as you did us at night
oh how you stretched and turned and re-arranged
your michigan spring faded curtain pieces
my father's santa fe work shirt
the summer denims, the tweeds of fall

in the evening you sat at your canvas
—our cracked linoleum floor the drawing board
me lounging on your arm
and you staking out the plan:
whether to put the lilac purple of easter against the
red plaid of winter-going-into-spring
whether to mix a yellow with a blue and white and paint
the corpus christi noon when my father held your hand
whether to shape a five-point star from the
somber black silk you wore to grandmother's funeral

you were the river current
carrying the roaring notes
forming them into pictures of a little boy reclining
a swallow flying
you were the caravan master at the reins
driving your threaded needle artillery across the
mosaic cloth bridges
delivering yourself in separate testimonies

oh mother you plunged me sobbing and laughing
into our past
into the river crossing at five
into the spinach fields
into the plainview cotton rows
into tuberculosis wards
into braids and muslin dresses
sewn hard and taut to withstand the thrashings
of twenty-five years

stretched out they lay
armed/ready/shouting/celebrating

knotted with love
the quilts sing on

ᴖ3ᴖ

I Should Be Trying to Start Some New Begonia Plants

There's the dirt my father
put in two grocery sacks
and
drove down 90 miles to me

and there
are the pots my mother
saved
for me.

So:
I should be trying to start some new begonia plants.

I should let them grow into pink or red blossoms
for you
and reach toward you in this way before
you go off into the fields
to organize the tomato pickers, beet pickers,
melon pickers, cucumber pickers, apple pickers…

who are out there
all
year
long
bending over,
tending other's crops/not growing begonias
in their back yards.

So:
I should be the crazy year/long gardener
plowing up my window box planter
growing begonias/sending them to you
for your desk piled high with sheets announcing
strikes, boycotts, marches.

You know what you are up to
and
I know what I am up to
for we are people
who have always bent down
to touch blossoms: of our own making

For Matisse

In my school
we were supposed
to color everything
within the lines
and outline Christmas bells
in black only.
We were paper-doll
cutters
working
with dull-edged scissors
and paper already outlined
for us
by
the mimeographing machine
down the hall.

So how could we have known
that you
were going out of the lines
like hell,
beautiful, crazy man
cutting strip upon strip
laying each
out
in
the
open
on huge canvases.

I passed third grade art classes
bearing a reverence for
stenciled
straight
marks
outlining
directions
in which artists should go.

Then

the first time
I saw your paper cut-outs,
I stood still
and
alone
and quite
happy
for a long time
in front of them.

ଔ

Untitled

the radio was
the best connection
to every dream we had

and Ruby who lived
just across the railroad tracks
from me
knew her Patsy Cline
songs by heart
had an emotional
mainline to fame in Nashville
(though no agent and no money)

but still she got to sing
her versions of 3-ton truck(er) blues/women
left-at-home songs
once a week
on local radio
falsetto style

my mother
with her own
wisdom
but mainly
her love of canciones mexicanas
flipped the radio dial assuredly toward
Chicano-laced trompetas
de amor
with no hope or idea
that I could
learn to carry the beat
of
Lydia Mendoza
y Augustín Ramírez—their art
churned out
on records cut in garage studios

coming at me with songs
that taught me
to love them and myself up here
away from the valley
in no man's land
calling on me
to join them on the dance floor

cs&o

Museum Pieces

Bones.
Adobe.
Straw baskets.
Facsimiles of our lives
as reported in the *National Geographic*.
That's what the curator
wants in the exhibition.
We nod in agreement.
Let her decide what we were.
Then that night
we dream about
lace and voile
bracelets
old tubes of lipsticks
cotton dresses made from flour sacks
doilies mamá got for starching and ironing all
twenty shirts for the men of the Falls mansion at one try.
We change our minds
but it's too late, the curator
informs us. They're already building the models,
sure that they will catch us at the right moment. This time
we cannot nod back. Now we know the difference
between suggestions and decisions.

On the following Sunday,
we open up the family trunk
and go through our museum.

Photo by Ted Polumbaum

Marjorie Agosín

Marjorie Agosín was born in Bethesda, Maryland, to Chilean parents who were then graduate students in this country. A human-rights activist, teacher and poet, Agosín maintains close ties with Chile, where she was reared. She received her Ph.D. from Indiana University and has taught Latin American literature for twelve years at Wellesley College. For the last fifteen years she has denounced human-rights abuses in Latin America; in 1990 she received the Jeanetta Rankin Award in human rights and the Good Neighbor Award from the Conference of Christians and Jews. Her poetry collections, *Conchalí* (1981) and *Zones of Pain* (1988), a finalist for the *Los Angeles Times* Book Award, powerfully portray the guilt of those who choose to look away. She has published numerous collections dealing with women's issues: *Brujas y algo más/Witches and Other Things* (1984); *Women of Smoke* (1988), and *Sargasso* (1993). *Hogueras/Bonfires* is a collection of poems that celebrate erotic encounters within a feminist context (1990). *Circles of Madness: Mothers of the Plaza de Mayo*, is a collection of prose poems with photographs by Alicia D'Amico and Alicia Sanguinetti (1992). Her forthcoming collection of family memoirs will be published in Santiago, where she has also recently published *La Felicidad*. Its translation, *Happiness* (1993), Agosín's first collection of fiction to be published in English, was translated by Elizabeth Horan. In this collection of lyrical pieces, Agosín introduces the reader to her European ancestors as they begin a new life in the New World. Agosín's speaking and writing has received critical acclaim on two continents. She lives in Wellesley, Massachusetts, with her husband and daughter.

Familiares en la pieza oscura

Marjorie Agosín

Jugábamos sin los primos a la pieza oscura. ¿Lo recuerdas, Rodrigo?
y así, nos encontrábamos entre los matorrales de almohadas
para descender perversos, sudando en la frondosidad rojiza de las
sábanas.
Debajo de ellas, éramos un túnel parecido a una escena de la playa,
éramos valientes entre las dunas de la piel. No lo olvides, Rodrigo.

En la pieza oscura, aceitábamos nostalgias, como en las mudas películas
nunca vistas.
Tú rojito, rosado evocabas el primer pubis durmiente,
la primera voz de niña, o esos senos largamente
arqueados como pequeñas bolsas de agua fresca. Repetíamos los
encuentros clandestinos en el manchado sofá de brocato, mientras
tú y yo viéndonos ruborizados, traviesos en la anomalía de
extraños adolescentes o en los espejos esfumados.

Ahora, tú y yo en esta pieza oscura, amarilla y enferma. Inocentes
nos queremos igual, aunque sea por el temor a quebrajar costumbres.
Soñamos a ser un cristal delirando entre las aguas. El deseo,
sin historias nos persigue como desfiladeros llenos de sangre y fuego.

En la pieza oscura, Rodrigo Díaz, lejos de la precocidad, con
la certeza que siempre habrá el abandonado, o el que quiere más
nos despedimos. Afuera nos aguardan ceremoniosos, los familiares:
la prima Eulalis, Cassandra, los hijos, Robin Hood, las alergias
de mi marido. En fin, los ancestros de otra pieza aún más oscura.

Family Members in the Dark Room

We used to play without the cousins in the dark room. Remember that,
Rodrigo?
and so we'd come together in the undergrowth of pillows
and snuggle down perversely, sweaty in the reddish jungle of the
bedclothes.
Burrowing beneath, we became a tunnel like a stretch of beach,
we were brave among the dunes. Don't forget, Rodrigo.

In the dark room, we stroked nostalgia, as in unseen silent movies.
You would summon up, all flushed and ruddy, the first
sleeping pubis, the first girl's voice, or those breasts,
swerving out like little pockets of cool water. We carried on
our secret meetings on the stained brocaded sofa, while
you and I glimpsed our reddened outlaw faces in the weirdness
of mixed-up adolescents, or in disappearing mirrors.

Now you and I in this dark room, yellowing and ghastly,
innocently take up love where we left off, maybe just from fear of
breaking habits.
We dream of being a delirious underwater crystal.
Desire with no past comes after us like mountain passes full of blood and
fire.

In the dark room, Rodrigo Díaz, far from these precocious moves, full of
the certainty that always comes to the rejected partner, the
one whose love is stronger, we say goodbye.
Outside, the members of the family are waiting for us ceremoniously:
cousin Eulalia, Cassandra and the kids, Robin Hood, my husband's
allergies.
That is to say: the forebears of another even darker room.

Ritual de mis senos

A Pablo Neruda

Hoy, aparezco
ante la redondez
tenue de mis senos.
Son dos variaciones
en pequeñeces,
guardan un olor
a encierro,
a lunas atormentadas,
que revolotean y encandilan
cuando Tú,
tiernamente los
guardas en
tus brazos
o los besas una y otra vez
como dos copas o cúpulas
de agua.

Mis senos,
guardan en su similitud,
dos soles incesantes,
un conjunto de arenas rosadas,
y se agrietan al alimentar al mundo,
al exhibirse solitarios
por un poco de pan y de miseria.

Yo los quiero, me acompañan
aunque pasan para mí desapercibidos,
los contemplo en sus imperfecciones,
mientras germinan o caen a la
tierra como las castañas de mis
deseos.

Mis senos,
desprendidos,
contorneándose en la
piel
son los espejos
de tus labios.

Ritual of My Breasts

to Pablo Neruda

Today, I stand
before the tenuous
roundness of my breasts.
Two variations on
the little things,
they retain a smell
of things kept shut away,
of tortured moons
that reel and flare
when You
enfold them
tenderly
in your arms
or kiss them over and again
like two goblets or two domes
of water

My breasts,
in their likeness, hold
two ceaseless suns,
a slather of pink sand
and they parch bone-dry when they feed the world,
when they're on display, alone,
for a little bit of bread and misery.

I love them, they come with me
without my giving them a thought
I contemplate them in their imperfections
as they're budding in or falling earth-
ward like the chestnuts
of my desires.

My breasts,
come loose,
modeling their curves
in skin,
are the mirrors
of your lips.

Mis pies

Hoy he vuelto
a detenerme
en mis pies,
son estrechos
como una niña
de la China,
o una mujer que nunca
pudo ser princesa,
mis pies
son dos enanos benignos
que me sujetan
mientres hago memoria
de parajes y océanos.

Mis pies son arqueados
como una espalda que desde
lejos nos besa,
tienen cinco dedos que los he
    llegado
a nombrar
de tanto quererlos,
de tanto guarecerlos
del sopor de la lluvia
o del sol
enlazado
con el agua
que los baña.

Hoy refrigero mi pies
en una poza de agua bendita
donde tantos otros
han vuelto
para pedir
favores, recuerdos,
o para poder caminar
otra vez sobre la tierra
y yo los miro,
son dos alas
que han anclado
los viajes
o dos faros acompañándome

Y hoy están conmigo,
los pellizco mientras les escribo
estos versos
parecen ser de verdad
como un camino
que van abriendo
por las ramas.

My Feet

Today I am back
on the topic
of my feet;
they are narrow
as a
Chinese
girl,
or a woman who
could never be a princess,
my feet
are two kindly dwarfs
who hold me down
while I hark back to
places and oceans.

My feet are arched
like a back that kisses us
from a distance;
they have five toes that I have
come to name
from loving them so much,
from saving them so much
from the drowse of the rain
or the sun
intertwined
with the water
bathing them.

Today I chill my feet
in a pool of holy water
where so many others
have come back
to ask for
favors, memories,
or to walk
the earth again
and I look at them,
they are two wings
that have anchored
journeys
or two lighthouses
that travel with me.

And today they are with me.
I pinch them as I write
these verses
they seem to be real
like my memory that
holds them
or like a path
they open
through the branches.

Los zapatos rojos

para Marilyn

Ya no cumple más
el mandato,
se desata el silencio
del flotido cabello.

Se alza estallada
con sus zapatos rojos, carmesíes,
granadas,
que estíran y rebozan
las orillas
de sus piernas,
zapatos rojos, sorpresivos,
rápidos recorriendo
aceras, marcando el rumbo
de una dirección un tanto ajena a
esos pies vendados
pero los zapatos enrojecidos,
la conducen a los
olores, a las ilusiones
tras las puertas, los estantes,
las cláusulas.

Ella con sus zapatos rojos,
corre, se hinca, bebe como desnuda,
hipnotizada
porque los zapatos
rojos acentúan
su mirada,
las caderas,
los tobillos de divagadora,
o de hechicera,
y los zapatos rojos
la dejan sin aliento,
y su boca
es un suspiro
rojizo
una hebilla
lanzada
en el
aire.

The Red Shoes

for Marilyn

She no longer
follows orders
the silence of her
flowering hair spreads free.

She rises shattered
with her red shoes, crimson
pulp-red,
stretching and binding
the edges
of her legs
red shoes, surprising,
swiftly running down
the sidewalks, heading
in a rather strange direction for
those bandaged feet
but the red-stained shoes
lead her to the
smells, the illusions
behind closed doors, the racks,
the clauses.

She with her red shoes
runs, kneels, drinks like a naked woman,
hypnotized
because the red
shoes bring out
the look in her eyes,
her thighs,
the ankles of a rambling woman
or a sorceress,
and the red shoes
leave her breathless,
and her mouth
is a reddish
sigh
a buckle
tossed out
to the
air.

La mesa de billar en New Bedford, Massachusetts

Ella entró vestida
era clara y encorvada como un día cualquiera
o como un otro día,
ella era redonda y joven
con algo de Eva y con algo de María.
Pero, ellos la vieron desnuda,
entraron bruscos por su pelo largo,
su pelo como cenizas
ellos la habitaban por las rendijas de sus ojos que se nublaban
mientras los falos asustados
la despedazaban como un trapo malgastado entre las cacerolas.

Ella entró vestida
como una luna
y le fueron deshojando sus misterios
sus faldas que se mecían
entre los dientes de los enanos rompiéndole, escupiéndola, acariciándola,
vagamente, torpemente.

Ella era celeste y vestía colores de río,
y ahora coagulada, fermentada, deforme
en una mesa de billar
New Bedford, Mass
pueblo de ballenas y hombres malolientes.

En las mesa de billar
ella flotaba eternamente abierta despojada de claridades
y ellos urgeteaban su vagina que ahora humeada como una cloaca
como una boca de ballena náufraga
incendiada entre los despojos.

Su blusa
era una ráfaga de humos chamusqueada
y ellos no la veían
ya no la veían desnuda
porque era una enrollada presa de colores púrpuros en
sus brazos inutilizados
no podrían colgarse del que tal vez le quiso
y ahora como una carne en una carnicería de velorios, amarrada a la mesa
de billar

Ella duerme desnuda.

The Pool Table in New Bedford, Massachusetts

She came in with her clothes on
she was as light and curving as any day
or as another day;
she was rounded and young,
a little bit of Eve and a little bit of Mary.
But they saw her naked,
they broke into her long hair,
her hair like ashes
they moved into her through the slits in her eyes that clouded over
while their frightened phalluses
ripped her up like a worn-out rag among the pots and pans.

She came in with her clothes on
like a moon
and they stripped away her mysteries,
her skirt torn back and forth
in the teeth of the dwarfs who were breaking her, spitting on her, stroking
her
vaguely, clumsily.

She was sky blue and wearing river colors,
and now clotted, spoiled, warped
on a pool table
New Bedford, Mass
a town of whales and bad-smelling men.

On the pool table
she floated forever opened up and stripped of light
and they harrowed her vagina, now steaming like a sewer
like a mouth of a beached whale
set on fire amid the rubble.

Her blouse
was a scorched gust of smoke
and they didn't see her
by now they didn't see her naked
because she was prey, folded up with purple marks on
her useless arms
could no longer cling to the one who perhaps loved her
and now like a piece of meat in a funerary butcher shop, pinned on the
pool table

She sleeps naked.

Estados Unidos

Estados Unidos,
yo no invoco tu nombre
en vano,
ni te acuso por
desvirginar tantas estrellas
solo me adhiero
a tus inmensas soledades
y entiendo que no es tu culpa
el haber inventado la vida en
ready-made
ni los anocheceres dorados
de Miss Monroe,
Aunque confiésate
que gozabas de la triste enfermedad
de los pueblos mansos
y trepaste hasta la vía andina
para llenarte de cobres, cromosomas, de fusil
pero pensándolo bien.
Me paseo por Managua, El Salvador
por la Avenida Providencia en Santiago de Chile
y todos vestimos botas de Cowboy
en un sordo diálogo de Rock and Roll.

United States

United States,
I do not take your name
in vain,
nor do I accuse you for
deflowering so many stars
I only follow
your immense lonely spaces
and I understand it's not your fault
that you invented ready-made
life
or the golden sundowns
of Miss Monroe.
But confess
that you enjoyed the sad sickness
of meek peoples
and you crept up to the Andes
to load up on copper, chromosomes, guns,
but thinking it all through,
I make my way down through Managua, El Salvador,
down the Avenida Providencia in Santiago de Chile
and we're all wearing cowboy boots
in a deafened dialogue of rock and roll.

(English translations by Naomi Lindstrom)

Rosemary Catacalos

Rosemary Catacalos, of Greek and Mexican ancestry, was born and reared in San Antonio, Texas. The author of a hand letterpress chapbook, *As Long As It Takes* (1984), Catacalos has received numerous literary awards. Her work has been widely anthologized and published in literary journals throughout the United States, including *The Bloomsbury Review, Southwest Review, Provincetown Arts* and *Parnassus: Poetry in Review*. In 1985, her full-length collection of poetry, *Again for the First Time*, received the Texas Institute of Letters Poetry Prize; its author was awarded the Dobie Paisano Fellowship by the Texas Institute of Letters and the University of Texas at Austin. She has been a Stegner Creative Writing Fellow in Poetry at Stanford University, and has been awarded a National Endowment for the Arts grant for her poetry. Catacalos has received three Pushcart Prize nominations and a Special Mention in *Pushcart Prize IX: Best of the Small Presses* (1985). A former newspaper reporter and arts columnist, Catacalos has also worked as a grant writer, publicist and development officer for non-profit organizations. From 1986 to 1989, she was Literature Program Director at the Guadalupe Cultural Arts Center in San Antonio, where she coordinated a citywide program of classes, workshops and readings and developed the San Antonio Inter-American Bookfair. Currently, Catacalos is Executive Director of The Poetry Center/American Poetry Archives at San Francisco State University, where she also teaches a creative writing process course based on The Poetry Center's reading series.

Katakalos

Rosemary Catacalos

The Old Man, we always called him.
We said it with respect.
Even when he embarrassed us
by wearing his plaid flannel work shirt
to church under the fine blue suit
one of his up-and-coming sons,
the three prides of his life,
had bought him.
Even when he spent hours
straightening used nails when
we could afford to buy him new ones
so he could build the hundreds
of crooked little plant stands
that still wobble in the corners
of our houses.

He had come off a hard island birthplace,
a rock long ago deserted by the gods
but still sopping with the blood
of its passing from hand to hand,
Greek to Turk, Turk to Greek
and back again,
as if everything had not always
belonged to the sea, he said,
and to the relentless light
that hurt the eyes
of statues and children alike.

He was brought up on routine whippings
every Sunday, before-the-fact punishment
to fit any crime. His father, the miller,
followed the wisdom that parents
can't be everywhere at once
and in seven days any boy is bound
to do something deserving a beating.
Besides, by his own admission
he was not such a good shepherd,
always getting sidetracked caring
for some sick bird or dog or donkey
that followed him everywhere ever after
and got mixed up with the goats and sheep.

A draft dodger from the Turkish Army,
he braved the maze of Ellis Island
alone at sixteen,
escaping with his last name intact
and his first name changed to Sam.
New York fed him dog food
those first few months
when he couldn't read the labels
and only knew from the pictures
that the cans were meat and cheap.
He used to laugh about that.
Said it was just as good as some of
that Spam and stuff they sell nowadays.
Anyway, Sam was
the darling of immigrant flophouses,
giving away counsel and sometimes money,
always finding someone who was
a little worse off than he was.

He hoboed all the way to Seattle
where he pretended to be a high-flying carpenter
and was saved by *Hagia Sophia* from a fall that
would otherwise have meant certain death.
Then he came to where they were
burning Greeks out of Oklahoma
and anyone who could kept moving
and opened a hamburger stand
a little farther south.
In San Antonio he rigged up
a brightly painted horse-drawn
popcorn and ice cream wagon
and made the rounds of the West Side,
never quite making more than a living
since he always told poor kids
to pay him whenever they got the money.
The hamburger stands came next.
The old cafe on Produce Row that some
old market hands still remember.
The Ideal Spot on South Presa,
where every hobo and derelict
from here to either coast
knew he could collect a free meal.
Good Old Sam.

But his wife was always angry.
She wanted a house of her own,
something more than glass beads.
She hated the way he was always
attracting winos and gypsies
and cousins from everywhere
who camped on her red velvet cushions
while he was out working hard
to give it all away.
She was from Lagos, Jalisco,
and when they'd met
it hadn't been so much about love
as it had been simply time to get married.
That's what she always said.
Sam never said much about it
one way or the other,
except to smile and tell us
she'd had a hard life.

Still, they must have had a
little something special going.
Seeing how back then
he spoke only Greek,
a little broken English,
and she spoke only Spanish.
They were married through an interpreter.
Sam wore an ill-fitting suit
and carried a brown paper bag
full of sandwiches he had made
so as not to let the few guests go hungry.

Years later when they were old
she had never learned English
and he had never bought her a house.
He'd spent years in his by-now-perfect
Spanish trying to get her to see
how there was always some poor devil
who needed just a little help.
When she complained the loudest
he just listened patiently
and went about setting out his
sugar water in bottle caps
to feed the ants.
A smiling survivor.
A fat soft heart.
The Old Man.
We still say it with respect.

ശ്ര

The History of Abuse, a Language Poem

Afternoon, two friends, nightshade flourishing outside the kitchen window
and fighting the sky for best color. Sobs rattle every cell in her, the whole world

in question. *Maybe it's just something simple and organic. The way all things die*
when it's time. He shakes his head, *It's not time, you know,* hands her a notebook

he's brought from Paris, frail lined pages bound with what we need to imagine:
canopies for shelter, bugles for announcing truth, mistletoe for possibility, cherubs

banging tambourines for joy. The way language makes us need to believe we can see
gifts and curses, that the difference between them means something greater than

each of us, something larger than any one constellation of cells that ends up, whether
combed and perfumed or beaten and in its own feces, like all compost. Because we have

language we know the undercover man in a blue raincoat carries a nervous little
laugh with him everywhere, that if we knew why, language would fail us as it so

often does. A man knowingly exposes his lover to life-threatening disease. A mother gives
her boyfriend a day with her twelve-year-old daughter, who is found in green leaf light,

eyes swollen, body bruised, bloody, smeared with semen, as the mother has often been;
dead, as the mother is not yet. She'd thought if she could be good enough, patient enough,

accommodating enough, the terror would stop. She'd thought this about her father,
two husbands, many lovers. The "merely personal" that has everything to do with how

the rooster shrieks at dawn when soldiers drag men from their beds to leave them
nameless, the luckiest in shallow graves. In Palestine, who but the Jews should know

better? In Salvador the soldiers have the same Mayan faces as their victims, have
mothers for whom they buy cheap blue sweaters, plastic rosaries at Christmas. And

the *silence!* Chasms, faults, fissures that put sanity at risk when the colonel vows
to rout and punish the guilty, when life goes on as if nothing had happened. And still

there is only language. Still there is the cruel beauty of basil and tomatoes, of an old man
peeing into a fountain in Barcelona, of someone who finds his dead wife's comb and

writes it so that we link hands across time. *The news that stays news* is no news at all,
is nonetheless nothing but emergency. History is the child locked in the closet who guards

the secret of locking *her* child in the closet. It's redwoods struggling for breath while they perfume
the world simply because this is how they're made. It's a monthly gathering in the desert, voices

wielding common and useless images of mother-rape against testing another bomb deep
in the earth. Just as it is a woman in failing light watching hundreds of bruises darken:

who insists on some kind of meaning from thick purple nightshade going black with ordinary
nightfall, each bloom's center marked with a tiny yellow star that can't be seen in the dark.

ଔ

Keeping the Vigil

for Naomi Shibhab Nye

The doors of the temple are ajar as
though a child had accidentally left
them that way. *People bring me*
food, medicine, music. Some dream
of me all night and also of giant
trees with visible roots. Others want me
to tuck white flowers into my hair
and dance on the poles of earth.
Some even say they will pray for me.

"We *need* some dancing," you say,
alarmed at the hole slit sideways
in my belly, the hole that will
not heal, not stop bleeding.
Sleep now, little sister.
The pain will have its long feast.
But your fat candle, glowing among
all the other loved ones' charms
hanging from the roots of the tree, will
help see to me.

Soon the morning will open
again in the simple sighing
of roses, in the beating of goatskin
drums like hearts. Soon the table
will be set outside under the trees,
this time for the Easter feast.
You will hold my hand, reach
for another. We will dance,
all of us, in the sight of the stars
that can only be seen by day.
We will all be learning the moonstruck
skills of gauze and hot water
again for the first time.

A Vision of La Llorona

for G.

I see your mother every week
now that you're gone.
Sometimes she knows me
and remembers to be polite.
But other times her eyes,
so like your eyes,
are already on the loose, already prowling
by the time she gets to me.
Then her gaze goes right past me.
I'm not what she's looking for.

Today your father was with her,
but she's not looking for him either.
She follows her eyes, so like your eyes,
all through the town,
turning their consuming blue
on the winos in football jerseys
and urine-stained pants
and on the old women who can't step up curbs.
She follows her eyes so like your eyes
into taco shops and libraries and bars,
scrutinizes the old men shooting the breeze
and killing time on Main Plaza,
even peers under the skirts
of our Lady of Grace and Our Lady of Sorrows.
She is alert to the possibility
of disguises. She examines everyone
with even a hint of a wing,
sometimes sneaking up from behind
and grabbing for their shoulders,
feeling for the supernatural bone
that resembles her own,
the telltale sign of flying.

Then she's deep in their faces,
the faces of all the fliers,
looking for her lost mirror,
the only water with the right reflection,
looking for her same eyes staring back at her,
looking for the only power
that since the day you were born
matches her own.

Your mother, looking for the blood
that will never dry,
her only son.

Photo © Copyright 1989 by Georgia McInnis

Lorna Dee Cervantes

Lorna Dee Cervantes writes poetry that is rooted in her Chicana heritage. A fifth-generation Californian of Mexican and Chumasch Indian ancestry, Cervantes has been closely identified with San Jose, the setting of some of her best-known poems. In the late 1970s, Cervantes learned the craft of printing in order to publish the work of other Chicano poets; *Mango* was the name she chose for both her press and her literary review. Her first book, *Emplumada* (1981), is a seamless collection of poems that move back and forth between the gulf of desire and possibility. *Emplumada* includes Cervantes' *ars poetica* in "Poem for the Young White Man Who Asked Me How I, an Intelligent, Well-Read Person Could Believe in the War between Races." In the concluding segment of *Emplumada*, Cervantes finds a balance in her search for identity. In *From the Cables of Genocide: Poems on Love and Hunger* (1991), the poet stretches the resources of language, imagery and the dialectics of love, hunger and aesthetics to express a penetrating feminist and human vision of her universe. *From the Cables of Genocide* received the Patterson Poetry Award and the poetry award of the Institute of Latin American Writers. Cervantes is working on a third collection, *Bird Ave*. She has received an A.B.D. in the History of Consciousness at the University of California in Santa Cruz and has been teaching creative writing at the University of Colorado in Boulder, where she is a co-editor of the literary review *Red Dirt*. Her poems are widely anthologized and are the subject of a chapter in Marta Sánchez's *Contemporary Chicana Poetry* (1985). Cervantes has been awarded the 1994-1995 Visiting Scholar Fellowship sponsored by the Mexican American Studies Program at the University of Houston, Central Campus.

Poem for the Young White Man Who Asked Me How I, an Intelligent, Well-Read Person Could Believe in the War Between Races

Lorna Dee Cervantes

In my land there are no distinctions.
The barbed wire politics of oppression
have been torn down long ago. The only reminder
of past battles, lost or won, is a slight
rutting in the fertile fields.

In my land
people write poems about love,
full of nothing but contented childlike syllables.
Everyone reads Russian short stories and weeps.
There are no boundaries.
There is no hunger, no
complicated famine or greed.

I am not a revolutionary.
I don't even like political poems.
Do you think I can believe in a war between races?
I can deny it. I can forget about it
when I'm safe
living in my own continent of harmony
and home, but I am not
there.

I believe in revolution
because everywhere the crosses are burning,
sharp-shooting goose-steppers round every corner,
there are snipers in the school...
(I know you don't believe this.
You think this is nothing
but faddish exaggeration. But they
are not shooting at you.)

I'm marked by the color of my skin.
The bullets are discrete and designed to kill slowly.
They are aiming at my children.
These are facts.
Let me show you my wounds: my stumbling mind, my
"excuse me" tongue, and this
nagging preoccupation
with the feeling of not being good enough.

These bullets bury deeper than logic.
Racism is not intellectual.
I can not reason these scars away.

Outside my door
there is a real enemy
who hates me.

I am a poet
who yearns to dance on rooftops,
to whisper delicate lines about joy
and the blessings of human understanding.
I try. I go to my land, my tower of words and
bolt the door, but the typewriter doesn't fade out
the sounds of blasting and muffled outrage.
My own days bring me slaps on the face.
Everyday I am deluged with reminders
that this is not
my land
and this is my land.

I do not believe in the war between the races

but in this country
there is war.

Beneath the Shadow of the Freeway

1

Across the street—the freeway,
blind worm, wrapping the valley up
from Los Altos to Sal Si Puedes
I watched it from my porch
unwinding. Every day at dusk
as Grandma watered geraniums
the shadow of the freeway lengthened.

2

We were a woman family:
Grandma, our innocent Queen;
Mama, the Swift Knight, Fearless Warrior.
Mama wanted to be Princess instead.
I know that. Even now she dreams of taffeta
and foot-high tiaras.

Myself: I could never decide.
So I turned to books, those staunch, upright men.
I became Scribe: Translator of Foreign Mail,
interpreting letters from the government, notices
of dissolved marriages and Welfare stipulations.
I paid the bills, did light man-work, fixed faucets,
insured everything
against all leaks.

3

Before rain I notice sea gulls.
They walk in flocks,
cautious across lawns: splayed toes,
indecisive beaks. Grandma says
seagulls mean storm.

In California in the summer,
mockingbirds sing all night.
Grandma says they are singing for their nesting wives.
"They don't leave their families
borrachando."

She likes the way of birds,
respects how they show themselves
for toast and a whistle.

She believes in myths and birds.
She trusts only what she builds
with her own hands.

4

She built her house,
cocky, disheveled carpentry,
after living twenty-five years
with a man who tried to kill her.

Grandma, from the hills of Santa Barbara,
I would open my eyes to see her stir mush
in the morning, her hair in loose braids,
tucked loose around her head
with a yellow scarf.

Mama said, "It's her own fault,
getting screwed by a man for that long.
Sure as shit wasn't hard."
soft   she was   soft

5

in the night I would hear it
glass bottles shattering the street
words cracked into shrill screams
inside my throat   a cold fear
as it entered the house in hard
unsteady steps   stopping at my door
my name   bathrobe   slippers
outside a 3 A.M. mist heavy
as a breath full of whiskey
stop it   go home   come inside
mama if he comes here again
I'll call the police

inside
a gray kitten   a touchstone
purring beneath the quilts
grandma stitched
from his suits
the patchwork singing
of mockingbirds

6

"You're too soft...always were.
You'll get nothing but shit.
Baby, don't count on nobody."

—a mother's wisdom.
Soft. I haven't changed,
maybe grown more silent, cynical
on the outside.

"O Mama, with what's inside of me
I could wash that all away. I could."

"But Mama, if you're good to them
they'll be good to you back."

Back. The freeway is across the street.
It's summer now. Every night I sleep with a gentle man
to the hymn of mockingbirds,

and in time, I plant geraniums.
I tie up my hair into loose braids,
and trust only what I have built
with my own hands.

For Virginia Chávez

It was never in the planning,
in the life we thought
we'd live together, two fast
women living cheek to cheek,
still tasting the dog's
breath of boys in our testy
new awakening.
We were never the way
they had it planned.
Their wordless tongues we stole
and tasted the power
that comes of that.
We were never what they wanted
but we were bold. We could take
something of life and not
give it back. We could utter
the rules, mark the lines
and cross them ourselves—we two
women using our fists, we thought,
our wits, our tunnels. They were such
dumb hunks of warm fish
swimming inside us,
but this was love,
we knew, love, and that was all
we were ever offered.

You were always alone
so *another lonely life*
wouldn't matter.
In the still house
your mother left you,
when the men were gone
and the television droned
into test patterns, with our cups
of your mother's whiskey
balanced between the brown thighs
creeping out of our shorts, I read
you the poems of Lord Byron, Donne,
the Brownings: all about love,
explaining the words

before realizing that you knew
all that the kicks in your belly
had to teach you. You were proud
of the woman blooming out of your
fourteen lonely years, but you cried
when you read that poem I wrote you,
something about our "waning moons"
and the child in me
I let die that summer.

In the years that separate,
in the tongues that divide
and conquer, in the love
that was a language
in itself, you never spoke,
never regret. Even
that last morning
I saw you with blood
in your eyes, blood
on your mouth, the blood
pushing out of you
in purple blossoms.

He did this.
When I woke, the kids
were gone. They told me
I'd never get them back.

With our arms holding
each other's waists, we walked
the waking streets
back to your empty flat,
ignoring the horns and catcalls
behind us, ignoring what
the years had brought between us:
my diploma and the bare bulb
that always lit your bookless room.

Astro-no-mía

The closest we ever got to Science
was the stars, like the Big Dipper
ladling hundreds of thousands
of beans and diamonds for some Greeks
long ago when law was a story
of chased women set in the sky:
Diana, Juno, Pleiades, las siete
hermanas, daughters, captives
of Zeus, and the children, the children
changed into trees, bears, scared into stars.
We wished ourselves into the sky,
held our breaths and stopped dreaming,
stopped stories, our hearts and escalated
up into that ash trip to heaven—seven
smoked rings of escape from the chase.
Y nada. Punto. We were never stars.
Our mothers would call, the fathers
of fate, heavy like mercury, would trash
our stomachs into our wombs. Cold.
We'd rollercoaster back down to the earth,
to the night before school, before
failed examinations y el otro
which is much harder to describe.
Study? Sure. We studied hard.
But all I could remember was that man,
Orion, helplessly shooting his shaft
into my lit house from the bow.
¿Y Yo? Hay bow. Y ya voy.

Pleiades from the Cables of Genocide

for my grandmother and against the budgets of '89

Tonight I view seven sisters
As I've never seen them before, brilliant
In their dumb beauty, pockmarked
In the vacant lot of no end winter
Blight. Seven sisters, as they were before,
Naked in a shroud of white linen, scented angels
Of the barrio, hanging around for another smoke,
A breath of what comes next, the aborted nest.
I'll drink to that, says my mother within. Her mother
Scattered tales of legendary ways when earth
Was a child and satellites were a thing of the
Heart. Maybe I could tell her this. I saw them
Tonight, seven Hail Marys, unstringing;
viewed Saturn
Through a singular telescope. Oh wonder
Of pillaged swans! oh breathless geometry
Of setting! You are radiant in your black light
Height, humming as you are in my memory.
Nights as inked as these, breathless
From something that comes from nothing.
Cold hearts, warm hands in your scuffed
Up pockets. I know the shoes those ladies wear,
Only one pair, and pointedly out of fashion
And flared-ass breaking at the toes, at the point
Of despair. Those dog gone shoes. No repair
For those hearts and angles, minus of meals, that
Flap through the seasons, best in summer, smelling
Of sneakers and coconuts, armpits steaming
With the load of the lording boys who garnish
Their quarters: the gun on every corner,
A chamber of laughter as the skag
Appears—glossed, sky white and sunset
Blush, and incandescence giving out, giving up
On their tests, on their grades, on their sky
Blue books, on the good of what's right. A star,
A lucky number that fails all, fails math, fails
Street smarts, dumb gym class, fails to jump
Through the broken hoop, and the ring
Of their lives wounds the neck not their

Arterial finger. Seven sisters, I knew them
Well. I remember the only constellation
My grandmother could point out with the punch
Of a heart. My grandma's amber stone
Of a face uplifts to the clarity of an eaglet's
Eye—or the vision of an águila
Whose mate has succumbed, and she uplifts
Into heaven, into their stolen hemispheres.
It is true.
When she surrenders he will linger by her leaving,
Bringing bits of food in switchblade talons, mice
For the Constitution, fresh squirrel for her wings
The length of a mortal. He will die there, beside
Her, belonging, nudging the body into the snowed
Eternal tide of his hunger. Hunters will find them
Thus, huddled under their blankets of aspen
Leaves. Extinct. And if she lives who knows what
Eye can see her paused between ages and forgotten
Stories of old ways and the new way
Of ripping apart. They are huddled, ever squaring
With the division of destiny. You can find them
In the stars, with a match, a flaring of failure,
That spark in the heart that goes out with impression,
That thumb at the swallow's restless beating.
And you will look up, really to give up, ready
To sail through your own departure. I know.
My grandmother told me, countless times, it was all
She knew to recite to her daughter of daughters,
Her Persephone of the pen.
The Seven Sisters
Would smoke in the sky in their silly shoes
And endless waiting around doing nothing,
Nothing to do but scuff up the Big Bang with salt
And recite strange stories of epiphanies of light,
Claim canons, cannons and horses, and the strange
Men in their boots in patterns of Nazis and Negroes.
I count them now in the sky on my abacus of spun duck
Lineage, a poison gas. There, I remind me, is the nation
Of peace: seven exiles with their deed of trust
Signed over through gunfire of attorney.
She rides
Now through the Reagan Ranch her mothers owned.
I know this—we go back to what we have loved

And lost. She lingers, riding in her pied pinto gauchos,
In her hat of many colors and her spurs, her silver
Spurs. She does not kick the horse. She goes
Wherever it wants. It guides her to places where
The angry never eat, where birds are spirits
Of dead returned for another plot or the crumb
Of knowledge, that haven of the never to get.
And she is forever looking to the bare innocence
Of sky, remembering, dead now, hammered as she is
Into her grave of stolen home. She is singing
The stories of Calafia ways and means, of the nacre
Of extinct oysters and the abalone I engrave
With her leftover files. She knows the words
To the song now, what her grandmother sang
Of how they lit to this earth from the fire
Of fusion, on the touchstones of love tribes. *Mira,*
She said, *This is where you come from*. The power
peace
Of worthless sky that unfolds me—now—in its greedy
Reading: Weeder of Wreckage, Historian of the Native
Who says: *It happened. That's all. It just happened.*
And runs on.

The Chumash who inhabited the Santa Barbara coast may have believed that they descended to earth from the Pleiades, also known as The Seven Sisters.

The Seven Sisters also refers to the seven big oil companies

Lucha Corpi

Lucha Corpi has many voices. Her poetry, written in Spanish, deals with the experience of being an immigrant, cut off from familiar surroundings and loved ones. But for fictionalizing events in recent Chicano history, she turns to English. Born in Mexico, Corpi came to Berkeley as a student wife when she was nineteen. She earned two degrees in Comparative Literature: a B.A. from the University of California at Berkeley and an M.A. from San Francisco State University. She lives in Oakland, where she teaches English to adults in the Oakland Public Schools. Corpi has received numerous literary awards, including a National Endowment for the Arts fellowship. She is past president of the Centro Chicano de Escritores (Chicano Writers Center) and a member of the international feminist mystery novel circle Sisters in Crime. Corpi has published two poetry collections, *Noon Words/Palabras de Mediodía* (1980) and *Variaciones sobre una tempestad/Variations on a Storm* (1990), both translated into English by Catherine Rodríguez-Nieto. The Third-World Student strike at Berkeley in the late 1960s serves as the background for her first novel, *Delia's Song* (1989). Her second novel, *Eulogy for a Brown Angel*, which opens at the height of the Chicano civil rights movement, was selected as Best Fiction for 1993 by the Multicultural Publishers Exchange. PEN/Oakland named *Eulogy* as its recipient for the Josefine Miles Award for Best Fiction. Corpi's third novel *Cactus Blood* will be published by Arte Público Press in 1995.

Romance negro

Lucha Corpi

Hay sabor de vainilla
en el aire dominical.

Melancolía de la naranja
que aún cuelga de la rama,
brillante y seductora,
sin esperanza de azahar.

Guadalupe se bañaba en el río
muy de tarde en un domingo.

Promesa de leche en los senos

Vainilla el olor de los cabellos

Canela molida el sabor de los ojos

Flor de cacao entre las piernas

Ah, la embriaguez de la caña
entre los labios.

El se acercó y la miró así
rodeada del agua
inundada de tarde

Y en instante arrancó la flor

Estrujó la leche hasta cambiarla
en sangre

Dark Romance

A flavor of vanilla drifts
on the Sunday air.

Melancholy of an orange,
clinging still,
brilliant, seductive,
past the promise of its blooming.

Guadalupe was bathing in the river
that Sunday, late,

a promise of milk in her breasts,

vanilla scent in her hair,
cinnamon flavor in her eyes,

cocoa-flower between her legs,

and in her mouth a daze
of sugarcane.

He came upon her there
surrounded by water
in a flood of evening light.

And on the instant cut the flower
wrung blood from the milk

Desparramó la vainilla por el
silencio de la orilla

Bebióse el candente liquido
de los labios

Y después . . . después desapareció
dejando sólo un rastro de sombra
lánguida al borde del agua.

Su madre la encontró y al verla
sacó de su morral un puño de sal
y se la echó por el hombro.

Y a los pocos días su padre
recibió una yegua fina de regalo.

Y Guadalupe . . . Guadalupe colgó
su vida del naranjo del huerto
y se quedó muy quieta ahí
con los ojos al río abiertos.

Hay sabor de vainilla
en el ambiente de la tarde.

Una nostalgia ancestral
se apodera de la mente.

De la rama cuelga una naranja
todavía sin promesa de azahar.

dashed vanilla on the silence
of the river bank

drained the burning liquid
of her lips

And then he was gone,
leaving behind him a trail of shadow
drooping at the water's edge.

Her mother found her, and at the sight
took a handful of salt from her pouch
to throw over her shoulder.

A few days later, her father
accepted the gift of a fine mare.

And Guadalupe…Guadalupe hung her life
from the orange tree in the garden,
and stayed there quietly,
her eyes open to the river.

an orange clings to the branch
the promise lost of its blooming.

Ancestral longing
seizes the mind.

A scent of vanilla drifts
on the evening air.

Los poemas de Marina

I. Marina Madre

Del barro más húmedo la hicieron,
al rayo del sol tropical la secaron,
con la sangre de un cordero tierno
su nombre escribieron los viejos
en la corteza de ese árbol
tan viejo como ellos.

Húmeda de tradición, mística
y muda fue vendida...
de mano en mano, noche a noche,
negada y desecrada, esperando el alba
y el canto de la lechuza
que nunca llegaban.
Su vientre robado de su fruto;
hecha un puño de polvo seco su alma.

Tú no la querías ya y él la negaba
y aquel que cuando niño ¡Mamá! le gritaba
cuando creció le puso por nombre "la chingada".

II. Marina Virgen

De su propio pie, junto al altar
del dios crucificado se hincó.
Como ella te amó, veía solamente
al ser sangrante. Y amaba en él
tu recuerdo secreto y enlutado.

Había querido lavar su pecado
con aqua bendita. Y arropaba
su cuerpo con una manta gruesa y nítida
para que no supieras que su piel
morena esaba maldita.

Alguna vez te detuviste a pensar
en dónde estaba su alma escondida.
No sabías que la había sembrado
en las entrañas de la tierra
que sus manos cultivaban—
la tierra negra y húmeda de tu vida.

The Marina Poems

I. Marina Mother

They made her of the softest clay
and dried her under the rays of the tropical sun.
With the blood of a tender lamb
her name was written by the elders
on the bark of that tree
as old as they.

Steeped in tradition, mystic
and mute she was sold—
from hand to hand, night to night,
denied and desecrated, waiting for the dawn
and for the owl's song
that would never come;
her womb sacked of its fruit,
her soul thinned to a handful of dust.

You longer loved her, the elders denied her,
and the child who cried out to her "mamá!"
grew up and called her "whore."

II. Marina Virgin

Of her own accord, before the altar
of the crucified god she knelt.
Because she loved you, she only saw
the bleeding man, and loved in him
her secret and mourning memory of you.

She tried to wash away her sin
with holy water, then covered her body
with a long, thick cloth
so you would never know
her brown skin had been damned.

Once, you stopped to wonder
where her soul was hidden,
not knowing she had planted it
in the entrails of that earth
her hands had cultivated—
the moist, black earth of your life.

III. La hija del diablo

Cuando murió, el trueno se reventó en el norte,
y junto al altar de piedra la noche entera
el copal ardió. Su mística pulsación para
siempre calló. Cayó hecho pedazos el ídolo
de barro sucio y viejo, y su nombre se lo llevó
el viento con un solo murmullo ronco:
su nombre tan parecido a la profundidad
salina del mar. Poco quedó. Sólo una semilla
a medio germinar.

IV. Ella (Marina ausente)

Ella. Una flor quizá, un remanso fresco…
una noche tibia, tropical,
o una criatura triste, en una prisión
encerrada: de barro húmedo y suave:
es la sombra enlutada de un recuerdo
ancestral que vendrá por la mañana
cruzando el puente con manos llenas—
llenas de sol y de tierra.

III. The Devil's Daughter

When she died, lightning struck in the north,
and on the new stone altar the incense burned
all night long. Her mystic pulsing
silenced, the ancient idol
shattered, her name
devoured by the wind in one deep growl
(her name so like the salt depths of the sea)—
little remained. Only a half-germinated seed.

IV. She (Marina Distant)

She. A flower perhaps, a pool of fresh water…
a tropical night,
or a sorrowful child, enclosed
in a prison of the softest clay:
mourning shadow of an ancestral memory,
crossing the bridge at daybreak,
her hands full of earth and sun.

Dos

Ahí
tras mi mesa de labores
donde
las arañas tienden sus telas a secar
y el relámpago pinta frescos sidra
y fantasmas en hogueras
inefable e inmediata
habita la palabra.

Diecisiete

Veinticinco años de querer llegar
y no pasar de las márgenes siquiera,
de arquear vértebra y espina
sin alcanzar el trasdós en la otra orilla,
veinticinco años de una vida prestada
que de tanta vivencia
en ausencia
he llegado a creer mía.

Voces

Mi padre me enseñó a cantar
mi madre a hilar versos
y de mi abuela aprendí
que se llega a la verdad
también por el silencio

Hay tantas voces en mí
tantas voces que bajan
a beber de mis sueños
en noches de invierno

Two

Behind my worktable
where
spiders stretch their webs to dry
and lightning paints amber frescoes
and phantoms in open fires
there
unsayable and immediate
lives the word.

Seventeen

Twenty-five years of wanting to go home
and never even crossing the boundaries,
of arching vertebrae and spinal cord
toward the outer curve of the opposite shore,
twenty-five years of borrowed life
such a long experience
in being elsewhere
have led me to believe is mine.

Voices

My father taught me to sing
my mother to spin verses
and from my grandmother I learned
that truth can be found
through silence as well

There are so many voices in me
so many voices going down
to drink at dreams' edge
on winter nights

English translations by Catherine Rodríguez Nieto

Verónica Cunningham

Verónica Cortez-Cunningham, a native of San Diego, California, celebrates the language of hearts in both her poetry and her art. In the mid-seventies, she was the valedictorian of her clownology class. Among her many performances as a clown, she counts as her most memorable her performances at a national conference of the National Endowment for the Arts for writers in the schools, and at the Gay and Lesbian Pride Festivals in San Diego. Her art has been on several covers of the *California Poets in the School* state-wide anthologies. One of the young poets associated with the literary component of the Chicano Movement, Cunningham felt that her subject matter was not encouraged and, for many years, she "disappeared" from the Chicano poetry scene. In the mid-seventies, however, she participated in four of the "Flor y Canto" Chicano Poetry Festivals—in Albuquerque, Austin, San Antonio and San Diego. Her poetry has appeared in various publications, including *Pacific Coast Times* and *Poetry Conspiracy*. Since 1982 she has taught poetry in San Diego County and in other districts in the state. As part of a Writing Magnet Program in San Diego, she has also worked with Russian exchange students and, in 1991, one week after the Russian coup, she went to teach creative writing at a special language school in Moscow. Her approach of integrating poetry with art and music encourages students and teachers to look into themselves and their world, and to take the risks of discovery. In her workshops and performances she explores the magic of poetry and the wonder of many voices. Presently, she is the area coordinator of California Poets in the Schools in San Diego, and a member of the Advisory Board of Directors for the statewide organization.

Poet

Verónica Cunningham

i am not a quiet poet.
i want to know Truths.
Hear the reason of Dreams
Hear the wonder of Questions
I want
to hear words that travel Heart
into the World
That reflect the lights
          and darks
Escaped, or allowed
Disguised or naked
Words
Reaching your sense of Words
Truth or lies, real or trusted
Poetry is language
The language of Our Lives

A Language of Survival

What if we created
a language
beyond curse or abuse
or the jagged judgments
of untended hearts
not pieces of hearts
not quilted hearts
not rock imitations
not a cancered heart
not the shadow of a heart
not the lie or the reflex
not a wooden corazón
not the rhinestone edition
not a glass see-through-object
not a damaged, erratic ticker
not a crazed sensitive bomb
but a language of *survival*
created with who we can be…
the Heart of Humanity
our most constant challenge
of Being.

ঙ৪ঌ

Porcupine Love

How can love so
tenaciously
be
that yearning
porcupine
swelling with a tenderness
beyond tenderness
an escaped contradiction
your soul tuning itself
into a sense of Beauty (of changing dreams)
What is the point of a porcupine's
loving?
Does it touch your memory?
scar? or song?
And do we love because we can
not help ourselves to push
against something that gives us
sign and gasp
and honors us
with tender acceptance

Heart Pieces

i have already
been inside your questions
and while I've had no answers
you have groaned and
survived the fire
of this journey
you craved the light
and
the fire
and walked a step in front of your fear
you were a lonely banquet
a contradiction
of feast
and
hunger.
i tasted the moon of your night
i ate stars until
people confused me with the
sun.
i was only a shy lover
of a startled moment.

El Beso

Close the door
open the window,
hearts wing
into sky blue dreams
imagined, final expression
that tongue that paints
fire inside of dreams

Angela de Hoyos

Angela de Hoyos, visual artist and poet, is a native of Mexico and a long-time resident of San Antonio, where she is co-editor of M & A Publications and of the literary review *Huehuetitlán*. In her poetry, published in both English and Spanish, De Hoyos is a verbal wizard, as she Hispanicizes the English language to suit her particular needs, expanding beyond the linguistic limits of the monolingual writer. Bryce Milligan, the San Antonio critic and author, has glowingly described his colleague and her work: "Angela de Hoyos, truly an angel in person, is a very demon when it comes to poetry. Oppression of any sort, superficiality in any form, these she faces down with authority and imagination—and humor. Her poetry is something of a *movimiento* in its own right, yet De Hoyos seldom lets passion outweigh craft." De Hoyos's early collections, *Arise, Chicano, and Other Poems* (1975) and *Chicano Poems: For the Barrio* (1975), convey the nationalistic and indigenist fervor of the Chicano movement of the mid-1960s to the mid-1970s in their testimonial rendition and reaction to the oppression of her people. *Poems/Poemas* (1975) and *Selecciones* (1979) bridge De Hoyos' nationalistic period with the feminist social analysis found in *Woman, Woman* (1985) in which she devotes full attention to a leitmotif present in most of her works: that dynamic tension which both unites and separates male and female. De Hoyos's poetry has also been published in India, England, Switzerland, and Australia, and is the subject of Marcella Aguilar-Henson's *The Multifaceted Poetic World of Angela de Hoyos* (1985).

To Walt Whitman

Angela de Hoyos

órale, carnal
mundo-poeta
demócrata profeta
te traje
una guitarra
—guitarra chicana—
pa' que te avientes una canción
a lo ancho del camino
donde quepa mi pueblo
—mi raza indígenamericana
que busco en tu verso
pero no la veo

A Walt Whitman

hey man, my brother
world-poet
prophet democratic
here's a guitar
for you
—a chicana guitar—
so you can spill out a song
for the open road
big enough for my people
—my Native Amerindian race
that I can't seem to find
in your poems

Arise, Chicano!

In your migrant's world of hand-to-mouth days,
your children go smileless to a cold bed;
the bare walls rockaby the same wry song,
a ragged dirge, thin as the air—

I have seen you go down
under the shrewd heel of exploit—
your long suns of brutal sweat
with ignoble pittance crowned.

Trapped in the never-ending fields
where you stoop, dreaming of sweeter dawns,
while the mocking whip of slavehood
confiscates your moment of reverie.

Or beneath the stars—offended
by your rude songs of rebellion—
when, at last, you shroud your dreams
and with them, your hymn of hope.

Thus a bitterness in your life:
wherever you turn for solace
there is an embargo.
How to express your anguish
when not even your burning words
are yours, they are borrowed
from the festering barrios of poverty

Tonantzín Morena

a la memoria de mi madre
a mis hermanas de sangre y de raza

en la casa de mi madre
no se perdía nada:
  when the milk went sour
  she made us cornbread
    ...en el chiquigüite grande
    apenas cabía
    el pan de maíz

the peach trees
cuajados de fruta
y nos hacía conserva
  ...trabajo pa todo el día
  bastante comida...
      always plenty to do
      plenty to eat
bajo el techo AmorMaterno

mi madre morena
con su hechura de diosa
dominando el espacio
  corazón abierto
  mente alerta
  manos a la obra
haciendo maravillas de manta:

¡ay mami, queremos ir al mitote
 de la onda proletaria!

...and she would spend
the night sewing
          Adelita blouses
adding peasant ruffles
  de retazos
  to lengthen
    our mini-skirts...

Mamá Tonantzín
always harnessing problems
always ready
with a sharp eye
for possibilities:
Oye, hija, ven acá!!!
a dónde vas
con esos costales...?

"Si amas, perdona—si no amas, olivada..."

that man
that vulgar luckless man
who spoke
with a savage tongue
(aunque el pueblo
estaba de fiesta)

who spat
those unkind words
when you approached him

no, no sé si es chicano
—podría ser
cualquier hombre—
pero ese hombre
que tú me pintas
así, tan distinto
no lo conozco

...still, he could be
someone's brother
he must be
somebody's father...

but supposing he were your own
hermano carnal
sólo que, por falta de luz
aquel día
en su espacio cúbico
en su mundo insólito
no te reconoció

or again, what if some day
you should happen
to come upon him
non-communicative
reduced
to the last corner of his
own private hell
—toothless eyeless voiceless
casi deshecho
barely a shadow
on the wall—

and what if he sees you
as the last
frontier of his hope

but you've come looking
for roses, as in poetry
for perfection, as in love

and he is only a derelict
devoid of all human dignity

so he has nothing
nothing to give you
beyond a blasphemous
inhuman
snarl.

Una mañana cualquiera

despiertas
satisfecho
en el cenit de tu vida
dejando atrás tus radiantes
conquistas
—y tal vez
un manojo de lágrimas
estratégicamente almacenadas
en algún rincón
donde no podrian
hacerte tropezar
y descubres

la muerte con su incansable hoz
insidiosamente escarbando
en el césped rebelde
de tu cuerpo.

Lo inaceptable

para M. R.

Desnúdate! Despójate de todo
hasta quedarte en tu pura esencia
—me aconsejaste—
o pasarás el resto de tus días
eternamente escondiéndote
en máscara.

Mas
cuando mostré
la pura, hermosa
esencia de mi verdad desnuda,
todos se alejaron
—sin comprender.

Spanish translations by Mireya Robles

One Ordinary Morning

you awake
satisfied
at the zenith of your life
with all your radiant conquests
behind you
(and perhaps a few
bucketsful of tears
strategically stored
in some remote corner
where they can't possibly
trip you)
and you discover

death with her diligent hoe
insidiously scraping away
at the unwilling turf
of your body.

On the Unacceptable

for M. R.

Strip! Strip all things
down to the pure essentials
—you advised me—
or you will spend your life
eternally hiding
behind facades.

And yet
when I revealed
my pure
my beautiful
my essential and naked truth
everyone turned away.
No one understood.

Invention of the Camel

for Mireya Robles

On the other side of water
in the desert
there was no life
worth mentioning

cactus had not yet learned
to produce wheels
the sky was a huge blanket
a dry and dusty blanket
and there were no stars

the myths had remained
just that
myths

—Jesus had not been cued
to make his
revolutionary appearance—

when one dreary morning
the sea awoke and yawned
she opened her dripping eyes
and sighed O my O me
what is this I see
these culturally-deprived
beings
are in trouble: no imagination
no sense no mobility: how
will they ever make it
to the Olympics on time?

I must call upon my old friend
the savvy Huitzilopochtli
at least he has first-hand
knowledge in the experience
of the instant birth
full-grown

and with a swish of
her frothy tail the sea
winked once, winked
twice and swam away with
a folio of kind and
gentle thoughts under her arm
—the newspapers exaggerated
called it a case of
divine intervention

but it was the sea
nuestra madre the sea
that rocks us to sleep—

it was the sea
our mother the sea
that conjured up
this legendary this
necessary creature.

(According to Aztec legend, Huitzilopochtli was the War God, principal deity of the Mexicans. The son of Coatlícue, mother of the gods, he was born full-grown and armed from head to toe, like the classic Minerva.)

Rhina Espaillat

Rhina Espaillat is a Dominican-born former high-school teacher of English. She resides in Newburyport, Massachusetts, with her husband Alfred Moskowitz, a sculptor and former industrial arts teacher. Espaillat, the daughter of a diplomat and a political exile, grew up in New York. When she was six years old, one year before her family moved to New York, she started to write poetry in Spanish; two years later, she began to write in English. At sixteen, she had the distinction of becoming the youngest member ever to have been inducted into the Poetry Society of America. She graduated from Hunter College and received an M.S.C. from Queens College, then taught in the New York City school system. Her poems have been widely published in reviews and anthologies, among them *Poetry*, *Merrimack: A Poetry Anthology* (1992), *Looking for Home: Women Writing about Exile* (1990), and *Sarah's Daughters Sing: A Sampler of Poems by Jewish Women* (1990). *Lapsing to Grace* (1992) is a collection of her poems with her own line drawings. Her work is also in *A Formal Feeling Comes: Poems in Form by Contemporary Women* (1994). Several of her poems in Spanish have appeared in newspapers in the Dominican Republic. Espaillat has won numerous awards, including one from The World Order of Narrative and Formalist Poets and two from the British magazine *Orbis*. In 1986 and again in 1989, the Poetry Society of America honored her with its Gustav Davidson Memorial Award. She describes herself as "one more exile with very little money and lots of old photographs." "The Ballad of San Isidro" is a hybrid poem. Stylized like a American ballad, its narrative is loosely based on events said to have taken place at the beginning of the century in her mother's home town, Jarabacoa.

Snapshots in an Album

Rhina Espaillat

I

Here are the elders,
looking out of
another place
as it was in a far summer.
Their time is before them.
Another time frames them,
but they do not know it.
I am a voice in their bones,
but they cannot hear me.

II

I am the small grim one
closing one eye against the sun,
clutching handlebars.
I don't like
whatever has just passed
on my left,
and the curve of the earth
is not to be trusted.

III

This woman is showing
an orange tree
she is growing from seed.
Dead forty years,
she will pick these oranges
when they ripen
and peel one, singing absently
the same five notes;
she will eat half
and give me half.
The pulp is sweet and sticky.

IV

This man lived
on his mule's back
where I sometimes perch
in the sweaty vice of his arms.
His farm smells of leather and heat.
A slow tide of straw hats
is flowing home around us
for the noon meal;
our ragged shadow rides under us,
pinned to our four hoofs.

V

This is the Virgin Mary
poised on a crescent moon.
She is shedding grace
like a fragrance
from both white hands.
Above her, lizards
patrol the wall for flies;
before her, votive candles bloom.
Someone is fingering beads:
the Virgin is pleased
with the small cool room,
pleased with the white pitcher
on its corner stand,
glad of the low voice
hailing her name.

VI

Here are the two of us,
looking out of now, this northern
autumn of wild cherry trees.
Most of our time is behind us.
Before us is more time
we wish ourselves into,
but it is your time, not ours.
You who are ours are somewhere
before us, adrift from our bodies.
We cannot see you, but
we are thinking out to you.

Where Childhood Lives

In my home town the nights are warm
and flies are watchful at the net,
as if Remember posted guards
along the borders of Forget.

And all night long in slow exchange
a dialogue of plunk and plink
from leaky roof to rusty basin
echoes what the raindrops think.

Along the wall where lizards hunt
mosquitoes urge their long complaint
and pious photographs commingle
the dead, the living and the saint.

One rooster, two, then five or six
from hill to valley rout the night,
and maids sigh up from creaky springs
to morning prayer and kitchen light

Along my narrow shuttered street
trot little donkeys gray with dust,
stopping to nuzzle here and there
at orange peel and cracker dust.

And morning takes the river road
down the bank where childhood lives,
where stones and water know my name
and stroke me with diminutives.

Translation

Cousins from home are practicing their English,
picking out what they can, slippery vowels
queasy in their ears, stiff consonants
bristling like Saxon spears too tightly massed
for the leisurely tongues of my home town.

They frame laborious greetings to our neighbors;
try learning names, fail, try again, give up,
hug then and laugh instead, with slow blushes.
Their gestures shed echoes of morning bells,
unfold narrow streets around them like gossip.

They watch us, gleaning with expert kindness
every crumb of good will dropped in our haste
from ritual to ritual; they like the pancakes,
smile at strangers, poke country fingers
between the toes of our city roses.

Their eyes want to know if I think in this
difficult noise, how well I remember
the quiet music our grandmother spoke
in her tin-roofed kitchen, how love can work
in a language without diminutives.

What words in any language but the wind's
could name this land as I've learned it by campfire?
I want to feed them the dusty sweetness
of American roads cleaving huge spaces,
wheatfield clean and smooth as a mother's apron.

I want to tell them the goodness of people
who seldom touch, who bring covered dishes
to the bereaved in embarrassed silence,
who teach me daily that all dialogue
is reverie, is hearsay, is translation.

The Ballad of San Isidro

In the village of San Isidro
they are gathered for a death.
A widow has called for her only son
and begs with her failing breath:

"I have promised you to God, my boy;
oppose me not in this.
Renounce the flesh and serve the Cross
and earn my parting kiss."

Shaken body and soul, he hears
his mother's final prayer,
for a body and soul and heart are bound
to a maiden's raven hair,

to a maiden's lips like a honeyed rose
and hands like an angel's nest,
and although he nods and bows his head
as his mother is laid to rest,
he longs to be on the silver cross
that lies on a budding breast.

A fortnight hence, by the river's edge,
her steps are swift and light.
"But where are my lover's eyes?" says she,
"for yours are not soft tonight."

"Farewell," says he, "my only dear,
for this is our final tryst,
and if you weep, you must weep alone,
for we must part unkissed."

She weeps, she weeps and calls after him,
but would she were alone,
for one has followed her from town,
whose heart is burning stone.

Her only sister's husband,
the herdsman Nicanor,
who's watched her from under his sullen brows
these seven years and more.

Seven long years to her sister wed,
and his thoughts are grim and dark,
for one sister's grown like a fat gray toad
but one is the morning lark.

"Let me pass, my sister's husband,
for you know we are close kin!
I cannot love my sister's man
nor lie with you in sin."

"Your love may shut me out," says he,
"but your body will let me in."

He mounts her like a battlement,
he leaves no gate untried.
The owl drifts down and swoops to find
what prey it was that cried,
and lucky the skittering tiny mouse
that knows a place to hide.

Heaven that bends above them both
is shining pure and clear.
"I shall not pray again," says she;
"for nothing there can hear,
can see, can feel for mouse or maid
who cries aloud in fear."

"Sister, sister, draw me a bath,
for tonight I slipped and fell."
"What fall is this that has left your eyes
like the shaft of a poisoned well?"

"Sister, sister, question me not,
for a serpent has frightened me."
"What serpent is this that has left more wounds
than the wounds of Calvary?"

Sister, the fall was your husband's fall,
the serpent Nicanor."
"A curse on your face that has tempted my man
until he could bear no more;
Pray God you do not warm his seed
and banish him from our door."

He does not come for the harvest
who did such fearful sowing.
There are those who hint they know not what,
there are those who play at knowing.
But after the town wears out the tale
the seasons forget his going.

"And what shall become of my boy and me
since you've sent my man to wander?"
"We will walk and walk on the points of spears
until we've traveled yonder.

We will make our peace, as the poor must do,
for the poor have scanty choices,
and labor as one for our fatherless brood
till the choir forgets our voices,
till our feet forget the dancing-floor
and our breath forgets how the world rejoices."

Her daughter is meek as a small gray dove;
she asks for nothing, ever.
But she's heard of the north, where dollars grow,
and her teachers call her clever.

"Farewell, farewell, my mother, my aunt,
my cousin who guides the plough,
I go to where dollars grow on trees
to pull them down somehow."
"Farewell, dear child, we have watched for you,
you must watch for your own self now."

"Fear not, my mother, my aunt," she writes,
"I am far from the honky tonks;
I have found a room like a cloistered cell
in a place they call El Bronx.

I spend my nights with an open book,
my days as a sickroom nurse.
The dollars shall be for sending home,
and the pennies for my purse."

In a Texas prison two thousand miles
from where she tends the sick,
there's a sullen man on death row
the guards call Spanish Nick

who could tell a tale, if he chose to tell,
but will soon tell nothing more,
for he's killed three men with a stolen gun
while robbing a liquor store.

In the village of San Isidro
they are gathered for a death.
The good old priest is babbling,
with every rasping breath,

of a maid alone by river's edge
and somebody cursed by prayer,
and somebody caught like a gasping fish
in a mesh of raven hair,

and wounds unhealed as the wounds of Christ
on hands like an angel's nest,
and somebody nailed to the silver cross
that lies on a budding breast.

You Call Me by Old Names

You call me by old names: how strange
to think "family" and "blood,"
walking through flakes, up to the knees
in cold and democratic mud.

And suddenly I think of people
dead many centuries ago:
my ancestors, who never knew
the dubious miracle of snow…

Don't say my names, you seem to mock
their charming, foolish Old World touch—
call me "immigrant," or Social
Security card such-and-such.,

or future citizen, who boasts
two eyes, two ears, a nose, a mouth,
but no manes from another life,
a long time back, a long way south.

Bodega

Bitter coffee, musty beans,
caramel and guava jam,
rice and sausage, nippy cheese,
saffron, anise, honey, ham,

rosemary, oregano,
clove, allspice and bacalao.
Fifty years have flown away:
childhood falls around me now,

childhood and another place
where the tang of orange sweets
golden on the vendor's tray
drifts like laughter through the streets.

Memory is filament
weaving, weaving what I am:
bitter coffee, musty beans,
caramel and guava jam.

Sandra María Esteves

Sandra María Esteves, born, raised and currently living in the Bronx, is a Puerto Rican-Dominican Latina whose poems have appeared in numerous anthologies and literary journals. Esteves is the recipient of poetry fellowships from the New York Foundation for the Arts (1985) and from CAPS (1980). Most recently she was the Executive Producer of the African Caribbean Poetry Theater, a Bronx-based arts organization, where she produced eight seasons of poetry readings and theater productions, and collaborated on artistic events with other arts organizations around New York City. Esteves is the author of three volumes of poetry: *Bluestown Mockingbird Mambo* (1989), *Tropical Rains: A Bilingual Downpour* (1984), and the revolutionary *Yerba Buena* (1981), which established an urban Latina aesthetic and thematic. A *Calyx* review of *Bluestown Mockingbird Mambo* describes Sandra María Esteves as a magician who pulls forty-eight poems out of her hat. "These poems do not go down easily for [...] naive readers: Esteves speaks with punch and politically-astute vigor about the realities of the urban poor. More importantly, the poetry draws a big distinction between one being economically poor and spiritually and culturally repressed. Esteves challenges all the societal devices that keep people down. She urges, yes, *dares* her people to celebrate, to maintain faith and strength against those powers that market their destruction." Sandra María Esteves's poetry readings are spectacular examples of the poetry reading as performance art.

Autobiography of a Nuyorican

Sandra María Esteves

for Lela

Half blue, feet first
she battled into the world.
Hardly surviving the blood cord twice wrapped,
tense around her neck. Hanging.
Womb pressing, pushing,
pulling life from mother's child.
Fragile flesh emerging perfect in blueness,
like the lifeline that sustained her,
yet limp, almost a corpse.

Her mother claims the virgin interceded.
Invoked through divine promise, in prayer,
that caused her dark eyes to open,
her tongue to taste air like fire,
as the blueness faded,
tracing death on the tail of an eclipse.

And as in birth from her darkness,
the free-giving sun inched slow to visibility,
revealing all color and form,
a great teacher, generous and awesome,
silent and reverent, loud and blasphemous,
constant,
sculpting edges of definition
in the shadow and light of multiple universes.

Half blue, feet first
she battled her way.
The world did not want another brown,
another slant-eyed-olive-indian-black-child.
Did not want another rainbow empowered song
added to repertoire in blue,
or azure, or indigo,
or caribbean crystal.
Did not want another mouth to feed,
especially another rock-the-boat poet,
another voice opened wide,
fixed on a global spectrum of defiance.

The meaning of war defined her. Gasping and innocent,
before she knew her mother,
before she discovered herself, barely alive,
gathering weapons into her being with each breath that filled her,
growing stronger,
determined
to beat all the odds.

Love Affair with a Welfare Hotel

A city breeds corruption
abundant,
like a dripping faucet,
spilling a payload of drug blood
into gutters where children play,
watching pushers
pushing nightmares into their dreams.

No money for wood and nails,
or for building new foundations.
No money for books, or pencils,
just enough to fill the coffers of greedy lords
who wait by desks that register the homeless.

While in Guatemala
fifty thousand dreams are shattered
into shades, shapes of fine glass
cut sharp, irregular.
Families dissipated into refugee camps,
severed from their roots,
replanted in artificial gardens
where no one has a name,
and nothing is known
but the interest rate
produced by slaves of the neonazichristianrepublicanstates
in the war that never ends.

What gives them the right
to displace people from their land,
destroy traditions built up over centuries,
redefine the borderline of priorities,
imposed, dictated, and controlled?

In Guatemala
you cannot call your brother in Santa Monica,
take a spin in your corvette,
shop Roosevelt Field on Sunday afternoons,
eating meat at least once a day.

In Guatemala
fifty thousand hopes for the future
wait for directions to the next relocation center
while others flee into jungles,
waiting to die for their liberation.

Sistas

Nina Simone, Celia Cruz, Billie Holiday, and Bessie
were all sistas growin' up,
keepin' her company through only-child-blues.
Afternoons spent laughin', cryin', dancin' motown
gold,
harmonizin' are-'n-be teen sweet melodies.

Aretha Franklin, La Lupe, Diana and the Supremes
stayed up nights at heartbreak hotel,
rappin' real close moonshine doo-waps,
patiently riffin' their lines till she learned all the
words.
Takin' it higher,
hittin' all the notes home.

Ronnie Scepter and Gladys Knight hung out too.
The first time ever she heard Roberta Flack,
knew they were fruit from the same feelin' tree.
How they loved her madly, without even tryin'.
Didn't have to be nobody. Didn't need to prove.
They never got tired, or complained about the volume,
or even cared who was listenin'.
Always by her side, no matter what.
Tight for days.
Gettin' it on. Gettin' down.

Sistas all the way.

Raising Eyebrows

for Frida Kahlo

Here we are Frida
Sisters face to face
You hanging on museum walls
Your canvass singing
Familiar womansongs
In bramble bush hair
Eagle eyebrow wings
Blood-stained wedding dress
Cloudy sky fan
Unspeakable man-suit
Where we met
Thru different times
Finding each other at last
Your colored visions seeing
Into my magic world
Under the surface
Where nothing much has changed

We are long lost sisters
In kinship without a doubt
Bloodlines thick
As Mexican mud
Your palette womb
Painting me over
Into myself
Into your twisted hair
Eagle eyebrows
Sky fan and man-suit
In our blood stained wedding dress
Staring into each other
Fighting to walk on water
Bring down rain
Behind the respectable door

I offer you this time
The way your brushstroke sacrifices
Offers your soul to us

Some called you crazy
What did they really know?
Opinionated woman
Shut into wrenching poems
Silenced into speaking paintings
Where I imagine
More than sisters
Seeing what you see
Seeing myself thru you
Clear as crystal
Drinking water from your brushstrokes
Reflections in the mirror.

☙❧

Amor negro

in our wagon oysters are treasure
their hard shells clacking against each other
words that crash into our ears
we cushion them
cut them gently in our hands
we kiss and suck the delicate juice
and sculpture flowers from the stone skin
we wash them in the river by moonlight
with offerings of songs
and after the meal we wear them in our hair
and in our eyes

Gringolandia

for Martin Espada

How I love to listen to north american intellectuals.
The way they utilize language, brutalize communication,
glibly flip speech from the tips of their flying tongues,
spontaneous maneuverings
on the precise order of perfection.
Always knowing. Absolutely aware
of the exact format of correctness.
Never failing. Never mistaking
a lie for anything not resembling it.
Commanding the copyright of thought communication
with presumptuous ownership.
Definitively dear on the ingredients of the perfect poem,
the metamorphosis of the superlative metaphor,
the inharmonious insistence on
control-domination-instinctive-twitch.

How I love to listen.
Remind myself there is more to the world.
The whole of it.
The multinational ethnicity of it.
The many prismed expression of it.
The strength and struggle of it.
How I have learned to grow from it.
To love and praise myself from it.
To let life force flow from it.
To be in tune as one to it.

Perceive the face of death whenever/wherever it stares
at me.
Then establish the rhythm of counterbalance,
the offbeat note of discovery at the crossroads
where montuno comes alive.

Ocha

Crawling through the ground,
hidden and covered in slime,
begins the metamorphosis of the butterfly.

Almost at the point of death,
dormant, frozen in its prison,
asleep and unaware of its future,
until its casing presses tight,
breathless against its skin
as it stirs in its initiation,
pushing at the walls that hold
like a sealed coffin,
finding need for its own rebellion,
heaving its liberation song with calculated force,
a ritual guided,
pulled forward through a slight crack
like a beacon barely sighted over a stormy sea,
like the tender promise of a lover's loss
after annihilation in the war of loneliness,
stretching out slowly,
limb after untrained limb,
emerging through its birth canal,
disoriented and dizzy,
unfolding one fan wing, then another,
to dry, visible and free over the fields,
revealing qualities of the prismatic universe
that powers it to flight,
to feast in the eternal garden,
empowered by itself
with beauty blazing mantle adorning its back,
head crowned luminous,
blessed by the eccentric wind,
blowing magnetically towards the midday sky,

receiving its final gift:
a left-sided wing
invisible, perfumed,
trailing a direct spiral into heaven.

Poem to My Therapist

I watch your eyes
Deep into mine
See the me
That lives in you
The you in me
That always returns again
To haunt the warrior
In your womansoul

You've already been
Where I begin
On a path
Familiar and well-traveled
Where I am lost
At the crossroad
Searching desperately
For the green light
To guide my next step

Already I caught myself
Walking backwards
Not knowing
Where the sun existed
Seeing and not seeing
Turned around
Believing in some other life
A creation I invented
Of a dream I once had

Now the desert bears my name
In each minute grain
That fell from the mountain
Where the cactus blooms
Only once a year

In the desert
A year is a lifetime
Water is more precious
Than gold
The rainfall waits
Near the distant horizon.

Religious Instructions for Young Casualties

Believe in yourself.
Be all that you can.
Look for your fate among the stars.
Imagine you are your best when being yourself
the best way you can.

Believe in yourself. Be all you want to be.
Open your mind, a window to the world,
different ways of thinking, seeing,
but be yourself— it's the best.

Become your dreams, visions to live by.
No matter what anyone says,
believe you can do it.
Day by day, a little at a time.
Be patient.

Believe you can find a way
to assemble the puzzle called life,
forming pictures that make some kind of sense.
Even when pieces fall scattered to the ground,
disappearing into the finite void,
forever lost, never to be found,
choosing your future from those that are left,
like one piece from some other dimension.

Maybe a corner triangle shape of sky,
or zigzag of ocean floor with seaweed and one school of fish,
or maybe a centerpiece on the table in some fancy dining room,
or patch of window lace curtain next to flowered bouquet,
wind blowing through sunlight, which some artist will paint someday.
Or bouncing feet on the moon,
walking in giant moon leaps, talking moon talk,
deep into research in your flying laboratory.

Be all that you can, but believe in yourself.
Climb the stairway of your imagination, one step after another.
Growing like the leaf, blossoming into a great tree,
complete with squirrels, nests, universe all around.

Be all that you can,
just believe in yourself.

Lourdes Gil

Lourdes Gil was born in Havana, Cuba, and has lived in the United States since 1961. She received an M.A. in Latin American Literature from New York University, and has worked as translator and editor for Hearst Publications in New York. With Iraida Iturralde, she has co-edited *Románica* (NYU's literary journal in the Romance languages) and the literary quarterly, *Lyra*. As a Cuban living outside of Cuba, Gil has been awarded an Arts International-administered Cintas Writer's Fellowship in 1979 and again in 1991. Widely published in numerous reviews, including *Michigan Quarterly Review, Inti, Linden Lane,* and *Brújula/Compass*, Gil is also the author of several collections of poetry: *Neumas* (1977), *Vencido el fuego de la especie* (1983), *Blanca aldaba preludia* (1989 and *Empieza la ciudad* (1993). Her work has appeared in the anthologies *Poetas cubanas en Nueva York/Cuban Women Poets in New York* (1991), *Los atrevidos: Cuban-American Writers* (1989), and *Poetas hispanoamericanas contemporáneas* (1989). Active in the Latin American Writers Institute of New York, Gil has been a member of the Literature Committee of the Ollantay Center for the Arts, and has coordinated several writers symposia for that organization. She is currently working on a book of essays on the transcendence of exile in Cuban literature and art. Critic Perla Rozencvaig notes that the experience of exile has brought Lourdes Gil a balance of losses and gains; her poetry displays a genuine revelation of the self in search of its milieu. Having written and published primarily in Spanish, Gil has recently started to write in English. Included here are her poems in their English original.

A Stranger Came

Lourdes Gil

Her sense of loss was like a chilling wind
across a hybrid landscape,
across the land she half-imagined years before,
the corollary of her sleepless nights,
her early vibrant colors fading
under the abstract light of wasted patience
on objects growing closer
in their subtler shades,
their greenish veins a strain over her eyes.

She told of dreams she had.
Of fragrant mango groves she never breathed again.
Of mythic, jewel-like birds,
gigantic lizards basking in the sun
with stomachs turned. And of two-headed swans
like two interrogation points
in a gyrating double helix
of erotic thrust.

She told of ancient voices hidden in the dust
she traveled to explore.
How they were furious that she ventured there.
And how their gift to her
was more misfortune than reward
—her name undone, her every vision
ruthlessly dispelled by sounds
of languages she conquered,
yet secretly despised.

During the interminable months she spent
among us, reality entered every room.
Windows to the east
and west, drenched in wintry light,
settled the stage for images we lost
and gained— the mute reflections
of places that we knew.

She left behind a trailing scent,
an elegy to spaces gone and found.
To sites transposed with their patina intact,
their stupor whole in every petal,
in every hummingbird transfixed
in its hypnotic interplay.

The landscape inadvertently acquired
a more familiar tone. The chill subsided
without warning, sights rearranged themselves
over the oleander, bones stretched
contentedly in the morning glow.
Time is the stranger now,
the invader of the flesh, the meddling presence
separating her from her past,
from the visiting child
no longer with us.

Mutation Comes by Water

He wrote to me (his written words
carefully different from his speech)
that there were pathways in the sky
and in the ocean for the bird
and for the fish
that human eyes cannot perceive.
And the thought grabbed me,
held me to him while the white surf
stroked our ankles.
This thirst, this paralyzing want
—I knew he had designed for me.
His fingers traced a mast above our heads.
I watched as he evoked
the elongated image of a palm tree, probing
the very substance of my pain.
Lines faintly emerged
from their invisible orbits: I saw
the sensuous arch engulfed by salt and sand
beyond the pink veneer of the horizon.
Our gestures swelled in secret motions,
their patterns now lucidly at rest
over the water.
A soundless, punctured tongue
described the unknown passages
to these primordial islands:
a muzzled count
of new erosions on the rocks, winds
wounded with rain, inflamed with purple light,
with scent of jasmine from the shore.
Darkness was gradually swallowing the boat
shrouding the slanted flight of sea gulls,
blurring the outline of the pier.
We were immersed in its black raspy throat.
How could I see, alone inside the vastness,
he had left
to follow his own path over the water?

Last Port

The Portuguese navigator
ended his visit of the isthmus.
The wispy chieftain's daughter hid
behind a cluster of marjoram trees
and watched him sail
en route to those scattered islands
of the Caribs, never to return.
She knelt and kissed the shadow
he left on the sand.
The convulsive shriek
of a red-necked parrot
pierced the vaulted skies.
She shuddered and looked up.
She saw his aura inflame the leaves
of the hibiscus, his soul
imprisoned in the golden boughs
of the Guamuhaya tribe.

This, My Last Thought

This is the unseen point
where the mysterious journey of the serpent
unravels in the mind,
where the relentless flesh invents
new crowning discs.
This is the fear of infinity, the end
of all the signs I have encountered:
spiral tails rising over roof tops,
long cirrus clouds spilling rain.
This is the final destination
of awkward longing, whenever I pass towns
resembling other towns—cities
smeared with honey, petrified cities
clutched in remote languages of clay;
translucent cities
where I encounter my own puberty
disguised in thinly painted glass.
This too is the epilogue
for walking corpses from the past
—faceless, half- dressed corpses
roaming indifferent by the boundary
of affliction. This, my last thought
of many places, innumerable times
the phosphorescence of memory:
the end to grotesque dreams
inside a bubble.
The last intent where gracious gods
flash their ancestral souls behind a mask
revealing primal Cuban myths;
where all submerged metaphors
rise raging over ruins like rolling waves.
This time surfaces crack
on every object, every wall now only
fallen bricks over the bougainvillea.

Carolina Hospital

Carolina Hospital was born in Havana. She came to live in Miami in 1961 when she was four years old. After completing her graduate studies at the University of Florida, she returned to Miami, where she teaches in the English Department at Miami Dade Community College. Her M.A. thesis, "The Children of Exile and Their Literature," has served as the point of departure for many of her articles on Latino literature of the United States. In addition, her own poetry and fiction have appeared in literary reviews throughout the nation, including *The Americas Review*, *Bilingual Review*, *Cuban Heritage Magazine*, *Linden Lane*, and the anthology, *Looking for Home*. Hospital has edited *Cuban American Writers: Los Atrevidos* (1989), an anthology to which she contributed prose and poetry. With Pablo Medina, she has also edited a bilingual edition of poetry by Tania Díaz Castro, *Everyone Will Have to Listen* (1990). In her introduction to *Cuban American Writers: Los Atrevidos*, Hospital views Cuban American writers of her generation as risk-takers, daring to belong to a future that acknowledges a new historical reality. Forced to develop their talents within two cultural and linguistic worlds, these authors write primarily in English about their legacy and cultural traditions at the same time that they demonstrate a vital exile consciousness. Hospital believes that such writers cannot be defined simply by their choice of language or their place of birth or residence. Rather, she emphasizes that their work must be contextualized within their cultural, social and linguistic legacies, then situated within both Cuban and North American literary traditions.

Hell's Kitchen

Carolina Hospital

for Angel Cuadra and Reinaldo Arenas, writers and ex-political prisoners in Cuba

The words drip down his lips:
Una Revolución sin odio.
A Revolution without hatred
is what he wanted.
In that dark cell, he learned to forgive.
For fifteen years, Angel forgave his youth
as it abandoned him, piece by piece.
He gave away his intimacy.
Ernesto helped him write metaphors of love
that fit into a matchbox.
The words flew on the wings of angels
and carried away his anger with his passions.
He stood firmly on the damp ground,
as Reinaldo scattered the sand.
Reinaldo found no angels,
only humans addicted to desire,
looking for the sum of all delights
in a place where no delights are possible.
The untempered pleasures of the flesh
offered him a respite,
but when I met him, death was already awaiting.
He had left hell to enter its kitchen
and there he died,
still eager as a twelve-year old boy.
Perhaps, one day angels and kings will meet
and need not speak.

A Visit to West New York

The Virgin of Charity, in blue,
and her three fishermen rest
on the wooden dresser.
I can hear salsa on
the neighbor's radio.
I try to decipher the faces
covering the night table.
The single bed hardly fits
in this room, cluttered,
clothes hanging, off the closet doors,
on the red felt armchair. I turn
to face the flowered wall
and sleep.

The ring of the phone, her voice,
loud and energetic, waken me.
I quickly dress, follow the scent
of espresso and buttered toast.
It's José's mother I meet in the kitchen,
her eyes glistening with mischief.
We have just met, but she talks of life
back home, her arms waving as she
urges me to eat more toast.
José seems embarrassed.

Then, it is time to leave.
He opens the door.
I confront the landscape:
a lean street with urinated curbs,
a jagged fence and skies of
worn and pitted bricks.

Dear Tía

I do not write.
The years have frightened me away.
My life in a land so familiarly foreign,
a denial of your presence.
Your name is mine.
One black and white photograph of your youth,
all I hold on to.
One story of your past.

The pain comes not from nostalgia.
I do not miss your voice urging me in play,
your smile,
or your pride when others called you my mother.
I cannot close my eyes and feel your soft skin;
listen to your laughter;
smell the sweetness of your bath.
I write because I cannot remember at all.

On the Last Stretch of the Journey

You recovered the forgotten smell of woman.
Tania Díaz Castro

On the last stretch of the journey,
I held the reins so tightly
my palms ached
and the mare gasped for air.
She struggled until I relaxed.
As first, she raced madly
across the grazing fields.
Gradually, she settled
on a steady trot
that returned us to the stables.
Her freedom delivered mine.

It was a moment of grace, said Father.
He held my hands and smiled,
as if my return after eighteen years
was a gift I had delivered him.
A spoiled child had abandoned
the stained glass windows
or sat waiting in an empty pew.
Now, he saw a woman approach him.
"Forgive yourself," insisted Father.
His hands on my head
released the fear,
the shame.
I stopped fighting my will.

I embraced the void,
the one that follows me like a lost child.
I awakened from a scream
to find you searching
for my purity.
You smelled my hair,
my naked flesh,
trying to recover a memory.
I tumbled into your arms.
We made love.
You were surprised
by the child in my eyes.

For a Sister Here

Six years ago I discovered her
in the ruins of the city,
wandering among the ashes
of burnt souls.
Then, I denied my sister,
a stranger.
I listened,
heard the silence of fear,
the sounds of aimlessness.
I could only wait,
wait for her to break the night.
One night, any night,
she called me.
"I'm worthless," she said.
What new words could I unleash
to keep her on the line.
I knew what she wanted.

911 found her,
babbling,
contorted in spasms by the phone booth.
In the ambulance, she was on her way out.
The I.V. lines replacing the coke lines,
the steel railings stiffened the whitish limbs,
powder-free air tubed up her nose.
My sister, confined
within the sterile order of life support,
arrived.
At the hospital, I waited.
All night, many nights.
She could not remember her bruises,
her missing chain with the Sacred Heart,
her last meal five days earlier.
Finally, she came out
packed with weary promises.
It's four days before Christmas;
her daughter, a fly on her arm, sits
by the door, ready
for their two week visit.
She never arrives.

It's easier to live
in the night,
where the dark conceals the ruins
and hides the residues of destiny.
Meaning splits in half and
the nearness of death
destroys all shame.
No longer my sister,
she becomes an accomplice
with the illusions,
falsehoods littered
across the cool counter of the bar.
Outside she tries to call home,
but she can't recognize the sidewalk.
Seven days and no word of her.
Will she get away this time?
Or will I find my sister
a hanging effigy
smiling upon the ruins?

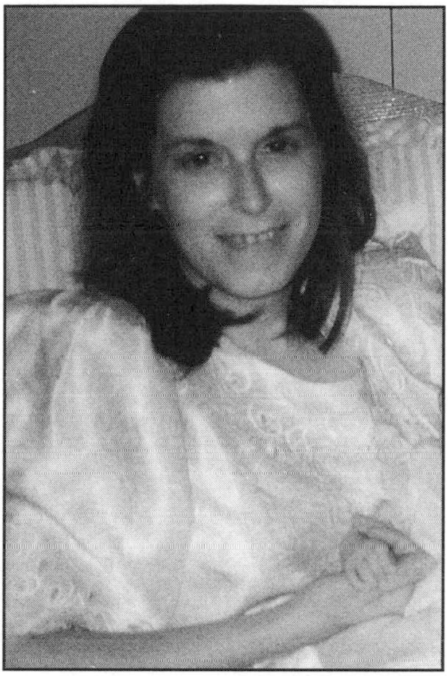

Iraida Iturralde

Iraida Iturralde came to this country from Havana in 1962 when she was eight years old, and now lives in New Jersey with her two daughters and her husband. She has received degrees in Political Science from New York University and Columbia University. With Lourdes Gil, she co-edited NYU's *Romanica* and later, the literary review, *Lyra*. She has received the Oscar B. Cintas Fellowship for Cubans living outside of Cuba, a Ford Foundation grant and the Mid Atlantic States Arts Consortium grant. Her poetry has been published in the United States, Europe and Latin America. The author of three collections of poetry—-*Hubo la viola* (1979), *El libro de Josefat* (1983) and *Tropel de espejos* (1989), Iturralde's work has appeared in several anthologies, among them *Fiesta del Poeta* (1977), *Poesía hispanoamericana en Nueva York* (1979), *Poetas cubanos en Nueva York* (1988), *Los Atrevidos: Cuban American Writers* (1989), and *Poetas cubanas en Nueva York/Cuban Women Poets in New York* (1991). She presently works as an editor for an international press agency. Of her life as an exile she says, "I was born in Cuba, an incidental fact, were it not for the passion its sun bestows on its progeny. There I took my first steps, read my first book, wrote my first word. I was snatched from its soil in 1962. Hence my ever-present bipolarity: melancholy and mirth. Coming of age was an awesome trial, and so long that it stretched out beyond its usual boundaries. Womanhood came to me almost imperceptibly, defined more by love than by the traditional parameters society dictates." Of her new poetry, in English, she says she is briefly forsaking her ancient verse to speak to her husband in his native language.

A Fragile Heritage

Iraida Iturralde

Not alone, at birth
when the upthrust of the sun claimed the eyelids
and I burst, tongue unfolding, from the shade
and then another and another, tufts of fallen vowels
ripe and open
claimed the sea edge—one long gentle earth
and the lips, tanned, half open
spoke and swallowed and spoke
and swallowed consonants tinged amber
by the sun (perched, like dove or antelope
on the forehead)

Yet you hardly met that child
now straying homeward like a chimney
her cheeks, two wailing shells
sallow from moonlight

Such countenance
was plain

The world below these waters had shed reeds
and behind their trail of silence came a still
and lonelier trail—
a new language (lips cracked-open)
unbraided the strange fabric of snow:
a run of painful, wily syllables
swerving seamless, like marbles, in the cold

Then I turned, my brow dawning
by another river:
your alien smell
nursing old wounds from memory

The Man Who Saved the Fish

The flood-tide pours in with a jolting swirl,
the waves leaping easily above his head.
Above this man's head, a clean absence of seaweed.

And above his eyes
the fish do somersaults in the misty space,
above the man's eyes, with the drowning smell
of a certain death.

Upon his palms, a sensuous flutter
and the man cups them into a potter's urn,
saving, by instinct, his tropical fish.

The children loved him on the sand
for in his splendid chivalry
this thin enamored man
looked so unlike the infidel.

Rite of Passage

For who's to say
when you and I caress, muffling
the sounds of the shepherds' flutes,
that I don't dance barefoot on your forehead
and you don't come sailing
unbound
into my womb.

Over a Baroque Portal: The Meow of the Offspring

She sat demurely, chiseled in gold
as if to say my smile is like a vestige
the memory of a land where palms sway gently
to the ocean's rippling blue.

The other, a sunlit fresco
imposing her marveled gaze upon the planet
as if to say, I bow
to the ultimate splendor.

Our children belie you.

The Obligatory Verse

This game of skills,
the mother, the wife, the woman
of your soul.
This earnest moon,
this planet for your cat.

She slithers in and out,
her daily potion spattered,
sweet.

Yet what is this mind,
confused, it seems too much
in awe.

Who is this monster,
this fragile resilience
she shows,
the opium on the earlobes,
our home a jumble
of uneven socks.

I dare say, you wonder
has she no skills
beyond
one giant thrust
of love.

On the Altars of Tikal

Legend has it that we were ancient,
that we sat cross-legged in the desert blizzard,
when only the rind of the errant moon
led the pupil to the twilled silk of darkness,
for we could hardly pierce the day—bathed in shadows—
while the sun rested on the slopes of time.

No one now remembers how a sturdy breed of unicorns
soared across the desert to slow the wind
and left an endless furrow of glyphs printed on the sand,
as if to lure us to the heavens,
for a splintered earth—sitting on the footstool of space—
was yet to blossom with temple-crowned pyramids on its lake beds.

But then you entered me,
and the archangels departed: and in the hour of silence
the sacred halo of a yellow star—bold and distant—
wrapped our bodies inside the sentimental gaze
of lusty creatures blessed,
the only phantom of the death to come.

It was later written in the Popol Vuh
that long before the Mayan rulers—in classic regalia—
wore the mask of the Sun God,
we were playing on conch-shell trumpets
the cadence of the universe:
I, the captive of your metaphor.

Natashia López

Natashia López was born in Portland, Oregon, and was reared as the daughter of a single-parent. Her mother was born in Mexico and was raised in Mexico City. As a teenager, Natashia was a Health Educator/Actress with Teens & Company, an educational theater company which performed across the state of Oregon, providing information on rape, safe-sex, family communication, and peer pressure. The show eventually was made into a television production and won an Iris Award. In 1988 she left Oregon to study at the University of California at Berkeley, where in 1992 she received her B.A. in Chicano Studies. As a student she was active in rape-prevention programs and in providing educational services to Chicano/Latino youth. In 1994, López completed her Master of Education in Risk and Prevention at Harvard University. In Boston, she worked with The Medical Foundation and the Governor's Initiative on Gay/Lesbian/Bisexual Youth, organizing conferences and workshops which focused on suicide prevention amongst gay youth. In her poetry, López writes about the peer pressures experienced by urban youth and their encounter with violence. She has published her poetry in student literary reviews and in *Chicana Lesbians: The Girls Our Mothers Warned Us About* (1991). Presently, she is living in San Francisco.

Epitaph

Natashia López

you were a girl that dreamed
of fame and fortune
at an early age
insisted on wearing tap shoes
around the house
and aluminum-foil crowns on your head
with red lipstick and blue shadow

at ten
you sang through a toy microphone
while big sister took photos you carried,
showing them off to friends

when drugs were popular
you became Ms. Marijuana
the one who always had a pipe in your pocket
a lighter in your purse
beer in your coat bulging at the waist,
at concerts you hid cocaine in your bra
a smokeless pipe down your pants
and pills in the side of your shoe;
once inside
you bragged about passing the search
emptied your bra and complained the music
wasn't loud enough,
there were never enough people puking to please you,
always wanting to see one more fight
a little more blood,
and the ambulance rushing in
something to talk about the next day;

you didn't care what you had to do
you wanted to be known
"I don't care if I have to go in one of
those sleazy magazines or be a call girl,
I'm gonna make it big someday"

and you felt big with men,
stroking their cocks
just the way they wanted
telling them how badly you wanted them
pretending to cum
digging your nails in their backs,
afterwards you closed your legs
returned home and didn't mind
if they never called back
but they always did
you played their games
hung up in their faces
wore the skirts they liked
and never pushed condoms

you were a girl that dreamed,
became a star for men and drugs
you could have charged money
but
in the end
what did it do for you?

All Body and No Soul

take my breasts
its all i have to offer
its not much
but its all i have
to offer
or you can have my legs
they're more shapely

i dont got no soul though
nothing inside
how did this happen to me
who made me a body
and took my soul
and how can i get
my soul back

Do you realize i cant keep eye contact
when my eyes are bare?

i need my mascara
my shadow
and powder

maybe its a personal problem
that i keep needing to peek
in my compact

i really do want to
offer you more
i really do have more
so much more to offer
than my body

but during conversations
i peek at my reflection
in windows and metal napkin holders
in doorknobs and other peoples glasses
im checking to see
if im showing
enough shoulder
as i speak
cause what good
is a brain
without a body

While i share my opinions with you im sucking in my tummy.

you said
you like
the way i express myself
sexually
not
the way i think
but
the way i fuck
basically
you like to fuck me

ya
ive been feeling like a fuck
been feeling like its
what i do
best
been feeling like
in the end
i always got that split
between my legs

i should have been
an inflatable woman
all body and no soul
a hole
hanging
between the videos and magazines
in that shop
called girls girls girls

maybe its not too late
to market myself
they say poetry writers
are in this year
i can tattoo a poem
down the middle of my chest
the end of the poem
will be at the tip
of my clitoris

that is
my mind
my creative side
will end
when you reach my cunt
cause isnt that what you like
so much more
so much more
like a whore
i feel sometimes
all body and no soul

From Between Our Legs

somewhere
in the third world
women bleed
wash their panties in the river
hang them between trees to dry
lie back flat on kitchen tables
and scream out babies
here
in the United States
I walk down Walgreen's "feminine hygiene" aisle
searching for my favorite pad or tampon
maxi or thin slender or regular
pregnant mothers attend birthing classes
I fight for condom machines in bathrooms
a Honduran woman vomits a clear white
the pill
makes her poorly nourished body sick
I worry about bloating
In El Salvador a mother
takes her sun-dried panties from the trees
mine are stuck on the side of a washing machine
with a sock and bra strap
somewhere
a woman is bending over in a field
hot blood running down the side of her leg
I feel it pouring
over the edges of my pad
everywhere/somewhere
we bleed
we were/are told we are witches
our pain is our "duty"
and it pours from between our legs.

For Women Who Need Strength

I want you to be strong
so strong that you could have survived a slave ship
with an inch above you
and an inch below you
with piss leaking over your head
and your own shit
squishing between your toes
I want you to be so strong
you can watch your child's fingers
get chopped at the ends
and see your sister
walk around with one ear

I want you to move things with your eyes
and speak in three voices
I want you to be able to travel miles
locked inside the trunk of a car
and still maintain your mind
I want you to endure
being buried alive
and dig yourself out
to talk about it
when your head gets chopped off
I still want you to talk
and when they rape you
again and again
i want you to leave your body
and come give mine a kiss

I want your nails to poke out eyes
and your feet to walk days
through muddy mountains
I want you to know how to use a gun
but also to feel secure
without one

I expect a lot from you
'cause sometimes my shoes
get holes on the bottom
and my feet
begin to freeze
other times
I lose my appetite
and my head
begins to drop
I need you strong to remind me
that even naked
I can walk through trenches
rain pouring over my head
I can eat rats if I have to
and live
even after the maggots appear.

Olga Elena Mattei

Olga Elena Mattei was born in Puerto Rico of a Colombian mother and a Puerto Rican father. She received her degree from the Universidad Bolivariana of Medellín, but for the last fifteen years she has lived in New York, where she is a member of the Institute of Latin American Writers. Her manuscript, entitled "Huellas en el agua," received the Café Márfil award in Spain. Her publications include *Sílabas de arena* (1962), *La gente* (1974), for which she received the national prize for poetry in Colombia, and *Cosmofonía* (1973), published bilingually in French and Spanish. French composer Marc Carles used *Cosmofonía* as the lyrics for his "Cantata," which was initially performed at the Maison Ronde in Paris, and aired in radio and television in France. *Cosmoagonía: Misa Cósmica*, in multimedia slide montage, with New Age music by Mexican composer Jorge López, has been performed in various planetariums, including planetariums in Bogotá, Toronto, Santo Domingo, Guadalajara, and San Juan, Puerto Rico. The newspaper, *El Columbiano*, of Medellín published the entire text of *Cosmoagonía* in its Sunday literary supplement on April 17, 1994. Her poetry will appear in a critical edition, *Colección de Autores Antioqueños* (1994). Recognized as one of the three most important contemporary Colombian poets, Mattei has done numerous readings in New York, including those at the Americas Society and the New York Public Library. While a resident poet at the International Writing Program at the University of Iowa, Mattei translated selections from her poetry into English, including the poems in this anthology. In her poetry and performances, she is interested in integrating humanistic values with the sciences and technology.

Ms. Bourgeois

Olga Elena Mattei

I am a bourgeois lady
and have a swollen belly.
I try to write my thoughts
despite my sore throat.

I behave
the way
some others want.
In common ground, the standard lie.
But,
for human beings
it is despicable to bear
labels which say:
"Dry clean only."
"Handle with care."

I have been a prodigious child,
a little brat,
a bad student,
a beauty queen,
a fashion model,
and one of those
that advertise
soups or sundries.

I got myself
into this inevitable mess,
by falling in love,
then sacrificing
a handsome man,
turning him
into a husband,
a sad situation.

(Not to mention
what kind of person
I have become!)

I have committed
an inconvenient
social crime:
adding five children to the crowd.

I have failed
as a mother,
and a wife,
as a lover,
as a reader
of philosophy.

All I can do,
with sad mediocrity,
is to be
a bourgeois wife,
unforgivably inconsequential,
deaf and blind:
a useless kind
of human mind.

And that
is
why
I always
have
a swollen belly,
and sometimes I want to scream
with such anger,
that my own raging words
do irritate my throat.

Then I write poetry
which has the sound
of a bass cord
inside my core.
Because
I know the truth:
that there's a war, and violence, and crime
each single day,
while I am
at the same time
sitting here
with no fear...
For dumb,
so doomed.
For deaf
so damned.

Not knowing what to do
I choose inertia.
I look the other way.
But inside myself, I cry.
Because
I remember
the hunger,
the children in tears
watching us
with open eyes...
far away or near,
the children
as real
as I.

At exactly
the same hour
we the ladies,
the socialites
keep sitting here
blinded,
surrounded
by disposable
happiness.

I do nothing
to see
if we can move the world
against poverty and drugs,
against violence and war!

Instead
there's this insanity,
staying still,
contented with being
just ass holes.

ઉજ્ઞ

The Angel of the Millennium
(Accident at the Nuclear Plant)

And so the Angel
came again.
One of those mysterious beings
whose deeds among men
are told in ancient books.
Now, this one came
to the country of great cities.
"Code Epsilon, thirteen to the seventh,
Z coordinate of minus 0.5, 8-5-3,
27 Submiriad";
"Michael" they called him
many centuries before.

He arrived camouflaged
in the secrecy of his mission,
Messenger of Chaos: To warn us.
In the center for "Knowledge and Sciences,"
He spoke to us, as a prophet though
it is no longer the age of prophets.
Men have stop believing
in this kind of weird thing.
We only believe in Science.
We have systems of exact prediction.
We forecast events, cycles,
the good seasons, the good times,
give ample warning of incoming dangers,
Prevent catastrophes.

But, still:
the politicians were angered,
the technicians insisted,
the leaders
made their manifestos.
And, the powerless, the people
of this great land,
were unmoved in their daily routine,
going and coming with their ethos
to earn, week after week,
the paychecks to pay their plastic-cards
which "our daily bread" has become.
It was necessary for the Angel,
Code Ep, 13 to the seventh, etc.
to change his robe
and live amongst us, as one with us,
as "one-of-us."

Michael, the forefathers had called him,
"The manly being dressed in linen,"
"The one of shining garments,"
"Messenger with heels of fire,"
"Winged being, angel clothed in bronze,"
"A demigod,"
"The one to aid us in battle."
We barely know of him from the scrolls,
from the traditions,
from the poets.
His heritage came down
to modern nations:
Ramayana, Mahabarata,
the Illiad, the Popul-Vuh,
the Bible.

The angels came,
but neither then, nor now
have we understood
Who they were or are.
Nor do we grasp
the range of their warnings,
since, in the present, or in recent years,
no one understood
they had to change tactics.
To speak to man grew day by day
more futile.
And every word spoken
was "classified"
for reasons defined as "political."
Foul misguidance.

Empires (Economic & Political Empires),
States (Private Wealth, Nation States,
Corporate Capital, State Capitals),
any and all, in their interest,
could dare:
to blow up mountains,
to burn the forests, and to dry the rivers,
to pollute their green environment,
to produce acid rain,
to exploit the land and degrade it,
to build unsafe atomic energy plants,
to explode the world.

Michael, the Archangel,
"Code Epsilon, thirteen to the seventh,
Z coordinate of minus 0.5, 853,
27 submiriad,"
changed his tactics.
He knew that his message
wouldn't work,
if delivered in gestures or words.
His logistic: to dress in the skin of the worker,
the technician, the programmer,
infiltrating himself in their milieu,
their offices, their plants, & their boards,
a bug in their systems,
crossing up the controls and the panels,
the wiring, the wave lengths,
the faxxing of messages, the spy satellites
& their receptors,
changing their conceptions, their charts.

No one can explain how it happened.
It began with a change in their systems,
rumbling all foundations.
What was thus unleased, no big deal,
was just panic around the world,
spreading from the East to the West,
and, later, to the South. No catastrophe.
Through all these upheavals,
his warning: The need of his coming,
the need for us all to understand it,
to open our minds.

And so they came. The thousands of protests,
demonstrations, debates, new alliances,
a change in the rules of their games:
The radio, the TV, the press,
all the media, the people, the governments,
the international gatherings,
the international sectors and groups,
the international agencies,
all, at once, clamoring, making promises.

But soon, the sensation died out.
Almost all was forgotten,
As it was, long ago, after Lot,
After the Buddha, after Confucius,
After all the Prophets,
As it was after the Christ. After Mahoma.
After both Luthers. After Ghandi. After Russell.
After the many other past missions
of Michael, Code-Epsi,
And all those who had come to warn us
against evil, and catastrophe...and...
The end!

Pat Mora

Pat Mora comes from the desert, a theme that runs through her poetry. A native of El Paso, Mora is the author of three poetry collections: Chants (1984), Borders (1986) and Communion (1991). Mora's imagery tends to be spare and minimalist, adding to the intensity of her poetry. Her poetry collections have won awards from the Border Regional Library Association, the National Chicano Studies Association and the Southwest Council of Latin American Studies. Twice she has received the Southwest Book Award. Mora was elected to the Texas Institute of Letters in 1987. As the recipient of a Kellogg National Fellowship, she has studied cultural conservation issues nationally and internationally, In 1993, she published her first collection of essays, Nepantla, which in Nahuatl (a language of the Aztecs, still spoken in parts of Mexico) means the place in the middle. She explains that she is in the middle of her life; she is the middle woman between her mother and daughter, and presently, she lives in the middle of the country, in Cincinnati, where her husband is a professor of archaeology at the University of Cincinnati. In The Nation (June 7, 1973), Ray González notes that "Nepantla is important because it allows a Chicana writer to present strong opinions, dreams and commitments—all of them backed by a tough voice of poetic experience." Mora has been very productive in children's literature, recently publishing *A Birthday Basket for Tía* (1992) and *The Desert is My Mother* (1994). Slated for publication are eight other children's books. The most widely anthologized Latina poet in this country, Pat Mora is also well-known for the healing quality she creates for her audience through her poetry readings.

Mi Madre

Pat Mora

I say feed me.
She serves me red prickly pear on a spiked cactus.

I say tease me.
She sprinkles raindrops in my face on a sunny day.

I say frighten me.
She shouts thunder, flashes lightning.

I say comfort me.
She invites me to lay on her firm body.

I say heal me.
She gives me *manzanilla, orégano, dormilón.*

I say caress me.
She strokes my skin with her warm breath.

I say make me beautiful.
She offers me turquoise for my fingers, a pink blossom for my hair.

I say sing to me.
She chants lonely women's songs of femaleness.

I say teach me.
She endures: glaring heat
numbing cold
frightening dryness.

She: the desert
She: strong mother.

The Eye of Texas

is white
as sun-bleached bone,
its one eye, a star
between two long horns,
was once two new eyes
that stared at one another until
the young bull could see only itself
reflected in those huge, soft mirrors
that grew together, hardened, a scar white

as its hoofs that trample deserts,
valleys, fields, shores, country roads,
the bull pausing to raise its
thick neck, its one white eye to the unseen
sky and bellow louder than the combined cries
of *coyotes*, wolves, mountain lions,
bellowing a dark bitter smoke
then charging on, crushing cotton, onions,
hierbabuena, trampling toys and children
in narrow dirt streets of the Rio Grande Valley,
deaf to the cries of old Mexican voices,

the bull seeking the smell of white
skin and chlorine, resting its loud body
by the acres of tinted, treated pools
owned by men who wrap their feet in snakes,
their legs in blue jeans, lull
the old, blind bull with their tales
tall as their hats that shade tongues
twanging like snapping guitar strings.

Curandera

They think she lives alone
on the edge of town in a two-room house
where she moved when her husband died
at thirty-five of a gunshot wound
in the bed of another woman. The *curandera*
and house have aged together to the rhythm
of the desert.

She wakes early, lights candles before
her sacred statues, brews tea of *hierbabuena*.
She moves down her porch steps, rubs
cool morning sand into her hands, into her arms.
Like a large black bird, she feeds on
the desert, gathering herbs for her basket.

Her days are slow, days of grinding
dried snake into powder, of crushing
wild bees to mix with white wine.
And the townspeople come, hoping
to be touched by her ointments,
her hands, her prayers, her eyes.
She listens to their stories, and she listens
to the desert, always the desert.

By sunset she is tired. The wind
strokes the strands of long gray hair,
the smells of drying plants drifts
into her blood, the sun seeps
into her bones. She dozes
on her back porch. Rocking, rocking.

At night she cooks chopped cactus
and brews more tea. She brushes a layer
of sand from her bed, sand which covers
the table, stove, floor. She blows
the statues clean, the candles out.
Before sleeping, she listens to the message
of the owl and the *coyote*. She closes her eyes
and breathes with the mice and snakes
and wind.

Tigua Elder

How do I tell my children:
there is worse than pain.

I bury pills.
Let my stomach burn.
I bury them in the sand by the window,
under the limp cactus.
Maybe it slipped into a long sleep instead of me.
I speak to my grandchildren in our language,
but they hear only the television, radio
in every room, all day, all night.
They do not understand.

How do I tell my children:
forgetting is worse than pain, forgetting
stories old as the moon; owl, coyote,
snake weaving through the night like smoke,
forgetting the word for the Spirit,
waida, waida, the sounds I hear in shells
and damp caves, forgetting the wind,
the necessary bending to her spring tantrums.

Afternoons I limp like a wounded horse
to the shade of the willow and wait for sunset,
for wind's breath, familiar, cool.
She eases this fire.

There is worse than pain.
There is forgetting
Those are my eyes in the mirror.
There is forgetting my own true name.

Tigua: a Native American Southwestern group

Picturesque: San Cristóbal de las Casas

No one told me about the bare feet.

The Indians, yes
the turquoise and pink shawls, yes
the men running lightly on thin sidewalks
hats streaming with ribbons, yes
the chatter of women sunning outside the church
weaving bracelets with quick fingers, yes

but no one told me about the bare feet.

The smiles, yes
the babies slung on women's backs,
the bundles of huge white lilies
carried to market: fresh headdresses,
the young girls like morning birds gathering
for a feeding, pressing dolls into my hands, yes

but no one told me about the bare feet.

The weavers, yes
the hands that read threads,
the golden strings pulled from bushes
in fresh handfuls to steal a yellow dye,
the houses in the clouds, in the high hills,
shuttles to-and-fro, to-and-
fro on tight looms, yes

but no one told me about the bare feet.

No one told me about the weaver's chair, a rock.
No one told me about the wood bundles bending
women's backs. No one told me about the children

who know to open their smiles
as they open their dry palms.

La Dulcería

Released into the season
of wildflowers, *zumban.*
Bees burst into petal scent,
gossip rumors of sweet platters,
glazed faraway place brimming
mountains of sugary crystals.

Zumban.

The swarm pursues an orange aroma,
and the pumpkins, figs, *tejocote*
simmering in syrups,
globes rolling in huge cauldrons
dark with bubbling and brewing gold
juices released in heat.

Bodies bumping and bruising
zumban, hundreds fly through tree
soughings, toward *leche quemada,*
pause only briefly to sip
fields flowering their yellow
spinning perfumes to the sun.

Zumban. Zumban.

They careen down streets and round
corners, veer at last, *zum-zum,*
into the *dulcería,*
round fruit gleaming like jewels, slide
on *ate de guava,*
sink into brown pools of *cajeta.*

Zumban y zumban.

Buzzing bodies nuzzle *coco*
and *jamoncillo,* as *la dueña*
en su delantal brushes
bumpings with, *"Es la temporada,"*
season of suckings and burrowings,
nectar irresistible.

San Cristóbal De Las Casas, 1993

Doña Feliciana

Ven. Come inside. *Es mi casa,*
two rooms I built from wood scraps.
Look at the nails, bent like my old fingers.
They spilled us like garbage, the landowners
with the big trucks, spilled us
in this bare field with our pots, sheets,
shoes stiff and old as tree bark.

At first, *niños* raced across the land,
mouths open to gulp in all the new wide air.
They ran laughing into the emptiness,
no trees, no mangos and avocados lying in the shade,
no houses, no plastic water buckets,
no tomato plants, no small fires, no chickens,
no thing, no thing in their way.

I brought just one plant, a little *cilantro,*
placed it in this blue, tin pot. Smell it,
even a little green smell helps in all this dust.
This is my house. I am my family, widow
without children. *Mis compañeros* and I have no land,
not even a stream of water thin as a thread.

The first nights in this bare place, mosquitoes
sucked and sucked until I had to build a house.
Alone at sixty-three. My arms hurt from dragging
boards. My head ached from banding,
but I lifted my house up, made myself a roof.
See? Two rooms: here I sleep, here I cook my rice.

Nights I lie in the dark and listen to the wind.
I whisper to my *viejo,* "I did it.
I built myself a house.
I hung my blue tin pot beside my door."

Honduras, 1993

Tornadé

Come to us through the green hill of Honduras.
Come to wave-swell warm as mothermilk.
Walk with us on the sand by the sea.

Boys splash in a small lagoon, their laughs rise
sunward like careless kites. Palms gossip,
their gray trunks, arms arching into the wind of Tornabé.

Walk with us, down dirt paths, by slatted wooden houses,
thatched roofs, pecking eyes of dogs, roosters, children;
head-scarves humming the islands.

"*Buenas tardes*," a Garifona says bending for centuries
into the smell of bread, into the blaring tin heat
of her makeshift oven, smolder of rocks and coconut shells.

Her black arms lift mountains, raise a blazing slab,
show you bread browning under the trees. Hot round puffs sweet
with coconut oil dissolve on your tongue. Swallow.

Come. Clouds dark with greed stream toward us. Listen
to tangled whispers of women who sleep with the sea, who dream
granddaughters and *mua's* red wind dancing to drum's old pulse.

mua: land in Garifona, the language of blacks who came to Honduras from San Vicente over two hundred years ago, who struggle to retain their lands, language, culture

The Young Sor Juana

I

I'm three and cannot play away my days
to suit my sweet *Mamá*. Sleep well, my dolls,
for I must run to school behind my sister's frowns.
She knows my secret wish to stretch. If only
I were taller. If only I could tell *Mamá* why
I must go, my words irresistible as roses.

My sister hears my tiptoes, knows her shadow
has my face. I tiptoe on, for I must learn
to unknit words and letters, to knit them new
with my own hand. Like playful morning birds
the big girls giggle, at me, the little tagalong.
I hear the grumble of my sister's frown.

I stretch to peek inside, to see
the teacher's face. How it must glow with
knowledge. Like the sun. A woman so wise
has never tasted cheese. She sees my eyes
and finally seats me near. My stubborn legs
and toes refuse to reach the floor.

At noon I chew my bread. Others eat soft
cheese. I've heard it dulls the wits. I shut
my lips to it. I must confess, when tired,
I slowly smell the milky moons, like *Mamá*
savors the aroma of warm roses. I linger,
imagine my teeth sinking into the warm softness.

II

I'm seven and beg to leave my sweet *Mamá,*
to hide myself inside boys' pants and shirt,
to tuck my long, dark hair inside a cap
so I can stride into large cities, into their
classrooms, into ideas crackling
and breathing lightning.

Instead of striding, I must hide from frowns,
from dark clouds in the eyes of my *Mamá.*
I hide in my grandfather's books, sink
into the yellowed pages, richer than cheese.
Finally, *Mamá* releases me to her sister.
I journey to the city. If only I were taller.

III

I'm sixteen and spinning in the glare of Latin
grammar. I cannot look away. Beware,
slow wits, I keep my scissors close,
their cold, hard lips ready to sink into
this dark, soft hair, punish my empty head,
unless it learns on time.

I'll set the pace and if I fail, I'll hack and
slash again until I learn. I'll pull and cut,
this foolish lushness. Again I'll feel my hair
rain softly on my clothes, gather
in a gleaming puddle at my feet.
My hands are strong, and from within I rule.

sor: member of religious community, sister
Sor Juana Inés de la Cruz: seventeenth century author, Mexico's most acclaimed woman poet

Mothers and Daughters

The arm-in-arm-mother-daughter-stroll
in villages and shopping malls
evenings and weekends
the walk-talk slow,
arm-in-arm
          around the world.

Sometimes they feed one another
memories sweet as hot bread
and lemon tea. Sometimes it's mother-stories
the young can't remember;

When you were new, I'd nest you
in one arm, while I cooked,
whisper, "What am I to do with you?"

Sometimes it's tug-
of-war that started in the womb
the fight for space
the sharp jab deep inside
arm-in-arm
          around the world,

always the bodytalk thick,
always the recipes
hints for feeding
more with less.

Photo © Copyright 1993 by Alyce Quiñónez-Rodríguez

Naomi Quiñónez

Naomi Quiñónez is a Los Angeles poet, educator and community relations expert. She has a B.A. in English from San Jose State University, a Masters in Public Administration from the University of Southern California and is a Ph.D. Candidate in American Studies at Claremont Graduate School; she is now a Dissertation Fellow/Lecturer at West Virginia Graduate College. With a high profile in community relations and education, Quiñónez was named to the Los Angeles Racial Harmony and Discourse Task Force and to the Mexican-American Advisory Commission of the California State Department of Education. She has received the Mayor's Award from the City of Monterey Park and a Congressional Award for Community Service. Quiñónez has participated in numerous readings and literary programs, including the Inter-American Bookfair and Literary Festival and the Los Angeles Festival of the Arts. Quiñónez has been a managing editor of *Caminos Magazine*, editor of *Chismearte*'s Southwest Issue, and the editor of *Invocation L.A., Urban Multicultural Poetry* (1989), which received the American Book Award from the Before Columbus Foundation. Her widely anthologized poetry has appeared most recently in *After Aztlán: Latinos Poets of the Nineties* (1992), *Infinite Divisions* (1993), *Colorado Review*, and *Latino Poets for the New Millennium* (1994). Quiñónez has received grants from the National Endowment for the Arts and the California Arts Council. Her poetry collection, *Sueño de Colibrí/Hummingbird Dream*, was published in 1985 by West End Press.

Ánima

Naomi Quiñónez

The fog in my mirror
slowly unveils
a woman of bronze
earth and fire.
The clouding of mystery
a shrouded face
breasts that Picasso
had seen and painted.
An eye dark as shadows
that bury the temples
deep in the image
of reflected haze.
Still wet from waters
of Aztec baptismals
an ancient face lingers
at the edge of my soul
          Suspended in time
          I wait in suspense
for the mirror to reveal
a forgotten woman.
Slowly the cheekbones
of an Indian face take form
rough hewn forehead
lips full and quiet
two eyes turn inward
to see what is born.
Hair black as ashes
of Wednesday's grim mourning
falls on the shoulders
that carried bronze babies,
infants in arms
that buried fierce warriors
with hands stained and bloody
that reached the gods.

Long broken fingernails
that clawed at the land
and trapped there forever
the clay…the sand….
Earthen face
color of fire
burns in the memory
of Coatlicue
burns into flame
and singes the hair
of my nostrils.
The nose of
a conquering Spaniard.
I breathe in the smoke
it changes to incense
Cathedrals are filled
with Indian perfume.
New names, old gods
my eyelids are heavy
the saints on the altar
all turn to Jaguars
the dove holy spirit
in Quetzalcoatl.
I open my eyes
the mirror is clouded
from ages of living
breathing and dying
eyes, hollow sockets
loins, dry as bone
but my soul
strong and fertile
will give birth
to my children.

La Llorona

When La Llorona comes to me
vulnerability turns to compassion
the haunting melody of her song
wanders as wounded and random
as her legend through the rivers
and alleyways of my existence.
La Llorona—madre perdida
who searches eternally,
the phantom murderess
who has killed her children,
the rejected mother
of disgraciados.
All-giving and all-loving
the all-forgiving part of my being
that is negated.
La madre bendita
La mujer fuerta
La puta madre
La soldadera
La india amorosa
La mujer dolorosa:
But who can understand
that a woman sentences to death
the child she brings
into the world.
La Llorona, the feminine
haunts us if we fear her
comforts us if we understand.
La madre who grieves
at bringing children into a world
that may destroy them
and will kill them.
La Llorona, contradiction
of the life and death,
who sacrificed her children
to haunt the weak
and comfort the giving.
La mujer sagrada
the defiled woman.
She makes her peace
with those who respect vulnerability
and draw from her strength.

Hesitations

I laugh
a glass of wine
between my legs,
dark, intensely burgundy,
glows from the warmth of my thighs.

I stare
into that crystal glass,
wait for it to reveal
past and future.
A fortuneteller
starring into herself
and finding nothing.

I feel
the tight vacuum of my womanhood
compressed
and kept between my legs
for no one to see,
for someone to anticipate,
for no one to see.

I am my own chastity belt,
and I laugh at that thought
into the dark red wine
that tells me nothing.

Before I grow confused,
and crush the glass
with my thighs,
I laugh again,
I look again
bring the wine to my lips
and take a long drink.

No Shelter

His explosion
was only temporary.
A moment, a blood clot
a red ribbon of anger
tied around her neck
a second of scorn
a fistful of hair.
His bruised ego
imprinted
its black and blue
on her face.
His words shot
like bullets
her spirit
cracked open
the blows
immediate, sharp
as she stumbled over
those few moments
and dragged herself
across the seconds
that split the shattered face
of time.

El Salvador

Does the sun still shine in El Salvador
where echoes of murdered children
run the width and breadth of rifle barrels?
Does it still rise to the senseless sounds
of machine guns that have made
even the morning rooster mute with terror?
Has the sun lost patience with madmen
who liquidate flesh for assets?
(The sad and angry sun that beats to boil
blood in thin crevices of cracked streets
while military police pull caps over eyes
clenching U.S. rifles to use on children
who will not cry tomorrow.)
Does the sun still shine in El Salvador?
Does it rise with the death toll
is it bleeding now, red with remorse
of an insane decade? Does it beat on those
who fight for justice, as well as on those
who know no justice?
They tell me there is a pallor of death
a stench of rotting bodies
thick enough to obscure the sun
from the apocalyptic vision
of our man-made infernos.
Thick enough to muffle the cries
of a people
who still wait for a savior.

Good Friday

Sage smoke circles
like a phantom
around my head.
Morning offering
unbridled thought
merge while muse
speaks softly to me
on this my good Friday.
Noon bells toll
it is the hour of sacrifice
to reflect on those crosses
large and small
I have carried.
This death is like a lover
a mad moment of passion
abandon and disintegration.
Blood and tears
are from the same source
they are the shadows of wounds
no one can see.
This death is like
a woman's labor
pain, wreathing
relief and joy.
On this my good Friday
I do penance on paper
and work my way to a rebirth
free of reason.
On this my good Friday
I treasure the tree of life
and give thanks
for the journey
and the destination.

Nina Serrano

Nina Serrano was born in New York City, where she grew up in the 1950s. While a student at the University of Wisconsin, she got married and had two children; twenty-seven years later she received her BA in Humanities at New College of California. Serrano holds the distinction of being the only woman closely identified with the Pocho Che Collective, a San Francisco East Bay group of cultural and political activists of the late 1960s. In the 1970s, Pocho Che redefined itself as the San Francisco Mission Poets—recognized for the far-reaching impact they gave to the Latino literary movement. Using poetry to advance the cause of peace and minority rights, Pocho Che/Mission Poets published poetry books and the review, *Tin Tan*. In 1972, Third World Communications—an associate of the Pocho Che Collective—and a group of women that included Serrano, published *Third World Women*, the first anthology of literature by women of color of the United States. In 1980 the Editorial Pocho Che Tenth Anniversary series included *Heartsongs: The Collected Poems of Nina Serrano (1969–1979)*. Through Comunicación Aztlán, Serrano produced two radio programs: "Reflecciones de la Raza" and "Como mis antepasados." Her poem, "Antepasados," which served as the weekly introduction to the radio series, grew out of this experience. As a film-maker, Serrano has co-directed two docu-dramas, each recognized internationally. "¿Qué hacer?" is set in Chile and "Después del terremoto/After the Earthquake" deals with Central American immigrants. With her daughter, Valerie Landau-Serrano, she has produced a video documentary, "Back from Nicaragua." At present, Serrano is working as a storyteller in the schools, producing radio programs and working on her first novel, *Down Nicaragua Way*, which reflects the solidarity of Latino artists in San Francisco with the liberation movements in Central America.

Antepasados/Ancestors

Nina Serrano

We are one
because America is one continent
tied by the slender curves
of Panama.
We are one people
tied by the buried bones of antepasados
the buried bones of ancestors.
        from Asia to America
        from Africa to America
        from Europe to America
Back to the first mothers and the first fathers
back to the first gardens of flowers and fruits,
where vegetables grew wild.
The soft thick grasses cushioned their bodies
when they lay down to love.
Warm water gurgled up from the earth
and spilled down into clear pools.
Feathers waved their heads
and floated across their bodies
as they strutted in the afternoon.

But then the snake of greed
grew like a weed
planted the seed
that made one person think that to fill their need
or to succeed
they had to use someone else's labor
for their own profit.
Wars came. Animals died.
Women and cattle became property,
Slaves were chained, put to work,
endless work
that finally built factories and smog,
rich parts of town and poor
built on the buried bones of antepasados
the buried bones of ancestors.
Shake the bones
hear their ghostly moans.
We learn from our past
to build our future.

Lolita Lebrón
(Puerto Rican Independence Fighter)

Back back back
to New York in the fifties
they were the times of hate
the times of fear.
Witchhunters flying
from town to town
from Washington to the electric chair
where the Rosenburgs sat.
On their execution day
people stood in solidarity,
the minutes till their death
counted over the loudspeaker.
Ten /
nine /
The police
cut the microphone.
By person to person relay
the word was passed
like a whisper heard by thousands,
the chant of life's last moments.
"Eight" runs through the crowd,
then "seven,"
the song of resistance.
Six / five /
"no names"
four / three / two /
Shock
electric shock
and then they were dead.

Those were times of fear,
times of hate,
teachers signing loyalty oaths.
Fear
that they might not teach
what the system would preach.

Front page headlines:
naming communists / banning books,
witchhunters flying in the moonlight.
The people were picking up the tab.
It was all on the expense account.
"Have plane fare, will testify."
The professional witness,
trained by Judas,
And will you name names?
And will you name names?
Names on blacklists
Attorney General's lists
subversive activities lists.
Didn't you belong to this committee?
Didn't you sign that petition?
Didn't you spend many years
in the company of a suspected communist
Who was your mother?
Smith Act trials and jailing.
"Are you now or have you ever been?"
And will you name names?
And will you name names?

The witchhunters flew
to the world of make-believe:
the movies, the pictures, the stars,
the Hollywood Ten.
"Not me, couldn't be."
Then who?
Point your finger at your ex-wife
your enemies
and you can keep on making
payments on your swimming pool,
and winning prizes.
And will you name names?
And will you name names?
Those who didn't went to jail.
Take the key and lock 'em up.
The witchhunters flew
in the dark and repressive fifties.

The 20th century just about halfway through
when the Taft-Hartley Act tied knots
around the picket lines
binding union power
purging unions with
"Are you now or have you ever been?"
Do you think he is?
What did she say? And to whom and when?
Labor and management must become one happy family,
signing sweetheart contracts.

But it was hard to have a happy family
on such a lousy salary
where Lolita worked.
The machines whirred in the garment factory
the faster the better
the fewer stitches to the inch
the greater number of workers per square foot.
Pay them by the piece.
Clothes are going to make it big this year,
as we go from wartime shortage
to the new look of the consumer society.
Skirts were longer again.
Women left the wartime plants
for flowerpots in the kitchen.
"Homework, I want to do homework,
instead of office work, I want
to work at home."

Lolita worked in one of those factories
where bits of thread
floated through the air.
The benches by the sewing machines
filled by the latest immigrants,
Borinqueños, Puerto Riqueños,
migrating when there was no work,
no harvest.
When the colony was squeezed
so hard
it spit out its population.

Lovely island of coco palms and sea,
wet song of the rain forest.
"Pepsi Cola hits the spot"
mingles with tropical laments.
La lee lo lei lo lai
La lee lo lai

Lolita looked at the moon
on hot nights
from her tenement roof.
She saw witchhunters fly by
but paid them no mind.
Her mind was on cutting the chains
tying her green island
to the greedy mainland,
pouring concrete on her country's fertile land
building military bases and factories,
sucking its rum
and sugar cane.
She was set on freedom.
She would bet on freedom,
take a chance
that the world would know her dream.
"Crazy-Loca" they called her.
When US bombers are blasting Puerto Ricans
and US citizens don't even know about it,
"What can one isolated act do?"
She made her plan with three others.
They needed a gun
to shoot off the word.
The word had to be heard.

Puerto Ricans wanted their independence.
"Are you sorry for what you did, Miss Lebrón?"
"I am not sorry for anything I do
to free my people."
And you, Irvin Flores
and you, Andrés Figueroa Cordero
and you, Rafael Cancel Miranda?"

"No, we are not sorry
about what we do
to free Puerto Rico."
No need to name names
"I take responsibility for all,"
she said,
in her accented English.

Elvis Presley howled
"I'm nothing but a hound dog"
and the shake, rattle and roll
of the yeah, yeah, yeah
was creeping into the music,
and the witchhunters flew straight
into the fires of the thaw
of the cold war.
Juke boxes turned their colored lights on.
TV sets filled every tract home and tenement.
Cars filled every street and parking lot.
The air turned black.

Peace in Korea.
War in Viet Nam,
always war.
The witchhunters were howled out of town
by crowds of demonstrators,
protestors.
The witchhunters circled around
and landed safe
in their offices.
Lolita went on a hunger strike
to back up the prisoners' rebellion
at Attica.
Meanwhile freedom is a constant struggle
and the witchhunters are just waiting,
waiting,
waiting for you.

Multi-Media Witch

to Isabel Alegría (Third World News Bureau) and
Elizabeth Farnsworth (Inter-news)

Electrical sparkles shine in my sky
My bracelets are cable connectors
My amulets are lavoleer microphones
My earrings are headsets
so I can share my truth with you
tune my message into your wave length
signal your beam
turn your head around
and flash it
back to you
back inside
the heart of you.

Woman Pirate

I hear there were women pirates out on the Caribbean
Now if there were women pirates I'd rather be 'em than see 'em
If I were a woman pirate I'd swagger around in boots
And wear two deadly pistols that I'd learn how to shoot.

Sailing out on the Caribbean out where the water's clear
I'd watch the colored fishes through waves of foamy beer
And when the deck was rocking and the winds began to blow
I'd be swinging in my hammock rocking to and fro.

I'd raise my spyglass when a ship came into view
Win the battle and the booty, sharing with my sister crew
The islanders would bring us mangos and coconuts
Invite us ashore for dancing and loving in their huts.

I could be a woman pirate and use you for a ship
I could rule you with a pistol, or else a long black whip
I could be a woman pirate and rock you 'til your cargo spilled
Rescue you from the gangplank and see that you weren't killed.

If I were a woman pirate I could lead you to shores unseen
And overthrow a junta in the name of freedom's queen.
But I'm not a woman pirate, I didn't seize the time
Didn't fly the Jolly Roger, a pity and a crime.

International Woman's Day

(March 8, 1975, Havana)

"CHI / cha cha cha
CHI / cha cha cha"
The men from our offices assault us,
It's an attack.
They come beating on tin cans,
"CHI / cha cha cha
CHI / cha cha cha"
One carries a guitar,
two share a handpainted sign
"Down with machismo"
it says.
They chant
"Down with machismo."
The guitar plays "Guantanamera."
We are being serenaded as we lean over banisters
leaving typewriters, dictionaries and telephones abandoned.
They speak in praise of women
of women as comrades,
They present us with a bouquet of flowers.
We cheer
They chant,"Down with machismo."
We agree.
They beat out a rhythm to send it to its grave.
They are gone.
"CHI / cha cha cha"
trails behind
with the perfume of the flowers.
We hear them attack our sisters in the other buildings.
Our typewriters click again,
Our thoughts click,
We are working,
We are smiling

Carmen Tafolla

Carmen Tafolla, a native of San Antonio, is a poet closely identified with the Chicano cultural nationalist movement. She received a B.A. and an M.A. degree from Austin College, and a Ph.D. from the University of Texas in Austin. Tafolla has been director of the Mexican American Studies Center at Texas Lutheran University and a professor of Women's Studies at California State University at Fresno. She has also worked as a folklorist, and has produced seven television screenplays. Tafolla brings the oral tradition to life by creating dramatizations of barrio personalities who speak in their voices about their struggles to self-affirm. Many of her poems emphasize the Native American roots of her people and deal with remembrances of ancestors and community elders. Tafolla's readings and performances have taken her to England, Spain, Germany, Norway and Mexico. Her early work appeared regularly in the San Antonio review *Caracol*, then in a collection entitled *Get Your Tortillas Together* (1976), which included the work of two other writers associated with *Caracol*: Reyes Cárdenas and Cecilio García-Camarillo. "La Isabela de Guadalupe y otras chucas" appears in *Five Poets of Aztlán*, edited by Santiago Daydí-Tolson (1985). Tafolla published two more collections: *Curandera* (1983) and *To Split a Human: Mitos, Machos y la Mujer Chicana* (1985). In 1987 her new poems, "Sonnets to Human Beings," won first prize in the poetry division of the Chicano Literary contest at the University of California, Irvine. A critical edition of *Sonnets to Human Beings and Other Selected Works* (1993) has been published in the United States and Germany. With her husband and child, she has recently relocated to the Río Grande Valley.

Right in One Language

Carmen Tafolla

"Write in one language," they say
and agents sit and glare hairy brows
over foreign words, almost trying hope,
say, "It's not French, is it?"

But it isn't.

Nor is my mind
when I try tight, clean line
manicured to be like Leave
it to Beaver's house
      straight sidewalks
      so square hedges
      and if there's one on
this side there's also one on that
Equally paced
         placed
         spaced
         controlled

"You seem to lose control of the line
in this one," he says, "it all explodes."
   I see bilingüe-beautiful
      explosions—
         two worlds collide
            two tongues dance
               inside the cheek
                  together
Por aquí, poquito and a dash allá también
salsa—chacha—disco—polka
Rock that Texan cumbia
in a molcajete mezcla!

But restrain yourself—
the Man pleads sanity—
Trim the excess—
just enough and nothing more
Think Shaker room and lots of light—
two windows, Puritan-clean floor, and chairs
up on clean simple pegs—three—
y
  las
    palabritas
      mías
        are straining at the yoke

  two-headed sunflowers
   peeking through St. Moderatius grass
    waiting for familias grandes
  garden growing wild
   with Mexican hierbitas, spices, rosas,
    baby trees nurtured así, muy natural
    —no one knows yet
     if they're two years old
     and should be weaned
                or pruned
                 or toilet-trained
    but they are given only
    agua y cariñitos,
    shade and sun and compañía
City Inspection Crew,
House and Gardens Crew,
Publications Crew agree
the lack of discipline
lack of Puritan
      purity
        pior y tí.

Chaucer must have felt like this,
 the old Pachuco playing his TexMex onto the page
and even then the critics said,
  "Write
  in one language."
But he looked at all that cleanness, so controlled,
 forms halved, and just could not deny
his own familia, primos from both sides,

weeds that liked to crawl
over sidewalks, pa' juntarse,
visit, stretch out comfy,
natural and lusty,
hybrid wealth,
and told them it was just because
he was undisciplined
unpolished
and did not know
how to make love
with just
one person
in the room
or
on the page.

And he, like me,
did what he wanted anyway
But
You, like they,
want Shaker hallways
and I grow Mexican gardens and backyards.
There are 2 many colors in the marketplace
to play modest, when Mexico and
Gloria Rodríguez say,
"¡Estos gringos con su Match-Match,
y a mí me gusta Mix-Mix!"
There are 2 many cariños to be
created
to stay within the lines,
2 many times
when I want to tell you:
There is room
here
for two
tongues
inside this
kiss.

MotherMother

(they see Hiroshima and speak of nuclear "defense")

Earth—
Your womb has been
cut open
just as mine
just as my mother's

Your child has died
in its halo of innocence
just as mine
just as my mother's

Your heart has pounded
angry, crying beats
in slaughtered grasps
for the child...
for your
soul

and drummed slowly
by the gravesite
in time to the warm pulse
of the rocking wind
which lulls
the child's
tomb.
Now—
That child is gone
That cut is mended
But let us
save
the next.

Nací la hija

Nací la hija
  de una hija
    de una curandera

Y la hija
  de un hijo
    de un obrero maestropastor

Mientras l'otrabuela
    crecía matas
  y l'otroabuelo
    forjaba metal.
Pues ni pa'qué preguntar porqué
  (is it any wonder then)
  frecuentemente me pongo
    a forjar remedios,
      predicando a las matas
        y

      tratando de
        curar
          metal.

Marked

Never write with pencil,
m'ija.
It is for those
who would
erase.
Make your mark proud
        and open,
Brave,
                beauty folded into
    its imperfection,
Like a piece of turquoise
        marked.

Never write
with pencil,
m'ija.
Write with ink
    or mud,
or berries grown in
gardens never owned,
  or, sometimes,
    if necessary,
      blood.

Allí por la Calle San Luis

West Side—corn tortillas for a penny each
Made by an aged woman
and her mother.
Cooked on the homeblack of a flat stove,
Flipped to slap the birth awake,
Wrapped by corn hands.
Toasted morning light and dancing history—
earth gives birth to corn and gives birth to man
gives birth to earth.
Corn tortillas—penny each
No tax.

Woman-Hole

Some say there is a
vacuum—a black hole—
in the center of womanhood
that swallows countless
secrets and has strange
powers

Yo no sé desas cosas
solo sé que the
black echo is music
is sister of sunlight
and from it
crece
vida.

In Guatemala

there are no political prisoners
only men's heads that show up sewed
into the now-pregnant bellies
of their fiancée's corpses

only hands that open
from the jungle floor,
fingers crying "Justicia!"
as they reach like vines trying
to break free

only butchered organs
pressed into the earth
beneath the feet
of "government" officers

only Ixil Indians in rebellion,
their red woven messages of humanness
in whole Indian villages corralled, beheaded,
for existing too full
of straight-backed dignity

There are no political prisoners
There are no problemas de derechos humanos
There are no repressions in free democracies
There are only Presidents
who scratch each other's backs,
blindfold each other's eyes,
laugh uncomfortably,
puffing the finest
popular-name cigars
and cutting too-human heads
from the non-human bodies
of non-justice.

Luz María Umpierre

Luz María Umpierre was born in Santurce, Puerto Rico. She received her Ph.D. in Latin American and Peninsular Literatures from Bryn Mawr College, and has done post-doctoral work under the auspices of the Ford Foundation and the Department of Education of the state of New Jersey. In 1984 she received tenure at Rutgers University; later, she chaired the Department of Foreign Languages and Folklore at Western Kentucky University, where she was also a professor of Women Studies and was selected "Woman of the Year." She is currently chair of Foreign Languages and Literatures at the State University of New York, Brockport. Umpierre is the author of five collections of poetry: *Una puertorriqueña en Penna* (1979), *En el país de las maravillas* (1985), *...y otras desgracias/...And Other Misfortunes* (1985), *The Margarita Poems* (1987) and *For Cristine* (1994). Recent articles on her "homocriticism," a theory of reading, have appeared in *Revista Iberoamericana* and *Collages and Bricolages*, which devoted an entire issue (1993) to her work. The National Writers Union, New York Chapter, honored the publication of this homage issue in December, 1993. A recipient of numerous awards, not only for her literary and critical work, but also for her human rights advocacy, she received a lifetime achievement award from the Coalition of Gay and Lesbian Organizations in New Jersey. Umpierre has been a guest writer at Harvard University, Wellesley College, Williams College and other colleges, as well as at grassroots organizations, such as the Museo del Barrio and the Mission Cultural Center. Widely anthologized, most recently in *Papiros de Babel* and *Puerto Rican Writers at Home in the U.S.*, Umpierre's poetry has been the subject of numerous critical studies.

To a Beautiful Illusion
Bella ilusión (danza)

Luz María Umpierre

for Sylvia Plath

I look at a picture of your grave full of wild weeds
and I want to dig in and press myself against your skeleton
and kiss each emptiness
and pretend that the grass growing is your sex.

I want to take you out walking down the streets of L.A., Sylvia,
I want you to smell the odor of gasoline in the air,
a premonition of yours nobody understood: the pollution of our minds,
of our bodies.
I want you to see people lined up for the psychiatrist,
the young suicides,
mothers who leave milk
for their children while they sleep;
mothers who had no choice,
mothers abandoned,
mothers empty
who weave another kind of stove gas
everyday without knowing
that you had shown them a way.

I want you to walk arm in arm with me
and raise your voice from
your skeleton
and whisper in my ear softly, arousingly,
that you want to make love on the beach at Cape Cod, under the sun,
and in Provincetown
city of ultraviolet power

where once they tried
    to lock you up
where you return today
    laughing, at my side,
    to watch barges and
    whales.

It's February again, Sylvia.
For the time being, it's not freezing;
stamps have gone up
in price and they have a different image
but they can still be bought in the middle of the night
by nocturnal poets
to send their poems home
to the mother.

Come take my arm, walk with me.
I too am returning this February
from far away.
Let's make love on the shore
while waves break and penetrate,
waves sent to us
from far away by an island.

I see your abandoned grave
and I want to press myself
                and I kiss
                and pretend
                and the salt
                and the calcic
                fill my mouth
                and I know, Sylvia,
                that on this night
                of this February warmer than usual
                I love you.

Translated by Patsy Boyer and Luz María Umpierre

[When will we bring the remains of Sylvia Plath home?]

Elliot's Sunset

for Sandra Gilbert

Elliot's sunset
the color of his shirt
reflected in the window—
orange light
yellow sun
violet clouds

What does one say to Death?

That stranger had a sense of humor
profound hilarity,
Elliot

The snow below, again;
another day of cold.
The plane swings towards the
left,
trembles
and I
write this letter

What makes the heart stop?

What light penetrates your pupils
that can no longer dilate beneath your long
eyelashes,
feminine eyelashes despite your grave voice?

I embraced you
and
you
left
like the others

Frozen
my blood once again in the snow
of a less damned country
because I recognized your cry.

You recognized,
you,
the worth of submerging
my feet
in painful truth.

"Macho," I am called by the men of my homeland.
"Macho" because my feet don't wear
high heels
and
they demand that I march to the rhythm of my mind.
"Macho" because I use this reddish ink to draw a path for a new world
orange
as your shirt.

The light
becomes opaque
Elliot
and
I
render my pain
still
Other shoulders
carry you
to
a
tomb
without a name
yet

The plane
descends
towards
the snow
and
your
body
comes to light in California

Shalom

Adiós,
man of profound hilarity,
both of us land:
I
in the snow
you
in the sun.

We live parallel lives.

Translated with Ellen J. Stekert

For Ellen

I don't know how to write you this poem
in a language of which you don't understand a word.
But this nerve opened between my legs
to receive your weight on a freezing night
in Minnesota asks me, begs me to write.

Painful nerve, nerve resistant to pressing
against a man, nerve my body forgot
how to contract.

And while you sought shelter between my legs
and fell asleep,
that nerve in my right leg
bore your years, the polio pain
of your legs, and I felt you close to my sex.
Still, I lay still while
you hung suspended over that nerve,
nerve weak in your legs
strong in mine.

And gradually, pain by pain, you entered
all my pores,
like a plant you took root
and drank from my veins and became
daughter, lover, mother and sister—
        daughter.

And passing down through the canal that never stretched
to give life,
you became life between my fingers,
salt, water, sea, and today, poem.

Translated by Luz María Umpierre and Patsy Boyer

Gloria Vando

Gloria Vando, a Puerto Rican poet who writes in English, received her B.A. at Texas A & I at Corpus Christi, and studied at New York University, the University of Amsterdam and the Academie Julian in Paris. She is the editor of *The Helicon Nine Reader*, an anthology featuring the best of *Helicon Nine* (a magazine she founded and edited from 1979-1989); currently she publishes Helicon Nine Editions. Vando won the 1991 Billee Murray Denny Poetry Prize and was a finalist in the Poetry Society of America's Alice Fay Di Castagnola Contest. Among her literary awards are a CCLM Editors Grant, the 1991 Kansas Governor's Art Award, a Kansas Arts Commission Fellowship in Poetry and a grant from the Barbara Deming Memorial Fund. With her husband, Bill Hickok, Vando has opened a Writer's Place in Kansas City, which has ties with Poets House in New York City and The Loft in Minneapolis. Vando's poems have appeared in numerous reviews and anthologies, including *Kenyon Review, Seattle Review, Looking for Home* and *Women of the 14th Moon*. She is a contributing editor to *The North American Review*. In 1993 she published her first collection of poetry, *Promesas: Geography of the Impossible. Publishers Weekly* (March 8, 1993) notes that "This collection introduces a newcomer whose voice is particularly sustained and developed. Vando is constantly searching for 'connections/between my parents' world and this one.' (...) Vando's is a universal voice expressing childhood anguish and passion." *Promesas* has been selected as the recipient of the Thorp Menn Award for Poetry for 1994. The poems herein are from *Promesas*. Vando is the daughter of Anita Vélez-Mitchell, whose work also appears in this anthology.

Divorce

Gloria Vando

On Saturdays her grandmother
would strip her bed and open
the windows while her grandfather
rolled the mattress up against
the head of the yellow iron frame
and carried her piggyback from
room to room. On this Saturday
she sneaks back into her room
and hides in the core of the striped
sleeve, wadding her body
into a rigid ball, small enough
and tight enough so no one
can find her; tight, tighter
so she can withstand the weight
of the horsehair, resist the steel
buttons embossing her flesh,
the fresh fumes of urine. Only
her blood boasts in the silence.
It is safe. She cannot see them
coming, cannot hear their reasons
why they're sending her away,
or hear their cries as they search
each empty room, while she—
ensheathed in the one bed they
will leave behind—awaits
the onslaught, hoping they'll forgive
whatever she has done, hoping
they'll forget that she must go.

Latchkey Kid

Instead of butterscotch caramels
glistening in Baccarat jar
her house is dark
bitter chocolate, so dark
shadows cringe in the corners,
clouds surround it low and hoarse
like a bad head cold in December.
At night insistent drafts lick
the threshold, stretching their
rough tongues across the hearth.
Her bones ache, feel like popsicle
sticks stained lime, sucked dry.
She never wants to go home.
It smells of death.
She goes instead to a friend's
house after school, outstays
her welcome through Fritolays,
pork chops, awkward
conversation as parents' eyes
exchange impatience. She lies
she will be going in a while, but
she's afraid and cannot tell them
her house is dark,
dark like her mother's blood,
dark like the crimson rose her father
sent for her seventh birthday,
a rose with a smudged note
he did not write.
She keeps its tall, brittle stem
in a bottle beside her bed. When
she turns on the light
it casts a shadow across her life.

At My Father's Funeral

My father, a free-thinker, who
insisted I be reared like him,
lies in his open casket,
the blood of Jesus dripping
on his clean white shirt,
El Grito de Lares pinned
to one lapel, *La Bandera*
to the other, and instead of
boleros or plenas permeating
the heavy incense of the chapel
a rosario of *Padre Nuestros*
and *Ave Marías* churns the air.

I study his hands, try to stroke away
the spots that will bury themselves
into my skin like spiders, brown
recluses, that will never let go.
Be careful, his doctor warns me,
your father died of skin cancer—
but at 93, I'd say he's entitled to go
as he pleases, and this ceremony
that accompanies his departure is
not my doing. I have no rights here.

My half sister removes the pins
from my father's lapels and presses
them into my hand like an omen.
You're the firstborn, she says.
We decided you should have them.
I pin them on my blouse.

At the cemetery, a handsome woman with
white hair stands on the sidelines
flanked by men in grey suits.
Lolita Lebrón, my sister whispers—

and it is 1954. I am in Holland
studying literature and art
when the news comes over the wires
and students at school start

asking me whether I'm ashamed being
Puerto Rican and I in turn ask them
whether they feel shame for Hiroshima
or Dresden or Dachau—because *I do*—
and they can't understand that
it *all* has to do with me, with them—

and here's Lolita Lebrón, patriot
or terrorist, take your pick—
though she never fired a shot
(*I didn't come to kill, I came to die!*
she proclaimed, ready to give
her life for *el gran ideal*),
her sole aim to publicize the plight
of her besieged island. They stormed
the Spectator's Gallery—she and
three men—waving German Lugers
and their outlawed flag and
shouting *Freedom for Puerto Rico!*—
when one of the men went berserk
and began shooting into the crowded
floor of the House—congressmen
diving for cover, under desks,
behind chairs, five hit, bleeding,
visitors screaming for help.

It was a suicide mission: born
in Lares, she felt it was her destiny—
but how could she have known
the sacrifice would be her children—
her son murdered during the trial,
her daughter killed in an accident,
or so they said, and she in and
out of solitary confinement
for thirty-five years, unable to eat
or sleep, unable to breathe,
her hair turning white overnight,
like her heart, a dead weight.

The roster at the grave site reads
like a who's who of better days.
The leaders old and infirm come
on crutches and canes—but they come.

My other sister tapes their tributes.
They recite my father's poems,
sing songs I didn't know he wrote.
When they sing *La Borinqueña,*
the one song I do know, my words
are all wrong—this is a new version,
Lolita's version— and my anthem,
my sweet anthem, is no longer
a *danza,* but a marching song.

Your father was a great man,
they all tell me, *a great man.*

I look cautiously around me
and spot them—one, two, maybe three
dark-suited men in the distance,
blending into the trees, documenting
our sorrows with hidden cameras
and tape recorders. No one
pays attention to them—the F.B.I
is as much a part of their lives
as the shadows their bodies cast
across my father's grave. I want to cry
out that I am innocent, that I
have nothing to do with the violence—
I'm there because we share a name,
a face—but when I look at my sisters

I see my *fate.* The next morning
my half brother waits at the airport.
He sees Papi's slogans like
stigmata bleeding on my lapels.
Ten cuidado, he warns me, *they might
not let you out.* We embrace
and I see our shadows on the sidewalk
merge—when I kiss him it is as if
I were kissing myself goodbye.

Cry Uncle

for Carlos Vélez-Rieckehoff

They say he was a revolutionary
in single-handed combat with contemporary
conquistadors who invaded his island's shores.
They say he was a radical, hitting hard,
baffling the foe, then running for cover
to the hills in and around Ciales, Novillo,
and points west where Yankee soldiers,
lost in the intricacies of hollows,
underbrush, and overload, deigned to follow.

They say, they say—but what they say is buried
like cloves of garlic deep into the diagonal slits
of my uncle's blue-grey eyes and what I see
across from me is a mild, bearded old man who sits
eating quiche at Columbus Restaurant, haunt
of the undaunted: Madonna, Penn, Baryshnikov—
a far cry from revolution, *patria, libertad*.

My uncle's pale suit matches his eyes.
My mother, her hands on her brother's,
tries to woo him with a clone smile.
In vain. He sees her coquetry as puerile
next to the manly courage his island demands.
(In the photo my husband later will take,
my mother will lean toward her brother, he
toward me, and I, stalwart as a tree,
try to keep the house of Medina from toppling down—
yes, I, the youngest, am doomed to pillarhood.)

Besides my uncle's suit and his eyes
and the veins straddling tendons
across the backs of his laced hands, another
blueness infiltrates his person, hones his mirth.
It bruises the edge of every gesture,
every word, pares slogans down to sighs.

He turns to me now. But I am dry,
rebellion sucked from my bones early on.
There's no one left to justify
his failure, to render his lifelong mission holy.

The "cry" in the title also refers to The Cry of Lares (*El Grito de Lares*), a symbol of Puerto Rico's ongoing struggle for independence.

Legend of the Flamboyán

1.

It was a good old-fashioned
victory—no massacres, no fires,
no children gunned down
in the streets of day,
no cameras to point a finger
and say *he* did it, or *they;*
it was calm, it was civilized—
they emerged from the ocean,
and claimed their paradise.

From the rain forest, naked and
trembling beneath scheffleras
and figs, perched like purple
gallinules among the low branches
of the jacarandas, the Taínos
watched the iron-clad strangers
wade awkwardly ashore, their
banners staking out their land.

Chief Agüeybana also watched,
the gold *guanín* glinting
on his chest like a target.
Who were these intruders and what
were they doing on this island?
Could they be cannibals like
the Caribes? Could they be gods?
Their bodies glistened like stars;
their eyes like the sea.

The Taínos met and argued
well into the night, weighing
the pros and cons of strategies—
if these were gods, to ignore them
might incite their wrath,
to fight them might invite death.
Best to rejoice then and welcome
the silver giants to Boriquén.

The Spaniards responded by
taking first their freedom,
then their land, then
using them as human picks to dig
for gold—gold for the crown,
gold for the holy faith,
gold for the glory of Spain.

2.

The darkness of the mines
consumed them, sapped
their laughter, their song,
locking them into perpetual night.
The women withdrew, drew in,
their hearts hard
against the longing they saw
in the strangers' eyes—
not to look, not to be seen—
they bowed their heads, folded
into themselves like secrets
whispered only in the safety
of brown arms.

3.

A wrecked vessel washed ashore
at Guajataca. The children raced
down to the beach looking
for treasures, looking under
torn sails, beneath coiled ropes,
turning over loosened boards,
and suddenly—a hand, then a face,
the skin pale and mottled, the eyes
staring up at them, opaque
like a fish, the color of the sea.

Something dead. Something *ungodly*.

The island echoed their cries.
That night the Taínos planned
carefully, knowing—
like those at Masada before them—
that there was no other way.
They drew straws.

The first Spaniard to awaken
was startled by the hush, as though
the earth itself had given up.
He stepped out into the chill,
into the stained silence,
but saw only flowers, thousands
of flamboyáns—

splashes of blood—

blooming all over the island.

Commonwealth, Common Poverty

. . . a name means continuity with the past and people without a past
are people without a name.
–Milan Kundera

for Zoltán Sumonyi

A visitor comes from Hungary as from outer space
dropping into my Midwestern world with poems
about himself and that bracketed place he hails from.
And though the gift he brings is veiled, submerged
in allegory and myth, I recognize myself. Say
to him: this poem you read is about me. He smirks.

He has read his poems before and not been heard.
He is weary, somewhat cavalier. His body is taut like
a gymnast's. His eyes form flat black mirrors of distrust
adjusting to what he perceives as enemy turf. It's August.
He sheds his jacket, rolls his sleeves above his biceps.
A pulse in his temple keeps rhythm with his words.

He tries again, leads me as he reads. I see us both,
two generations earlier, perhaps three, running down once
familiar streets with new strange names, and I am plagued
by what I might have been had nothing changed,
had Teddy's boys not made it to the top of San Juan
Hill. Like him I, too, yearn for connections

between my parents' world and this one, long for
a tie, cut short by strangers—does it matter
that his were Russian, mine American; or that
his lines allude to Greeks and gifts of death, while
mine—because our history has yet to be revamped—
still lament the Massacre of Ponce? Here we sit

in a Kansas City motel, hearing what we say
translated by a man we have to trust—could be
a friend, could be a secret agent— a clean-cut man
in a banker's suit who keeps his jacket on,
claims he walked away from Budapest to freedom, and
converts our pain into passionless sounds. Yes,

here we sit, feeling as our ancestors surely felt
the day their world shifted in its global socket
and everything they cherished perished in the quake,
leaving them disfranchised, disconnected from
their past, from each other, from themselves. How
they must have searched then for a look, a gesture,

a familiar word to ease their terror: the arch of a brow,
a jawline—*something* to bind them to their captors,
something so slight it might have gone unnoticed
had all remained whole. And we, their progeny, now
sit here immersed in Russian and American symbols:
we, their future, have become what they most feared.

Faith

for Philippe

Sometimes when I witness the blindness of faith
I feel cheated,
Robbed of a liturgical heritage that should have been mine.
But I've been exiled to a prosebyterian plane—insensate,
Incenseless, devoid of hocus pocus
With water no holier than Perrier.
I've had to endure tedium without *Te Deum,*
Listen to scriptures
In a raptureless take-it or-leave-it vernacular. I left it,
Protesting its blandness, rejecting not faith
But the leveling down of faith to a line so fine it ceases
To divide the inner from the outer life—as though
The noises of the street
And the turmoil of the soul were interchangeable.

I have a friend, a good Catholic, who gets off on ritual,
Ritual for its own sake,
Much like good theater, where you're so transported
By the trompe l'oeil sets, paste jewels, electric sunlight,
It doesn't matter whether the words fade
Before they reach your second-to-the-last-row seat—
The magic stays—night after night.
So, too, the magic of Hail Marys on the rosary or
The Latin Mass every Sunday of your life,
Fish on Friday, Benediction on Thursday—a predictable,
Dependable, inspiring show (makes you want to sing
And dance up the aisle, beating
Your breast and snapping your fingers to *Mea culpa*).

Oh, it should have been mine!

But I grew up in other people's homes, learned early
To distrust the permanence of words
And stones and flesh, not to mention
The father, the son, or the holiest of ghosts.
I *know* the curtain falls on all things. Still,
Sometimes, something deep within me hums
In a minor key,
Mouths syllables I don't fully understand or even hear and
When I least expect it, stuns me
With a right hook in the eye of reason.

Anita Vélez Mitchell

Anita Vélez-Mitchell has had a distinguished career in the arts. As a child, she once transcribed into verse, for her absent mother, the Spanish picaresque novel, *Lazarillo de Torme*. Born and reared in Puerto Rico, Vélez-Mitchell was a dancer in Xavier Cugat's San Juan shows. At Lincoln Center, she directed "West Side Story" and performed the role of Anita; she also directed the open-air musical "Salsa of Hispanic Women," at Lincoln Center. Equally successful as a poet, her bilingual poetic piece, *Primavida: calendario de amor*, received the *Revista Sin Nombre*'s "Premio Julia de Burgos" award in 1978. On the linguistic level, *Primavida* reveals the author's biculturalism through renditions that are astutely different, yet alike, in each language. She has received three Ibero-American awards for short stories and the 1991 Poetry Award from the Institute of Puerto Rico. The editor of an *Antología de trece cuentos puertorriqueños de autores contemporáneos*, Vélez-Mitchell has most recently capped her success in the New York theater by receiving the 1993 "Inky Award" for Playwrighting from La MaMa, E.T.C., the Off Broadway Theater Company. She has presented numerous one-act plays at La MaMa, E.T.C., and has translated and directed Norma Aleandro's premiere play, "Kids Want In." For the Puerto Rican Traveling Theater, she translated lyrics for a musical directed by Susana Tubert. Vélez-Mitchell is currently preparing, for the Latino Playwrights Company, a film treatment of her play "Ripples of the Mind," which focuses on child abuse and the treatment of mental illness through hypnotherapy. She is a member of PEN, Feministas Unidas, and the American Academy of Poets. Included here are four of the twelve sections of *Primavida*.

April

Anita Vélez Mitchell

In Central Park
the trees sheltered
our smooching
We ventured out in herds
shepherded by the moon
We didn't know yet how to kiss
Later the lamplight glowed
on our clown-like faces
denouncing our awkward kisses
and we'd laugh ourselves hysterical
ending in tearful laughter
Then seized with those innocent rousings of childhood
we'd go up in the swings
'til the earth met the sky
and on to race barefoot
on the dampened green grass

Remember the rainfall of stolen kisses
under umbrellas as we queued up
to see Frankenstein and Dracula?
It was then we realized
we knew each other only by
our voices and our faces and
we discovered legs and stances
and affected poses of
sexy body language
Such fun
such ardor
reveling in the pulse
of springtime!

The game was joy
under the stars
under the sun
and enduring love song
Such a feverish desire to drain the enchantment
of life's prime season!
We didn't know of hate or boredom
Life was breathtakingly full of that
optimism that sets all hope afire

"Luis, I cannot wait for your graduation
let's get married now...*enseguida*
But Luis had promised Sandro he would
let me finish my studies
Sandro was already courting Hibis
and I wondered what she saw in Sandro
when one day suddenly I saw myself in his place
So much was I like my brother
Amado too had a crush on Hibis but
he wouldn't declare himself
out of loyalty to Sandro
They were best of friends
So that "Take my sister out, Amado"
a demand coming from Sandro
was a joke on both of us
Amado ached to be near Hibis, and Sandro
didn't have to spy on his ward!

A quiet smile masked my impatience
and anxiety and anger
bloomed in Primavida and
all because of Sandro!

It was at the costume ball the stranger
pressed his body to mine
Two pieces of a puzzle
two fitting continents of a world
yet to be explored

June

School time was over
we graduated
We flocked to the streets shouting
"All we want is *libertad*
space and freedom!"
Then we looked for work
Our working papers
our ignorance and innocence
Soon wiser voices cautioned
"there is but one rite of spring
and one must drain it
to the core!"

Hibis the exotic South Sea Island girl
knew how to kiss
She kissed Sandro
rapturously
We drooled as in the movies over the soulful kisses

Wise in legendary pleasures
one night Hibis taught me how to kiss
the way she kissed my brother
Initiated in the art of kissing
I fell in love with Hibis
dazzled by her beauty
I couldn't care less that she was
like me a woman
¡era amor!

Just like Titania in *Midsummer Night's Dream*
love-blinded
my senses veiled and
there began that unspeakable "amour fou"
of Primavida
ancient poets haloed in their songs
Love submerged in the divine waters of creation
The apple bitten but never swallowed
Mystic hours of incense
silent vigils on life and death
chanting to tom-toms
and hand-clapping
mimicking nature at its best
palm trees
waves and rivulets

And then the mantra and the hum
"Truth within us
our souls rise to the gods
an everlasting stream
of gentle thought
breathed in peace and love"
We sang songs of the islands
hands held in bond
of apparent joy yet
facing painful reality

I was in love with Hibis
and Hibis loved Sandro
Amado also loved Hibis
but Maíza loved Amado
Mark loved Lili
and Lili loved Darío
and Darío dutiful to his organ
had no time for love
Emmanel loved Maíza
Allegra loved Luis
but Luis loved me
Bombón had a secret crush
on Sandro or was it Emmanuel?
Only Maga loved no one
she laughed at us all
teasingly turning off and on

So that a tactic anguish spread over
our rose-honeyed meetings
face-to-face
And it remained there unseen
nurturing and shaping us
emptying us of
youth-sap
Deep into the night we invoked the gods
in silence

"Here we lie revealed...*esperando*
We sleep awake
ready to meet the challenge
of the unfolding of our
golden dreams"

ઉଷଚ

October

The parish priest
caught up with us
in the street
wringing in his reverend hands
the secret he must reveal
"It's Darío"
he confided with dried-tears
"He tried to commit suicide!"
Pobre Darío...they put him away
where even life forgets itself

We had been chastised
for being cumbersome
when virtuous now
we were light-weights!
Could it be virtue outweighed everybody?
Waiting to lose the purity of soul
our moral virtue was
superfluous
we shed it without restraint

And the leaves began to fall
on vain hopes
Who was there to replenish our faith?
What had we done in our flowering
to deserve such punishment?
Yet the gods went mercilessly on
plucking the heart
of our beloved world!

And Maga cradled her aborted child
Bombón became obese to protect her soul
Lili's sepia beauty was disfigured
in a car accident
Allegra stripped her tender hopes in a
burlesque
Maíza posed in the nude for art students
Luis left for parts unknown
to become a man

Mark became a traveling salesman
for pharmacopoeia
Amado, whom mama referred to as a "ne'er do well,"
gambled and drank
Emmanuel was deep into religion
Sandro joined the merchant-marines
Only Hibis and I remained
virginal
pure and, we thought,
wise
And from our love just enough
to trace a voluptuous design
of happiness life
gleaned its meaning

...And the wizardly ripener
took off in a blaze of colors
stealing all our joys
in a golden armful.

December

Amado was the first
for the love of Hibis
to forget
I poured my heart out
over the clouds reflected
in the Central Park lake
next day because now
I could make pronouncements

Man is strong
woman softer
and a lover should be
a wise and tender creature
a shadowless being
grasping from heaven
and earth the salt
and sweetness of
mutual perfection
to become life's truth

And Sandro who was always
into everything
came to fetch me
"Don't you know, silly gander,
that 'Love' is God's great game?
One cannot sit there and bleed
because of an experience
Love has a perennial mystery
a butterfly one picks up gently
between two fingers and places it
with grateful tenderness
back into the cupped hands of God

"Brave words!" I murmured, lighting
a cigarette and turning
to hide a rush of tears
And I thought...
"Why didn't you remain
the hero you were
when I was a child
instead of growing up
to become a spy of
my joys and sorrows?"

"Sis, the United States has declared war
The Marines were called in this morning."
I turned to see his blurred image
in the pit of the lake
His brave words
sounded like a huge wave
in a giant sea-shell
held to the ear of time
And with a wave of the hand
he was gone forever

Soon came the love-beggars
asking for alms...
All but Sandro.
They had a rendezvous with the end
of an era
going to conquer peace,
where dressed in fire
honor would soon wreak havoc

"No...I will not
give into lust!
Bring me love and peace,
muchachos

How many times I grieved
over the tremor
of a handshake
held in the shock of time!

And stilled in contemplation
I remained waiting
waiting like a perpetual
Sunflower.

Ah, Primavida
my mind is much too small
to hold your vehement heart

Then the fieriness
blazed itself out turning
half the world
to ashes and etching
with its dust
this "memento mori"
at the year's end.

Abril

En el Parque Central, los árboles cobijaban nuestros abrazos
Aún no sabíamos besar. Caminábamos en grupos como cachorros
pastoreados por la luna. Los besos a boca cerrada relucían
más tarde bajo la luz, y éramos payasos con bocas grotescas
de pintalabios. Reíamos hasta llorar. Si aún nos quedaba
esa pureza de la niñez que nos columpiaba hasta unir cielo
y tierra, y nos corría por la grama descalzos.

¡Ah, aquel día lluvioso de besos ocultos tras los paraguas!
¡Las grandes esperas en fila para ver a Frankenstein y a Drácula!
Nos dimos cuenta de que sólo nos conocíamos por la voz,
la cara, y descubrimos las piernas, las actitudes, y cómo cada uno
se expresaba. ¡Qué bullicio, qué alegría, ardía la sangre primaveral!
Todo era amor, al sol, a las estrellas, todo era canción. Delirio
de escanciar la savia virgen de la temporada. No conocíamos
ni el odio ni el hastío. ¡La vida era tan bella, plena de ese
intenso optimismo que aviva la esperanza!

—¡Luis, no puedo esperar hasta tu graduación, nos casamos hoy
mismo!—
Pero Luis le había dado su palabra a mi hermano Sandro de dejarme
estudiar. Sandro era novio de Hibis, y yo buscaba en Sandro lo que Hibis
veía y me encontraba yo. ¡Tan parecida era yo a mi hermano!
También Amado estaba loco por Hibis, pero no se le había declarado,
por respeto a Sandro. Eran muy intimos, y por eso— Acompaña tú a
mi hermana Vilia—le decía Sandro a Amado, y eso a mí no me valía de
nada.
Amado no me quería y Sandro me velaba. Y una dulce sonrisa
enmascaraba
mi impaciencia, y la ansiedad, la tristeza, retoñaba ya en primavida.
¡Todo por Sandro!

Fue en aquel baile de fantasía, donde el desconocido
unió nuestros cuerpos como dos continentes para formar
un mundo no explorado aún. Ardorosos, las sienes pulsantes
nuestros pasos sincopaban con la voz soñadora, urgente, del cantante.

You'll never know
just how much
I love you…

Y el desconocido la traducía a mi oído dulcemente…

Nunca sabrás
cuánto yo
te amo…

Y el mutuo aliento nos humedecía la palma de la mano y se vaciaba
en el supra sentido, el del recuerdo, en el frenesí instante.
De repente, Sandro, bailando con Hibis muy de cerca, me maltrató
con el pie. —¡Salvaje!— le grité, y provoqué una porfía que los
amigos tuvieron que aplacar. ¡Nada, que me quedé como dicen, pintada
en la pared, el resto de la fiesta…por el maldito Sandro!

—Vas a aprender que soy hembra y con tanto derecho como tú al placer.
¿Qué edad tenía Julieta, y no murió de amor? Pero yo no voy a morir
de amor, voy a vivir para amar…No voy a sacrificarme, no y para que
luego venga el hombre a hacerme esposa y madre, pantalla para expiar
sus pecados! ¡Dios mío, qúe martirio! ¿Cómo escaparme de la jaula
de oro de esa mente, donde me tenía prisionera ese maldito macho.

Junio

Pasó la época de las competencias y nos graduamos.
Íbamos sueltos por las calles, en bandadas, vociferando,
—¡No nos briden otra cosa que libertad y espacio!
No crean, buscamos trabajo, sin otra carta de referencia
que la ignorancia, la inocencia. Pronto aprendimos de bocas
pródigas que sólo hay una adolescencia y que había que disfrutarla.

Hibis, la exótica marsureña, sabía besar. . . y besaba a Sandro
como en un rapto. Era un beso entrelazado, de película, y nos
extasiábamos mirándolos. Niña sabia de placeres legendarios,
una noche Hibis me enseño a besar como besaba a mi hermano.
Inciada en el arte del beso, me enamoré locamente de Hibis
como Tatania en "Un Sueño de Verano". Me prendí de su belleza.
¡Que importaba que fuese como yo mujer, ciego el amor, mis
sentidos se nublaron! Y ahí comenzó esa indecible amorosa
amistad de primavida a la que cantan los poetas de antaño.
Amor que se clava en la mordida manzana que nunca se traga.
Amor sumergido en las aguas sublimes de nuestra creación.
Meditábamos en su cuarto inciensado entonando en caricia
de voces cantos sagrados, a tom-tom, ukelele y ritmos de mano.

—Le verdad está en nosotros mismos y nos une al dios por una sarta
de pensamientos mutuos bañados en paz y amor. —Luego cantábamos
"La Canción de las Islas".

Y entre nosotros aparentemente todo era paz y amor.
Pero al salir y toparnos con la punzante realidad...

Yo amaba a Hibis,
Maíza amaba a Amado,
Amado amaba a Hibis,
Mark amaba a Lili, mas
Lili amaba a Darío, y Darío
amaba su órgano sagrado,
Emanuel amaba a Maíza, pero
Maíza amaba a Amado
Allegra amaba a Luis,
y Luis, a mí me amaba,
Bombón secretamente
amaba a Sandro, y Maga,
aún no amaba a nadie,
y se reía de todos. . .
lo estaba pensando.

Y la enemistad se escurría por entre los colores rosados
y melados que la naturaleza nos había prestado, tal cual
si estuviera dentro de nosotros, nutriéndonos, formándonos…
Y en la noche invocábamos al dios amor en silencio,

Aquí estamos
iluminados…
aquí vamos
con la faz ardiente de fe
en pos de sueños dorados.

ఆ

Octubre

Un día nos alcanzó en la calle, el cura. En sus reverendas manos
estrujaba algún secreto que nos debería confesar.
—Es Darío—nos dijo con lágrimas ya secas,— se ha querido suicidar.
¡Pobre Darío! Lo encerraron por vida. Allá,
donde la muerte se olvida de sí misma.

Nosotros, los que antes éramos "pesados" por virtuosos,
ahora éramos "ligeros" al perder la virtud, tal como si la virtud
le pesara a todos. En la espera de perder la pureza del alma,
la virtud moral era superflua. Nos la dimos ya sin tregua.

Y comenzaron las hojas a caer...hojas dispares, de esperanzas
vanas. ¿Quién nos devolverá la fe, y que hicimos para merecer
maltrato? Mas los dioses seguían despiadados, desgajando
el corazón de nuestro mundo ufano.

> ...Y Maga acunó un aborto, fruto de sus amores con Luis.
> Bombón se puso obesa para proteger su alma.
> Lili de un choque se desfiguró su linda cara sepia.
> Allegra quemaba su juventud en un burlesco.
> Maíza modelaba desnuda en el Art Student's League.
> Luis se fue a su patria a hacerse "grande".
> Mark viajaba como vendedor de productos nuevos.
> Amado a quien mamá llamaba mequetrefe, jugaba y bebía.
> Emanuel estudiaba y Sandro se enlistó en la Marina.

Sólo quedábamos Hibis y yo puras, vírgenes y sabias.
De nuestro amor, sólo lo necesario para trazar
un diseño voluptuoso de la felicidad, la vida
tomaba su significado

...Y el sabio madurador se alejó triunfante tras una feria
de colores, llevándose nuestra alegría en un dorado abrazo.

Diciembre

Amado fue el primero. Nuestro amor por ella nos unió, en el dolor.
Y al día siguiente volqué mis sentimientos sobre las nubes
que se reflejaban en el lago del Parque Central. ¡Ah,
porque ya yo podía hacer celebraciones!...

—El hombre es duro,
la mujer es tierna,
y el amante debiera ser
una criatura de ternura sabia
con un cuerpo sin sombra,
que arrebatara del cielo
y de la tierra, la sal
y la dulzura de mutua
perfección, para así ser vida.

Y Sandro que todo lo adivinaba vino en mi busca:
—¿No sabes, tonta, que la vida es así? No puede uno sangrar
por culpa de una experiencia. El amor tiene su intimo misterio,
una mariposa que recoge delicadamente con dos dedos
y la devuelve con inmensa ternura a las manos de Dios.

—Bravas palabras—murmuré prendiendo un cigarrillo
y volviéndome de espaldas para esconder la lágrima que rodaba
hacia el abismo de la nada. Y pensé: —Por qué no vuelves a ser mi héroe
como cuando era niña, y no ser espía de mi felicidad y mi desgracia.
—Hermana, los Estados Unidos han declarado guerra abierta.
Se avisó ya a la marina esta mañana. Me di vuelta y vi que su imagen
se desvaneció en el seno del lago. Dijo algo así que sonó
como un caracol rotundo en el oído del tiempo, y con un gesto
de adiós se alejó para siempre.

...Y vinieron los mendigos a pedirme una limosna de amor.
Iban a un rendezvous con el fin de una era, a conquistar
la paz donde vestido de fuego, el honor haría estragos.

—¡No! No voy a ceder a la lujuria. Tráiganme amor y paz.
Os quiero demasiado. ¡Que Dios los bendiga, muchachos!—
¡Ay, cuántas veces me hirió el trémolo de una mano envuelta
en el sibido del tiempo!

Y me quedé contemplando la desvanecencia, y esperando,
esperando, como un girasol perpetuo y solitario.

¡Ah, primavida, tu corazón palpitante no me cabe
entre
las
manos!

Y aquella fogosidad
que se apagó de incendio,
dejó medio mundo incinerado,
mas yo guardé su polvo de oro
como "memento mori" al terminarse
el año.

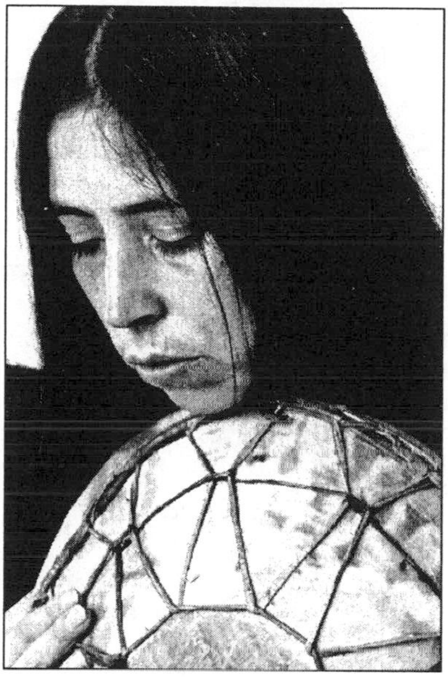

Photo by Nina Subín

Cecilia Vicuña

Cecilia Vicuña, a poet and artist from Chile, belongs to a generation of Latin American writers in exile in the United States, and elsewhere. Born in Santiago, she studied Fine Arts at the University of Chile. She went to London on a British Council scholarship in 1972; the military coup of 1973 forced her to remain in England, where she was active in opposition movements. In England she published *Sabor a Mí* (1973), her first bilingual book of poetry, and exhibited at the Institute of Contemporary Arts. Under an assumed name, she was the subject of a BBC documentary. In 1975 she returned to South America, basing herself in Columbia. Traveling throughout the continent, she studied Andean shamanism, oral traditions, mythology and herbal lore. Vicuña moved to New York in 1980, where she continues to live. She received the Human Rights Award from the Fund for Free Expression in 1985, and was invited to the Bellagio Study Center in Italy in 1990. Her poetry was the subject of a one-hour documentary in the Rohm & Hass "Poets Vision" series. In New York, she is active in the Latin American Writers Institute, and PEN. Her work has been featured in the *American Poetry Review* and in numerous publications on three continents. *Palabrarmás* (1984) was born from a vision in which individual words opened to reveal their inner associations, thus allowing ancient and newborn metaphors to come to light. Using an association of words (*palabra*, word; *labrar*, to work; *armas*, arms; *más*, more), Vicuña uses words as weapons. In 1992, she published her first extensive bilingual collection of works, *Unravelling Words and the Weaving of Water*, a selection of three of her seven books of poetry, prose, and performance "events."

Entering

Cecilia Vicuña

I thought that all this was nothing more than a way of remembering.

To remember (*recordar*) in the sense of playing the strings
(*cuerdas*) of emotion.

Re-member, *re-cordar*, from *cor*, *corazón*, heart.

ര

First there was listening with the fingers, a sensory memory: the shared bones, sticks and feathers were sacred things I had to arrange.

To follow their wishes was to rediscover a way of thinking: the paths of mind I traveled, listening to matter, took me to an ancient silence
waiting to be heard.

To think is to follow the music, the sensations of the elements.

And so began a communion with the sky and the sea, the need to respond to their desires with works that were prayers.

Pleasure is prayer.

If, at the beginning of time, poetry was an act of communion, a form of collectively entering a vision, now it is a space one enters, a spatial metaphor.

ര

Metaphor stakes out a space of its own creation.

If the poem is temporal, an oral temple, form is a spatial temple.

Metapherein: to carry beyond
to the other contemplation:
to con-temple the interior and exterior.

Space and time, two forms of motion that cross for a moment, an instant
of doubled pleasure, concentration, con-
penetration.

The precarious is that which is obtained through prayer.

To pray is to feel.

"The quipu that remembers nothing," an empty string, was my first precarious work.

I prayed by making a quipu, offering the desire to remember.

Desire the offering, the body is nothing but a metaphor.

In ancient Peru the diviner would trace lines of dust in the earth, as a means of divination, or of letting the divine speak through him.

Lempad, in Bali, says: "All art is transient, even stone wears away." "God tastes the essence of the offerings, and the people eat at the material remains."

To recover memory is to recover unity:

To be one with the sea and sky
To feel the earth as one's own skin
Is the only kind of relationship
That brings her joy.

(New York, 1983-1991)

Translated by Eliot Weinberger

quipu: a form of measurement used in Ancient Perú using knots on string

The Origin of Weaving

origin
from *oriri:* the coming of the stars

weave
from *weban, wefta,* Old English
weft, cross thread
web

the coming out
of the cross-star

the interlacing of
warp and weft

to imagine the first cross
intertwining of branches and twigs
to make a nest
to give birth

the first spinning of thread
to cross spiraling
a vegetable fiber imitating a vine

the first thread coming out of fleece trapped in
vegetation

the first cross of warp and weft
union of high and low, sky and earth,
woman and man

the first knot, beginning of the spiral:
life and death, birth and rebirth

textile, text, context
from *teks*: to weave, to fabricate, to make wicker or
wattle for mud-covered walls (Paternosto)

sutra: sacred Buddhist text
thread (Sanskrit)

tantra: sacred text derived from the Vedas: thread

ching: as in *Tao Te Ching* or *I Ching*
sacred book: warp
wei: its commentaries: weft

Quechua: the sacred language
derived from *q'eswa*:
rope or cord made of straw

to weave a new form of thought:
connect
bring together in one

Translated by Eliot Weinberger

Precarious

And if I devoted my life
to one of its feathers
to living its nature
being it understanding it
until the end

Reaching a time
in which my acts
are the thousand
tiny ribs of the feather
and my silence
the humming the whispering
of wind in the feather
and my thoughts
quick sharp precise
as the non-thoughts
of the feather.

Translated by Eliot Weinberger

Poncho: Ritual Dress

hilo de agua
thread of water

hilo de vida
thread of life

they say woolly animals
are born high in the
mountain springs

water and fiber
are one

wool & cotton
downy fiber
an open hand

the Cotton Mother textile goddess in Chavín is a plant creature with snake feet, eyes and heart radiating from the center like a sun

the poncho
is a book
a woven
message

a metaphor
spun

white stones found in the mist, the *illa* and the *enqaychu* are the emblems of the vital force within the woolly animals themselves but only the poor and haggard can find them by the springs.

[Written in English]

De Palabrarmas

Primero vi una palabra en el aire
sólida y suspendida
mostrándome
su cuerpo de semilla

Se abría y deschacía
y de sus partes brotaban
asociaciones dormidas
                    Enamorados
                              en amor, morado
                              enajenados

Encantándome se sucedían
domos y cúpulas de encanto
cantaban en mí

Ascendía en el vértigo
desbarrancándome
en el quiebre
entre canto y dome
canto y en

Entraba y salía
por palacios desiertos
viendo la imagen
del canto y el entrar
el principio y el final.

La imagen tiene muslos
en su fractal
caderas y llagas
por donde entrar

Ella es madre y ventolera
su cuerpo fino
acomete y espera

From Palabrarmas

I saw a word in the air
solid and suspended
showing me
her seed body

She opened up and fell apart
and from her parts sprouted
sleeping thoughts
                                        of love, livid
                                                                        in love, living
                                                                        out of love

came madder violet

Enchanting me
nipples and cupolas
chanting in me

She ascends in a spiral
as I fall in the break
between chants and cupola

In and out
of deserted palaces I wander
seeing the image of chanting
and entering
the beginning
                                the end
                                                the word

The fractal image has thighs,
hips and wounds
to enter

She is mother and wind
her lean body
stalks and waits

Busca y atiende
la puerta
con silbante solicitud
la urge amándola
y al golpe terso
del portal
entra rodando
a su lugar

Nadie vería el mismo palacio
una vez cruzado el portal
nadie observaría las mismas flores
más que por un don
de ubicuidad

La coincidencia es un alcance
milagroso del azar
el cruce de dos vectores
poco cuidadosos quizás

Cada palabra
aguarda al viajero
que en ella
espera hallar
senderos y soles
del pensar

Esperan silentes
y cantarinas
cien veces tocadas
y trastocadas
agotadas por un instante
y vueltas a despertar

Perdidas o abandonadas
esplenden de nuevez

Cuerpos celestes
cada una
en su movimiento

She seeks
the door
whistling in love
pushing it
with a terse blow as
the door rolls
                    in place

No one will see the same palace
once the threshold has been crossed
no one will see the same flowers
except through the gift
of ubiquity

Coincidence is a miracle
of chance, the crossing
of two vectors,
carelessly placed perhaps

Each word
awaits the traveler
hoping to find
in her
trails and suns
of thought

They wait
singing in silence
one hundred times touched
and changed
exhausted for a moment
then revived

Lost or abandoned
they shine again

Celestial bodies
each
in its orbit

Estructura cuárzica
al oído y al tacto
interior

Música corporal
sus formas transforman
nacen y mueren
y se solazan
en la unión

Espacio
al que
compenetramos

Amos del com
pene y entrar

Amos y dueños
del palabrar
o aman ellas
nuestro labrar

Lo desean
como nosotros
a ellas.

Quartz structure
sensed by touch
and the inner ear

Body music
forms transform
born to die
enjoying
their conjugation

Space
that we penetrate

Lords of pen
in trance

Lords of words
or do they
love our works?

Do they
desire us as we
desire them?

Translated by Suzanne Jill Levine

Evangelina Vigil-Piñón

Evangelina Vigil-Piñon, the Assistant Editor of *The Americas Review*, was born and reared in San Antonio. She received her B.A. in English from the University of Houston, then did graduate work at St. Mary's University and the University of Texas at San Antonio. Vigil has been a Writer-in-Residence in Austin, Galveston and Houston. An arts administrator and community affairs media expert, Vigil has been Project Coordinator of the Mexican-American Cultural Center in San Antonio. In Houston, over a twenty-year period, she has hosted and produced numerous radio talk shows, and, since 1988, has been Public Affairs Manager of the Cultural Arts Council of Houston. She is also an Adjunct Lecturer in the English Department/Mexican American Studies at the University of Houston. Widely published in national and international reviews and anthologies, Vigil has three collections of poetry, *Nade y Nade* (1977), *Thirty an' Seen A Lot* (1983), which received the American Book Award from the Before Columbus Foundation, and *The Computer Is Down* (1987). Editor of and contributor to the anthology, *Woman of Her Word: Hispanic Women Write* (1983), she has done the English translation of the late Tomás Rivera's *And the Earth Did Not Devour Him* (1987). Vigil has received many literary honors, including a National Endowment for the Arts Fellowship for Creative Writers. Her early poetry was published in several issues of *Caracol*, the San Antonio review identified with Chicano literary nationalism. A poet preoccupied with the essence of space, in those early poems she captured the core of Mexican-American life in her native city. Then she depicted life in a fast-paced metropolis. Through her nature poems she renders still an entirely different sense of place.

El Mercado en San Antonio Where the Tourists Trot

Evangelina Vigil-Piñón

el otro día
me levanté yo bien temprano
y una buena caminata di
por la plaza y el mercado
y en una banca de madera me senté
a desenmarañarme el pelo
y, hijo, que sí batallé

y luego como casi media hora
me pasé entretenida
viendo por entre vidrieras
aterradas y pañosas
de tiendillas y boticas
ya abandonadas
pero nunca olvidadas
donde en años del pasado
se vendían comics
anillos importados
y velitas y novelas
santitos y rosarios

y de repente me di cuenta
qué tan hondo me encontraba
en recuerdos del pasado
cuando una voz tan de repente
tan cercas que se oyó—
voz que penetró mi espacio
voz que me espantó
me estremeció

dice la voz artificial
oiga, señorita,
perdone la molestia
pero por casualidad
¿no traerá usted un nicle
que me pueda dar?

me sorprendo
y volteo
y veo al señor
barbudo, flaco, hambreado y crudo
adicto del licor
vagabundo solitario
perdido al mirar

y la realidad absurda
me estruja
y obedezco mi impulso—
pero ay, pregunto yo,
dígame, señor,
¿en qué le va a servir un sólo nicle?

con ojos brillosos como espejos
me da una mirada penetrante
y como entre sonrisa y dolor
la voz artificial me informa:

pues nunca sabe uno
un poquito aquí
un poquito acá
quién diga quizás junte
suficiente pa'—

and I smile from heart
comprendiendo que 's verdad
y le doy una peseta
y el comprende el respeto
y yo la claridad cristal

el mercado queda
por la calle Produce Row
y la plaza queda
en el corazón del centro
por la calle de Comercio
de Comercio y Soledad

Legacy

to the memory of César Chávez

waste not the fruit
of sacrifice
la vida es una
waste not the fruit
el sudor en la palma
lineas de arena colorada
el río es grande
puños de tierra gris mojada
polvos de pozos
escarbados
a pico y pala
waste not the broken backs
siembra
waste not the broken dreams
que la espiga se da
make something of the pain
make something of the toil
sueña tu historia:
  revolucionarios al partir del siglo
  desesperados de los veintes y treintas
  olvidados de los cincuentas
  refugiados de los sesentas
  desaparecidos de los ochentas
  recién llegados de hoy y de mañana
  y de siempre
aprecia tu deber
escarba
tear the earth with your nails
escarba
tear the truth with your hands
más hondo
aguanta
ignore the scrape of rock against
the raw flesh of your hands
escarba
usa tu poder
comprométete
el destino no se hace solo
es tu vida

es tu derecho
waste not the fruit
of sacrifice
escarba
no pares
para descanso hay tiempo
escarba
el destino no se halla
se hace
waste not the fruit
la vida es una

Daily Progress

inner city youths
gather at the stop
some hold books
others blasters
their lean bodies emanating
rhythm

a dude strolls by at a paced
yet uncertain gait
he wears a pastel green shower cap over his 'fro
intermittently he snaps his finger
with down-cast eyes
looking 'bout and over his shoulder
then steps up his pace
anew

still and timeless as a black and white photo
barely visible under dark morning shadows
six old timers sit
on the steps of a dilapidated red brick house
waiting for "they rides to woik"
they watch the 8 a.m. traffic speed by
"shootin' de breeze"
discussing last night's poker game
in few words
making plans for the night
plotting a way out of the day
into tomorrow

at the corner
an elderly woman stands
leaning slightly on a cane
her features are contained by a flowered silk scarf
her stance alert
eyes sharp
cheekbones high
skin smooth, dark
with fine lines

the white-washed structure of a baptist church
stands bare and erect in the background
its steeple pointing
the way

across the street
two tall, lanky boys walk in synchronized strides
they nudge each other
talking and laughing loudly
waving their arms in sporadic gestures
each carries a varsity gym bag

down the street
rows of shotgun shanties lean
in odd directions
ramshackled by shifting foundations
layers of paint, brittle and chipped
exposing ashen-brown weathered wood
as in the hue of the skin
of the aged hands of a white-haired woman
in a pastel blue house dress
now tending to her roses
and humming a spiritual
"mmmmmmhhhh-mmmhhhmmmmmhh. . ."
sprinkling droplets of water
from a Folger's coffee can
on the thorny-stemmed bushes

an old battered station wagon
approaches the order of the day
its rectangular rear window frames silhouettes
five middle-aged men
their stout bodies crowded
each gazing in distinct directions
at red lights
one leans forward to talk to the driver
who responds with words and gestures
the tapping of ashes off his cigarette
out the window onto the street
his eyes fixed straight ahead
the light turns

the '59 wagon floats over bumps and dips
like a boat over water
cast to the toils of a Tuesday

"KTSU-U-U-you-you"
sensuous stereophonic voice echoes
female jock
on cue
her t's
and sibilants distinct
in digital delay
"...we are effective
efficient
and provocative..."
fades into
expansive percussive world rhythms:
in the distance
a group of children prance
and skip across the school yard
in perfect timing with the music
they can't hear

eyes right:
in the tiny porch of a small frame house
a lonely figure of a man
sitting erectly on a wooden stool
his hands resting idly on his lap
palms up
exposing traveled lines of destiny
he watches time zoom by
cars, vans, buses and trucks
bikers, people on foot
all in a hurry
they must all hurry
his eyes, now blurred of vision
have seen more than most
he's lived here all his life
the "Wa'd" is as it's always been
"...save a few Spanish folks an' Vietnamese
dats moved into de neigh'hd
he'ah an' the the'ah..."

a car idles at the light
its muffler rumbles loudly
Motown bass progressions resound
the driver turns the volume down
leans out the window
grins widely at a heavy, big-boned girl
who's swaggering by
"Say!
Say, girl!
What's yo' name?
I be talkin' to you.
You, in the red!"
at the DON'T WALK
she stops
then slowly, nonchalantly
turns her head to look at him
coolly, "What chu want, fool?"
"Shoot! What chu mean,
'fool'!?
Shoot! You gonna be that way, baby,
I won't even look achu!"
the light turns green
the smart dude speeds off in his blue Impala
burning rubber
feigning triumph

at Emancipation Park
an evangelist hails a bible in one hand
a megaphone in the other
with fervor he preaches to motorists and pedestrians
to "Repent!"
"Repent and See the Light
and Walk that Golden Path to Salvation!"
when there are no pedestrians or motorists
he directs his sermon seemingly to the heavens
and doesn't hesitate to kick aside a stray pup
that meekly tries to huddle at his side

the next block is bustling
office workers scurrying into buildings
African American beauties in high fashions
kiss their husbands or lovers a morning good-bye
lipstick glossy fresh

with poise they step out of elegant cars
they strut off with their stuff
in smart high heels
contours vanishing into the depths
of AT&T corridors
but not before men's eyes
check out the merchandise
theirs and others'
as long as it remains in view
while motorists in lanes behind them
honk their horns impatiently
"Move it, buddy!
Move it on!"

little old white ladies watch
nervous as birds
in fifties sweaters
translucent scarves
wide-rim glasses
apprehension painted on their powdered faces
they stand alongside middle-aged black working women
with patience in their eyes
they've seen much
"Mmmm-huhh. Yes, indeed."
their hefty arms crossed at their chests
"I gots time."
some wear white starched uniforms and nurse's shoes
some hold shopping bags and large purses
"You best not mess wit' me,"
one glares at a bum not to be trusted
in line behind her
she clutches her purse
tighter

clusters of black and Latino teenagers
approach with reluctance
their designated threshold to alternative
success
the Contemporary Educational Training Center
two Chicanas linger behind
hurriedly they share the last drags
it's Kool affirms the All-American handsome overhead
in his western provocative pose

while at the next street corner
handsome teenagers in designer fashions
await buses en route to a distinct destiny
like models in a catalog they pose
some have music cases at their sides
others stacks of books
their every glance a snap
of the fast motion of human traffic
a hint of future in their eyes
in their minds the echo
of serious advice
"You best study ha'd,
don't be a fool, son.
I've woiked ha'd to give you
the opp'tunity we din git.
You make somethin' of yo'self, son,
and make yo' Momma and
yo' Daddy
proud."

1993

Equinox

in the center of August
the cicadas
restively
chitter chatter
lazily
back and forth

somewhere far away
the cotton must be high
nearby
trout jump
their silver bodies
splashing above emerald waters

on the parched summer grass
tall pecan trees
choreograph their poses
graceful inconspicuous persuasion
motioning
advancing shadows

far away
in a starlit space
the sun burns fiercely
compelling eyes
east

next, a baby child stirs
in the center of afternoon dreams
that will not be remembered
nor known

and the cicadas
lazily
chitter chatter
back and forth
in the lush green shadows
of pecan trees

Omniscience

autumn leaves scatter in swirls
gulf gusts flap
press
caress

a lady bug cuts blank space and intercepts this poem
its rounded shell bright orange cellophane
a count of dusty lavender spots

eyes cast across the quiet
where ashen-brown Victorian houses lean on time
ghostly against sharp, angular cuts
of futuristic backdrop
obsidian monoliths
waterglass elegance
empowered
design pressing for space
against weathered ramshackled shanties with vacant eyes
what's left
of life
gone by

above,
on faded violet rooftops
pigeons gurgle and croon
their black brown silhouettes assembled in a line
some face east
some west
some each other
one now shrugs and flutters wings
streams across grey space

below,
a garden once tended
in now a tangle of ivy and weeds
smothering
the irises
shrouding
the shrubs
while from the dark of deep green morning shadows
the pallid faces of tea roses peek
wide-eyed
for a glance
a glimpse
a clue

there's something here

Photo by Wilfredo O. Castaño

Alma Luz Villanueva

Alma Luz Villanueva, of Yaqui, Spanish and German ancestry, was born and reared in the San Francisco Mission District. She has an MFA in writing from Vermont College of Norwich University and teaches fiction and poetry at the University of California at Santa Cruz. Recognized for her fiction and her poetry, Villanueva's work has appeared in many major anthologies, most recently in *The Before Columbus Foundation Fiction Anthology* (1992) and *No More Masks!* (1993). In 1977, she published *Bloodroot*, and her *Poems* won the UC, Irvine's Third Chicano Literary Prize. In *Mother, May I?* (1978), an autobiographical poem and Villanueva's best-known work, the poet transforms concrete experience into personalized myth by recounting the life of a woman's cyclic changes and emergence to wholeness and hope. The quintessential feminist poet, Villanueva is dedicated to her search for a universal female community, a quest she continues in her poetry collections, *La Chingada* (1985), *Lifespan* (1985), and *Planet* (1993), which has been coupled with the reprint of *Mother, May I?* Concerned with eco-feminism, the poet—in *Planet*—also shines a glaring light on such issues as poverty, sexual abuse, and racism. In addition to her poetry collections, Villanueva has also published two novels, *The Ultraviolet Sky* (1988), recipient of the American Book Award of the Before Columbus Foundation, and *Naked Ladies* (1994). *The Ultraviolet Sky* has been reissued by Anchor Doubleday. Her latest book, *Weeping Woman: La Llorona and Other Stories* (1994), a collection of short stories, reflects a world that is ravaged by racism, sexism and violence. Nonetheless, the characters possess a strength and a spirituality that allows them to triumph.

An Act of Creation

Alma Luz Villanueva

to César Chávez

They keep rounding them up
through the centuries, killing
the innocent, so easily-

the babies, the children,
the screaming mothers-
the men who do not beg

for mercy. Yes, yes, they
keep rounding up the victims,
again and again—their only

heirloom, possession: poverty.
When I was a young mother, I
didn't fully realize this-
in my stupidity, I thought

the children were spared.

And when I thought of wolves
and lambs, I thought of
one or the other. A wolf.
A lamb. One bloodthirsty, eating
raw, red meat. One gentle, nibbling

grass. Now, twenty years later, they
still round up the innocent, or
corral them (as in South Africa),
slowly starving their flesh and
spirit to death. The enemy

kills the enemy's children.

A stubborn man fasts for
the farmworkers—their children
are not born whole, and ours
will not be born whole. That

is an act of creation.

Like painting a mural, a
watercolor, like composing
a symphony, like writing
a story, a poem.

That is when the lamb
and the wolf lay down,
together, and make extraordinary,
exquisite, ecstatic love.

Until the next round-up.

Or until we learn better-
that without the lamb, the
wolf starves, and without the
wolf, the lamb grows fat
and stupid. Yes, I understand

why the stubborn man
does not eat, pretending
to be a lamb, inviting
the wolves to feast
upon his sweet, brown

flesh. His spirit.

Trust

I wouldn't be surprised if I opened
the front door and nuclear winds
were blowing, the sky a crazy color,

like a tornado, everything swept away—
my child, myself and everyone else
(this is only fantasy, now) (I know

the power of words, I know)—the sun
strolling down the street, tired of her
place, a distant star—she wants to embrace

us, make us disappear—well, okay, what
does this mean?

Who do you trust when love turns its
back on you? When the ozone tatters,

bit by bit? When wars are more popular than
teaching children? When people have no memory

of what a bed was like, clean sheets? When
children, everywhere, go to sleep hungry? When

the children of Baghdad are slaughtered?
When South Africa comes to its senses?

When the rain forests curse the sky?
When all the murdered in Latin America

return to their families, intact and singing?
When the radiation at Chernobyl stops killing

the innocent? When children in our cities
stop dying for lack of hope, stray bullets,

the crack dealers' promises, our leaders'
promises, their convenient lies

to the children of the poor, the forgotten?
When our Drug Wars turn into Fierce Peace:

medical coverage, dental coverage, food, clothing,
shelter, real, substantial, *free* education? When

the birds become mute and tired of flying? When
Spring turns her back on us, withholding her

matrix, source; whispering in the wind,

"There was a web, but you destroyed it-

there was a seed, but you crushed it-

there was a way, but you forgot."

Oh, and me standing in the sun, praising her
to the very end.

Indian Summer Ritual

I was born in the Indian Summer,
by the sea, at sun set-

I slid from my mother's womb,
face to the sea-

I felt a dolphin leap
from the sea for joy-

I cried in agony because
I was naked, cold, beached-

It was Indian Summer
and the clouds were purple-

It was Indian Summer
and Venus glowed in the west-

It was Indian Summer
and the moon rose, a ripe, gold melon-

It was Indian Summer
and fire was in the ascendant-

It was Indian Summer
and I danced and danced with dolphins

all the first night of my birth,
until the eagle's cry brought the sun-

It was Indian Summer;
light wolves and dark wolves howled
through the day-

It was Indian Summer
and a snake shed its skin.

Then, and only then, was I properly
human.

Photo by Margaret Randall

Marie Elise Wheatwind

Marie Elise Wheatwind describes herself as a "coyote" of mixed heritage: she is half Chicana, one-quarter Swedish and one-quarter Russian Jew. She has a B.A. in Creative Writing from San Francisco State University and an M.A. in English from the University of California, Berkeley. She has worked as a poet, teacher, and Santa Barbara regional coordinator for the California Poets in the Schools program. Her poetry has been published in numerous small press magazines, journals and anthologies, including *Blue Mesa Review 5* (1993), *Onthebus* (1993), *Chicana Lesbians: The Girls Our Mothers Warned Us About* (1991), *New Chicana/o Writing I* (1992), and *She Who Was Lost Is Remembered* (1991). Wheatwind has been the recipient of two California Arts Council grants in literature and a PEN Syndicated Fiction Prize. A regular contributor to *The Women's Review of Books*, she currently lives in New Mexico and teaches at the University of New Mexico.

Abortion

Marie Elise Wheatwind

Our grandmothers remember
women who suffered
coat hangers, quinine,
an angry shove
from their husbands,
or children, unplanned,
unwanted.

Now we have this
medicinal ritual:
noisy machines and
antiseptic instruments
probing the uterine walls.
Dark cells, holding life
sentences, are opened up,
set free.

Out of your body,
a single cycle
mistaken,
leaves one soul
one spirit
to compromise,
and survive.

You resume your life
tired, frightened,
careful.
No time for tenderness,
or hot compresses
of cotton soaked in tea:
chamomile
yarrow
comfrey.

You hear the slap
of hands, and dream
of mudpie biscochitos,
play-dough tortillas,
fry bread floating
in a cast iron pan.

Outside, little girls play
pat-a-cake
while you keep secret
count, breathing
This
is my body;
This
is my blood.

Perverted Villanelle

She's only made for sex, the way she's dressed
on billboards, magazines, in neon lights.
Her open mouth, those luscious lips suggest

curvaceous entrance, a soft place to rest,
a sumptuous menu offering tasty bites.
She's only made for sex. The way she's dressed

to bring you drinks, leggy and statuesque,
serves just to whet your growing appetite.
Her smiling mouth, those luscious lips suggest

she's waiting for your clever lines. Possessed
with lust, she'll liven up your lonely night.
See how she's intentionally half-dressed,

then coyly turns away when she's caressed?
Just tell her what you want. (Why be polite?)
Her silent mouth, those ruby lips suggest

she's heard it all. Her tired walk means "yes."
You know she wants it, pretending to fight—
she's only meant for sex—get her undressed.
Her bleeding mouth's just what those red lips suggest.

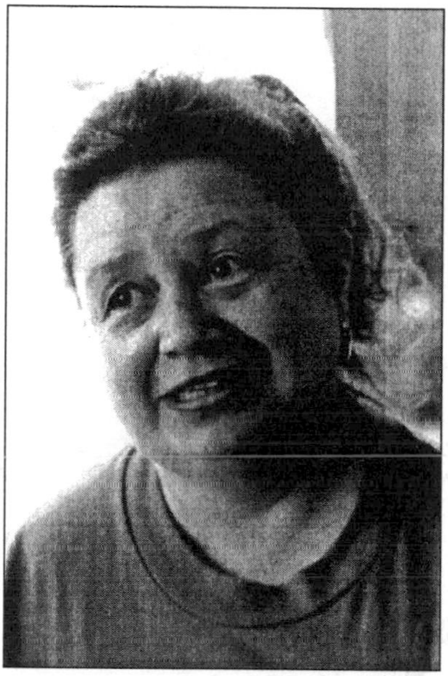

Photo by Susan Bradley

Bernice Zamora

Bernice Zamora has a considerable reputation as a poet, based primarily on *Restless Serpents* (1976), a book that is made up of two collections of poetry, Zamora's and José Antonio Burciaga's. Her poetry, the subject of numerous critical studies, has been widely anthologized, primarily in Chicano movement journals of the 1970s, such as *El Fuego de Aztlán, De Colores, Atisbos, Mango,* and *Caracol*. She was born in Aguilar, a village in the coal-mining region of Colorado, and grew up in Pueblo, Colorado, where cultural life centered around the church and its traditions. After high school, she got married and raised two girls. At twenty-eight, Zamora began her studies at Southern Colorado University, earning her first degree in English and French, then an M.A. from Colorado State University in Fort Collins. She began her doctoral program at Stanford University, then left Palo Alto for Albuquerque to help edit the journal *De Colores,* and to document and support the Chicano poetry movement. In 1986 she received her Ph.D. in English and American Studies from Stanford. While on the doctoral program, Zamora taught at Stanford, the University of California, Berkeley, and the University of San Francisco. Presently, she teaches ethnic and world literatures at the University of Santa Clara. Zamora's poetry in *Restless Serpents* explores such topics as Chicano cultural traditions, language, and the experience of women in that culture; in these poems she shows that her primary anger is against oppression in all its forms. In 1994, Bilingual Press published her long-awaited second collection of poetry, *Releasing Serpents*. To *In Other Words* Zamora has contributed new poems.

Above Aguilar

Bernice Zamora

The albinoed are edgy.
Above Aguilar trees were seen burning
New tundra lines, unevenly.

Trees blaze here when the unmatchable
Marry. Snow melting whets
thirst especially when winter lifts.

Grandmother blesses an arch of sunbeams
Spring brings. Creek beds and tundra
Line their living space. The blazing
Trees salute the sunbeams, the summer
To come, the breath of worlds swirling
Holy water in cascades upon the earth.
Raul and Teresa wed the way it was like
Inside Grandmother's whisper.

Shade

Plastic slats
Swish the wind
Into this dark room,
The sound of playing cards
Into the morning;
The white-out smells
Of a Requiem Mass;
The knowledge that midnight
Syncopates beyond midnight;
This sound
    like slapping wood planks
    to brace a country coffin
    like waiting for dawn or death
    like waiting for life to live
        or suicide
    like the shade of an oak tree
    sounds its own swish.

Summer's Rage

Near Lake Echo, snow
On Independence Day!
The Mississippi floods and floods
Heat waves in Houston
And frogs are disappearing.
We adults race fatigued
From reality to betrayal.
Our children respect our confusion.
The Medieval plague in our midst
Is medievally confronted
Our children respect our confusion.
Our Elders are drugged or dying.
Our children know our confusion.

Open Gate

I may know things.
I don't wish to know.
I know the elm tree will outlive
The pain in my other heart
And the news of what else I know.

She will don a blue and white cap.
Happily amid friends and standing before
triple mirrors, she will sweep her head
around. I believe that's how things happen
Walking past an open gate into mirrors,
angled as memory eaves.

Peatmoss

The plague of repression may satisfy peatmoss;
In a cheerless universe,
A woman's laugh is the envy of Heaven.
Howls by the ladies' gravesides
Do not unsmirk the male mirth.

Original Seeding

For one full fast hour
I have puzzled at the will
Happy at the slow plague
Slowly seeding man to man
Man to woman, woman to child
Like English history, language, lore,
Degendering the whole of human life.

Piles of Sublime

Cordial slavery, too, is a vision bent.
The dogs bark, unwilling to herd for massacre.
Icicles forest the chapels of unexamined history,
And sometimes children search for futures
In landscapes idled by barbarians.

The endangered are not species.
The endangered is beauty,
Unfrozen.

A Willing Abdication

A hazard in the kitchen
Is my reputation.
Buttered toast is not so essential
To my *té de cota*.
This writing hand is a sphinx in the place
Men place women. Except for an occasional
Crashing snatch at the sherry,
I dare not hold the crystal. There is that
Room where jousting reigns, I move unprettily
Fogging its interior with quasi-meals.
Bedeviled, the fairies forage on principle
On my behalf.

Our Instructions

Beyond the China Wall
In Mongolian highlands
I comb the edge of a lake
In periodic dreams.
Few women cross the desert dunes
To set a foot path with history's hordes
We are told. We are a class of pupils
Tracing spirits of women and female children.
Striations of their images serve as our guides,
Our instructors. At such altitudes our own
Spirits' auditory range wanes in turn with
Visions of snow gardens as we train to scale reality.

Part Two:
Essay

Gloria Anzaldúa

Gloria Anzaldúa, a Chicana lesbian-feminist poet and fiction writer, is widely recognized for her ground-breaking, theoretical works: *This Bridge Called My Back: Radical Writings by Women of Color*, co-edited with Cherríe Moraga, (1981), an anthology which received the Before Columbus Foundation American Book Award; and *Borderlands/La Frontera: The New Mestiza* (1987), selected as one of the Best Books of 1987 by *Library Journal*. In *Technologies of Gender*, critic Teresa de Lauretis notes that *This Bridge Called My Back* contributed to a "shift in feminist consciousness" in the United States. Writing in prose and poetry about her childhood along the Texas-Mexico border, Anzaldúa describes the experiences of being caught between two cultures, of being an alien in both. *Borderlands/La Frontera* is a meeting ground for all people who, like its author, realize that the work of the twenty-first century will be about the coming together of diverse cultures. Anzaldúa is also the editor of *Making Face, Making Soul/Haciendo Caras: Creative and Critical Perspectives by Women of Color* (1990). The *Women's Review of Books* has said that Anzaldúa "has chosen the most difficult task, that of mediating cultures without concession or dilution." She lives in Santa Cruz, where she is completing a Ph.D. in the History of Consciousness at the University of California. Her dissertation is a theoretical extension of her unusual combination of scholarly research, folk tales, personal narrative, poetry and political manifesto. Anzaldúa is also the author of a bilingual children's picture book, *Prietita Has a Friend/Prietita tiene un amigo* (1991).

La Conciencia de la Mestiza/ Towards a New Consciousness

Gloria Anzaldúa

Por la mujer de mi raza
hablará el espíritu.[1]

José Vasconcelos, Mexican philosopher, envisaged *una raza mestiza, una mezcla de razas afines, una raza de color—la primera raza síntesis del globo.* He called it a cosmic race, *la raza cósmica,* a fifth race embracing the four major races of the world.[2] Opposite to the theory of the pure Aryan, and to the policy of racial purity that white America practices, his theory is one of inclusivity. At the confluence of two or more genetic streams, with chromosomes constantly "crossing over," this mixture of races, rather than resulting in an inferior being, provides hybrid progeny, a mutable, more malleable species with a rich gene pool. From this racial, ideological, cultural and biological cross-pollenization, an "alien" consciousness is presently in the making—a new *mestiza* consciousness, *una conciencia de mujer*. It is a consciousness of the Borderlands.

Una lucha de fronteras / A Struggle of Borders

Because I, a *mestiza,*
continually walk out of one culture
and into another,
because I am in all cultures at the same time,
alma entre dos mundos, tres, cuatro,
me zumba la cabeza con lo contradictorio.
Estoy norteada por todas las voces que me hablan
simultáneamente.

The ambivalence from the clash of voices results in mental and emotional states of perplexity. Internal strife results in insecurity and indecisiveness. The mestiza's dual or multiple personality is plagued by psychic restlessness.

In a constant state of mental nepantilism, an Aztec word meaning torn between ways, *la mestiza* is a product of the transfer of the cultural and spiritual values of one group to another. Being tricultural, monolingual, bilingual, or multilingual, speaking a patois, and in a state of perpetual transition, the mestiza faces the dilemma of the mixed breed: which collectivity does the daughter of a dark-skinned mother listen to?

El choque de un alma atrapado entre el mundo del espíritu y el mundo de la técnica a veces la deja entullada. Cradled in one culture, sandwiched between two cultures, straddling all three cultures and their value systems, *la mestiza* undergoes a struggle of flesh, a struggle of borders, an inner war. Like all people, we perceive the version of reality that our culture communicates. Like others having or living in more than one culture, we get multiple, often opposing messages. The coming together of two self-consistent but habitually incompatible frames of reference[3] causes *un choque*, a cultural collision.

Within us and within *la cultura chicana*, commonly held beliefs of the white culture attack commonly held beliefs of the Mexican culture, and both attack commonly held beliefs of the indigenous culture. Subconsciously, we see an attack on ourselves and our beliefs as a threat and we attempt to block with a counterstance.

But it is not enough to stand on the opposite river bank, shouting questions, challenging patriarchal, white conventions. A counterstance locks one into a duel of oppressor and oppressed; locked in mortal combat, like the cop and the criminal, both are reduced to a common denominator of violence. The counterstance refutes the dominant culture's views and beliefs, and, for this, it is proudly defiant. All reaction is limited by, and dependent on, what it is reacting against. Because the counterstance stems from a problem with authority—outer as well as inner—it's a step towards liberation from cultural domination. But it is not a way of life. At some point, on our way to a new consciousness, we will have to leave the opposite bank, the split between the two mortal combatants somehow healed so that we are on both shores at once and, at once, see through serpent and eagle eyes. Or perhaps we will decide to disengage from the dominant culture, write it off altogether as a lost cause, and cross the border into a wholly new and separate territory. Or we might go another route. The possibilities are numerous once we decide to act and not react.

A Tolerance For Ambiguity

These numerous possibilities leave *la mestiza* floundering in uncharted seas. In perceiving conflicting information and points of view, she is subjected to a swamping of her psychological borders. She has discovered that she can't hold concepts or ideas in rigid boundaries. The borders and walls that are supposed to keep the undesirable ideas out are entrenched habits and patterns of behavior; these habits and patterns are the enemy within. Rigidity means death. Only by remaining flexible is she able to stretch the psyche horizontally and vertically. *La mestiza* constantly has to shift out of habitual formations; from convergent thinking, analytical reasoning that tends to use rationality to move toward a single goal (a Western mode), to divergent thinking,[4] characterized by movement away from set patterns and goals and toward a more whole perspective, one that includes rather than excludes.

The new *mestiza* copes by developing a tolerance for contradictions, a tolerance for ambiguity. She learns to be an Indian in Mexican culture, to be Mexican from an Anglo point of view. She learns to juggle cultures. She has a plural personality, she operates in a pluralistic mode—nothing is thrust out, the good the bad and the ugly, nothing rejected, nothing abandoned. Not only does she sustain contradictions, she turns the ambivalence into something else.

She can be jarred out of ambivalence by an intense, and often painful, emotional event which inverts or resolves the ambivalence. I'm not sure exactly how. The work takes place underground—subconsciously. It is work that the soul performs. That focal point or fulcrum, that juncture where the mestiza stands, is where phenomena tend to collide. It is where the possibility of uniting all that is separate occurs. This assembly is not one where severed or separated pieces merely come together. Nor is it a balancing of opposing powers. In attempting to work out a synthesis, the self has added a third element which is greater than the sum of its severed parts. That third element is a new consciousness—a mestiza consciousness—and though it is a source of intense pain, its energy comes from continual creative motion that keeps breaking down the unitary aspect of each new paradigm.

En unas pocas centurias, the future will belong to the mestiza. Because the future depends on the breaking down of paradigms, it depends on the straddling of two or more cultures. By creating a new mythos—that is, a change in the way we perceive reality, the way we see ourselves, and the ways we behave—*la mestiza* creates a new consciousness.

The work of *mestiza* consciousness is to break down the subject-object duality that keeps her a prisoner and to show in the flesh and through the images in her work how duality is transcended. The answer to the problem between the white race and the colored, between males and females, lies in healing the split that originates in the very foundation of our lives, our culture, our languages, our thoughts. A massive uprooting of dualistic thinking in the individual and collective consciousness is the beginning of a long struggle, but one that could, in our best hopes, bring us to the end of rape, of violence, of war.

La encrucijada / The Crossroads

A chicken is being sacrificed
    at a crossroads, a simple mound of earth
a mud shrine for *Eshu*,
    Yoruba god of indeterminacy,
who blesses her choice of path.
    She begins her journey.

Su cuerpo es una bocacalle. La mestiza has gone from being the sacrificial goat to becoming the officiating priestess at the crossroads.

As a *mestiza* I have no country, my homeland cast me out; yet all countries are mine because I am every woman's sister or potential lover. (As a lesbian I have no race, my own people disclaim me; but I am all races because there is the queer of me in all races.) I am cultureless because, as a feminist, I challenge the collective cultural/religious male-derived beliefs of Indo-Hispanics and Anglos; yet I am cultured because I am participating in the creation of yet another culture, a new story to explain the world and our participation in it, a new value system with images and symbols that connect us to each other and to the planet. *Soy un amasamiento*. I am an act of kneading, of uniting and joining that not only has produced both a creature of darkness and a creature of light, but also a creature that questions the definitions of light and dark and gives them new meanings.

We are the people who leap in the dark; we are the people on the knees of the gods. In our very flesh, (r)evolution works out the clash of cultures. It makes us crazy constantly, but if the center holds, we've made some kind of evolutionary step forward. *Nuestra alma el trabajo*, the opus, the great alchemical work; spiritual *mestizaje*, a "morphogenesis,"[5] an inevitable unfolding. We have become the quickening serpent movement.

Indigenous like corn, like corn, the mestiza is a product of crossbreeding, designed for preservation under a variety of conditions. Like an ear of corn—a female seed-bearing organ—the *mestiza* is tenacious, tightly wrapped in the husks of her culture. Like kernels she clings to the cob; with thick stalks and strong brace roots, she holds tight to the earth—she will survive the crossroads.

Lavando y remojando el maíz en agua del cal, despojando el pellejo. Moliendo, mixteando, amasando, haciendo tortillas de masa.[6] She steeps the corn in lime; it swells, softens. With stone roller on metate, she grinds the corn, then grinds again. She kneads and moulds the dough, pats the round balls into tortillas.

We are the porous rock in the stone *metate*
squatting on the ground.
We are the rolling pin, *el maíz y agua,*
la masa harina. Somos el amasijo.
Somos lo molido en el metate.
We are the *comal* sizzling hot,
the hot *tortilla*, the hungry mouth.
We are the coarse rock.
We are the grinding motion,
the mixed potion, *somos el molcajete.*
We are the pestle, the *comino, ajo, pimienta,*
We are the *chile colorado,*
the green shoot that cracks the rock.
We will abide.

El camino de la mestiza / The Mestiza Way

Caught between the sudden contraction, the breath sucked in and the endless space, the brown woman stands still, looks at the sky. She decides to go down, digging her way along the roots of trees. Sifting through the bones, she shakes them to see if there is any marrow in them. Then, touching the dirt to her forehead, to her tongue, she takes a few bones, leaves the rest to their burial place.

She goes through her backpack, keeps her journal and address book, throws away the muni-bart metromaps. The coins are heavy and they go next, then the greenbacks flutter through the air. She keeps her knife, can-opener and eyebrow pencil. She puts bones, pieces of bark, *hierbas*, eagle feather, snakeskin, tape recorder, the rattle and drum in her pack and she sets out to become the complete *tolteca*.[7]

Her first step is to take inventory. *Despojando, desgranando, quitando paja.* Just what did she inherit from her ancestors? This weight on her back—which is the baggage from the Indian mother, which is the baggage from the Spanish father, which is the baggage from the Anglo?

Pero es difícil differentiating between *lo heredado, lo adquirido, lo impuesto.* She puts history through a sieve, winnows out the lies, looks at the forces that we as a race, as women, have been a part of. *Luego bota lo que no vale, los desmientos, los desencuentos, el embrutecimiento. Aguarda el juicio, hondo y enraízado, de la gente antigua.* This step is a conscious rupture with all oppressive traditions of all cultures and religions. She communicates that rupture, documents the struggle. She reinterprets history and, using new symbols, she shapes new myths. She adopts new perspectives toward the dark-skinned, women and queers. She strengthens her tolerance (and intolerance) for ambiguity. She is willing to share, to make herself vulnerable to foreign ways of seeing and thinking. She surrenders all notions of safety, of the familiar. Deconstruct, construct. She becomes a *nahual,* able to transform herself into a tree, a coyote, into another person. She learns to transform the small "I" into the total Self. *Se hace moldeadora de su alma. Según la concepción que tiene de sí misma, así será.*

Que no se nos olviden los hombres

> *"Tú no sirves pa' nada—*
> you're good for nothing.
> *Eres pura vieja."*

"You're nothing but a woman" means you are defective. Its opposite is to be *un macho.* The modern meaning of the word "machismo," as well as the concept, is actually an Anglo invention. For men like my father, being "macho" meant being strong enough to protect and support my mother and us, yet being able to show love. Today's macho has doubts about his ability to feed and protect his family. His "machismo" is an adaptation to oppression and poverty and low self-esteem. It is the result of hierarchical male dominance. The Anglo, feeling inadequate and inferior and powerless, displaces or transfers these feelings to the Chicano by shaming him. In the Gringo world, the Chicano suffers from excessive humility and self-effacement, shame of self and self-deprecation. Around Latinos he suffers from a sense of language inadequacy and its accompanying discomfort; with Native Americans he suffers from a racial amnesia which ignores our common blood, and from guilt because the Spanish part of him took their land and oppressed them. He has an excessive compensatory hubris when around Mexicans from the other side. It overlays a deep sense of racial shame.

The loss of a sense of dignity and respect in the macho breeds a false machismo which leads him to put down women and even to brutalize them. Coexisting with his sexist behavior is a love for the mother which takes precedence over that of all others. Devoted son, macho pig. To wash down the shame of his acts, of his very being, and to handle the brute in the mirror, he takes to the bottle, the snort, the needle, and the fist.

Though we "understand" the root causes of male hatred and fear, and the subsequent wounding of women, we do not excuse, we do not condone, and we will no longer put up with it. From the men of our race, we demand the admission/acknowledgment/disclosure/testimony that they wound us, violate us, are afraid of us and of our power. We need them to say they will begin to eliminate their hurtful put-down ways. But more than the words, we demand acts. We say to them: We will develop equal power with you and those who have shamed us.

It is imperative that mestizas support each other in changing the sexist elements in the Mexican-Indian culture. As long as woman is put down, the Indian and the Black in all of us is put down. The struggle of the mestiza is above all a feminist one. As long as *los hombres* think they have to *chingar mujeres* and each other to be men, as long as men are taught that they are superior and therefore culturally favored over *la mujer*, as long as to be a *vieja* is a thing of derision, there can be no real healing of our psyches. We're halfway there—we have such love of the Mother, the good mother. The first step is to unlearn the *puta/virgen* dichotomy and to see *Coatlapopeuh-Coatlicue* in the Mother, *Guadalupe*.

Tenderness, a sign of vulnerability, is so feared that it is showered on women with verbal abuse and blows. Men, even more than women, are fettered to gender roles. Women at least have had the guts to break out of bondage. Only gay men have had the courage to expose themselves to the woman inside them and to challenge the current masculinity. I've encountered a few scattered and isolated gentle straight men, the beginnings of a new breed, but they are confused, and entangled with sexist behaviors that they have not been able to eradicate. We need a new masculinity and the new man needs a movement.

Lumping the males who deviate from the general norm with man, the oppressor, is a gross injustice. *Asombra pensar que nos hemos quedado en ese pozo oscuro donde el mundo encierra a las lesbianas. Asombra pensar que hemos, como femenistas y lesbianas, cerrado nuestros corazones a los hombres, a nuestros hermanos los jotos, desheredados y marginales como nosotros.* Being the supreme crossers of cultures, homosexuals have strong bonds with the queer white, Black, Asian, Native American, Latino, and with the queer in Italy, Australia and the rest of the planet. We come from all colors, all classes, all races, all time periods. Our role is to link people with each other—the Blacks with Jews with Indians with Asians with whites with extraterrestrials. It is to transfer ideas and information from one culture to another. Colored homosexuals have more knowledge of other cultures; have always been at the forefront (although sometimes in the closet) of all liberation struggles in this country; have suffered more injustices and have survived them despite all odds. Chicanos need to acknowledge the political and artistic contributions of their queer. People, listen to what your *jotería* is saying.

The mestizo and the queer exist at this time and point on the evolutionary continuum for a purpose. We are a blending that proves that all blood is intricately woven together, and that we are spawned out of similar souls.

Somos una gente

Hay tantísimas fronteras
que dividen a la gente,
pero por cada frontera
existe también un puente.
—Gina Valdés[8]

Divided Loyalties. Many women and men of color do not want to have many dealings with white people. It takes too much time and energy to explain to the downwardly mobile, white middle-class women that it's okay for us to own "possessions," never having had any nice furniture on our dirt floors or "luxuries" like washing machines. Many feel that whites should help their own people rid themselves of race hatred and fear first. I, for one, choose to use some of my energy to serve as mediator. I think we need to allow whites to be our allies. Through our literature, art, *corridos,* and folktales we must share our history with them so when they set up committees to help Big Mountain Navajos or the Chicano farmworkers or *los nicaragüenses,* they won't turn people away because of their racial fears and ignorances. They will come to see that they are not helping us but following our lead.

Individually, but also as a racial entity, we need to voice our needs. We need to say to white society: We need you to accept the fact that Chicanos are different, to acknowledge your rejection and negation of us. We need you to own up to the fact that you looked upon us as less than human, that you stole are lands, our personhood, our self-respect. We need you to make public restitution: to say that, to compensate for your own sense of defectiveness, you strive for power over us, you erase our history and our experience because it makes you feel guilty—you'd rather forget your brutish acts. To say you've split yourself from minority groups, that you disown us, that your dual consciousness splits off parts of yourself, transferring the "negative" parts onto us. (Where there is persecution of minorities, there is shadow projection. Where there is violence and war, there is repression of shadow.) To say that you are afraid of us, that to put distance between us, you wear the mask of contempt. Admit that Mexico is your double, that she exists in the shadow of this country, that we are irrevocably tied to her. Gringo, accept the doppelganger in your psyche. By taking back your collective shadow, the intracultural split will heal. And finally, tell us what you need from us.

By Your True Faces We Will Know You

I am visible—see this Indian face—yet I am invisible. I both blind them with my beak nose and am their blind spot. But I exist, we exist. They'd like to think I have melted in the pot. But I haven't, we haven't.

The dominant white culture is killing us slowly with its ignorance. By taking away our self-determination, it has made us weak and empty. As a people we have resisted and we have taken expedient positions, but we have never been allowed to be fully ourselves. The whites in power want us people of color to barricade ourselves behind our separate tribal walls so they can pick us off one at a time with their hidden weapons; so they can whitewash and distort history. Ignorance splits people, creates prejudices. A misinformed people is a subjugated people.

Before the Chicano and the undocumented worker and the Mexican from the other side can come together, before the Chicano can have unity with Native Americans and other groups, we need to know the history of their struggle and they need to know ours. Our mothers, our sisters and brothers, the guys who hang out on street corners, the children in the playgrounds, each of us must know our Indian lineage, our afro-*mestizaje*, our history of resistance.

To the immigrant *mexicano* and the recent arrivals we must teach our history. The 80 million *mexicanos* and the Latinos from Central and South America must know of our struggles. Each of us must know basic facts about Nicaragua, Chile and the rest of Latin America. The Latinoist movement (Chicanos, Puerto Ricans, Cubans and other Spanish-speaking people working together to combat racial discrimination in the market place) is good, but it is not enough. Other than a common culture we will have nothing to hold us together. We need to meet on a broader communal ground.

The struggle is inner: Chicano, *indio*, American Indian, *mojado, mexicano*, immigrant Latino, Anglo in power, working class Anglo, Black, Asian—our psyches resemble the border towns and are populated by the same people. The struggle has always been inner, and is played out in the outer terrains. Awareness of our situation must come before inner changes, which in turn come before changes in society. Nothing happens in the "real" world unless it first happens in the images in our heads.

El día de la Chicana

> I will not be shamed again
> Nor will I shame myself.

I am possessed by a vision: that we Chicanas and Chicanos have taken back or uncovered our true faces, our dignity and self-respect. It's a validation vision.

Seeing the Chicana anew in the light of her history, I seek an exoneration, a seeing through the fictions of white supremacy, a seeing of ourselves in our true guises and not as the false racial personality that has been given to us and that we have given to ourselves. I seek our woman's face, our true features, the positive and the negative seen clearly, free of the tainted biases of male dominance. I seek new images of identity, new beliefs about ourselves, our humanity and worth no longer in question.

Estamos viviendo en la noche de la Raza, un tiempo cuando el trabajo se hace a lo quieto, en lo oscuro. El día cuando aceptamos tal y como somos y para a dónde vamos y por qué—ese día será el día de la Raza. Yo tengo el conpromiso de expresar mi visión, mi sensibilidad, mi percepción de la revalidación de la gente mexicana, su mérito, estimación, honra, aprecio, y validez.

On December 2nd when my sun goes into my first house, I celebrate *el día de la Chicana y del Chicano*. On that day I clean my altars, light my *Coatlalopeuh* candle, burn sage and copal, take *el baño para espantar basura*, sweep my house. On that day I bare my soul, make myself vulnerable to friends and family by expressing my feelings. On that day I affirm who we are.

On that day I look inside our conflicts and our basic introverted racial temperament. I identify our needs, voice them. I acknowledge that the self and the race have been wounded. I recognize the need to take care of our personhood, of our racial self. On that day I gather the splintered and disowned parts of *la gente mexicana* and hold them in my arms. *Todas las partes de nosotros valen.*

On that day I say, "Yes, all you people wound us when you reject us. Rejection strips us of self-worth; our vulnerability exposes us to shame. It is our innate identity you find wanting. We are ashamed that we need your good opinion, that we need your acceptance. We can no longer camouflage our needs, can no longer let defenses and fences sprout around us. We can no longer withdraw. To rage and look upon you with contempt is to rage and be contemptuous of ourselves. We can no longer blame you, nor disown the white parts, the male parts, the pathological parts, the queer parts, the vulnerable parts. Here we are weaponless with open arms, with only our magic. Let's try it our way, the mestiza way, the Chicana way, the woman way.

On that day, I search for our essential dignity as a people, a people with a sense of purpose—to belong and contribute to something greater than our pueblo. On that day I seek to recover and reshape my spiritual identity. *¡Anímate! Raza, a celebrar el día de la Chicana.*

El retorno

> All movements are accomplished in six stages,
> and the seventh brings return.
> —I Ching[9]

> *Tanto tiempo sin verte casa mía,*
> *mi cuna, mi hondo nido de la huerta.*
> —*"Soledad"*[10]

I stand at the river, watch the curving, twisting serpent, a serpent nailed to the fence where the mouth of the Rio Grande empties into the Gulf.

I have come back. *Tanto dolor me costó el alejamiento.* I shade my eyes and look up. The bone beak of a hawk slowly circling over me, checking me out as potential carrion. In its wake a little bird flickering its wings, swimming sporadically like a fish. In the distance the expressway and the slough of traffic like an irritated sow. The sudden pull in my gut, *la tierra, los aguaceros.* My land, *el viento soplando la arena, el lagartijo debajo de un nopalito. Me acuerdo como era antes. Una región desértica de vasta llanuras, costeras de baja altura, de escasa lluvia, de chaparrales formados por mesquites y huizaches.* If I look real hard I can almost see the Spanish fathers who were called "the cavalry of Christ" enter this valley riding their burros, see the clash of the cultures commence.

Tierra natal. This is home, the small towns in the Valley, los pueblitos with chicken pens and goats picketed to mesquite shrubs. *En las colonias* on the other side of the tracks, junk cars line the front yards of hot pink and lavender-trimmed houses—Chicano architecture we call it, self-consciously. I have missed the TV shows where the hosts speak in half-and-half, and where awards are given in the category of Tex-Mex music. I have missed the Mexican cemeteries blooming with artificial flowers, the fields of aloe vera and red pepper, rows of sugar cane, of corn hanging on the stalks, the cloud of *polvareda* in the dirt roads behind a speeding pickup truck, *el sabor de tamales de res y venado*. I have missed *la yegua colorada* gnawing the wooden gate of her stall, the smell of horse flesh from Carlitos' corrals. *He hecho menos las noches calientes sin aire, noches de linternas y lechuzas* making holes in the night.

I still feel the old despair when I look at the unpainted, dilapidated, scrap-lumber houses consisting mostly of corrugated aluminum. Some of the poorest people in the U.S. live in the Lower Rio Grande Valley, an arid and semi-arid land of irrigated farming, intense sunlight and heat, citrus groves next to chaparral and cactus. I walk through the elementary school I attended so long ago, that remained segregated until recently. I remember how the white teachers used to punish us for being Mexican.

How I love this tragic valley of South Texas, as Ricardo Sánchez calls it; this borderland between the Nueces and the Rio Grande. This land has survived possession and ill-use by five countries: Spain, Mexico, the Republic of Texas, the U.S., the Confederacy, and the U.S. again. It has survived Anglo-Mexican blood feuds, lynchings, burnings, rapes, pillage.

Today I see the Valley still struggling to survive. Whether it does or not, it will never be as I remember it. The borderlands' depression that was set off by the 1982 peso devaluation in Mexico resulted in the closure of hundreds of Valley businesses. Many people lost their homes, cars, land. Prior to 1982, U.S. store owners thrived on retail sales to Mexicans who came across the border for groceries and clothes and appliances. While goods on the U.S. side have become 10, 100, 1000 times more expensive for Mexican buyers, goods on the Mexican side have become 10, 100, 1000 times cheaper for Americans. Because the Valley is heavily dependent on agriculture and Mexican retail trade, it has the highest unemployment rates along the entire border region; it is the Valley that has been hardest hit.

"It's been a bad year for corn," my brother, Nune, says. As he talks, I remember my father scanning the sky for a rain that would end the drought, looking up into the sky, day after day, while the corn withered on its stalk. My father has been dead for 29 years, having worked himself to death. The life span of a Mexican farm laborer is 56—he lived to be 38.

It shocks me that I am older than he. I, too, search the sky for rain. Like the ancients, I worship the rain god and the maize goddess, but unlike my father I have recovered their names. Now for rain (irrigation) one offers not a sacrifice of blood, but of money.

"Farming is in a bad way," my brother says. "Two to three thousand small and big farmers went bankrupt in this country last year. Six years ago the price of corn was $8.00 per hundred pounds," he goes on. "This year it is $3.90 per hundred pounds." And, I think to myself, after taking inflation into account, not planting anything puts you ahead.

I walk out to the back yard, stare at *los rosales de mamá*. She wants me to help her prune the rose bushes, dig out the carpet grass that is choking them. *Mamagrande Ramona también tenía rosales*. Here every Mexican grows flowers. If they don't have a piece of dirt, they use car tires, jars, cans, show boxes. Roses are the Mexican's favorite flower. I think, how symbolic—thorns and all.

Yes, the Chicano and Chicana have always taken care of growing things and the land. Again I see the four of us kids getting off the school bus, changing into our work clothes, walking into the field with Papi and Mami, all six of us bending to the ground. Below our feet, under the earth lie the watermelon seeds. We cover them with paper plates, putting *terremotes* on top of the paper plates to keep them from being blown away by the wind. The paper plates keep the freeze away. Next day or the next, we remove the plates, bare the tiny green shoots to the elements. They survive and grow, give fruit hundreds of times the size of the seed. We water them and hoe them. We harvest them. The vines dry, rot, are plowed under. Growth, death, decay, birth. The soil prepared again and again, impregnated, worked on. A constant changing of forms, *renacimientos de la tierra madre.*

This land was Mexican once
was Indian always
and is.
And will be again.

Notes

1. This is my own "take off" on José Vasconcelos' idea. José Vasconcelos, *La Raza Cósmica: Misión de la Raza Ibero-Americana* (México: Aguilar S.A. de Ediciones, 1961).

2. Vasconcelos.

3. Arthur Koestler termed this "bisociation." Albert Rothenberg, *The Creative Process in Art, Science, and Other Fields* (Chicago, IL: University of Chicago Press, 1979), 12.

4. In part, I derive my definitions for "convergent" and "divergent" thinking from Rothenberg, 12-13.

5. To borrow chemist Ilya Prigogine's theory of "dissipative structures." Prigogine discovered that substances interact not in predictable ways as it was taught in science, but in different and fluctuating ways to produce new and more complex structures, a kind of birth he called "morphogenesis," which created unpredictable innovations. Harold Gilliam, "Searching for a New World View," *This World* (January, 1981), 23.

6. *Tortillas de masa harina*: corn tortillas are of two types, the smooth uniform ones made in a tortilla press and usually bought at a tortilla factory or supermarket, and gorditas, made by mixing masa with lard or shortening or butter (my mother sometimes puts in bits of bacon or chicharrones).

7. Gina Valdés, *Puentes y Fronteras: Coplas Chicanas* (Los Angeles, CA: Castle Lithograph, 1982), 2.

8. Richard Wilhelm, *The I Ching or Book of Changes*, trans. Cary F. Baynes (Princeton, NJ: Princeton University Press, 1950), 98.

9. *"Soledad"* is sung by the group, Haciendo Punto en Otro Son.

10. Out of the twenty-two border counties in the four border states, Hidalgo County (named for Father Hidalgo who was shot in 1810 after instigating Mexico's revolt against Spanish rule under the banner of *la Virgen de Guadalupe*) is the most poverty-stricken county in the nation as well as the largest home base (along with Imperial in California) for migrant farmworkers. It was here that I was born and raised. I am amazed that both it and I have survived.

Photo © Copyright 1994 by Georgia McInnis

Roberta Fernández

Roberta Fernández is a native of Laredo, Texas. She received a B.A. and an M.A. from the University of Texas, Austin, and a Ph. D. in Romance Languages and Literatures from the University of California, Berkeley. An arts advocate, she has worked at The Mexican Museum in San Francisco, directed a Bilingual Arts Program in the Oakland schools, and at Mills College founded *Prisma: A Multicultural, Multilingual Women's Literary Review* (1979-1982). Coordinating partnerships between academic and community groups, Fernández has directed two conferences with funding from state humanities councils: "The Cultural Roots of Chicana Literature, 1780-1980" (Mills College, 1981) and "Latinos in the United States: Cultural Roots and Present Diversity" (Brown University, 1985). Currently an editor at Arte Público Press, she also teaches in Modern and Classical Languages at the University of Houston, where in 1992 she curated "Twenty-Five Years of Hispanic Literature of the United States, 1975-1990," an exhibit selected by the Texas Humanities Resource Center for one of its traveling exhibits. A three-time resident at the MacDowell Colony, she was named in 1991 to the Texas Institute of Letters. Her work has appeared in many anthologies, among them *The Stories We Have Kept Secret: Tales of Women's Spiritual Development* (1986), *Short Fiction by Hispanic Writers of the United States.* (1993), and *Barrios and Borderlands: Cultures of Latinos and Latinas in the United States* (1994). Multicultural Publishers Exchanged selected her book, *Intaglio: A Novel in Six Stories,* about the transmission of women's cultural expressions on the Texas/Mexican border, as Best Fiction for 1991; her own Spanish version of *Intaglio* will be published in Mexico in the near future. Fernández has been awarded the 1974-75 post-doctoral fellowship sponsored by the center for Mexican-American Studies at the University of Texas in Austin.

(Re)vision of an American Journey

Roberta Fernández

> *"What is it for?" Isabella is said to have asked, in a burst of practicality, when Nebrija's book was presented to her by a royal courtier. "Your Majesty," the courtier is reported to have answered, "language has always been the companion of empire."*[1]

Stimulating, sometimes heated, late-night conversations with friends were frequent fare in candle-lit cafés in Berkeley, where quite often our discussions revolved around theoretical solutions to Third World social problems. A complex situation, we agreed, but not unsolvable, as we too grappled with our own identity as people of color actively challenging the hegemonic structure and our own relationship to it within "the belly of the monster." Self-identity did not come easily as we strove to balance our academic endeavors with the nitty-gritty explorations we carried on outside the classroom. In general, we tended to straddle between a nationalist identity and an internationalist world view.

As an extension of this struggle, I chose to focus my dissertation research on the theories of cultural and literary nationalism espoused by the social philosopher José Carlos Mariátegui; and in the academic year 1974-1975, I went to Peru to begin my investigation in earnest. At that point, life in the Third World took on a different dimension, as I confronted one challenge after another in the capital city of Lima. Theoretical solutions were far from my mind, as I dealt with such basic experiences as getting around a city that was undergoing rapid demographic transformation under the "revolutionary" leadership of the Velasco Alvarado government.

My daily existence in Lima, on a graduate student budget (which nonetheless surpassed that of the average Peruvian), forced me to come face to face with a reality that was entirely different from the one I had known previously. For example, the act, once assumed as simple, of getting around a city often proved to be physically exhausting. I had to figure out how to get on—and even more difficult, how to get out of—the slick, foreign-made buses that, teeming with passengers, often bypassed the bus-stops, making it impossible to keep to any projected schedule. Daily I made my way through main pedestrian thoroughfares where residents of the *pueblos jóvenes,* the shantytowns ringing the parameters of the city, took up entire sidewalks with cheap plastic wares, the sale of which promised their vendors a meal for yet another day. I learned to concentrate in the reading room of the Biblioteca Nacional, where the open windows forced the library patrons to study amid the noise and pollution emitted by the constant parade of buses rumbling up and down Abancay Street. Intellectual work in the Third World, I found out, demands an unrelenting yet flexible commitment; its challenges are, for the most part, unimagined within the academic institutions of the United States, where general comfort and accessibility to materials are almost always taken for granted.

I soon realized that as demanding as the physical adjustment to the capital city was, often I was more worn out by psychological stress, a response to the value system I encountered in many of the people I met from the bourgeoisie. At the *pension* where I ate and conversed with students from the colonial city of Arequipa, I often felt sick with the way the entire household treated the fifteen-year-old, round-faced youth and the equally young maid in uniform, both of whom had come to Lima from Puno in the Lake Titicaca area. From early morning to late evening, the *señora* kept the young *serranos* constantly at work. I was aware that the two servants never got a chance to rest, as in silence, never raising their gaze, they repeated the same chores day after day. When they finally would go off to their rooms, their overworked bodies would rest in a narrow, hard cot with two-inch pilings for mattresses.

A few days before I returned to the United States, much to the consternation of the *señora,* I gave all my clothes, including my well-worn Spanish boots, to the young *serranos. ¿Cómo pudo hacer eso?"* she asked me in disbelief, and I figured that, after I was gone, she would probably lay claim to my clothes. I should have realized she would have this reaction, for the overvaluing that was given to products imported from the United States and Europe had become apparent to me soon after I arrived in Lima. I had been unprepared for this overconcern with appearances, coming as I was from years of living in a rarefied society in the United States, where people delighted in boasting of their nonmaterialistic lifestyle; in contrast, I had been surprised at the great number of professional women and young women of the bourgeoisie who told me they made at least one trip per year to Miami to shop for clothes.

Now that I live in Houston, I periodically read in the newspapers about wealthy Mexican tourists who come to this city for a weekend of shopping at the Galleria stores, under the pretext, of course, of spending a few days away from the smog in Mexico City. These Mexican shoppers remind me of articles in *Unomasuno*, the Mexico City daily, describing the latest aspiration of the Mexican middle-class: to give their children the best of all presents—a trip to Disneyland. In Peru, the desired vacation spots were the cosmopolitan cities of Buenos Aires and Caracas.

As I recall this bent toward *artificio* and *apariencia*, I am reminded of the sad humor in an experience I had with another common mechanism used in colonialized societies to maintain control over the masses: the preoccupation with *abolengo*, or the importance given to ancestry and the "right name," remnants of the old Spanish concern with being an *hidalgo*, an *hijo de algo*. In Lima, I had been told by the Office of Foreign Ministry that in order to extend my tourist card for a third time, I had to find a sponsor who would vouch for me. I also needed to bring in the required documentation accompanied by a notarized signature.

Based strictly on the convenience of the address, I had selected a notary public out of the phone book, for his office was on my way to the library. When I called the person who had agreed to vouch on my behalf to advise him of our meeting spot, my friend quickly told me that the notary public I had picked would be exorbitantly expensive because the firm was associated with one of the "old names" of Peru. I listened to his suggestions of other places, but in the end opted for the convenience of the address.

The following day we met at the designated office. I presented my documentation, got the required signature, and was asked for a minimal fee. My friend was astounded. "Many *Limeños* would gladly pay ten times as much to have that name on their official papers," he told me more than once. At that point, I felt I had a sense of how this emphasis on *apariencia* manifests itself on the daily lives of the people in a society that has undergone a period of colonialism.

In the last few days, I have been reminded of some of the experiences I had in Lima as I read *Dogeaters*, Jessica Hagedorn's brilliant satirical novel of life in the Philippines during the Marcos regime. Hagedorn's Manila is a world very much like the one I found in the Peruvian capital city, where things were "slightly off, carefully posed and artificial,"[2] a world in which people's motto tended to be "Adaptability is the simple secret of survival,"[3] a philosophy of life symbolized in *Dogeaters* by the fragile, transparent snakeskin that the young witness/narrator Rio finds in her mother's garden. In a society that has suffered through colonialism, Hagedorn implies, changes of skin are common occurrences.

Dogeaters has led me to reflect further on the Columbus legacy and the heritage it has left in the New World. A description of Manila made by the voice of the Filipino opposition, Senator Domingo Avila, reminds me of the comparable situation I encountered in Lima: "We Pinoys suffer collectively from a cultural inferiority complex. We are doomed by our need for assimilation into the West and our own curious fatalism..."[4]

A brief passage in the novel makes me ponder. It is entitled "President William McKinley Addresses a Delegation of Methodist Churchmen, 1898"; here, the mind-set of colonialism is synthesized into a generic encapsulation as Hagedorn shows how the colonialist tends to rationalize how his own version of civilization justifies his actions.

> ...And one night it came to me this way...that we could not give them (the Philippine Islands) back to Spain—that would be cowardly and dishonorable; two, that we could not turn them over to France or Germany—our commercial rivals in the Orient—that would be bad business and discreditable; three, that we could not leave them to themselves—they were unfit for self-government—and they would soon have anarchy and misrule over there worse than Spain's was; and four, that there was nothing left for us to do but to take them all, and to educate the Filipinos, and uplift and civilize and Christianize them, and by God's grace do the very best we could by them, as our fellow men for whom Christ also died. And then I went to bed, and went to sleep and slept soundly.[5]

Remembering how personally wearing it had been to deal with the social repercussions of colonialism as I encountered it in the Peruvian metropolis, I pause to consider that about every six weeks I would escape for a few days to interact with the healthier, more authentic peoples of the *sierra* and the *selva*. The trip that left the deepest impression on me was a visit to Yarinacocha, a rough and tumble city in the oil-rich *selva* of the highlands. All the stepping stones for that trip were laid as a result of my interest in language and languages.

In January of 1975 an international congress of philology met in Lima. I attended some of the sessions, particularly drawn to one dedicated to the Spanish language in the United States. In that session a leading Latin American linguist from the University of Texas, basing his work on the patterns established by other immigrant groups in the United States, came to the conclusion that the use of Spanish was fated to disappear in the United States. I knew I had to challenge the speaker, for I felt that he had marred his conclusion by his sociological interpretation of the question-at-hand. So, when the floor was open for discussion, I walked to the microphone and introduced myself as a Chicana from Texas, studying in California and researching in Peru. Then, I proceeded to tell the audience about the constant regeneration of the Spanish language that occurred every time a new wave of immigrants arrived in the United States from Mexico, or from other parts of Latin America. I summarized information about the new social movements for reclaiming Latino heritage, which had inspired a whole new generation to look to its cultural past; and finally, I referred to the role that bilingual education was having in keeping the Spanish language alive among the youngest speakers of Spanish in the United States. "We know," I concluded, "that whether a language lives or dies is, at root, a political question, and that as a people we can impact on the fate of our language."

I had not realized, as I had been speaking, that what I had been describing in reference to the future of the Spanish language in the United States paralleled the Peruvian preoccupation with Quechua, their own unofficial national language. Therefore, I was unprepared for the reception to my comments, but was pleased when the audience cheered and clapped for a long while; and I immediately understood the implications that my remarks had for their own situation.

With that ten-minute commentary I unexpectedly broke the isolation I had been feeling as an independent research scholar. A student leader from the Universidad Nacional Autónoma de San Marcos offered to teach me Quechua, and for about two months, until he was forced to go underground, we had a two-hour language lesson on a weekly basis in which I learned the language of his country and listened to his interpretation, from a Maoist perspective, of the Peruvian reality which, I felt, complemented my library research on Mariátegui's preoccupation with national questions in the 1920s.

Also at the congress I met a number of young people from the United States who became my good friends: Becky Van Hooten, from Wisconsin, who was teaching English at the University of Trujillo; Martha Beane, who was also teaching English at the Universidad Nacional in Lima, and later continued her work in the barrios of Los Angeles; and Peter Landerman, whose research on proto-Quechua allowed him an association with the Peruvian branch of the Summer Institute of Linguistics, a group of linguists-missionaries who, in Peru, work primarily in the jungle.

A few months after Peter and I met, and fortuitously, a couple of weeks before my anticipated journey into the *selva*, Felisa Kazen, one of my childhood friends from Laredo, came to Lima to speak as part of the lecture series sponsored by the Instituto Cultural Peruano-Norte Americano. Her presentation focused on the Congressional law that funded bilingual education programs in the United States, and it was attended by the entire group associated with the Summer Institute of Linguistics (SIL). At that event Peter introduced me to the leaders of the SIL, who upon hearing that I was planning a trip to Pucallpa, invited me to stay at the SIL center bordering a lagoon in Yarinacocha.

Little did I anticipate what awaited me on that much-needed excursion, where I would be privy to the story of the encounter of two completely different cultures. I was to have the good fortune to be told about this encounter by someone directly associated with the experience.

On my fourth day in that village center in the high *selva* of northern Peru, I sat in the small SIL library, the sole listener to the story of the Mayorunas, a people characterized (like other peoples native to the Americas) as "primitive" in the Spanish colonial chronicles. More recently, in the early twentieth century, the Mayorunas had been described as foragers into the territories of neighboring tribes, where they raided for food and women. Their practice of female infanticide eventually unbalanced their population, causing them to engage in additional "aggressive" activities. They had last been sighted in 1910, the period of the rubber boom, when the Mayorunas had responded to the invasion of Western adventurers by moving deeper into the jungle. By the end of the first quarter of the century, the Mayorunas were considered extinct.

The person telling me the story was a white American missionary-linguist, dedicated, like her colleagues, first to learning the unwritten languages of the people in the jungle, then to painstakingly transcribing those languages into grammar texts. With those texts, their goal of bringing the word of the Christian bible to the residents of the high *selva* came closer to becoming a realization. As she spoke, I would occasionally glance at the images of the Mayorunas in the album she had set down in front of me. Mostly, though, I listened attentively to the story she was willing to share with me.[6]

By the time I went to Yarinacocha, I had already been to the Amazonic lowlands, to Iquitos, a city associated, in the early twentieth century, with the prosperous years of the rubber-barons. Built up as an elegant city in the *selva*, Iquitos was then left to stagnate when the Asian *caucho* market lowered the price of the Peruvian product, described by the natives of the rain forest as the "tears of the trees." In Iquitos I had signed up to take a commercial trek into the rain forest. But when I had shown up at the early hour designated for departure, I had found out that no one else had requested the trip, and I was to be the sole passenger on the excursion that would take the boatman, the guide, and me in an aluminum canoe along the black waters of the Amazon into the rain forest.

On that trip, whose delights I could not have fantasized, we visited several sparsely inhabited communities of roof-thatched huts where the residents with painted faces and decorated bodies had demonstrated the art of blow-shooting poisoned darts. While I had loved every minute of that journey, particularly the instances where we were enveloped by the sounds of the birds and fauna of the rain forest, I had been aware at all times that on one level or another I was experiencing what some clever entrepreneur had dreamed up as my "two days in the jungle." Still, in spite of my wariness about the trek, I had left Iquitos feeling that on that particular excursion I had experienced the high point of my trip to Peru, an evaluation I would have to alter after the visit to Yarinacocha and its environs.

In Yarinacocha I immediately felt privileged to be in contact with people in their natural habitat. I was touched by my interaction with the Shipibo people, a so-called primitive society forced to interact with the slickness and conniving mores of the world in which I lived, my world whether I wanted to claim it or not. In San Francisco, a village that was several hours away by canoe from Yarinacocha, I had looked at the serene and simple lifestyle of the Shipibos (who reminded me of the Lacandones of Chiapas) and had wondered how they would be able to make the jump across centuries in one or two generations. I had listened intently as Teófilo Tapia, the Peruvian bilingualist administrator who had accompanied me to San Francisco, constantly reminded his listeners that they were indeed Peruvians. It is important to convey a sense of national identity to them, he reassured me, for the Shipibos viewed themselves strictly as a tribal people. In order to incorporate them into the national reality, the Peruvian government had to convince them that they were an important part of the nation; and, for this process to take effect, the Shipibos also had to be taught to conduct themselves in Spanish outside of their own immediate circles. The solution would not be easy, he reassured me.

Several years later, back in the United States, I was told that the Shipibos were doing quite well in adjusting: they were fast learners and were earning a "good" living installing tiny chips into computer boards for foreign corporations. I did not know of this *barbaridad* as I listened to the story of the Mayorunas, who had been inhabiting a world far older than that of the Shipibos. Until circumstances had forced them to make contact with the outside world, the Mayorunas had lived in a completely circumscribed world, their existence known only to other tribal people in whose territory the Mayorunas foraged.

I looked at the photographs in the album provided me by my narrator, a kindly and well-meaning middle-aged person, eager to share details of the encounter that had so affected her life and the lives of all her colleagues. We sat in the tiny library, next to the language lab, as the setting sun streaked shadows on the photos of a type of people with whom I had come into previous contact only through illustrations in *National Geographic*. The Mayoruna men and women, who had stared directly into the camera, were pictured with thin reed spears piercing the area around their mouths. In this way, they had created catlike whiskers on themselves, no doubt to show their *nahual* connection to that particular species of the animal world.

As I listened to the story, I kept turning the pages of the album, looking both at the people who had recently made contact with a world unknown to them and at the face of the narrator, describing the singular experience of two groups who had met across cultural and temporal borders. Her side had become aware of the Mayorunas when a scouting party had found a young man, of about sixteen, abandoned in the jungle by his people after having been bitten by a snake. Assuming he was dead, the Mayorunas had left him behind in his hut, but he had eventually made his way to a road, where the linguists had found him. His infected leg had been nursed back to health, and over many months of contact, the Americans had learned both his language and about his people.

During the three years that intervened from the time the young man was found to the moment that direct contact was made with the Mayoruna group, the SIL staff learned about the beliefs of the people they were seeking. They found out that the Mayorunas believed that when a member of their group died, they had to abandon the immediate area and strike up a home in a new place. Because the diseases of the world from beyond the jungle had penetrated into their habitat, the Mayorunas were losing their people at a rapid pace. Thus, they were constantly on the move, going around in circles throughout the jungle.

At the time the young man had been found, the leaders of the Mayorunas—by now various groups numbering several hundreds—had come to the conclusion that they needed to go past their own confines into the world beyond their own, a world whose existence was verified for them by myths, rumors, and their own findings.

The SIL linguists decided that they too needed to find the Mayorunas. As a group they concluded that women would be perceived as less physically threatening to the tribal people, and an expedition of two volunteers was sent out. Armed only with the language they had learned from the young man, two women—Harriet Fields and Hattie Kneeland—

headed into the jungle in search of a people who they now knew were also looking for them.[7]

During this time, each group kept finding the signs that the other party was leaving behind in strategic locations. Eventually, my narrator explained, only a river separated the two. One night, the linguists heard the menacing cries of jungle cats, but assuming that pumas could not swim, they went to sleep, albeit lightly as they anticipated a possible meeting on the following day.

"Those women were so brave," I heard my narrator say, a brusque interruption to the scene I had been envisioning from the point of view of the Mayorunas.

"At least they knew what they might expect to meet," I said by way of reply, "while the Mayorunas had no idea about what lay ahead for them."

The women continued camping on the banks of the river, my narrator continued. Then, on their second morning by the river, they awakened to find a delegation of Mayorunas standing a few feet away. In simple speech the women greeted the Mayorunas, inviting them to share their food.

By the end of that day in the late 1960s, the two parties had crossed the river on a canoe. Greetings had been extended between the women and the rest of the Mayorunas, and a new delegation had been sent back with the linguists to the center at Yarinacocha. Additional food and medicine were sent to the people in the *selva*, again with new delegations of women. Eventually, the men also met each other; and the young man who had served as language and cultural informant was reunited with his people. With Western medicine combating the Western diseases that had infiltrated into the jungle, the Mayorunas managed to break the cycle of death that had been plaguing them for years.

"What will happen to the Mayorunas?" I asked. "It must be so difficult for them to traverse temporally into the twentieth century, and I doubt that they will be left alone to continue with their own ways of life. Westerners will find it hard to believe they have anything to learn from these tribal people, and yet we might learn something if we only opened ourselves to them."

"They are adjusting well," my narrator said with a smile. "We have brought the word of Christ to them. That young man quickly learned our language, then served as interpreter between both parties. We think they were led to us by Divine Providence."

"Won't they just wind up being exploited?" I asked. "Everyone expects the give and take associated with 'discovery' to go only in one direction. They give and give in. We take and take out. But, realistically, how will they survive economically?"

"The Peruvian government is seeing to their integration into the greater world," she replied. "The Mayorunas are very smart. Like the Shipibos, they are being processed to enter into civilization. And, like the Shipibos, the Mayorunas are doing extremely well in adapting to Western culture."

At the time, I did not realize what her statement really implied. But, in retrospect, I am reminded of a comment made by the famous Berkeley anthropologist A. L. Kroeber: "It is pleasant to believe in progress. It makes my times and ways superior to all others."[8]

I converse with my friend and colleague Benito Pastoriza, a Puerto Rican poet, at a café in Houston. I tell him about the Mayorunas, about more recent information I have obtained regarding the instruction the Mayorunas have been receiving in bilingual education programs. In these schools they have learned to read and write in their own language; then, their new skills are transferred to the target language—Spanish, the official national language in Peru. The ultimate goal of this standard bilingual education program is to have the Mayorunas use Spanish for social and official transactions. One might assume, then, that in subsequent generations, their original language will be lost. This is the same conclusion, I remind Benito, that the linguist from the University of Texas reached in regard to the future of the Spanish language in the United States. The difference is that, in the United States, new groups from Latin America constantly regenerate the current use of the Spanish language. The situation of the Mayorunas is not quite the same.

By the 1970s, the Mayorunas were recognized as a community numbering several hundreds composed of different bands, all of whom had been contacted by the SIL linguists. An airstrip was built by the government near the area identified as Mayoruna territory; soon the various bands congregated near the airstrip. It became evident that the Mayorunas needed to have their territory officially recognized, for once their raiding of other tribes stopped, colonizers from the outside world—Peruvians and others—began to claim the land previously inhabited by the different bands. As a result of these invaders, the Mayorunas were forced to learn about Peruvian law to stake their claim to their lands. In such situations, there is always a conflict of forces at work, I was told, for it is easy for the Mayorunas to lose their culture and come into the national culture at the lowest level possible. In practice, their needs must be met as the process of acculturation goes on.

The outside world also discovered that the Mayorunas refer to themselves and to their language as *Matse*. However, this same outside world continues to use the Quechua word *Mayoruna,* meaning "river people," to refer to this recently "discovered" group.

"Their survival no doubt depends on many factors, including what we all do to save the rain forests," I say to Benito.

"*Imagínate,*" he responds with a wry smile.

We wonder, then, if the Mayorunas will wind up losing their own language in subsequent generations because of the infiltration of Western languages and cultures into their lives. We think of our own people—the Mexicans and the Puerto Ricans—in the process. And of our own individual situations, for we both have made an effort to be truly bilingual and bicultural; in fact, we have striven to become multilingual and multicultural.

We discuss our Tejano students, native-speakers of the Spanish language who identify themselves as "Mexican-Americans." We note how generally they are closer to the roots of their culture of origin than is the general tendency among students in California who call themselves "Chicanos." Benito and I have both taught some of the course for native-speakers of Spanish. Of the two, I think he is the better teacher in this particular area.

"Every day I look at my students," he tells me, "and I get so angry when I see how hard they struggle to reclaim their language. If they had been taught to read and write in Spanish all the way from elementary school to the present, by now they would be completely proficient in oral and written communications in Spanish. I have no patience when it comes to waste, and that is what the educational system has done. It has wasted human talent. For two hundred years." He gives emphasis to his voice. "When are these people going to accept the fact that the Mexicanos in this area have been speakers of Spanish ever since they got here more than two-hundred years ago?"

"Let's not forget the other, older languages," I remind him. "As a people we did wind up losing our Indian tongue, didn't we?"

Then I recall the question posed by Yolanda Broyles González, a friend in Santa Barbara who chairs the Chicano Studies Department at the University of California, Santa Barbara. When she found out that I was teaching a course for native-speakers of the Spanish language, she sincerely inquired: "What do you do with them in such a course? The Mexicanos in Tejas have such a special way of expressing themselves. Yet, these Spanish departments insist on changing their speech. 'So that they may be well understood in Buenos Aires and Caracas,' they rationalize. More than likely, our students will be using the language only within their own cultural sphere. So, why do these educators insist on colonizing the Mexicanos by way of their language usage? They so demean us in the process."

I tell Benito that I sympathize with my friend's question, that she and I have discussed ways of strengthening our students' knowledge of Spanish from a positive point of departure. And I recall two incidents I recently witnessed: the spontaneous outburst of the entire class during an oral presentation when a student enthusiastically described a character in a short story by Carlos Flores as "*Es un huevón.*" Turning red in reaction to the class's response, the young woman explained that this was the only word in her repertoire to describe the father in the story. Empowering her, I wrote *perezoso* and *flojo* on the board. In another instance, a student was able to describe a long-haired person only as *greñudo* or *con mechones largos*. Yet, his passive knowledge of the language allowed him to select, from a list provided, a variety of ways to get his point across.

We need to give our students the ability to make different choices in vocabulary usage, Benito and I agree, in order to broaden their choices in life. "But, in regard to most choices, particularly linguistic choices, one must choose on the side of the open, of the positive," I remind him. "Let's take Richard Rodriguez. He chose on the side of closeness, on the side of the negative."

I know Chicanos tend to have a visceral contempt for Rodriguez and for his book, *Hunger of Memory: The Education of Richard Rodriguez*; yet, for a number of reasons that will soon become evident, I teach the book in several of my literature classes and always refuse to permit my students to attack the author on the basis of what he has to say about bilingual education and affirmative action. That's the easy way out, I tell them, for, if you believe in these social programs, then you will tend to disagree with him. But others who do not support the programs will disagree with you. So, the discussion will come down to one based strictly on personal opinion, albeit one based on statistics from both sides of the argument.

I try to contextualize Rodriguez's mindset within the American assimilationist experience, also an undebatable perspective to my way of thinking, for I believe that he has as much right to view himself as a middle-class Mexican-American as a Chicano has the right to align himself with the working class and its culture. Even Rodriguez's pathetic relationship with his parents cannot be truly debated, for it is a point in fact in the life of this author. As a consequence, he provides the reader with a description of a dysfunctional family, not unheard of in your typical case of the American assimilation process in which members of different generations, each with a different world view, come into conflict with one another.

For the first-generation or even the second-generation American, this cultural separation from one's parents tends to be the price that is paid for becoming "an American"; it is the price paid for turning one's back on personal and group history and for opting to live, in a cultural vacuum, strictly in the present and for the future. But, again, to berate Rodriguez on his choice in this matter means that one would still be involved in value judging; in this instance, one would be making a value judgment on a choice made by the great majority of people in the United States.

Even his self-portrayal as a person disproportionately concerned with appearances, with *apariencia* and *artificio*, can leave us with a sense of pity. He describes how his preoccupation with symbols of status was passed down from parent to child.

> ...In their manner, both my parents continued to respect the symbols of what they considered to be upper-class life. Very early, they taught me the *propria* (sic) way of eating *como los ricos*. And I was carefully taught elaborate formulas of polite greeting and parting. The dark little boy would be invited by classmates to the rich houses on Forty-fourth and Forty-fifth Streets. "How do you do?" or "I am very pleased to meet you," I would say bowing slightly to the amused mothers of classmates. "Thank you very much for the dinner; it was very delicious."
>
> I made an impression. I intended to make an impression, to be invited back. (I soon noticed that the trick was to get the mother or father to notice me.) From those early days began my association with rich people, my fascination with their secret.[9]

Like Jessica Hagedorn's Pinoys and some of the people I met in Lima and in other places, Rodriguez comes across as the quintessential colonized person, predisposed to being outer-oriented, preoccupied with appearances and with symbolic changes of skin.

> This man. A man. I meet him. He laughs to see me, what I have become.
>
> The dandy. I wear double-breasted Italian suits and custom-made English shoes. I resemble no one so much as my father—the man pictured in those honeymoon photos. At that point in life when he abandoned the dandy's posture, I assume it. At the point when my parents would not consider going on vacation, I register at the Hotel Carlyle in New York and the Plaza Athenée in Paris. I am as taken by the symbols of leisure and wealth as they were. For my parents, however, those symbols became taunts, reminders of all they could not achieve in one lifetime. For me those same symbols are reassuring reminders of public success. I tempt vulgarity to be reassured. I am filled with the gaudy delight, the monstrous grace of the nouveau riche.[10]

His confession is at least honest, not without a sense of irony, not without a sense of distance as he looks in the mirror to confront the man he has become. The educational process he has undergone has produced a colonized individual, a person who bows down to hegemonic rules. We last see him in the book as a man without a family, without real friends, without a job.

Rodriguez's premises regarding the goals of the educational system can indeed be questioned. He pretends to criticize the system when in fact he succumbs to it and is its logical-end product. In setting up the binary divisions of private self versus public self, of private language versus public language, he chooses on the side of the negative and the closed. In his convoluted self-hatred, he winds up giving the reader an example of what American education can produce and does in fact produce in the majority of cases: a monolingual and monocultural person.

Paralleling Hagedorn's Pinoys and, generally, people in colonized societies, including those within the United States, Rodriguez suffers from the inferiority complex of those who accept the norms set up by the colonialist; his need for assimilation into the hegemonic culture has narrowed, rather than broadened, his choices in life. In the end, his concluding that the restriction of one's self is a better choice than its expansion, that negation is better than affirmation, winds up being an altogether unacceptable solution to a problematic situation.

The philosopher María Lugones further enlightens this reaction to Rodriguez's work, stating "that to be educated is to be monocultural is an untenable proposition. Education should instill cultural flexibility in us. It should instill cultural fluency: the ability to appreciate in different cultural modes. It should enable us to go back and forth between worlds with different logics, different values, different ways of perceiving."[11]

Unfortunately, the goal of colonialism has always been the opposite of what Lugones tells us is the ideal of education, the ideal of what a society should offer its people and their future, based on their singular history and their present reality. Colonial systems strive to erase the cultural and linguistic base of groups that have the misfortune of being perceived as detriments to the system's deluded sense of progress. For five-hundred years the Americas have witnessed a legacy of conquest and colonialism as the aftermath of Columbus's journey. The Native peoples have experienced the imposition of the outsider's language, religion, and values; and the colonialist's fantasy of "otherness" has shaded his vision of the people he has colonized: the Tainos, the Aztecs, the Incas, the Shipibos, the Mayorunas, the present-day Mayas, the Filipinos, the Navajos, the Cherokee, the Creeks, and the Chicanos. The list goes on.

But, as we near the end of the twentieth century, the various Calibans of the New World are arising to curse the colonialists in the particular languages in which they have been educated. We are reclaiming our cultures and languages, which have survived in spite of centuries of outside imposition. The quincentenary of the so-called discovery of the Americas has provided a forum for the discourse on the politics of identity, a response of the voice of "the other," which insists on the politics of ethical difference. For the moment, in some circles, the politics of identity is superseding the politics of erasure. Perhaps we too will wind up going to bed and sleeping soundly, free for a while at least of having to live with the repercussions of the delusion of hegemonic sameness.

Notes

1. Kirkpatrick Sale, *The Conquest of Paradise: Christopher Columbus and the Columbian Legacy* (New York: Alfred Knopf, 1990), p. 18. Sale describes Nebrija's 1492 grammar of the Castilian language as "a typical work of what one might call the encyclopedic mentality to which Renaissance Europe aspired and that was to sustain its vaunted scientific method: it is intended to be all-inclusive and exhaustive, neutral and non-judgmental, ostensibly without political point of view or social purpose, and meant only to be a list, a catalogue, an inventory." (p. 18)

2. Jessica Hagedorn, *Dogeaters*, (New York: Pantheon Books, 1990), p. 35.

3. Ibid., pp 8-9.

4. Ibid., p. 101.

5. Ibid., p. 71.

6. On April 21, 1975, I wrote about my visit to Yarinacocha in a letter to my friend Margaret Shedd. Born in 1899 in Persia, now Iran, of American missionary parents, Margaret Shedd lived in many different cultures and wrote about them in nine novels. She was founder and director, for eighteen years, of the Centro Mexicano de Escritores. After the Tlatelolco massacre in Mexico City, she left the Centro and returned to Berkeley, where she was one of the founding members of Aztlán Cultural, an organization in which I was very active.

The following comments record my evaluation of the staff at the Summer Institute of Linguistics immediately following my visit to Yarinacocha:

"Did you have contact in Mexico with the Summer Institute of Linguistics? If so, what is your opinion of the work they do? I went to Yarinacocha with lots of reservations about the work of the Institute, but soon my doubts were replaced with admiration for the people themselves, although I still question the nature of their work. I thought of you during my visit there, for I figured that the childhood you described in *Hosanna Tree* was probably lived in the atmosphere of love, gentleness, and fervor I found at Yarinacocha.

"The physical atmosphere is beautiful: lots of green lawns, small houses carefully screened and upkept, with no frills but with all the basic necessities, little barefooted children all over the place, and these gringo missionary-linguists whose lifework is translating the New Testament into the 'exotic' languages of the world. They have the most personally balanced lives I have yet seen in which all the different aspects of life truly come together—a sense of mission, hard work and the realization of one's labor in tangible form: giving the power of literacy to the tribal peoples and embarking them on their path to 'civilization.' The linguists seem to live in full realization of their being, guided by the motto: 'The Lord wills it so.' With such a personal world view, what problems can then exist?

"There are a few Peruvian representatives of the Ministerio de Educación here. Their self-realization also comes from putting their socialist ideas into tangible form. This is what I always thought a revolution could be like; for the first time I had a sense that something indeed might be coming out of this Peruvian revolution, but one doesn't really experience the positive changes in Lima. Some of the people I've met here have told me that the government is striving to build a base in the Sierra and the Selva first; then it will deal with the cities.

"I think it will take me a long time to process through these experiences, to have a sense that I truly understand what it is I have been seeing and doing."

7. According to Petru Popescu in *Amazon Beaming* (New York: Viking, 1991), the photographer Loren McIntyre, intrigued by stories that were coming out of the SIL center in Yarinacocha, set out on his own to make contact with the Mayoruna. McIntyre has spent the last forty years exploring and photographing Latin America. As such, he has visually documented the southern continent more than any other living photographer and is also recognized for having experienced Amazonia in greater depth and scope than any other living North American journalist. He has written and photographed for many articles in *National Geographic*. Wanting to record the Mayorunas with his camera before they could be dragged into "the basement of Western culture" (p.17), McIntyre tends to have a rather sardonic view of "the two Harriets" as he repeatedly refers to the linguists Fields and Kneeland. "If these (the people he encountered on his own) were Mayoruna, they were related to the ones first sighted in 1966 in Peru, doggedly pursued since by a missionary pair from the Summer Institute of Linguistics known as the two Harriets. Harriet Fields and Harriet Kneeland kept flying over the Peruvian jungle calling in Mayoruna through an airborne loudspeaker the way an alien ship would call to the earth race in a science fiction movie." (p. 17)

Popescu, Romania's most provocative young writer and filmmaker before defecting from the Ceausescu regime, met fellow filmmaker McIntyre in Brazil and set out to tell the story of his Latin American explorations, focusing primarily on the American's discovery in 1971 of the source of the Peruvian tributaries of the Amazon. Now officially named Laguna McIntyre, the fountainhead of the Amazon, in Peru, is close to the site where the rivers Apurimac and Ucayali meet. *Amazon Beaming* is a fascinating book, targeted at a New-Age readership active in ecological concerns. In this way, it tangentially addresses some of the issues connected with the ecological destruction of the New World brought on by the "discovery" of America; these questions inform the point of view in Kirkpatrick Sale's *The Conquest of Paradise* and Herman Viola's *Seeds of Change* (Smithsonian, 1991), books closely associated with the plethora of "discovery/encounter/legacy" publications that are appearing in 1991 and 1992.

8. Quoted in *Amazonia*, photographs and text by Loren McIntyre (San Francisco: Sierra Club Books, 1991), p. 158.

9. Richard Rodriguez, *Hunger of Memory: The Education of Richard Rodriguez* (New York: Bantam Books, 1983), p. 122.

10. Ibid., p. 136.

11. Common reading presentations made by María Lugones, Jackson Bryce, and Deborah Appleman on *Hunger of Memory* by Richard Rodriguez (Northfield, Minn.: A Carleton College publication of papers presented at The Carleton College New Student Convocation, September 3, 1990).

Cherríe Moraga

Cherríe Moraga, born and reared in Los Angeles, is a Chicana poet, playwright, and essayist. Her work is highly politicized, intensely personal and eloquently honest. With Gloria Anzaldúa, she had the perspicacity to envision the highly original and much needed challenge to American feminism, *This Bridge Called My Back: Writings by Radical Women of Color* (1981), which won a Before Columbus American Book Award. An indefatigable cultural worker, Moraga helped found Kitchen Table: Women of Color Press, which in 1983 published *Cuentos: Stories by Latinas* (1983), edited by Alma Gómez, Moraga, and Mariana Romo-Carmona. That same year she published her first collection of works, *Loving in the War Years/Lo que nunca pasó por sus labios*. With Norma Alarcón and Ana Castillo, Moraga edited *The Sexuality of Latinas* (1989) and the new edition and translation of *Bridge* entitled *Esta puente mi espalda*. She has received awards from the Fund for New American Plays and the National Endowment for the Arts Theatre Playwrights' Fellowship for her plays, which include *Shadow of a Man* and *Heroes and Saints*. Her latest book, *The Last Generation*, argues for a reconceptualization of gender, sexuality, race, art, nationalism, and the politics of survival. As is characteristic of Moraga's work, the political analysis developed in *The Last Generation* builds a compelling case for a radical transformation of consciousness and society. Crossing literary genres and moving freely between Spanish and English, Moraga ruminates on her identity as a lesbian writer/activist and her role in the Chicano community, weaving a rich tapestry of ancestors, lovers, poetry and life on the streets. Moraga lives in San Francisco and teaches at the University of California, Berkeley.

Art in América con Acento

Cherríe Moraga

I write this on the one week-anniversary of the death of the Nicaraguan Revolution.*

We are told not to think of it as a death, but I am in mourning. It is an unmistakable feeling. A week ago, the name "Daniel" had poured from *Nicaragüense* lips with a warm liquid familiarity. In private, doubts gripped their bellies, and those doubts they took finally to the ballot box. Doubts seeded by bullets and bread: the U.S.-financed Contra War and the economic embargo. Once again an emerging sovereign nation is brought to its knees. A nation on the brink of declaring to the entire world that revolution is the people's choice betrays its own dead. Imperialism makes traitors of us all, makes us weak and tired and hungry.

I don't blame the people of Nicaragua. I blame the U.S. government. I blame my complicity as a citizen in a country that, short of an invasion, stole the Nicaraguan revolution that *el pueblo* forged with their own blood and bones. After hearing the outcome of the elections, I wanted to flee the United States in shame and despair.

I am Latina, born and raised in the United States. I am a writer. What is my responsibility in this?

ଓ

Days later, George Bush comes to San Francisco. He arrives at the St. Francis Hotel for a $1,000-a-plate fund-raising dinner for Pete Wilson's gubernatorial campaign. There is a protest. We, my camarada and I, get off the subway. I can already hear the voices chanting from a distance.

*An earlier version of this essay first appeared in *Frontiers: A Journal of Women Studies*, XII:3 (1992). It was originally presented as a talk given through the Mexican-American Studies Department at the California State University of Long Beach on March 7, 1990.

We can't make out what they're saying, but they are Latinos and my heart races, seeing so many brown faces. They hold up a banner. The words are still unclear, but as I come closer to the circle of my people, I am stunned. "¡Viva George Bush! ¡Viva UNO!" And my heart drops. Across the street, the "resistance" has congregated—less organized, white, middle-class students. *¿Dónde está mi pueblo?*

A few months earlier I was in another country, San Cristóbal de las Casas, Chiapas, México. The United States had just invaded Panamá. This time, I could stand outside the United States, read the Mexican newspapers for a perspective on the United States that was not monolithic. In the Na Bolom Center Library I wait for a tour of the grounds. The room is filled with *norteamericanos.* They are huge people, the men slouching in couches. Their thick legs spread across the floor, their women lean into them. They converse. "When we invaded Panama..." I grow rigid at the sound of the word "we." They are progressives (I know this from their conversation.) They oppose the invasion, but identify with the invaders.

How can I, as a *Latina*, identify with those who invade Latin American land? George Bush is not my leader. I did not elect him, although my tax dollars pay for the Salvadoran Army's guns. We are a living, breathing contradiction, we who live *en las entrañas del monstruo*, but I refuse to be forced to identify. I am the product of invasion. My father is Anglo; my mother, Mexican. I am the result of the dissolution of blood lines and the theft of language, and yet I am a testimony to the failure of the United States to wholly anglicize its *mestizo* citizens.

I wrote in México, *"Los Estados Unidos es mi país, pero no es mi patria."* I cannot flee the United States, my land resides beneath its borders. We stand on land that was once the country of México. And before any conquistadors staked out political boundaries, this was Indian land and in the deepest sense remains just that: a land *sin fronteras.* Chicanos with memory like our Indian counterparts recognize that we are a nation within a nation. An internal nation whose existence defies borders of language, geography, race. Chicanos are a multiracial, multilingual people, who since 1848, have been displaced from our ancestral lands or remain upon them as indentured servants to Anglo-American invaders.

Today, nearly a century and a half later, the Anglo invasion of Latin America has extended well beyond the Mexican/American border. When U.S. capital invades a country, its military machinery is quick to follow to protect its interests. This is Panamá, Puerto Rico, Grenada, Guatemala...Ironically, the United States' gradual consumption of Latin America and the Caribbean is bringing the people of the Americas together. What was once largely a Chicano/Mexicano population in California is now *guatemalteco, salvadoreño, nicaragüense.* What was largely a

Puerto Rican and Dominican "Spanish Harlem" of New York is now populated with *mexicanos* playing *rancheras* and drinking *cerveza*. This mass emigration is evident from throughout the Third World. Every place the United States has been involved militarily has brought its offspring, its orphans, its homeless, and its casualties to this country: Vietnam, Guatemala, Cambodia, the Philippines...

Third World populations are changing the face of North America. The new face has a delicate fold in the corner of the eye and a wide-bridged nose. The mouth speaks in double negatives and likes to eat a lot of chile. By the 21st century our whole concept of "America" will be dramatically altered, most significantly by a growing Latino population whose strong cultural ties, economic disenfranchisement, racial visibility, and geographical proximity to Latin America discourages any facile assimilation into Anglo-American society.

Latinos in the United States do not represent a homogenous group. Some of us are native born, whose ancestors precede not only the arrival of the Anglo-American but also of the Spaniard. Most of us are immigrants, economic refugees coming to the United States in search of work. Some of us are political refugees, fleeing death squads and imprisonment. Others come fleeing revolution and the loss of wealth. Finally, some have simply landed here very tired of war. And in all cases, our children had no choice in the matter. U.S. Latinos represent the whole spectrum of color and class and political position, including those who firmly believe they can integrate into the mainstream of North American life. The more European the heritage and the higher the class status, the more closely Latinos identify with the powers that be. They vote Republican. They stand under the U.S. flag and applaud George Bush for bringing "peace" to Nicaragua. They hope one day he'll do the same for Cuba, so they can return to their patria and live a "North American-style" consumer life. Because they know in the United States they will never have it all, they will always remain "spics," "greasers," "beaners," and "foreigners" in Anglo-America.

As a Latina artist, I can choose to contribute to the development of a docile generation of would-be Republican "Hispanics" loyal to the United States or to the creation of a force of "disloyal" *americanos* who subscribe to a multicultural, multilingual, radical re-structuring of América. Revolution is not only won by numbers, but by visionaries. And if artists aren't visionaries, then we have no business doing what we do.

ଊ

I call myself a Chicana writer. Not a Mexican-American writer, not an Hispanic writer, not a half-breed writer. To be a Chicana is not merely to name one's racial/cultural identity, but also to name a politic, a politic that refuses assimilation into the U.S. mainstream. It acknowledges our mestizaje—Indian, Spanish, and Africano. After a decade of "hispanicization" (a term superimposed upon us by Reagan-era bureaucrats), the term Chicano assumes even greater radicalism. With the misnomer "Hispanic," Anglo America proffers to the Spanish surnamed the illusion of blending into the "melting pot" like any other white immigrant group. But the Latino is neither wholly immigrant nor wholly white; and here in this country, "Indian" and "dark" don't melt. (Puerto Ricans on the East Coast have been called "Spanish" for decades and it's done little to alter their status on the streets of New York City.)

🙠

The generation of Chicano writers who produced the literature being read today sprang forth from a grass roots social and political movement of the sixties and seventies that was definitely anti-assimilationist. It responded to a stated mandate: art is political. The proliferation of *poesía, cuentos,* and *teatro* that grew out of El Movimiento was supported by Chicano cultural centers and publishing projects throughout the Southwest and in every major urban area where a substantial Chicano population resided. The *teatro* that spilled off flatbed trucks into lettuce fields in the sixties and the *Flor y Canto* poetry festivals of the seventies are hallmarks in the history of the Chicano cultural movement. Chicano literature was a literature in dialogue with its community. And as some of us became involved in feminist, gay, and lesbian concerns in the late seventies and early eighties, our literature was forced to expand to reflect the multifaceted nature of the Chicano experience.

The majority of published Chicano writers today are products of that era of activism, but as the movement grew older and more established, it became neutralized by middle-aged and middle-class concerns, as well as by a growing conservative trend in government. Most of the gains made for farm workers in California were dismantled by a succession of reactionary governors and Reagan/Bush economics. Cultural centers lost funding. Most small Chicano presses disappeared as suddenly as they had appeared. What was once a radical and working-class Latino student base on university campuses has become increasingly conservative. A generation of tokenistic affirmative-action policies and bourgeois flight from Central America and the Caribbean has spawned a tiny Latino elite who often turn to their racial/cultural identities not as a source of political empowerment, but of personal employment as tokens in an Anglo-dominated business world.

And the writers...? Today more and more of us insist we are "American" writers (in the North American sense of the word). The body of our literary criticism grows (seemingly at a faster rate than the literature). We assume tenured positions in the University, secure New York publishers, and our work moves further and further away from a community-based and national political movement.

ɞ

A writer will write, with or without a movement. Fundamentally, I started writing to save my life. Yes, my own life first. I see the same impulse in my students—the dark, the queer, the mixed-blood, the violated—turning to the written page with a relentless passion, a drive to avenge their own silence, invisibility, and erasure as living, innately expressive human beings.

A writer will write, with or without a movement, but at the same time, for Chicano, lesbian, gay, and feminist writers—anybody writing against the grain of Anglo misogynist culture—political movements are what have allowed our writing to surface from the secret places in our notebooks into the public sphere. In 1990, Chicanos, gay men, and women are not better off than we were in 1970. We have an ever-expanding list of physical and social diseases affecting us: AIDS, breast cancer, police brutality. Censorship is becoming increasingly institutionalized, not only through government programs, but through transnational corporate ownership of publishing houses, record companies, etc. Without a movement to foster and sustain our writing, we risk being swallowed up into the "Decade of the Hispanic" that never happened. The fact that a few of us have "made it" and are doing better than we imagined has not altered the nature of the beast. He remains white and male and prefers profit over people.

Like most artists, we Chicano artists would like our work to be seen as "universal" in scope and meaning and reach as large an audience as possible. Ironically, the most "universal" work—writing capable of reaching the hearts of the greatest number of people—is the most culturally specific. The European-American writer understands this because it is his version of cultural specificity that is deemed "universal" by the literary establishment. In the same manner, universality in the Chicana writer requires the most Mexican and the most female images we are capable of producing. Our task is to write what no one is prepared to hear, for what has been said so far in barely a decade of consistent production is a mere *bocadito*. Chicana writers are still learning the art of transcription, but what we will be capable of producing in the decades to come, if we have the cultural/political movements to support us, could make a profound contribution to the social transformation of these Américas. The *reto*, however, is to remain as culturally specific and culturally complex as possible, even in the face of mainstream seduction to do otherwise.

Let's not fool ourselves, the European-American middle-class writer is the cultural mirror through which the literary and theatre establishment sees itself reflected, so it will continue to reproduce itself through new generations of writers. On occasion, New York publishes our work, as it perceives a growing trend for the material, allowing Chicanos access to national distribution on a scale that small independent presses could never accomplish. (Every writer longs for such distribution, particularly since it more effectively reaches communities of color.) But I fear that my generation and the generation of young writers that follows will look solely to the Northeast for recognition. I fear that we may become accustomed to this very distorted reflection, and that we will find ourselves writing more and more in translation through the filter of Anglo-American censors. Wherever Chicanos may live, in the richest and most inspired junctures of our writing, our writer-souls are turned away from Washington, the U.S. capital, and toward a México Antiguo. That is not to say that contemporary Chicano literature does not wrestle with current social concerns, but without the memory of our once-freedom, how do we imagine a future?

I still believe in a Chicano literature that is hungry for change, that has the courage to name the sources of our discontent both from within our raza and without, that challenges us to envision a world where poverty, crack, and pesticide poisoning are not endemic to people with dark skin or Spanish surnames. It is a literature that knows that god is neither white nor male, a literature that recognizes no reason to rape anyone. If such ideas are "naive," (as some critics would have us believe) then let us remain naive, naively and passionately committed to an art of "resistance," resistance to domination by Anglo-America, resistance to assimilation, resistance to economic and sexual exploitation. *An art that subscribes to integration into mainstream America is not Chicano art.*

All writing is confession. Confession masked and revealed in the voices and faces of our characters. All writing is hunger. The longing to be known fully and still loved. The admission of our own inherent vulnerability, our weakness, our tenderness of skin, fragility of heart, our overwhelming desire to be relieved of the burden of ourselves in the body of another, to be forgiven of our ultimate aloneness in the mystical body of a god or the common work of a revolution. These are human considerations that the best of writers presses her finger upon. The wound ruptures and ... heals.

One of the deepest wounds Chicanos suffer is separation from our Southern relatives. Gloria Anzaldúa calls it a "1,950-mile-long open wound," dividing México from the United States, "dividing a pueblo, a culture." This *llaga* ruptures over and over again in our writing, for we are Chicanos in search of a México that never wholly embraces us. "Mexico gags," poet Lorna Dee Cervantes writes, "on this bland pocha seed." This separation was never our choice. Presently we witness a fractured and disintegrating América, where the Northern half functions as the absented landlord of the Southern half and the economic disparity between the First and Third Worlds drives a bitter wedge between a people.

I hold a vision requiring a radical transformation of consciousness in this country, that as the people-of-color population increases, we will not be just another brown faceless mass hungrily awaiting integration into white Amerika, but that we will emerge as a mass movement of people to redefine what an "American" is. Our entire concept of this nation's identity must change, possibly it must be obliterated. We must learn to see ourselves less as U.S. citizens and more as members of a larger world community composed of many nations of people and no longer give credence to the geopolitical borders that have divided us, Chicano from Mexicano, Filipino-American from Pacific Islander, African-American from Haitian. Call it racial memory. Call it shared economic discrimination. Chicanos call it "Raza,"—be it Quechua, Cubano, Colombiano—an identity that dissolves borders. As a Chicana writer, that's the context in which I want to create.

I am an American writer in the original sense of the word, an American *con acento*.

Judith Ortiz Cofer

Judith Ortiz Cofer was born in Puerto Rico, the daughter of a Navy man who, in the 1960s, moved his family to Paterson, New Jersey, where she lived as a bicultural, bilingual child. She received her B.A. in English from Augusta College. A fellow of the English Speaking Union of America, she studied at the Summer Graduate School at Oxford University, then completed her M.A. in English at Florida Atlantic University. Ortiz Cofer is the author of *The Line of the Sun* (1989), the first original novel published by the University of Georgia Press, which also published her collection of prose and poetry, *The Latin Deli* (1993). In addition, she has published a collection of personal essays and poems, *Silent Dancing* (1990), two collections of poetry, *Terms of Survival* (1987) and *Reaching for the Mainland* (1987), as well as *Peregrina* (1986), a winning manuscript in the Riverstone International Chapbook Competition. Ortiz Cofer has published in numerous national reviews, including *Prairie Schooner, The Kenyon Review, Antioch Review* and *The Southern Review. Silent Dancing* was awarded a PEN American/Albrand Special Citation in the category of best non-fiction by an American author in 1991. Its title essay was selected by Joyce Carol Oates for inclusion in *The Best American Essays 1991. Silent Dancing* was also chosen as one of the "Best Books for the Teen Age" by the New York City Public Library, which in 1989 selected *The Line of the Sun* as one of the "25 Books to Remember." Ortiz Cofer is a member of the associate teaching staff at the Bread Loaf Writers' Conference. She teaches English and Creative Writing at the University of Georgia.

Silent Dancing

Judith Ortiz Cofer

We have a home movie of this party. Several times my mother and I have watched it together, and I have asked questions about the silent revelers coming in and out of focus. It is grainy and of short duration but a great visual aid to my first memory of life in Paterson at that time. And it is in color—the only complete scene in color I can recall from those years.

We lived in Puerto Rico until my brother was born in 1954. Soon after, because of economic pressures on our growing family, my father joined the United States Navy. He was assigned to duty on a ship in Brooklyn Yard, New York City—a place of cement and steel that was to be his home base in the States until his retirement more than twenty years later.

He left the Island first, tracking down his uncle who lived with his family across the Hudson River, in Paterson, New Jersey. There he found a tiny apartment in a huge apartment building that had once housed Jewish families and was just being transformed into a tenement by Puerto Ricans overflowing from New York City. In 1955 he sent for us. My mother was only twenty years old, I was not quite three, and my brother was a toddler when we arrived at *El Building*, as the place had been christened by its new residents.

My memories of life in Paterson during those first few years are in shades of gray. Maybe I was too young to absorb vivid colors and details, or to discriminate between the slate blue of the winter sky and the darker hues of the snow-bearing clouds, but the single color washes over the whole period. The building we lived in was gray, the streets were gray with slush the first few months of my life there, the coat my father had bought for me was dark in color and too big. I sat heavily on my thin frame.

I do remember the way the heater pipes banged and rattled, startling all of us out of sleep until we got so used to the sound that we automatically either shut it out or raised our voices above the racket. The hiss from the valve punctuated my sleep, which has always been fitful, like a nonhuman presence in the room—the dragon sleeping at the entrance of my childhood. But the pipes were a connection to all the other lives being lived around us. Having come from a house made for a single family back in Puerto Rico—my mother's extended-family home—it was curious to know that strangers lived under our floor and above our heads, and that the heater pipe went through everyone's apartments. (My first spanking in Paterson came as a result of playing tunes on the pipes in my room to see if there would be an answer.) My mother was as new to this concept of beehive life as I was, but had been given strict orders by my father to keep the doors locked, the noise down, ourselves to ourselves.

It seems Father had learned some painful lessons about prejudice while searching for an apartment in Paterson. Not until years later did I hear how much resistance he had encountered with landlords who were panicking at the influx of Latinos into a neighborhood that had been Jewish for a couple of generations. But it was the American phenomenon of ethnic turnover that was changing the urban core of Paterson, and the human flood could not be held back with an accusing finger.

"You Cuban?" the man had asked my father, pointing a finger at his name tag on the Navy uniform—even though my father had the fair skin and light brown hair of his northern Spanish family background and our name is as common in Puerto Rico as Johnson is in the U.S.

"No," my father had answered, looking past the finger into his adversary's angry eyes, "I'm Puerto Rican."

"Same shit." And the door closed. My father could have passed as European, but we couldn't. My brother and I both have our mother's black hair and olive skin, and so we lived in El Building and visited our great-uncle and his fair children on the next block. It was their private joke that they were the German branch of the family. Not many years later, that area too would be mainly Puerto Rican. It was as if the heart of the city map were gradually colored in brown—*café-con-leche* brown. Our color.

The movie opens with a sweep of the living room. It is "typical" immigrant Puerto Rican decor for the time: the sofa and chairs are square and hard-looking, upholstered in bright colors (blue and yellow in this instance, and covered in the transparent plastic) that furniture salesmen then were adept at making women buy. The linoleum on the floor is light blue, and if it was subjected to the spike heels as it was in most places, there were dime-sized indentations all over it that cannot be seen in this movie. The room is full of people dressed in mainly two colors: dark suits for the men, red dresses for the women. I have asked my mother why most of the women are in red that night, and she shrugs, "I don't remember. Just a coincidence." She doesn't have my obsession for assigning symbolism to everything.

The three women in red sitting on the couch are my mother, my eighteen-year-old cousin, and her brother's girlfriend. The "novia" is just up from the

Island, which is apparent in her body language. She sits up formally, and her dress is carefully pulled over her knees. She is a pretty girl, but her posture makes her look insecure, lost in her full-skirted red dress which she has carefully tucked around her to make room for my gorgeous cousin, her future sister-in-law. My cousin has grown up in Paterson and is in her last year of high school. She doesn't have a trace of what Puerto Ricans call "la mancha" (literally, the stain: the mark of the new immigrant—something about the posture, the voice, or the humble demeanor making it obvious to everyone that that person has just arrived on the mainland; has not yet acquired the polished look of the city dweller). My cousin is wearing a tight red-sequined cocktail dress. Her brown hair has been lightened with peroxide around the bangs, and she is holding a cigarette very expertly between her fingers, bringing it up to her mouth in a sensuous arc of her arm as she talks animatedly with my mother, who has come to sit between the two women, both only a few years younger than herself. My mother is somewhere halfway between the poles they represent in our culture.

It became my father's obsession to get out of the barrio, and thus we were never permitted to form bonds with the place or with the people who lived there. Yet the building was a comfort to my mother, who never got over yearning for *la isla*. She felt surrounded by her language: the walls were thin, and voices speaking and arguing in Spanish could be heard all day. *Salsas* blasted out of radios turned on early in the morning and left on for company. Women seemed to cook rice and beans perpetually—the strong aroma of red kidney beans boiling permeated the hallways.

Though Father preferred that we do our grocery shopping at the supermarket when he came home on weekend leaves, my mother insisted that she could cook only with products whose labels she could read, and so, during the week, I accompanied her and my little brother to *La Bodega*—a hole-in-the-wall grocery store across the street from *El Building*. There we squeezed down three narrow aisles jammed with various products. Goya and Libby's—those were the trademarks trusted by her Mamá, and so my mother bought cans of Goya beans, soups and condiments. She bought little cans of Libby's fruit juices for us. And she bought Colgate toothpaste and Palmolive soap. (The final *e* is pronounced in both those products in Spanish, and for many years I believed that they were manufactured on the Island. I remember my surprise at first hearing a commercial on television for the toothpaste in which Colgate rhymed with "ate.")

We would linger at *La Bodega*, for it was there that mother breathed best, taking in the familiar aromas of the foods she knew from Mamá's kitchen, and it was also there that she got to speak to the other women of El Building without violating outright Father's dictates against fraternizing with our neighbors.

But he did his best to make our "assimilation" painless. I can still see him carrying a Christmas tree up several flights of stairs to our apartment, leaving a trail of aromatic pine. He carried it formally, as if it were a flag in a parade. We were the only ones in El Building that I knew of who got presents on both Christmas Day and on *Día de Reyes*, the day when the Three Kings brought gifts to Christ and to Hispanic children.

Our greatest luxury in El Building was having our own television set. It must have been a result of Father's guilt feelings over the isolation he had imposed on us, but we were one of the first families in the barrio to have one. My brother quickly became an avid watcher of Captain Kangaroo and Jungle Jim. I loved all the family series, and by the time I started first grade in school, I could have drawn a map of Middle America as exemplified by the lives of characters in "Father Knows Best," "The Donna Reed Show," "Leave It To Beaver," "My Three Sons," and (my favorite) "Bachelor Father," where John Forsythe treated his adopted teenage daughter like a princess because he was rich and had a Chinese houseboy to do everything for him.

Compared to our neighbors in El Building, we were rich. My father's Navy check provided us with financial security and a standard of life that the factory workers envied. The only thing his money could not buy us was a place to live away from the barrio—his greatest wish and Mother's greatest fear.

In the home movie the men are shown next, sitting around a card table set up in one corner of the living room, playing dominoes. The clack of the ivory pieces is a familiar sound. I heard it in many houses on the Island and in many apartments in Paterson. In "Leave It To Beaver," the Cleavers played bridge in every other episode; in my childhood, the men started every social occasion with a hotly debated round of dominoes: the women would sit around and watch, but they never participated in the games.

Here and there you can see a small child. Children were always brought to parties and, whenever they got sleepy, put to bed in the host's bedrooms. Babysitting was a concept unrecognized by the Puerto Rican women I knew: a responsible mother did not leave her children with any stranger. And in a culture where children are not considered intrusive, there is no need to leave the children at home. We went where our mother went.

Of my pre-school years, I have only impressions: the sharp bite of the wind in December as we walked with our parents towards the brightly lit stores downtown; how I felt like a stuffed doll in my heavy coat, boots and mittens; how good it was to walk into the five-and-dime and sit at the counter drinking hot chocolate.

On Saturdays our whole family would walk downtown to shop at the big department stores on Broadway. Mother bought all our clothes at Penny's and Sears, and she liked to buy her dresses at the women's specialty shops like Lerner's and Diana's. At some point we would go into Woolworth's and sit at the soda fountain to eat.

We never ran into other Latinos at these stores or eating out, and it became clear to me only years later that the women from El Building shopped mainly at other places—stores owned either by other Puerto Ricans, or by Jewish merchants who had philosophically accepted our presence in the city and decided to make us their good customers, if not neighbors and friends. These establishments were located not downtown, but in the blocks around our street, and they were referred to generically as *La Tienda, El Bazar, La Bodega, La Botánica.* Everyone knew what was meant. These were the stores where your face did not turn a clerk to stone, where your money was as green as anyone else's.

On New Year's Eve we were dressed up like child models in the Sears' catalogue—my brother in a miniature man's suit and bow tie, and I in black patent leather shoes and a frilly dress with several layers of crinolines underneath. My mother wore a bright red dress that night, I remember, and spike heels; her long black hair hung to her waist. Father, who usually wore his Navy uniform during his short visits home, had put on a dark civilian suit for the occasion: we had been invited to his uncle's house for a big celebration. Everyone was excited because my mother's brother, Hernán—a bachelor who could indulge himself in such luxuries—had bought a movie camera which he would be trying out that night.

Even the home movie cannot fill in the sensory details such a gathering left imprinted in a child's brain. The thick sweetness of women's perfume mixing with the ever-present smells of food cooking in the kitchen: meat and plantain *pasteles,* the ubiquitous rice dish made special with pigeon peas—*gandules*—and seasoned with the precious *sofrito* sent up from the island by somebody's mother or smuggled in by a recent traveler. *Sofrito* was one of the items that women hoarded, since it was hardly ever in stock at La Bodega. It was the flavor of Puerto Rico.

The men drank Palo Viejo rum and some of the younger ones got weepy. The first time I saw a grown man cry was at a New Year's Eve party. He had been reminded of his mother by the smells in the kitchen. But what I remember most were the boiled pasteles—boiled until the plantain or yucca rectangles stuffed with corned beef or other meats, olive, and many other savory ingredients were ready, all wrapped in banana leaves. Everyone had to fish one out with a fork. There was always a "trick" pastel—one without stuffing—and whoever got that one was the "New Year's Fool."

There was also the music. Long-playing albums were treated like precious china in these homes. Mexican recordings were popular, but the songs that brought tears to my mother's eyes were sung by the melancholic Daniel Santos, whose life as a drug addict was the stuff of legend. Felipe Rodríguez was a particular favorite of couples. He sang about faithless women and broken-hearted men. There is a snatch of a lyric that has stuck in my mind like a needle on a worn groove: "De piedra ha de ser mi cama, de piedra la cabecera...la mujer que a mí me quiera...ha de quererme de veras. Ay, Ay, corazón, ¿por qué no amas...?" I must have heard it a thousand times since the idea of a bed made of stone, and its connection to love, first troubled me with its disturbing images. The five-minute home movie ends with people dancing in a circle. The creative filmmaker must have asked them to do that so that they could file past him. It is both comical and sad to watch silent dancing. Since there is no justification for the absurd movements that music provides for some of us, people appear frantic, their faces embarrassingly intense. It's as if you were watching sex. Yet for years, I've had dreams in the form of this home movie. In a recurring scene, familiar faces push themselves forward into my mind's eye, plastering their features into distorted close-ups. And I'm asking them: "Who is she? Who is the woman I don't recognize? Is she an aunt? Somebody's wife? Tell me who she is. Tell me who these people are."

"No, see the beauty mark on her cheek as big as a hill on the lunar landscape of her face—well, that runs in the family. The women on your father's side of the family wrinkle early; it's the price they pay for that fair skin. The young girl with the green stain on her wedding dress is *La Novía*—just up from the island. See, she lowers her eyes as she approaches the camera like she's supposed to. Decent girls never look you directly in the face. *Humilde,* humble, a girl should express humility in all her actions. She will make a good wife for your cousin. He should consider himself lucky to have met her only weeks after she arrived here. If he marries her quickly, she will make him a good Puerto Rican-style wife; but if he waits too long, she will be corrupted by the city, just like your cousin there."

"She means me. I do what I want. This is not some primitive island I live on. Do they expect me to wear a black *mantilla* on my head and go to mass every day? Not me. I'm an American woman and I will do as I please. I can type faster than anyone in my senior class at Central High, and I'm going to be a secretary to a lawyer when I graduate. I can pass for an American girl anywhere—I've tried it—at least for Italian, anyway. I never speak Spanish in public. I hate these parties, but I wanted the dress. I look better than any of these *humildes* here. My life is going to be different. I have an American boyfriend. He is older and has a car. My parents don't know it, but I sneak out of the house late at night sometimes to be with him. If I marry him, even my name will be American. I hate rice and beans. It's what makes these women fat."

"Your *prima* is pregnant by that man she's been sneaking around with. Would I lie to you? I'm your great-uncle's common-law wife—the one he abandoned on the island to marry your cousin's mother. I was not invited to this party, but I came anyway. I came to tell you that story about your cousin that you've always wanted to hear. Remember that comment your mother made to a neighbor that has always haunted you? The only thing you heard was your cousin's name and then you saw your mother pick up your doll from the couch and say: 'It was as big as this doll when they flushed it down the toilet.' This image has bothered you for years, hasn't it? You had nightmares about babies being flushed down the toilet, and you wondered why anyone would do such a horrible thing. You didn't dare ask your mother about it. She would only tell you that you had not heard her right and yell at you for listening to adult conversations. But later, when you were old enough to know about abortions, you suspected. I am here to tell you that you were right. Your cousin was growing an *Americanito* in her belly when this movie was made. Soon after she put something long and pointy into her pretty self, thinking maybe she could get rid of the problem before breakfast and still make it to her first class at the high school. Well, *Niña*, her screams could be heard downtown. Your aunt, her Mamá, who had been a midwife on the Island, managed to pull the little thing out. Yes, they probably flushed it down the toilet, what else could they do with it—give it a Christian burial in a little white casket with blue bows and ribbons? Nobody wanted that baby—least of all the father, a teacher at her school with a house in West Paterson that he was filling with real children, and a wife who was a natural blond.

Girl, the scandal sent your uncle back to the bottle. And guess where your cousin ended up? Irony of ironies. She was sent to a village in Puerto Rico to live with a relative on her mother's side: a place so far away from civilization that you have to ride a mule to reach it. A real change in scenery. She found a man there. Women like that cannot live without male company. But believe me, the men in Puerto Rico know how to put a saddle on a woman like her. *La Gringa*, they call her, ha, ha, ha. *La Gringa* is what she always wanted to be..."

The old woman's mouth becomes a cavernous black hole I fall into. And as I fall, I can feel the reverberations of her laughter. I hear the echoes of her last mocking words: *La Gringa, La Gringa!* And the conga line keeps moving silently past me. There is no music in my dream for the dancers.

When Odysseus visits Hades asking to see the spirit of his mother, he makes an offering of sacrificial blood, but since all of the souls crave an audience with the living, he has to listen to many of them before he can ask questions. I, too, have to hear the dead and the forgotten speak in my dream. Those who are still part of my life remain silent, going around and around in their dance. The others keep pressing their faces forward to say things about the past.

My father's uncle is last in line. He is dying of alcoholism, shrunken and shriveled like a monkey, his face is a mass of wrinkles and broken arteries. As he comes closer, I realize that in his features I can see my whole family. If you were to stretch that rubbery flesh, you could find my father's face, and deep within that face—mine. I don't want to look into those eyes ringed in purple. In a few years he will retreat into silence, and take a long, long time to die. *Move back, Tío,* I tell him. *I don't want to hear what you have to say. Give the* dancers *room to move, soon it will be midnight. Who is the New Year's Fool this time?*

Part Three:
Fiction

Elena Castedo

Elena Castedo has lived on four continents. She was born in Barcelona, Spain, and reared in Chile. In 1968 Castedo received an M.A. with honors from the University of California, Los Angeles; her Ph.D. is from Harvard University. The former editor of the *Inter-American Review of Bibliography*, she is also the author of a critical study of Chilean theater. Castedo is married and lives in McLean, Virginia, near her children and grandchildren. Her first novel, *Paradise* (1990) was a finalist for the National Book Award. The *Washington Times* described it as follows: "There is Mark Twain's Huckleberry Finn and Harper Lee's Scout in *To Kill a Mockingbird*. To the roll of important or noteworthy youths of American literature add Solita, the protagonist of Elena Castedo's enchanting debut novel, *Paradise*...a unique hybrid of the best of America and Latin America combined." Castedo uses the lessons of her own life—her parents' escape from Franco's Spain and her Chilean childhood—to create a brilliant satire of Latin American hegemonic society. In the following excerpt from *Paradise,* the characters experience a nocturnal earthquake. El Topaz, the hacienda to which Solita's mother Pilar has brought the girl and her brother Niceto, is full of visitors on this particular night: Tía Merce, the proprietress of El Topaz, and her daughters Patricia, Grace and Gloria; Berta, Solita and Niceto's nursemaid; Madame, the French governess who is totally out of her element in El Topaz; and sundry other visitors who pair up in ever-changing cycles. The reader also encounters Papi, Solita's father, a socialist and a union leader. Finally, there is the *guanaco*, a llama-like creature, who is one of the delights in the book.

from *Paradise*

Elena Castedo

Cavernous noises sounding like giant tarantulas came from the ground. Berta's yells cut my dream, right when I was about to throw a bucketful of goo on a pack of huge ostriches coming at me with stretched necks. My bed rocked away from the wall. Berta screamed, stumbled, pulled my brother, grabbed my hair, yelled, "Little girl! Wake up! Get up! Get out! Have mercy, Santa Rita, Santa Lucía, San Gregorio, Santa Catalina, *mártir y virgen*, have mercy! Little girl! Get out!" She stumbled toward the door carrying my half-asleep brother.

My dream bucket of spit turned into a real bucket of iced water going through me; I headed after them. Was this war? Walls moved like giants; dust showered from the ceiling; my bed followed me creaking, as if angry at me for leaving it before morning; the night table opened its door, letting out the chamber pot; the dresser danced to the music made by the basin and the pitcher banging against each other. While I was passing through it, the doorway moved sideways. I leapt across the veranda to the front garden.

Near and distant screams, people and shadows poured out of doors and corridors. A creamy moon spilled eerily over the front gardens. The cook and some chamber girls hit the gravel on their knees, like ghosts in their raw cotton gowns. Young maids cried; older ones punched their bosoms with their fists, looking up and yelling, "Mea culpa, mea culpa, Lord Father, forgive, mercy, have mercy!" Half-dressed gardeners, butlers, chauffeurs and helping hands leapt over bushes, staying away from creaky trees. Maximiliano ran buttoning his tasseled jacket, not nearly as impressive without pants. Gabriel, the back-gardens gardener, ran naked with a burlap bag clumsily wrapped around his middle to the huge oak and started the bell talk: fast ding-ding-ding-dings, for disasters.

The girls came out in their ruffled nightgowns, pulled and pushed by la Mamota, who crossed herself with frenzied eyes. Someone tripped out of Tío Juan Vicente's room, removing a chin-to-head contraption.

It was he. María Pía floated like a ghostly puma wrapped in silk. Mlle. Vicky erupted in her flimsy nightgown, her face a white skull, yelling, "Save me! Save me, someone! Don't let me die unmarried!" Men came out trying to act composed. At the sight of them, Mlle. Vicky wiped off the white from her face. Ladies with curled bangs and the Genius avoided the dogs, who howled at the moon, maybe imitating the servants. Beethoven pranced, wagging his tail and barking gently to reassure everyone he was on top of the situation.

Madame ran up and down the veranda screaming, *"Au secours! Ce pays sauvage!"* Tío Juan Vicente grabbed her and brought her down. Madame fidgeted frantically with a bathrobe, furious at us, as if we had planned the event just to scare her to death. She mumbled about civilization as if earthquakes were the result of backward governments. There were none in Paris, ever, she cried; presumably the Parisians simply wouldn't stand for it.

Tía Merce, pulling the frightened hipless poet by the hand, wobbled, bemused by the screaming scene. "Thank Goodness Pablo left, this would have given him a dreadful impression."

"Watch the ground for cracks, little girl!" Berta warned. "You fall in one and it closes, and it'll make flat *charqui* out of you, mercy, mercy, San Gregorio!" I told her I had to tell my mother to come out, and rescue my foil ball. "Don't you dare, you foolish little girl. The houses can fall any second! Señora Pilar'll come out. Protect us, Santa Rita, Santo Tomás!"

As if the prayers had worked, Tío Juan Vicente stumbled to my mother's window. "Come back here!" la Mamota shrieked. "What if a loosened roof tile decapitates you! Remember what happened to Elias Cabezón, the cheese maker!" He came back saying Pilar refused to get up. Terror hit me. I remembered a refugee saying that Pilar ignored the sirens and never went to bomb shelters.

When I started to whine, the tremors subsided and suddenly the earth was still, as if bombing planes had left. Voices yelled at my mother to come out. With a candle, she looked through the window's ironwork at us as we shivered in the moonlight, now more frightened than when the earth was shaking. "Can't a person get any sleep around here?" she asked.

Everyone was dumbfounded. Tía Merce chuckled with delight. I wished I could be brave like my mother, like a Spaniard had to be. Niceto was like her; he slept on Berta's lap.

"Pilar, come out, come out," Tía Merce ordered. "First tremors aren't always the worst..."

The psychiatrist shouted, "Pilar, enough of this bravery nonsense. We aren't under siege from the Moors or the fascists; this is an earthquake, you know."

"I don't want to catch a cold," my mother said. "If it gets bad, I'll come out."

Tía Merce laughed happily and ordered the men to go inside, grab blankets from the beds and bring her guitar. She talked to Werther secretively. The men came out, and everybody wrapped themselves up and prayed. Tía Merce and Werther went toward the bungalow playhouse, and one of Tía Merce's songs could be heard.

There was another tremor, more wailing and chest-pounding. What would my father say about all this? A good thing he was safe in Galmeda. Or was he? "Make the sign of the cross again, my little ones. Don't falter, Spaniards always bring bad luck," la Mamota told the girls. In the moonlight, their heads were wild escarole plants, appearing less powerful and more dangerous at the same time. No wonder it took so long every morning for the nannies to tame that flaming chaos into their magnificent curls. "Promise the Good Virgin," la Mamota ordered, "to be good girls if She prevails upon the Heavenly Father to stop for good."

Grace, the closest to me, prayed. The tremor stopped. There was an opportunity here. I asked Grace, "Did you promise to be good?"

"Of course, you dunce. Didn't you see that after my promise the tremor went away?" There was no doubt that Grace had unlimited confidence in her power. So much the better.

I asked if that meant good to everybody. She thought for a moment, then said with reluctance, "I guess so," but added, "I'll do what la Mamota says." That would be of no help to me.

I asked if being good meant being nice and sharing things, including secrets. She agreed. "Well, then, you have to tell me those things you know about me." She was appalled. I had to try it with her sisters. It was like a field of flowers to think of three meek girls.

Patricia said, "We don't mean just anybody. For instance, we don't pray for the peasants. And anyway, we're very fair and always give people what they deserve."

Gloria agreed to be good. She took me aside; she could let me know one secret. They had heard their Mumsy confide to her friend Mónica on the phone that she was taking Pilar to El Topaz to get her away from her brother-in-law Armando, because she feared Pilar could catch him. Then Pilar would have no use for her. As for the other secrets...another tremor started. Grace shouted to her, "If this one keeps up and Madame's study falls down, we won't have to have classes."

Finally my mother came out, tripping on the shifting veranda steps, her black hair down to her waist. The men helped her once she was away from falling roof tiles. Something crashed noisily in the dark. The air sponged up noises from underground. In the salon, furniture traveled around as if having a dance class, or banged against the walls as if complaining about the noise from next door. Several walls cracked; our room's wall crumbled. I wished the houses would be swallowed forever by a crater, even if my foil ball disappeared. Then, abruptly, there was an eerie calm.

"Ifigenio, see if this's the end of it," la Mamota told him. A small man who worked in the hothouse put his ear to the ground. Everybody watched him. Would my father include this in what he called "bizarre religion?"

As if reading my thoughts, Tío Juan Vicente said, "Ifigenio learned to be an underground noise expert from my viñas' expert, who's never been wrong yet."

After a while Ifigenio said, "It's the end of it. Won't be another one this night."

Everyone got up, hugged, cried, thanked a list of those Up Above and discussed where they should go to drink something hot.

Tío Armando grumbled, "A poorly built house in an earthquake zone; I'm never coming back to this godforsaken place." The earthquake was bringing good things!

The Genius said he liked this country because they left geniuses in peace and didn't expect them to discover anything. The guanaco nibbled on his collar, and he slapped it away.

Tío Merce arrived back from the play bungalow and announced, "This divine tremor will change everything. Come inside; wait until I tell you the news!"

Gabriel went to the huge oak to toll the bell; slow ding-dong-dings told everyone in El Topaz the earthquake was over and they could go back to bed. If there were beds to go back to.

La Mamota gave instructions about debris and beds.

"Mamota, how's everything going to change, like Mumsy says?" Gloria asked, true to form.

"None of your concern, you nosy child; none of your concern. You better thank the Good Virgin, who prevailed upon the Almighty Lord to lift only one finger this time," la Mamota sighed.

"One finger?" Grace disagreed. "It seemed like three to me."

"No, child, that was one finger He lifted, two at the most. If He had lifted three fingers, the houses would have flattened."

Berta carried sleeping Niceto on her shoulder. She was glad the Basilisco hadn't gotten away with anything. That featherless, roosterlike *ánima* slid through canyons on its snake tail, promoting earthquakes in cahoots with the Devil, so he could expand his territories. In the moonlit dust, all those things you couldn't see seemed more plausible: the *ánimas*; the crowd Up Above; the floating souls who influenced humans; the girl's rules. In El Topaz, bad, evil, and the weird weren't in mad political parties, in deranged tyrants, weren't remote and clear-cut, but confusing, unpredictable. Would the twins keep their promise to be good, and Tío Armando his to never come back?

La Mamota told servants to make maté and be ready for anything that might be requested. They headed for the kitchen, repeating to each other, "I knew this morning there'd be trembling. First such heavy air, then that wicked moon. Can't say the Saint didn't warn us plenty..."

"I knew yesterday! I told everybody, remember? I said..."

"That big one that crumbled half the houses in El Topaz; I warned everybody for days. But not a soul listened; nobody ever listens to me, then they're plenty sorry..."

"A day like this, back before Terencio, the old butler, died, remember? And I kept saying, 'It's earthquake time,' but nobody paid any attention, but I was sure of it..."

"...and the wall fell over María Quiñones' baby, remember?"

"...and that big elm just crushed the poor boy, remember?"

"...and Victorina Soto was swallowed by that ditch that's still there, near the sheep's bath, pregnant and all, remember?"

"...and the entire room collapsed on me, but I stood right under the doorway, and that's how I'm here to tell the story."

Their chatter drifted past the corridor.

My mother and the guests waited in front of the salon for servants to clear away debris and broken glass. I sneaked toward them, anxious to find whether Tía Merce's big news was that my father was being invited to live here, or that now the houses were unlivable and we had to leave. Maybe it had to do with the other big secret the girls didn't want to tell me.

The salon's door was blocked by furniture packed like animals trying to get out. The grown-ups settled in the gallery. A couple of chamber girls managed to light two candelabra with their shaky hands. Tía Merce grabbed my mother's arm, whispering, "I did it! I did it! A double coup! At last, I got my lovely bard, and what I had long wished for, a workout during an earthquake!" She chuckled. "And I managed to keep that lovely slim body going—la Madre! what leaps!—and he threw a torrent like the Mapu-Mapu River, right up into my lungs. I'll drip for a week..." She saw a chamber girl nearby. "Tell Manuel to come light the fireplace."

The chamber girl started to leave, then mumbled to another one, maliciously, "There's no lack of kindling around."

Judging by her manner, Tía Merce had said something naughty. Someone had nearly drowned her, but she wasn't angry. I couldn't ask the girls because it had to do with their mother, and you didn't do that. They did, but it was wrong.

Manuel lit a fire and a chambermaid threw a basket of chestnuts on it. Sofa chairs, with figures wrapped in sheep-smelling blankets like mummies, moved closer. I hid in a dark corner. "What do you think happened out in the mountains?" Mlle. Vicky cried with agitation, but no one answered.

"Europeans criticize us for being lazy," the Walrus complained defensively, "but what's the point of building great things when we know they're going to crumble periodically?"

"Then you rebuild. You have a rebirth; build something better," the psychiatrist said. This was a cheerful idea.

"That's exactly what I wanted to tell you," Tía Merce said.

"I kept wondering *oú* Mercedes was." Tío Juan Vicente readjusted his satin pajamas. "I feared she *and* Werther'd been swallowed by an earthquake ditch." He looked impishly at the hipless poet wrapping his blanket up to his ears, then motioned to a chambermaid. "Bring *cedrón* brew for Mlle. Vicky, my dear, to calm her nerves, and bring me some hot chocolate."

Orders came from everyone. I badly needed some hot chocolate, but if I didn't keep quiet, they would send me to bed.

A chambermaid asked Tía Merce shyly, "Should I send a couple of girls to do some cleaning up?"

"No, no," my mother said. "It's more interesting this way. This is like penetrating inside an ancient pyramid."

Tío Juan Vicente kissed my mother's hand. "Divine Spaniard, you find enchantment even in a roomful of earthquake dust!"

Tío Armando fretted, "We're right next door to a volcano-ridden ridge, a perfect place for earthquakes." His bald spot was dusty. I wished a brick had fallen on it. He said to María Pía, draped over the sofa as if she were an empty silk bathrobe, "And for you to come at this time; I shudder." He removed his blanket and put it carefully over her.

Tío Popsy appeared at the door in a bathrobe. I almost leapt to my feet. "I need a chambermaid to redo my bed," he said sleepily. "It's full of dust. Good night, my friends." He left. The gallery felt empty.

"He slept right through," Melons said. "Whiskey turned the rocking into la Mamota's young arms, and noises into a lullaby."

Tía Merce clapped, "*Mes chers amis*, permit me to make my wonderful announcement. This tremor caused me to realize I've been acting too much like a matron. I'm young! Really, I'm just a girl enchanted by life...and poetry. And—"

"Naturally," Melons interrupted. "An earthquake makes one think about one's life." Melons should have thought about shutting up.

"I'm revitalizing El Topaz," Tía Merce exulted, "turning it into a creative force, a haven for poets! We'll have readings, unveil young talent! Isn't it the most divine idea?" She looked at the hipless poet, who observed the fire gloomily.

So, these were the big news and big changes announced by Tía Merce with such fanfare? Who cared about poetry! Wasn't Tía Merce going to release that terrible power she had over my mother so we could leave? It made me so angry...

When I woke up, I was in a strange bed. Outside, the sun appeared feebly between clouds as heavy as the bottom of ships.

With debris everywhere and the guests changing rooms, the confusion was wonderful, but the girls had gathered no news about what was going on, except that the hipless poet had announced he would leave with the first departing guest. We had too much important detective work to do to worry about him. We met at the avocado orchard. "Solita, did you see or hear anything about your mother and Tío Armando? We haven't seen them together since María Pía showed up."

I would have eaten a prickly pear, skin and all, rather than tell them anything about my mother. I asked, "Do you know about a torrent like the Mapu-Mapu River near your play bungalow?" They didn't, or weren't telling, either. We would get nowhere this way. We ate fallen avocados, whose black skin peeled out like a satin glove, leaving a dark, almond-tasting aura around the juicy flesh, the perfect gateway for the guarded sweetness that followed.

"I heard Tío Armando and Tío Juan Vicente talking, and maybe it was naughty," Gloria said. This was a word that made you pay attention. "Tío Armando said he was fed up with hard-to-get dames. He said, 'Our own women are far more sophisticated; they get to a romp as fast as we do.'" She ground an avocado pit with a rock.

"Well, go on. That doesn't say anything."

"Tío Juan Vicente said, 'They are also fickle; your wispy beauty has left you twice already—first Jorge, then the baron.'"

"And?" Patricia packed her pipe with the pit grounds.

"Then he said something and laughed his way that's so funny, knotting his face with teeth in the middle, you know?"

"But what did Tío Armando say?" She burned the grounds.

"Nothing. I laughed so hard at Tío Juan Vicente's face, they noticed me and stopped. That's how I know it was naughty."

"Gloria, you turkey, you always gather useless info."

All we got was a sore throat and a raspy voice from smoking avocado pits. The Genius was consulted about our throats and said it was due to the climatic and air-pressure changes brought about by the earthquake. Everyone was impressed.

Madame jolted us by handing me a new book with pictures, saying I would do work for my age. The girls would stay in remedial, but although she had recuperated from a *crise nerveuse* due to the *sauvage* earthquake, they wouldn't write compositions, as her nerves couldn't take it. The new book showed Earth with layers, all the way to a pit of fire! Having me on a higher level made the girls sit on a pit of fire, and me happy. But jumpy.

Depending on her mood, Madame made them write twenty *"Je suis une fille paresseuse"* or *"lente."* The next time we went on a funereal march, Patricia dallied, so we arrived at the center of a field just at the time the irrigation water was let go. We ran to a hill, then watched Madame calling us, until the water hit her up to her calves. She held her skirts up to slosh through the field. This cost us one hundred *"Je suis..."* After we started, Patricia made a special nod and all three bounced their legs against the table, making the floor tremble. Patricia gave me a kick; I joined them.

Madame stiffened up, then stampeded out of the classroom and down the veranda, screaming, "Earthquake! *Au secours*! Help! Help!" After screaming up and down the veranda a few times, she realized everyone stood looking at her as if her brains had crumbled. She was mortified. We observed her from the classroom door, thrilled.

Thereafter, when we made the floor tremble, Madame never knew whether it was for real and tried to act calm. We kept it up. She continued to tell the girls about farms, but sooner or later her nerves piled up and she rushed outside in a cold sweat. She couldn't punish us with one hundred *"Je suis* a treacherous earthquake fraud and sadistic savage," because it would be a recognition that she had swallowed our bait. It made me happy to see someone else scared.

Patricia told Madame not to worry about the tricks the twins and I played on her, because in El Topaz earthquakes came only every three months or so. Madame called la Mamota and told her to go directly to Madame Larraín and inform her she was leaving as soon as a car could take her back to Galmeda. Fine, Tía Merce said, she'd bring the real governess. It turned out that this Madame was not the one chosen by Tío Toto, the one who had a subscription to *Astronomy News* and had been a friend of the famous painter's brother. Tío Armando had decided that that one was a screwball and had taken it upon himself to bring this one instead. We didn't know how Patricia came up with such brilliant ideas.

Papi gulped his coffee while standing up. He handed back his demitasse to a serving girl. Instead of hugging me, asking me where Niceto was, or taking me with him to the park, where the grown-ups were, he rushed out, telling me to wait in my room. The front wall to our two rooms had collapsed. The little bathroom had crumbled; only the toilet was left, presiding over the calla-lily field. I sat on a step at the people's entrance, closer to the park than the vehicle's entrance, feeling like an earthquake aftermath. But it was thrilling; everything would be fixed now.

Under la Mamota's command, the houses were being assaulted by repair brigades. Broken glass, knickknacks, branches and debris disappeared, furniture pieces went back into place, cracked adobe walls closed up. Dusters, sweepers, patchers, painters and trimmers cheerfully shared what they'd been thinking right before the tremors started, and what they did next. My nose was tickled with a barrage of exotic fumes.

I got tired of waiting and went to the park. Through the trees I spotted my father by the tiled fountain. He seemed very upset. Everyone looked at him and at Tío Armando, who one minute had a neck like a fighting rooster and the next a superior goose smile.

My mother came closer to the fountain. "Of course, Julian, I'm very pleased about your job offer with a lawyer, but I have no intentions of leaving for the time being." The fountain's waterfall drowned their words, but his body was angry. She said something. He turned around and headed toward the houses, his eyes and jaw about to pop out. Everyone looked at him; some seemed amused.

Tío Juan Vicente, his patches bouncing, followed him, distressed. "Congratulations on your job, old boy, but you are truly mad. Most roads are impassable. Stay awhile, Julian."

My father didn't slow down. He jumped on the motor bicycle and left before I could catch up with them. I was greeted by the dry smell of dust settling on the road.

I swung the white chains flanking the entrance steps. Underneath, some vicious scorpion flies sucked the defeated body of a millipede with their long mouths. The millipede squirmed in pain and despair. After a while the crunching of pine needles and voices got near. "It takes an earthquake to have Julian come to see his family." "You know very well that other earthshaking news brought him here." "Ironically, he hadn't heard the last one."

Earthshaking news? And he hadn't told me? The millipede died. One of the two white chains made a rusty sob as I swung it, and swung it, and swung it.

Madame showed up at the veranda, jerking her parasol, followed by a butler with her suitcase. "I'm not surprised to be leaving so soon," she said haughtily. "Nobody in this country takes education seriously. Or anything else, for that matter." When the girls saw Madame's hat with the cherries settled in the back of Tío Popsy's car, they ran up and down the gallery a hundred times, yelling, "Je suis a happy girl!" I ran too. The German photographer promised to bring back the new Madame.

The guanaco, on the rear seat of the Walrus's car, and Tío Popsy's bald head were being removed from us. His departure didn't cause the girls any visible grief. It was a cruel blow to me, although nothing had really happened with respect to Tío Popsy. What I expected of him wasn't even clear. The maids couldn't reconcile themselves to the loss of the tasseled chauffeur. La Mamota wiped tears, waving at her Miguelito. Tía Merce waved a perfumed handkerchief, mumbling, "Good-bye, my poet, *mon beau* Eros...," then turned to my mother: "I must say, Pilar, it's all your fault for having a consort who drives everybody away with his maniac macho scenes. Well, my revenge is that now you have neither one and will have to stay here." My mother had the same face as when she'd tell Papi, "You're wrong, just wait and see." Whatever it was, my mother was always right.

That night Tía Merce and the girls went to their well-lit quarters, the only ones fully restored. My mother, Niceto and I were given rooms next to the salon, which had been cleaned but still needed repairs. I checked on my rescued foil ball under my pillow; it shone like a moon. The wall between my mother's room and ours had a crack. I could hear her breathing, awake. What was left here was the wreck of our part of the houses.

On one side of a big earthquake ditch was my mother, and on the other side my father. They refused to jump across, and I was too dumb to convince them with my begging and crying, so I decided to show them by jumping myself, but I fell inside and the ditch closed forever.

Lucha Corpi

Lucha Corpi has many voices. Her poetry, written in Spanish, deals with the experience of being an immigrant, cut off from familiar surroundings and loved ones. But for fictionalizing events in recent Chicano history, she turns to English. Born in Mexico, Corpi came to Berkeley as a student wife when she was nineteen. She earned two degrees in Comparative Literature: a B.A. from the University of California at Berkeley and an M.A. from San Francisco State University. She lives in Oakland, where she teaches English to adults in the Oakland Public Schools. Corpi has received numerous literary awards, including a National Endowment for the Arts fellowship. She is past president of the Centro Chicano de Escritores (Chicano Writers Center) and a member of the international feminist mystery novel circle, Sisters in Crime. Corpi has published two poetry collections: *Noon Words/Palabras de Mediodía* (1980) and *Variaciones sobre una tempestad/Variations on a Storm* (1990), both translated into English by Catherine Rodríguez-Nieto. The Third World Student strike at Berkeley in the late 1960s serves as the background for her first novel, *Delia's Song* (1989). Her second novel, *Eulogy for a Brown Angel*, was selected as Best Fiction for 1993 by the Multicultural Publishers Exchange. PEN/Oakland named *Eulogy* as its recipient for the Josefine Miles Award for Best Fiction. *Eulogy for a Brown Angel* opens at the height of the Chicano civil-rights movement. The tear gas sprayed at the Chicano Moratorium in Los Angeles has barely settled and Gloria Damasco, a young Chicana activist, finds a four-year old child dead on a street. Excerpted here is Chapter Two of this exciting novel.

from *Eulogy for a Brown Angel*

Lucha Corpi

Little Michael David Cisneros had been identified by his mother and father, Lillian and Michael Cisneros, about six hours after Luisa and I found him. His maternal grandmother, Otilia Juárez, who had reported him missing at 2:45 that afternoon, claimed he'd been taken from the porch of her house on Alma Avenue, about three blocks from Laguna Park.

We had found him less than two miles from Otilia Juárez's house, approximately the length of the area swept by the police during the riot as they forced the crowd from the park back towards Atlantic Park where the march had originated.

Joel had insisted on going back with me to that spot. Michael David's body was there, still with no more company than Luisa and the flies. I knelt down to fan them away so that Joel could take pictures of the scene. He didn't seem to have the same reaction I'd had when I first looked at the body, but his hands shook as he snapped photo after photo.

Luisa assured me that nothing had been disturbed. No one had passed by, for the area was quite isolated. A building rose to a height of about three floors on the side of the street where we stood. It was one of those windowless low-budget plaster fortresses where unwanted memories are stored and sometimes forgotten. Across the street, a number of small neighborhood stores had been closed because of the disturbance. Even under ordinary circumstances this was an out-of-the-way street, a good ten blocks from the main thoroughfare.

Suddenly I saw a Chicano teenager standing at the corner, smoking a cigarette and glancing furtively in our direction. He was wearing a red bandana, folded twice and tied around his head, a black leather vest, no shirt, and black pants. Just then, he turned around and I noticed that a skull with a halo above it and the word "Santos" were painted on the back of his vest. He seemed no older than eighteen, most likely a "home boy," a member of a youth gang. What was he doing here, I wondered.

Luisa told us she'd seen him cross that intersection twice since she'd been there. It was obvious the young man didn't seem disturbed by our surveillance and, after a few minutes, he began to walk in our direction. Luisa instinctively retreated behind me, and I behind Joel. Finding himself suddenly cast in the role of defender, Joel put his camera in its case and began searching his pockets for something to use as a weapon.

Two years before, after a couple of attempted rapes of students at Cal State Hayward, Luisa and I had taken a self-defense course for women and, as a reward for our good performance, we had received a small container of mace, a permit to carry it, and a whistle. I reached for the whistle and Luisa grabbed the mace from her purse. Seeing our weapons, Joel gave a sigh of relief. Then he frowned as though he recognized the young man.

"Is this guy someone you know?" I asked Joel. He shook his head.

With a slow stride, the young man approached, then stopped a few feet away from us.

"*Soy Mando,*" he said, and looked straight at Joel. But his eyes took in everything between the wall and the opposite sidewalk. He threw a quick glance at the body, then at me. "*El chavalito este. ¿Es tuyo?*"

"No," I replied, "it's not my child." This Mando was much younger than he'd seemed from a distance, not quite fifteen. Not a bad young man either, I sensed, and relaxed a little.

"The dude who brought the *chavalito* here dropped this." Mando handed me a folded newspaper clipping which had turned yellow and was already showing signs of wear at the creases. No doubt it had been kept for a long time in a wallet.

My heart beat wildly and my hands shook as I reached for the clipping. Almost automatically, I closed my eyes. I suddenly sensed the presence of a man. I saw his shadow, then a small house surrounded by tall trees. Somewhere in the area children were laughing. The scene passed and I felt nauseous, but I managed to overcome the desire to vomit. Still I had to hold on to Luisa.

My strange behavior disconcerted her, but Mando didn't pay any heed to it. Perhaps he had witnessed stranger things, seen a lot of pain or wanton cruelty in his short life. I doubted there was much left in this world that would shake him, except perhaps the death of the child. Why had he decided to give *us* the clipping? And why did I trust him? Instinctively I felt he had nothing to do with the death of the child.

"Did you see the person who did this? Can you tell us what he looked like? Joel took a small memo pad and pencil from his pocket, flipping for a blank page. Like my husband, who was also left-handed, Joel held the memo pad in the hollow of his right hand, across his chest.

"I didn't see nothing. Understand? *Nada*." Mando looked at Joel's hand, put his palms out, and took a couple of steps back.

"How do we know it wasn't you who killed this *chicanito*?" There was a double edge of contempt and defiance in Joel's voice, which surprised both Luisa and me.

Mando stood his ground across from us. His eyes moved rapidly from Joel's face to his torso and arms, locking in on the camera hanging from his neck. A wry smile began to form on Mando's lips. He spat on the ground, wiped his mouth with the back of his hand. "Later, *vato*," he said, waving a finger at Joel.

"*Cuando quieras*," Joel answered back, accepting the challenge. "Any time," he repeated.

Irritated with their childish confrontation, Luisa commanded, "Stop it! Both of you!" She looked at Joel, then added, "A child is dead. That's why we're here."

Joel's face flushed with anger, but he remained quiet. Mando turned slightly to the left, cocking his head. The only noise was the distant clattering of the waning riot. Mando moved close to me and whispered in my ear, "The dude—the one who brought the *chavalito*? He wasn't a member of the Santos. I know 'cause he was wearing a wig. *Era gabacho*. He had a scar, a *media luna*, a half-moon on his right arm."

Looking over his right shoulder, Mando began moving swiftly down the street, every muscle in his body ready for either attack or defense. I was fascinated, yet sad. A mother would be crying for him sooner than later, I thought. Not many gang members live long enough to bury their mothers.

"I'll see if I can get some more information from him," Joel said. He ran off in pursuit of Mando, who was already turning the corner when Matthew Kenyon's unmarked car stopped with a screech beside us.

Why is it that cops and tough men, young or old, have to brake or start up a car with a screech, I wondered. Do they think they are establishing turf, like moose or sea elephants?

I looked towards the corner. How had Mando known the cops were on their way? I had a feeling I would never have a chance to ask him.

So I gave my full attention to Kenyon. He was a lanky man, six feet tall, with very short red hair already graying and a pallid, freckled face. Everything seems to be fading in this man, I thought, as I focused on his Roman nose, his only feature that seemed atypical.

With Kenyon was another man who answered to the name of Todd, obviously from the crime lab since he was already marking the place where the body lay. A third man, driving a car marked with the seal of the Los Angeles County Coroner's Office, pulled up behind Kenyon's car. He, too, got out and began to examine the body.

Before questioning us, Kenyon helped Todd cordon off the area. Actually, he hardly paid any attention to us at all until Todd referred to the vomit on the sidewalk and I claimed it as mine.

"Ah, yes. Gloria Damasco?" Kenyon said. It amazed me that anyone besides Marlon Brando and Humphrey Bogart could speak without moving his upper lip in the slightest. True, it is easier to do that in English than in Spanish, because of the closeness in quality of English vowels; but Kenyon's case, next to Brando's and Bogie's, was definitely one for the books. He had soulful, expressive eyes, and perhaps because of that I expected his voice to reveal much more emotion.

"Yes," I said, "I'm Gloria Damasco."

I asked Luisa for the clipping Mando had given us and was about to hand it to Kenyon when I was seized by the same kind of fear I had felt when I had tried to take it from Mando earlier. Again, I saw the house, but this time I saw the word "park" carved into a board next to it. In my haste to get rid of the clipping before I became nauseated again, I threw it at the policeman. "Here. I think the murderer might have dropped this."

"So much for fingerprints," Todd muttered, shaking his head.

"I told you not to disturb anything." Despite his perfectly controlled tone, Kenyon's eyes showed anger, but I didn't care since I was more preoccupied with the realization that I was experiencing something out of the ordinary every time I touched that clipping. Perhaps it was only the product of what my grandmother called my "impressionable mind," her term for an imagination that could easily develop a morbid curiosity for the forbidden or the dark side of nature. Even a liking for death. These possibilities distressed me.

I must have looked pretty distraught because Kenyon invited Luisa and me to wait in his car. Since he had already taken note of our names and addresses, perhaps he simply wanted us out of the way until he had time to question us, I thought.

We got into the back seat and I lowered the window so I could hear what Todd and the Coroner were telling Kenyon, who was now putting Michael David's body on a stretcher and covering him with a cloth. "Well, Dr. D., was he strangled?"

Dr. D., whose full name, according to his tag, was Donald Dewey, nodded, then shook his head, making the detective raise an eyebrow. "Whoever did this wanted to be extra sure the boy would die. So the boy was drugged. I'm almost sure. This is all preliminary, you know. I'll have more for you in the morning."

"That soon?" Kenyon smiled. "They're putting the others in the deep freeze, huh?" He flipped the pages in his notebook and read aloud: "Rubén Salazar, Angel Díaz and Lynn Ward."

"Looks that way." Dr. Dewey picked up his equipment and headed towards the coroner's wagon. "Just buying time, I suppose. They got themselves into a real jug of *jalapeño* this time." I wondered if "they" referred to the police or to the demonstrators. Dr. Dewey came back after putting everything in the vehicle, then called Kenyon aside.

Trying not to be too conspicuous, I stuck my head out the window but I could hear only fragments of the conversation since both men were speaking in a low voice. "...Second opinion. You never know. You'll have to tell them...soon." Dr. Dewey patted Kenyon on the shoulder.

"Maybe Joel was right," I concluded. "Maybe it was a mistake to call the cops."

"Someone was going to do it anyway," Luisa said in a reassuring tone.

Todd and Kenyon picked up the stretcher and headed towards the wagon.

"Before I forget," Kenyon said to the coroner, "will you find out as much as you can about the fecal matter?"

"Try my best," Dr. Dewey answered. "Need about two weeks, though." He shook his head. "Real backlog and two lab boys just went on vacation." Kenyon nodded and waved at the coroner.

I made the sign of the cross, closed my eyes and said a silent prayer for the dead child. My eyes were burning inside my lids. I opened them again and looked at my watch. It was now 5:15. The sun was still beating down on the streets and the sirens of ambulances and patrol cars were still wailing in the distance.

I had aged years in just a few hours. By sundown, I would be as old as Mando.

For Rubén Salazar, Angel Gilberto Díaz, and Lynn Ward there was no going home, and the horror that would make the living toss and turn for many nights was of little consequence to them now. They were lying on autopsy slabs, side by side, waiting for their bodies to be opened and drained of blood, their insides emptied, then studied and tested to determine the exact cause of death.

In time, perhaps someone would admit to the real cause of what happened that day. But perhaps we already knew the name of the insidious disease that had claimed three, perhaps four, more lives that late August afternoon.

More than ever before, I wanted to go home, to hold my daughter and seek the comfort of Darío's arms. But the spirit of the dead child had taken hold of me. I would no longer be able to go about my life without feeling his presence in me.

Beatriz de la Garza

Beatriz de la Garza was born in northern Mexico but moved to Laredo, Texas, when she was eight years old. While still in high school, she began to write fiction and to win recognition for her short stories, including two awards from *Seventeen Magazine*. She received a B.A., an M.A. and a Ph.D. in Spanish from the University of Texas in Austin, where she also graduated from the School of Law. De la Garza is a licensed attorney and has worked both in the academic and the legal fields. In 1988 she was elected to serve on the Board of Education of Austin, Texas. Presently she serves as the President of the Board of Trustees of the Austin Independent School District. In 1994 she published her first collection of short fiction, *The Candy Vendor's Boy and Other Stories. Publishers Weekly* (February 21, 1994) referred to De la Garza as "an important new voice in Mexican-American literature (one who can stand alongside such better-known practitioners as Rudolfo Anaya and Miguel Méndez) and leaves readers wanting to hear more of her rooted, feminine voices." Her stories are situated in Texas and take place in many eras, but the problems the people encounter reflect a calculated consistency to racism. "Margarita" is a story from her recent collection.

Margarita

Beatriz de la Garza

Margo had always hated the time and place in which she was born. She did not really wish she had been born someone else since she had a warm, affectionate family of whom she was truly fond, but if she could have transported them all to Paris or New York, or if they could have all lived in fifteenth-century Spain, or been French or Anglo-Saxon whenever, she would have been happy. But to have been born in South Texas, to live in Texas in 1964, in the shadow of the Alamo—both the building and the movie—as a Mexican, that was to be one of fortune's stepchildren.

She was born Margarita Ancira, twenty years earlier, in Los Encinos, Texas, population 3,000, a place as dry and dusty as only a small town in South Texas can be. Hot for at least nine months out of the year, bitterly cold for perhaps two weeks in the winter, and always gray. Gray blowing dust, gray thorny brush that belied the town's name, since not a solitary oak was to be found. Except for the sky; the sky was always blue. The horizon in Los Encinos was infinite, and that limitless expanse of blue crushed Margo with a sense of desolation. Margo would pray for rain, as did her father, but for different reasons. Rain, mist, fog, would have blurred the horizon, broken the monotony, but the rain, like change, seldom came.

At the moment Margo also hated the time and place she was in, although she was not in Los Encinos. She was in the library of the University of Texas at 7:30 on a June evening, too late to find a place at a study table. She circled around the room in a miserable mood, hating herself for arriving late, hating herself for being at the University of Texas at all. She felt so adventuresome, enrolling for the summer session at the big university instead of spending the summer with her family at Los Encinos. They were hurt that she had not chosen to be with them for the summer after having spent the spring in Europe, studying in Madrid and traveling through Spain and France with a dozen other girls from Sacred Heart College in San Antonio, where she would be a senior in the fall.

Margo had the notion when she enrolled for the summer session that she would perhaps transfer to the university in the fall for good. She felt she was ready for a big coed school, where the students came from all parts of the state, even from all parts of the country, and even from abroad. She had become impatient with Sacred Heart, a school so much like home, where her friendships were confined to nice, Catholic girls, mainly from South Texas and northern Mexico, her dates circumscribed by the limits of her classmates' male relations, all nice Catholic boys. How she wished now, as she looked at the blank stares and indifferent faces, that she was back home, relating her European experiences to her family and making plans to return to Sacred Heart in the fall.

She thought she saw a vacant place at a table for two at the back of the room. She hurried towards it; she must find a place to study for her test on Milton tomorrow. She arrived, almost breathless in her hurry, and set down her books in front of the empty chair, across from a bowed blond head. Eyes as blue and as cold as a mountain lake looked into hers as the occupant raised his head and said curtly, "That place is taken."

Margo felt her face grow hot, and she knew it must be glowing red. She stood immobile for a second or two. Perhaps he noticed her embarrassment because he added, "Sorry," but as an afterthought.

She clutched her books to her chest as if they could shield her from rebuffs and hurried away from the table and out of the room. She was so stupid, so incredibly stupid, she lashed out at herself. Two weeks she had been in this place, and she had not made a single friend. Why did she ever come here? People didn't give her the time of day; they walked past her on the street, on the campus, as though she wasn't there. And now they wouldn't even let her sit at a library table.

She had not even made friends with her roommate, who was never in the room. Perhaps that was a good thing now. She could go back to her room and study, safe in the knowledge that she would be alone and without interruptions. But something in her balked at this solution. It was like falling off a horse; you had to get back on it again. If she went back to her room now, she knew that she would not dare come back to the library tomorrow, and she would end up being a prisoner in her room, afraid to go out and risk any more rebuffs like tonight's. She walked up the stairs to the next floor and circled that room till she came to a table with a couple on one side and a girl on the other, next to an empty chair. She set down her books and pulled out the chair, almost defiantly. Nobody looked up or even gave a sign that they noticed her. She sat down, opened her book, and read Milton.

She was back at the dorm by ten, amply making curfew, and had already showered and was in her nightclothes when her roommate came rushing in, muttering about how the old hag of the housemother almost locked her out. Margo's roommate had a hectic social life, was seldom in for meals, sometimes checking out for the evening, and had, so far, been away every weekend. Margo, however, did not know what her roommate did, or where she went, or if she ever went to class. Her name was Consuelo, and, though she was friendly to Margo, she was never in long enough for Margo to have learned anything about her.

When Margo first arrived at the dorm, before the summer session started, she found the two names posted on the door to the room: "Consuelo and Margo." She had groaned to herself, "Consuelo—another girl from back home. Will I never meet anybody else?" But Consuelo Wolf was not from back home, that much Margo had learned almost immediately. Consuelo was tall, between five-ten and five-eleven, and slender, with beautiful pale white skin, jet black hair, worn piled up high on her head, and enormous blue eyes fringed by dark eyelashes and black eyeliner.

No, Consuelo was nothing like the girls she had grown up with in Los Encinos, nor like Teresita, her roommate at Sacred Heart. Teresita was from the border, plump and friendly, and with those remnants of tomboyishness that Margo had come to associate with girls who had attended convent school since childhood. Teresita was not pretty or glamorous by any means, but Margo envied her, nonetheless. She envied Teresita's complete unself-consciousness and self-assurance. Whether a girl—or even a boy—was from Texas or Tennessee, whether the name was Smith or Sánchez, it was all the same to Teresita. Of course, Teresita's family was well off, being in the import-export business in Laredo, as well as having land, which, no doubt, went a long way to making her self-assured. But Margo's family was not so different from Teresita's in that respect.

Margo's mother's family, the large García clan, still held on to the lands of their forefathers, and of others' forefathers, who had been imprudent or profligate. The Garcías were boisterous, aggressive, and the shrewdest cattlemen and traders. Margo's father, Rafael Ancira, was a quiet man, in contrast to his wife's family, with a good head for accounting and business. Unlike his wife and her family, whose roots went back some two hundred years in Texas, he was a relative newcomer, having arrived from Mexico in 1930 as a young man of eighteen, penniless but with a good education. The young Rafael had gone to work as a clerk in his future father-in-law's feed store and had eventually married the daughter of the family. He had stayed on in Los Encinos where, together with his wife's brothers, he soon acquired the local cattle auction house, which, in addition to the feed store and the cattle, made them all a comfortable living and paid Margo's college tuition and European trip without any hardship. Yet, with all this, Margo hated what she was, or what people thought she was—a Mexican in Texas. Born and bred in the place, with a pedigree longer than the life of the state, but still an outsider.

The following evening found Margo at the library before seven. She had hurried through dinner to make sure she would find a place to study on the second floor of the library, which, for some reason, suited her better than the others. It was an attempt, she realized, to make something familiar and more her own if she went to the same spot every evening. Tonight it was the French Symbolists that she had to read, and she set about doing so with the minimum use of the dictionary. To her gratified surprise, she was able to read the poetry almost fluently and with enjoyment. At nine, she allowed herself a break, first spreading out her books as a sign of possession, lest someone think the place had been vacated. "What a place," she thought, "you spend all your waking hours fighting just to keep what you have."

She went out in the lobby to smoke a cigarette. She had taken up smoking that spring in Europe, not because she particularly enjoyed it, but because it gave one something to do with the hands. Better than standing about with arms hanging limply at the sides. She allowed herself only one cigarette per break and was almost at the end of it when the rude acquaintance from the previous evening approached the bench she was sitting on, apparently to use the same standing ashtray she was using. He did not seem to recognize her, and she looked down, busying herself in stubbing out her cigarette. As she reached for her handbag in preparation for leaving, she looked up and noticed that he was staring at her with a puzzled expression. "Don't I know you from somewhere?" he asked.

She felt her face grow hot again, but, as her grandmother would say, the blood of the Garcías showed through, and her embarrassment turned to anger.

"I don't know. Do I know you?"

"I'm sorry. I guess that sounded rude. It's just that I thought I had met you somewhere. Maybe from a class. My name is Mike," he continued, oblivious to the fact that she stood, handbag over her shoulder, in a pose of arrested departure.

"No, I don't think we have any classes together. I'm only taking two, and I'm new here."

"Oh, where did you transfer from? Or, are you a freshman?"

"I'm here for summer school; I don't know if I'll transfer. I'm a junior, will be a senior next fall."

He looked at her expectantly, waiting for her to finish furnishing the information requested, and she found that politeness demanded that she do so. "The reason we are always at a disadvantage with the Gringos," she had heard her father say once with exasperation, "is that we were brought up to be polite. They always take advantage of that." Margo understood now what her father meant.

"I came here from Sacred Heart in San Antonio," she finally said, as she started to walk away.

"Wait, how about going out to get some coffee?" She noticed that people at the university always said they were going for coffee, even if they drank Cokes.

She shook her head, "I've got a report due tomorrow."

"Okay, how about tomorrow? I'll meet you here at nine-thirty." She was beginning to shake her head again when he added, "All right, I've just realized it was you I was rude to last night. I'm sorry. I was having a hard time with my chemistry, and I had promised to save a seat for a friend. But I am sorry."

Politeness was truly her undoing, she thought, but how to refuse an apology. She smiled, "Fine. Nine-thirty," and started to walk away for the second time.

"Wait," he said. "What's your name?"

"Margo," and this time she left.

She arrived at nine-thirty-five, and he was already waiting. During the day she had told herself he would probably not show up, but if he did appear, she would go to the student union with him or at most to the coffee shop across the street from the campus, nowhere else. She did not know him; she did not know the city. Her mother's warnings about picking up strange men came echoing back. He suggested the coffee shop across the street, saying only oddballs frequented the union at this time of evening. It was fine with her.

He got coffee for both of them, and they sat at a booth at the back of the long room. At this time of the evening the place was still fairly full, but nothing like in the mornings when all the tables were crowded with large, noisy groups from the sororities and fraternities who excluded anyone else, as Margo had found out the first week of school.

He sat across from her and suddenly smiled at her. It was as if a bright light had illuminated his face from within, she noticed, with a tightening at her throat. A mirror on the opposite wall reflected them both. He was not so different from her. They were both slender, the same delicate bones—too delicate for him, perhaps?—the same fine mouth and straight nose. His eyes were clear blue, though, transparent as the mountain lakes she had been reminded of before, his hair a pale blond, where both eyes and hair were a rich brown in her, his skin of the fairness that burns rather than tans, while hers was already a warm gold. The differences were obviously greater than the similarities, she concluded.

"And now tell me all about yourself. Why are you here, what is your major, what do you want to do?"

She told him again about going to Sacred Heart, and she thought for a moment that he was going to give her that knowing smile she sometimes got from non-Catholic boys when she told them that she attended a Catholic girls' college. One air force lieutenant she had gone out with in San Antonio—her one Anglo date—had kept asking her if the nuns really shaved their heads and if Catholic-school girls were really as wild as people said. This time there were no questions about the nuns, so she told him, instead, that she had a double major in French and Spanish and a minor in English, and that she would probably end up being a teacher, although perhaps she might be a translator or an interpreter.

He told her his name was Mike Anderson, and he was a pre-med major. His father was a doctor, and he had two younger sisters. What a coincidence, she had two younger brothers. He was having a hard time with organic chemistry. She had never taken it, never would, if she could help it. What was her last name? Margo's heart sank to her stomach at the question that had ended friendships before. There was no sense in muttering it; she would only have to repeat it. She would not disguise it with an English-sounding pronunciation; she had too much pride for that.

"Ancira," she said clearly. It was not a common name.

"Ancira," he repeated, but not sounding like her. "Is that Italian or Spanish?"

"Spanish."

"Are you Spanish?"

Margo winced at the euphemism. In Texas there were no Spaniards, or very few, but people thought they were sparing your feelings if they called you Spanish instead of Mexican. Margo's father understood the sentiment behind the words (although they only considered your feelings if your skin was light), but he always set them straight. "No," Don Rafael would say courteously, "we have been in the New World some three or four hundred years, even longer, we have Indian blood; Spain was too long ago." But Margo was not made of the same stuff as her father, so when asked if she was Spanish, she said, "Yes."

Mike's family lived on the Gulf Coast, just outside Corpus Christi, and he had never been to Los Encinos, although he knew that it was about a hundred miles away from Corpus Christi. What a coincidence, both of them being from South Texas. Mike's grandparents had come to South Texas in the 1920's and had started farming irrigated land. His mother, though, was born in Minnesota, where the older Andersons had come from originally.

Mike talked and Margo listened to him, superimposing on his face that of another boy named Mike she had met in her senior year in high school. His name was Mike Perkins, and he had had a round, friendly face that freckled in the sun. Blond hair and blue eyes, too. Mike Perkins had come to Los Encinos his senior year in high school. His father worked for the oil company that had a big field near Los Encinos. Because the family moved often, Mike had gone to three different high schools. They were, what Margo's father called, itinerants.

That Mike had not known how things stood in Los Encinos. He had asked Margo to help him in geometry class and, then to repay her the favor, he had asked her to go for a Coke with him and his friends after school. Mike's friends of course, were the Anglo kids from whom came the football captain and the homecoming queen, the ones that, although in the minority, ran things in the school, just as their parents did in the town and in the county. Margo had gone with them to the Dairy Queen for a Coke, and they were not unfriendly to her, but she could see the raised eyebrows. Margo's friends, too, had asked themselves what she was doing with the Gringos.

She looked at her watch. It was ten-twenty, four years later. She needed to rush to make curfew by ten-thirty. She thanked Mike for the coffee and said she must run. He protested that they had to continue their conversation, and said he would meet her again the following evening, same place, same time.

He did, and they went back to the same table and resumed the conversation from the night before. He told her his father was an obstetrician and had delivered thousands of babies in South Texas. He did a lot of charity work among the Mexicans. Mike, as the only son, was expected to follow in his father's footsteps. But Mike wasn't sure he wanted his father's life—out at all hours, seldom having a meal or an evening at home.

She told him about her father, a quiet, courtly man, who seemed out of place in the rough cattle country. He had come to Texas in 1930, during the strife that had erupted between the Mexican government and the Catholic Church. Her father had been a young seminarian, not quite eighteen years old, but active in protesting anticlerical government policies. He had to flee the country, fearing for his life. He took the wrong train out of Monterrey and ended up in rural South Texas, instead of in San Antonio, where he had intended to go.

Mike seemed fascinated. Her father was a priest! No, no, she corrected him. Her father had never been a priest. He was studying to be a priest, but he had to drop out of the seminary. He had never taken any vows. That explained why Margo went to Catholic school; her family must be very religious. Not particularly, she told him. They went to church on Sunday and kept the major holy days, but that was not the reason she attended Sacred Heart. It was only with the Sisters that her parents would allow her to live away from home. It had been very difficult to convince them to let her come to Austin for summer school. Even here she was supposed to stay at the Catholic dorm, but it was full. It was not so much a question of being religious as it was of being a proper, well-brought-up young lady. Not like the Americans, as her mother would say, who are ill-bred and immoral. But she did not say this. It would not have been polite.

The conversation ended, again, with her impending curfew, but this time he walked with her back to her dorm. The dorm was actually a large privately owned boarding house that prided itself in the personal attention and genteel atmosphere it offered girls. It was not inexpensive, but the food was good and the maid service prompt. Mike remarked that he knew a girl who lived in Margo's dorm, and she asked him who it was, but the name meant nothing to her. It turned out that the girl was away for the summer, anyway. She felt a pang of wistfulness and envy. Who was he when he was among his friends, in his own environment and not in isolation, as she knew him? It must be wonderful, she thought, to belong in the world, to feel the country was yours, to never question who you were. Under the porch light that was already flashing, he smiled his brilliant smile at her again, and they shook hands in the friendliest manner as they said good night.

That Friday evening, she watched television with two other girls in the dorm who did not have dates either. Saturday she was in the midst of washing her hair and polishing her nails when she was called to the telephone. She still did not know people well enough for anyone to call her, she thought. It was Mike. He was apologetic. He knew it was very late, but, perhaps, if she was free, would she like to go to a movie? Her pride debated with her inclination, and her pride lost. She accepted. He said he would pick her up at seven.

It was their first formal date, she told herself, and as such, special. She finished drying her hair and set it briefly on large rollers before going through her closet to decide on what to wear. She settled on a sleeveless linen shift, pale ivory like her skin and guaranteed to bring out the rich cocoa brown of her hair and eyes. She made up her face carefully, outlining her eyes with a soft brown pencil, but nothing like Consuelo would. The air force lieutenant she had dated in San Antonio had once remarked that he found the Catholic school girls' ladylike appearance "damned sexy." And as she finished dressing—crisp dress, pale stockings and beige pumps—and combed out her hair, shining and fresh-smelling, flipping up at the ends, almost touching her shoulders, she knew that the Sisters at Sacred Heart would find nothing to complain about in her appearance. They insisted on turning out ladies, as well as scholars, at Sacred Heart, but they also turned out sexy girls, as the lieutenant had said.

She was ready by six-thirty, and when he arrived at quarter to seven, she was already waiting for him in the parlor. They smiled shyly at each other, a little embarrassed at their own eagerness. But underneath his embarrassment she could also sense admiration.

"You look so nice," he finally said. "I thought we could walk to campus, go to the union movie, but if you'd rather not, I'll go get my car and we could go somewhere else. I'm not dressed for it, but I could go get a coat, and we could go dancing."

She was touched by his apology, but she didn't think he was inappropriately dressed—neat khaki trousers and freshly ironed madras shirt. She said he looked fine and going to the union movie was fine, too. And, since campus was only four blocks away, they would walk.

They were forty-five minutes early for the next feature, so they sat out on the student union patio, under large oak trees, and talked. She had come to love their talks, the probing of each other's personality, the gradual discovery of each other's lives and pasts, a little at a time, almost like a mental strip tease.

He told her about his grandparents, the Minnesota farmers who had come to South Texas with little money but much determination and had bought land to farm. At first they had relied on the unreliable rains, but soon they had put in irrigation wells, which allowed them to produce more and to buy more land. Then oil was discovered on the land in the 1940's, and by the end of the decade, the older Andersons had moved from their modest farmhouse to a fine house on Ocean Drive, overlooking the Bay of Corpus Christi. Mike's grandfather had been dead for ten years, and his oldest son, Mike's uncle Bob, now lived in the house with his family. His widowed grandmother also lived with them. Mike recalled the family barbecues on the lawn when the four Anderson children, Mike's uncle Bob, Mike's father, and two aunts and their children—twelve cousins in all—and their friends would gather for family holidays. On the Fourth of July and Labor Day, in particular, they would have barbecues. The children would play out on the lawn under the indulgent eyes of the grownups until the late afternoon became night, and then they played and laughed under the moonlight with the constant roar of the waves in the background.

Margo repressed a sigh as she listened to this description. She could see it all, just like a movie, a Hollywood movie with blond all-American actors, or maybe it was like "Giant," with the Anglo-Saxon masters and the Mexican serfs.

He was talking now about picnics on the beach. Did she go to the beach often?

Should she tell him about the time her mother and grandmother had gone to Corpus Christi to see a doctor for her grandmother's arthritis?

Her father did not like for his wife to drive those desolate country roads, so the two women had taken the bus to town. They had come back tight-lipped and pale, and Margo's mother had said, her voice shaking in hardly more than a whisper, that they had been forced to sit at the back of the bus, where the "coloreds" sat, as the driver said.

No, Margo felt the anecdote would not be conducive to a lighthearted exchange of reminiscences. It would probably embarrass him, and it certainly humiliated her.

Mike was already on to another question. "Margo," he was musing, "that's an unusual name. I've never known a girl named Margo before. Is it your real name or a nickname?"

It was the name she had chosen as preferable to "Margarita," which was as Mexican as the drink, but superior to "Margie," the name given to her by the teachers at the Los Encinos Sam Houston High School.

"It's short for Margot," she fibbed. "That was my grandmother's name—my father's mother, who was part French." Her grandmother had been another Margarita, and the story of the French soldier who had come with the Emperor Maximilian and who had stayed behind in Mexico and married an Ancira girl had never been confirmed.

Margo realized that in the game of mental strip tease they might play, she hid more than she revealed. But was he hiding anything? Did he have a girlfriend, for example, who had left him free for the summer? She did not ask any questions, though; she might not have liked the answers.

They sat through the movie, which was a comedy with a European location. Their shoulders brushed against each other until, in the time-honored fashion, he rested his arm on the back of the seat and then gradually let it slide down until it came to rest around her shoulders. Afterwards, they walked out of the theater hand in hand, and he suggested they stop at a coffee house recently opened. The place was lighted by dim red and blue bulbs, the light made more hazy by the thick smoke in the room. People sat on large cushions on the floor and listened to a Black blues singer while waitresses brought cups of espresso or cappuccino. She thought that he seemed out of place in these bohemian surroundings and wondered why he had brought her there.

They left the coffee house close to midnight and walked slowly back to her dorm, still hand in hand. He did not say good night upon arriving, however, but lingered on the veranda and gradually steered her to the short leg of the "L" of the porch, where the light was dim. He kissed her there and, without much prompting, she kissed him too. They began hesitantly, but soon their fervor increased. The intensity of her reaction surprised her. She suddenly realized how much she had been wanting him to kiss her. They remained pressed close against each other, their mouths searching eagerly for each other's lips, ears, throat, any non-forbidden part of the anatomy, until the porch lights flickered to signal curfew. Mike pulled himself away and said good night.

They fell into the habit of meeting every evening at the library and going for coffee afterwards. He would then walk her to the dorm where they would say good night on the dark end of the porch. She began to feel that they had always been together.

One evening, contrary to her custom, Consuelo was present at dinner. After the meal, she further surprised Margo by going upstairs with her and announcing that she was going to the library. As Margo was obviously preparing to do the same, she felt compelled to invite her roommate to join her. All the way to the library, while Consuelo chatted about people and places Margo did not know, Margo mentally kicked herself. She did not want Consuelo along when she was going to meet Mike. Consuelo was not a girl easily overlooked. Mike would probably fall for her. For once, the French Symbolists did not hold her attention as she read her assignment.

Shortly before ten, she saw Mike walk into the room; he knew where she usually sat and now scanned the room in her direction. When he caught her eye, he waved and gestured that he would be in the lobby. Margo gathered her books and, walking a fine line between inclination and courtesy, informed Consuelo that she was going to meet a friend.

"I think I'll go too," said Consuelo, stifling a yawn. Margo emerged from the reading room trailed by her roommate. There was nothing to be done but perform the introductions. Mike graciously included Consuelo in the invitation to go for coffee. Margo's heart sank further when Consuelo accepted.

They walked across the street to the coffee shop and, once inside, found their usual table. Mike went to the serving counter and got three coffees for them, and then and there began the usual preliminary conversation of what is your major and where are you from. Margo found, to her surprise—for she had yet to have a sustained conversation with her roommate—that Consuelo was majoring in anthropology, at least for the time being, and minoring in archeology. "Ruins fascinate me, you know. Especially in South America. Machu Picchu and the Incas. It's a good excuse to travel, anyway." Her father, she continued, was an engineer with an international construction company, and her family had lived in or visited most parts of the world. What other fascinating revelations Consuelo would have made were left in suspense when she spied three foreign students walking in the door and interrupted her conversation to wave at them.

"That's Ahmad," she said, "let me go say hello to him." After a few minutes of talking to the trio, she walked with them to a table.

Mike and Margo had fallen silent, watching the encounter, and now Mike finally said, "She seems to know them very well. Some girls really go for those desert jocks. Must be all the money they have." Margo was not sure whether to be glad that Consuelo was thus dismissed from his thoughts or to feel uneasy at his reason for doing so.

When it came time to leave, Margo caught Consuelo's attention and gestured, pointing to the door to convey their intention. Consuelo walked back to the table and picked up her books. "I'll catch up with you later at the dorm. I'm staying a little longer. We're having a fabulous conversation."

The following evening Consuelo reverted to her routine, and Margo went alone to the library to meet Mike. They studied together and, at nine-thirty, in unison, they put away their books and went for their usual nightcap. Later, as he walked her to the dorm, he asked her if she thought Consuelo would like to go out with his friend Jay. They could double date on Saturday evening. Margo had seen Jay only once, and briefly. She remembered him as tall and wiry, with dark hair and eyes and very black eyebrows. She thought him somewhat sardonic, but she could not be sure from the brief introduction. Margo agreed, somewhat tentatively, to broach the subject to Consuelo, which she did when Consuelo made her last minute arrival. To Margo's surprise, Consuelo agreed readily.

Saturday, at seven o'clock in the evening, the sun still lingered, streaking the western sky with orange where it met the hills. The late June heat rose from the pavement as a reminder of the day it had been—and would be again on Sunday. By seven, Consuelo and Margo were ready. Consuelo wore a bold print of cobalt and green, a sleeveless shift that barely reached her knees, and Margo a pale yellow sundress. Both were festive but casual, since they did not know what the evening plans would be. "We'll probably go drink beer," Consuelo prophesied, "or buy a bottle and go somewhere for setups and dancing." She was right the first time.

Mike and Jay had decided to go to Scholz's beer garden, a traditional watering hole for politicians and students for almost a hundred years. Margo, who did not like beer, kept from saying so. She had heard so much about the place that she was glad to be finally going there, even if she had to nurse one beer all night long.

As they approached the beer garden, Mike, who was driving, turned to her and said. "I hope you girls have ID's. They're pretty sticky about them here."

Margo shook her head. "I'm not twenty-one yet."

"Well, neither am I," said Consuelo, "but that's no problem, I've got an ID."

Margo turned around to look at her roommate, and Consuelo hastened to explain: "My older sister and I look very much alike. She's out of the country, and she let me use her driver's license."

Jay, who had been silent after the introductions, put his arm around Consuelo's shoulders and gave her a quick squeeze, saying, "A girl after my own heart."

At Scholz's they sat in metal folding chairs around a picnic table under large pecan trees while waiters ran constantly from the bar, which was inside (and undoubtedly air conditioned, thought Margo longingly), carrying two or three heavy pitchers of beer at a time. They ordered a pitcher and three glasses and a Coke for Margo. All the tables seemed to be full. Conversation was difficult over the babble of voices, music amplified by loudspeakers concealed in the tree branches and the incongruous sound of falling bowling pins. Mike explained that there was a bowling alley next door.

During a lull in the music, while Consuelo remarked on the absurdity of not being able to get a mixed drink in Texas and of having to lug a bottle of bourbon in a brown paper bag when you went to a club, the talk turned to bars they had visited. Margo found herself the center of conversation when she mentioned the only bar she had ever been in, the Cadillac Bar in Nuevo Laredo. It was a hit; Mike had been there too. It was a real classic, he said. They had Pancho Villa's saddle there. Everybody should visit the Cadillac Bar, at least once. The drinks were great too. Yeah, Jay said, almost snickering, there was nothing like going to Mexico for a good time. Why don't we go to Mexico? Margo was momentarily puzzled until she realized that when these people said Mexico, they did not mean Mexico City, as people back home did. They were talking about the border.

Soon Consuelo was asking, "Well, why don't we go to Mexico?" Mike said, "Fine, but when?" And then the logical answer presented itself: "Next weekend, of course. It's the Fourth of July."

"We would have to leave on Friday." Mike was already planning. "Friday afternoon at the latest. It's about a four-hour trip, to drive to Laredo, I mean. We don't want to spend the Fourth on the road."

Margo's thoughts were racing. Could she go? Would her parents approve of the trip? No, of course not, they would never approve of an overnight trip, a weekend with three people they had never met, two of whom were of the opposite sex. She didn't have to tell her parents about it, but what if they found out? How? An accident on the road, or she might run into somebody they knew. . . .

"What about it, Margo, will you go?" Mike was asking.

"I don't know . . . I don't know if I can." Inspiration came suddenly. "I have a paper due on Monday after the Fourth."

"We'll be back on Sunday afternoon. And we'll make sure you start working on it tomorrow. C'mon, honey, say you'll go." He put his arm around her waist and gave her a gentle squeeze to punctuate his plea.

"I'd like to," she said softly, "let me see if I can."

"It's a date," Jay pronounced, pounding on the table. "We'll go to Mexico. We'll have a great time—get drunk, visit Boys' Town."

Margo started to shake her head and began to say she probably couldn't go, but Mike gave her another hug and told her not to mind Jay, he was just being an ass. Jay would behave himself, Mike would make sure of it.

On the way back to the dorm, Mike held her hand in between shifting gears. He smiled at her and whispered, "Say yes. I don't want to go without you," which made her knees go weak. Consuelo and Jay nuzzled in the back seat and generally acted as if they were very glad they had met. They kissed good-night, briefly, because the curfew light was already flashing. Margo promised Mike she would let him know her decision about the trip by Wednesday, at the latest.

On Tuesday evening he told her that he loved her while he kissed her. She was not even sure he had realized what he was saying, but that answered the question for her. The following evening, as soon as she saw him in the library, she told him she had decided to go to the border with them after all. The next thing was to devise the strategy to keep her parents from accidentally finding out about the trip.

They left Friday at mid-afternoon because Margo had stubbornly refused to cut her one o'clock class. By three o'clock she and Consuelo were signed out for the weekend, giving the name of a friend of Consuelo's parents as their destination.

"She lives in San Antonio," Consuelo explained, "and I always go there on weekends. I mean, I always put down that there is where I am going."

They rode in Mike's car, a 1960 Chevrolet Impala, which had been his mother's until she had gotten a Cadillac for her birthday and given the Impala to him. The car windows were rolled down, by necessity, and the wind that rushed in burned their faces like the exhaust from a furnace. Mike told them his mother's new car had a wonderful air conditioner. His next car would be air conditioned, for sure. They were all in high spirits, though, joking and singing along with the Beatles on the car radio, even as they were driving into the sun.

After they came out of San Antonio, they left behind the rolling pasture land and the hills that had followed them in the distance. Oaks and elms now gave way to stunted mesquites and an occasional huisache. This was the beginning of the brush country, thick, thorny scrub brush, as impenetrable as a forest in parts. Where the brush had been cleared by some enterprising rancher, though, the grass was singed brown. They passed small towns, some of only a few hundred people and with one paved street—the one they were on. They all reminded Margo of Los Encinos. At one of them, midway between Austin and Laredo, they stopped for gasoline and Cokes. As they stood out on the pavement, while the attendant filled up the car, Jay began to complain. What a God-forsaken place, how could people live here, nothing but heat and dust, not even a single shade tree. He knew it was hot all over Texas, but this must be the deepest pit in hell.

"Now you know why the Spaniards called this country the *brazada*," said Margo, surprising herself for remembering this little-known fact of Texas history. She did not know where she had heard it, probably from her grandmother.

"What's that? You know I don't speak the lingo," Jay responded suspiciously.

"It means a bed of coals."

"You can say that again. We should have let Mexico have it. You might as well be in Mexico, anyway, the way they chatter down here." This was directed at the two service-station attendants who carried on their conversation in Spanish, oblivious to their audience. Margo was glad when Mike got his change, and they got back in the car. She had not wanted another lecture about "this is America, why don't they speak American." Consuelo, Margo noted, had yet to complain about the heat or the scenery; this perhaps portended well for her future as an anthropologist or archeologist.

It was not yet eight o'clock and even hotter still when they reached Laredo. They debated whether to eat first or find a motel with reasonably priced rooms. They drove up and down the main street, passing some ten or twelve motels before stopping at one that looked clean but modest. They were not in luck; it was full. They began again, and with the same results. By the fourth or fifth try they began to get anxious.

"It's the Fourth of July weekend, and we're full of tourists. They're having bullfights across the river on Sunday," one reception clerk finally explained. Margo told herself she should have thought of that. Jay was definitely on edge now, and even Consuelo began to fret, complaining that she was dying for a shower.

They must have tried all ten or twelve motels without any luck. However, at one of them, among the least prepossessing, the clerk said he was holding two rooms, but the people had not arrived yet. If they were not checked in by nine, he would let them have the rooms. Mike suggested they go get something to eat in the meantime; they would be back before nine, he assured the clerk. They had hamburgers and Cokes at a restaurant some two blocks away from the motel they had dubbed "The Last

Chance." The restaurant was air-conditioned, and the cool air revived them briefly. At ten to nine, while they were still eating, Mike said he would just drive back to the motel to be sure he was there at nine so the clerk wouldn't give the rooms to somebody else.

He left, and Jay and Consuelo soon fell into a rather querulous conversation while Margo relived her main concern of "what if my parents found out." Mike returned some thirty minutes later to a cold, half-eaten hamburger, but he had two room keys. They paid for the food and got back in the car for the two-block drive. After Mike had parked the car, and they were unloading their bags, Consuelo turned to Margo and said, "I'll toss you to see who gets the shower first. After that it's sleep for me." Margo smiled at her, genuinely liking her for the first time and mentally thanking her for so swiftly answering the awkward questions that hung unasked of who would sleep with whom.

"Yes," she agreed, "I'm falling asleep on my feet," and they left the men to go find their own room.

The next morning they went back to the same restaurant, and while they ate breakfast they discussed the itinerary for the day. They were going across the river, to Mexico, as Jay said, there was no question of that, but what to do first once there. They decided to let Margo be their guide, and her suggestion was that they should park the car close to the International Bridge, on the U.S. side, and then walk across the bridge. They would avoid the heavy Saturday traffic that way.

They left the car by the old plaza around which the city had been founded in the mid-eighteenth century and set out walking. A soft breeze was blowing, alleviating the heat of the sun that was already beating down on them, and the walk was not unpleasant. The bridge was crowded with pedestrians and cars going in both directions. Consuelo and Jay stopped, along with other tourists, midway across the bridge to look down at the Rio Grande, flowing sluggishly below, but Margo averted her eyes. Heights gave her a queasy feeling. Jay was disappointed; the river was not very big, contrary to its name. Margo explained that there was a large dam upstream that controlled the flow.

At last they were across, barely nodding at the customs guard in passing, and the sounds and smells that Margo always associated with Mexican towns surrounded them. The smells were a mixture, she thought, of diesel fumes and the fruits from the street-vendors' carts. The sounds were a confused din of shouts from the newspaper boys and lottery-ticket vendors, car horns and the music blaring from record shops. She suggested that they walk up and down the main street first, just looking and window shopping. The sidewalks were crowded with tourists and vendors offering them everything from cheap leather wallets to paintings of bullfighters done on velvet. Margo told them they should wait before buying anything until they had looked in the shops.

By lunch time, they must have visited every shop on a five- or six-block stretch, Margo thought. They went to the Cadillac Bar, which Jay had wanted to visit from the moment they had set foot in Nuevo Laredo. It was full of tourists, and they had a long wait before they were served, but the food was good. They had seafood and roast *cabrito*, and Margo introduced them to the Ramos Gin Fizz, which tasted like a milk shake with a kick. They duly admired the saddle that was prominently displayed and that was reputed to have belonged to Pancho Villa. They read about the origins of the Cadillac Bar in New Orleans and about how, with the advent of Prohibition, it had relocated in Nuevo Laredo.

It was after two o'clock when they emerged from the cool dimness of the bar, and the sun beat down on them as if it had a personal grudge against them. They agreed that they would probably get sunstroke if they tried walking back to the car then, so they ambled down the main street again, staying under the awnings of the shops for shade as much as possible until they came to a plaza. It was relatively empty at that hour, only mad dogs and Americans being out in the sun then, and they sat on a marble bench under the largest tree. They carried on a fitful, disjointed conversation, punctuated by fanning themselves with a magazine they had found lying on the bench. Consuelo pointed out a café on the other side of the plaza, and they decided to stop suffering and go in there and drink something. Mike said he was thirsty, but didn't want to drink the water, so Consuelo told him to drink beer. This was some of the best beer in the world.

They sat there some two hours, drinking beer. Margo drank lemonade, to Mike's consternation; he kept saying the water in it would probably make her sick. She assured him she always drank lemonade "if the place looked clean." Jay had discovered the merits of Mexican beer, and they eventually left the café to get him to stop drinking it. He weaved slightly as he walked, and Margo began to worry about making it back to the car. They finally hit upon the idea of riding back to the bridge in one of the horse-drawn buggies that carried tourists around downtown. Jay's spirits soared, and he enjoyed himself immensely, waving at pedestrians and cars and insisting loudly that he wanted to visit Boys' Town and see the whores. Margo, afraid that the driver would take him seriously, hastened to assure the man that they wanted to go to the bridge. She began to wish they had never made the trip, and only prayed they would get across the bridge and through customs safely and without further embarrassment. As they walked across the bridge, though, Jay seemed relatively subdued, merely trying on the same stale joke on the customs guard: when asked if they were bringing back any liquor, he replied, patting his stomach and grinning, "Only inside." The guard had heard it before; he waved them on without a smile.

As they drove back to the motel, Jay asked if there would be any fireworks that evening.

"I don't think so," said Margo. "I've never heard of them having fireworks on the Fourth of July. New Year's Eve, yes."

"We might as well be in a foreign country. It's un-American to have bullfights for the Fourth of July but no fireworks," Jay continued to grumble.

"It's probably too hot for fireworks," Consuelo said calmly. "Anyway, the bullfights are tomorrow—and they are in another country. Mexico is across the river."

"You couldn't tell it. It all looks the same on both sides of the river."

"Why don't we go swimming when we get back to the motel?" Consuelo had stepped into the role of peacemaker, thought Margo, and she was glad of it.

As soon as they were back at the motel, Consuelo and Jay got into their swimsuits and jumped in the pool, calling to Margo and Mike to join them. Margo shook her head; she had not even brought a swimsuit. Instead, she went to her room and stepped into the shower. Her head was beginning to ache from the heat, but the water trickling down her face and the back of her neck was soothing. She felt much better by the time she had dried off and put on fresh clothes.

Margo went outside and watched the two in the pool until Mike joined her, soon afterwards. He had obviously showered and changed and had that air of crispness that seldom left him. Margo looked up affectionately at him. He motioned her to sit next to him on a glider under the scanty shade of a palm tree. They sat in silence, his arm draped around the back of the glider, his fingertips lightly touching her bare shoulder, until the other two, laughing and breathless, came out of the water and dried themselves. The sun was going down, and the heat now was more like the afterglow of embers rather than the fire raining down from above it was earlier. Jay and Consuelo spread out their towels on a small patch of grass at Mike and Margo's feet and lay on their backs. Margo caught fragments of their conversation, disjointed words only, and thought she must be dozing off.

Consuelo finally sat up and announced she was going back to her room to get out of her wet suit. Jay reached up and pulled her down again, and there followed a playful struggle that threatened to leave Consuelo with only a fragment of her swimsuit on. She finally got up and, rather crossly, told Jay to keep his paws off her and walked away. He scrambled up and ran after her. Soon they were out of sight as they rounded the corner that hid their rooms from view of the pool.

A family with three children then came out and took over the pool. In spite of their shouts, Margo felt herself lulled by the gentle rocking motion of the glider as Mike pushed it back with his foot. A feeling of contentment spread over her as they sat there, their bodies only brushing against each other.

She was glad the day was over; she doubted that she was particularly suited to be a tourist guide. Jay had been difficult, but, still, she was glad to be there with Mike in what was more her natural environment than Austin. It was good to hear Spanish again and to speak it. She remembered the first time she was away from home without her family. It was a school trip for a convention in West Texas. Three days of hearing and speaking only English. She told her best friend afterwards that her face muscles had begun to ache with the strain of smiling all the time and speaking nothing but English. At school they were forbidden to speak Spanish, received demerits (even whippings in grade school) if they were caught doing so, but after school Spanish was all they spoke. It was only when she went away to college that she realized that she spoke "with an accent," as someone put it. She immediately started working on shedding the telltale "Spanish accent," asking her speech teacher for help, imposing on herself the discipline of speaking only English, even with Teresita. Her face muscles became used to it.

It occurred to her that Consuelo and Jay had been gone much longer than necessary to change out of their wet swimsuits, and she wondered if they were in one of the rooms together. A mixture of excitement and unease went through her, and she thought, "I wish I knew how to handle this like Consuelo," and then, "I'm happy just as we are now," for Mike was speaking softly and had his arm around her.

She did not pay close attention to everything he said; it was enough that she could hear his voice and feel him next to her. He was talking about being out in the open sea in the Gulf, fishing; about his uncle Bob's boat, the Yacht Club, sailing in the bay. She wondered what her father would think of this Mike; this Mike was not an itinerant. Her mother would be pleased that he was going to study to be a doctor. Should she ask him home for Thanksgiving? She would be home for Labor Day. Would he be sailing out in the bay then? Perhaps he could come home to see her during the Labor Day weekend. He was telling her now about his mother, how crazy she was about taking photographs, especially at family gatherings. Last year on the Fourth of July they had had a cookout in the backyard, by the pool. She was taking pictures and wanted the perfect pose—he and his sisters and his father, all together. His mother kept walking backwards and looking through the lens until she fell, backwards, in the water, the deep end. The water was above her head, but she held up the camera as high as she could, kept it dry. They helped her out, laughing at her all the time. She was furious with them for laughing at her, but finally she ended up laughing, too, really good, a sport. Margo smiled, too, at the image she conjured of his mother, wet and angry but blond and beautiful, like her son.

"She sounds like a lot of fun," she heard herself saying, drawling out the words lazily. "I can't wait to meet her."

"Oh, but I couldn't take you home. . . ." His words hung in the air for several seconds before she felt their impact like a solid blow. She went very still then, and felt as if she were shrinking in size by the minute. It was just like the time when she had first met him. The harsh words had come out of him without apology, and then the delayed contriteness followed. She felt the muscles in his arms contract now with tension, and then he said, sounding more regretful than contrite, though, "Oh, God, I am sorry. I didn't mean it like that . . ."

But how did he mean it, she asked herself as she got up, slowly and stiffly, like an old woman. "I am going back to my room. The heat is giving me a headache," she said in a tight, flat voice, unlike her own. He made as if to stop her, but then he let his arm fall, and she walked away, holding herself very straight.

As she approached her room, the thought struck her that Jay and Consuelo might be in there. "I'll kick them out if I have to," she thought, savagely, for she had begun to feel her face burning red, and anger shook her body. The room was empty, though, cool and dark. The two must be next door in the dim, cool room, on fresh-smelling sheets . . . She closed the door behind her and shot the deadbolt.

She walked into the bathroom and turned on the light, peering at herself in the mirror above the sink. The color was draining from her face, leaving only a red flush on her throat. She slammed her hand against the edge of the sink. "You stupid fool, you damned, stupid fool. And to think I was falling for him," she whispered, still looking at herself in the mirror. "And to think I would have probably gone to bed with him," was her next thought. She felt a cold sweat break out all over her body, and nausea gripped her for a minute. "Oh, God, it was that damned seafood," she said and, turning on the cold tap, stuck her head under the water. She felt better after a minute or so. Finally, she straightened up and, taking a towel, rubbed her face and her hair dry.

"And now what are you going to do? What am I to do? Those two will eventually emerge from the passion pit next door, and what will I do then? I just couldn't bear to face them. I must think of a way to get away, get back to Austin without them." In moments of crisis, Margo resorted to these conversations with herself. "But how, where can I go?" She could not see herself walking, overnight bag in hand, to another hotel. She had enough money to ride the bus back to Austin tomorrow, but what to do tonight? She was staring at the telephone when inspiration struck. Teresita, of course.

She dialed Teresita's number and knocked on the table, hoping it was wood and not plastic. A young voice answered in Spanish. Yes, Teresita was home, wait a minute, said Teresita's sister. Margo was so relieved, she sat down weakly on the bed. A minute went by while she gripped the receiver anxiously, and then there was Teresita, exclaiming with delight, what a wonderful surprise, haven't seen you since last Christmas, where are you, you've got to come over. Margo explained. She had come down for the weekend with these other three people from Austin, a boy and a couple who wanted to see the border, but—here she hesitated—she didn't like the way they were acting. Ah, Teresita understood, give them an inch and they take a yard. Why didn't Margo come and stay with her; she would come and pick her up, where was she? Margo told her.

Hastily, Margo stuffed her belongings into the overnight bag and then, unable to shake off ingrained courtesy, wrote a short note to Consuelo, explaining that she was going to visit an old roommate and would return to Austin on her own. She propped up the note against Consuelo's makeup case, certain that it would be found there. Some twenty minutes later Teresita was knocking at the door. Margo opened it cautiously, then, seeing who it was, grabbed her bag and quietly closed the door behind her. Anyone seeing her would assume she was sneaking out without paying the bill, which in a way she was, she thought.

Teresita wanted to talk before they went home, since her brothers and their girlfriends were there, and it was a madhouse. They went to a drive-in restaurant and asked for curb service. They both ordered Cokes, and Margo, suddenly realizing she had not had supper, also ordered a cheese sandwich. "So, now tell me about Europe. What about tonight, though, did you end up with some creep; was he lecherous?" Mike's face, his voice, his scent were suddenly before Margo once more, and something wrenched inside her, but then she felt her cheeks burning again, as if he had left the imprint of a slap on her face. She told Teresita that she had described the situation just right, and then went on to tell her about the spring semester in Europe.

As they drove home through the dark streets, Margo tasted humiliation, bitter as gall, rising again in her throat, in a surge of self-loathing. The next moment, though, she thought, "I can't go on like this for the rest of my life. I am who I am. If others don't like me, it's their problem. I belong in this country as much as they do, down here even more than they because we were here first."

She wondered what explanation Mike would eventually give to Jay for her sudden departure. The García blood reasserted itself in her then, shoving aside good manners, and she thought, "I don't care what they think about my leaving tonight. If they don't like it, screw them." She repressed an impulse to giggle. "Or better still: don't screw them."

They left the car in the driveway and went into the house, where all the lights were blazing. Teresita's younger sister and older brother were sprawled out on the living room floor, playing Monopoly, while her parents sat around the dining table, conversing with their son's fiancée. There were handshakes and hugs as Margo greeted each one, until Teresita broke in and said that she wanted to show Margo to the guest bedroom.

Margo followed her friend up the stairs, but before they reached the room, she asked, "Do you mind if I call my parents? I'll make it collect."

As Margo heard the telephone ringing, one hundred miles away, she felt a great desire to cry. "Not now," she told herself, and then she heard the soft sound of her father's voice saying, "Hello" in an accent that was noticeable even in his surroundings.

"Papá," she said, "this is Margarita."

Margarita Engle

Margarita Engle was born and raised in Los Angeles. Her father, an artist, traveled in the late 1940s to the picturesque town of Trinidad, Cuba, where he met and married Margarita's mother. As a child, and again in 1991 and 1992, Engle visited relatives in Cuba. A botanist who achieved tenure as a professor of agronomy at California State Polytechnic University, Engle has won numerous scientific honors. She has worked as an irrigation specialist in Southern California, and has published many non-fiction articles related to plants and soil science. Since 1982, her opinion columns have been syndicated by the Hispanic Link News Service to over two hundred newspapers. Engle has published short stories in various reviews, among them *Nuestro*, *The Americas Review*, *Chiricú* and *Revista Interamericana*. Her haikus, published in the United States and Japan, have received awards from the Haiku Society of America and the American Poetry Association. *Singing to Cuba* (1993), Engle's first novel, is based on her recent travels to Cuba as a journalist. The central character in the novel encounters much more than she expected, as her family's dilemma becomes her own personal drama, cast in a modern mystery play of good versus evil. "Bonaventura and the Fifteen Sisters" and "Cimarrón," the two short stories included here, are based on Engle's research into Afro-Cuban history. They are imbued with a particularly Cuban tradition of *lo real maravilloso* in which the natural setting appears to be "magical." In actuality, what we have is a realistic rendition of the island's fauna and flora filtered through the oral traditions of a racially plural society. Engle lives in Fallbrook, California, with her husband and two children.

Buenaventura and the Fifteen Sisters

Margarita Engle

Imagine fifteen sisters shut inside their house for three years.

"Another rebellion is starting," their father told them, "and the tyrant's police are swarming like bees. You must not leave the house for any reason."

The sisters crept to the windows after their father left for work. They gazed beyond the grillwork of iron bars at the hordes of young men running and shouting. They backed away from the windows and listened only to the sounds inside the house. They listened to the whistling island breeze and the distant chants of vendors.

The sisters quarreled at first, but soon they realized that they were all alone and needed each other.

From the streets came the clash of *machetes* and the clamor of riots and rebellion.

Their father went to work every day. Their brothers disappeared. Their mother sat all alone, as far from any window as she could get, embroidering unicorns and castles and maidens with hair the color of wheat.

"Singing is now forbidden," their father announced one day after work. "Do not sing in this house under any circumstances."

So the chants of vendors ended. The dark woman who used to stop at the windows every day still came with her orange mamey, purple *caimitillo*, tiny red bananas, immense *fruta bomba*. But she no longer sang praises for her fruit, no longer danced at the window to make the sisters notice her. She no longer reminded the sisters of sunshine and wilderness. She seemed a different person.

Knowing that they should not sing, the fifteen sisters began to remember the words of old songs.

"Ugly people can't come to my party," they sang.

"I'm going away with you, dark Saint," they sang, "if you'll carry me to eternity. You want to leave me here. I don't want to suffer. With you I'll go my Saint, even though it means I have to die."

Their father heard them one day as he was coming home from work, and he was furious.

"No singing!" he reiterated, but the fifteen sisters soon forgot.

"Mamá, I want to know, where do the singers come from?" they sang. "Mamá, they come from the hills, Mamá, they sing in the flatlands. I find them very gallant, and I want to get to know them."

When their father came home and found all fifteen sisters singing robustly, he warned and pleaded.

"On every block the bodies of troubadours are rotting," he insisted.

Their father worked as a reader in a cigar factory, so the fifteen sisters decided to demand that he entertain them with stories.

"All day," he told them, "I have to read melancholy poems and silly love stories to foolish girls who cannot work without daydreaming at the same time. So much do they care about these stories that they are willing to each pay me a percentage of their wages just to read to them and keep them from being bored. But how difficult they are! If I forget to express with sufficient passion the flowery praises of some dashing hero, they threaten to replace me. So you see, it's not an easy job telling stories to women, and now you expect me to come home and start it all over again, reading to another pack of amazons?

"Ask Buenaventura to tell you her stories. You'll see, she knows much better stories than I do and, what's more, hers are all true."

So the fifteen sisters approached the maid, a very old, very fat, very black woman who had been born a slave and had been named for a ray of hope that good luck might be just around the corner. The maid had been in the sisters' house for thirty years, but she had seldom spoken to anyone.

When they had pestered her for three months, she said, "Well, okay, I'll tell you a story about a pilgrimage I once made to the shrine of the Miraculous Virgin of Copper. The shrine has windows of colored glass, and the floor and walls are carved from thirteen different kinds of marble from thirteen different faraway lands. The Virgin herself is a miracle, only as tall as the length of a man's arm. She is plump and very pretty, with her dress so fancy, all decorated with jewels. On her head is a golden crown, and she wears an enormous diamond in her hair.

"They fished her from the sea. Imagine, an Indian and an African and a Spaniard, very long ago.

"She stands on a silver pillar, and in one hand she holds a cross with an emerald this big, and in the other a little baby Jesus.

"At her feet are all the gifts she has ever received—butterflies, guns, hats, braids from the heads of little girls, ribbons, medals, shoes.

"I had nothing to give at all, so that is when I broke off this tooth, see, and left it there for her glory.

Buenaventura laughed. "Despite my name," she said, "I haven't had much good fortune."

The sisters, who were not satisfied with the story, but had no other hope for entertaining themselves, escorted the old woman out of the kitchen and into the parlor, where they sat her in their father's most comfortable chair and presented her with a silk fan. They gave her a glass of sherry, and one of their father's best cigars.

So she told them about the *ñáñigos* of the wild backlands, voodoo priests who could swallow flaming candles and smokey cigars.

"They used to walk across a bed of fire," she told the fifteen sisters. "They danced like this, with knives twirling over their heads."

She rose from her chair to show them the dance. Kitchen knives went spinning through the air and clattered against the tables and floor.

"They acted so wild, you would never have known they were just ordinary slaves. When they ate fire, they ate up the evil spirits too, and that is how the spirits were destroyed. Later the *ñáñigos* would calm down and receive their payment in beads and feathers, which they traded for coins. Some were able to save enough coins to buy their freedom, and they started to save more, to buy the freedom of their children."

Every day became a journey into the old woman's past. The fifteen sisters asked for dances too, and ceremonies, and rituals, and mysterious beliefs.

"Once," Buenaventura told them, "there was a man who was in love with a monkey. He had been away to sea, and to the North Pole, and Africa, and Spain, and China. Everywhere he went he killed ferocious animals and stuffed them and sent them to museums in great cities. When he returned, all he had was one live monkey and the skin of a snow leopard. He spread the skin on the floor of his room and sat with the monkey in the window, looking out, just looking out, all day. When a fruit vendor came by dancing and singing, he would buy a banana for the monkey, or a mango. One of the vendors was a wild young brown woman who fell in love with him, but he would have nothing to do with her. He seemed very happy just as he was, with his monkey friend and the ghost of that dangerous creature waiting there on his floor.

"There's no explaining men," the old woman told the sisters. "I wouldn't even want to share my room with a gentle ghost, and certainly not with the spirit of something angry.

"And the strange part is," Buenaventura swore, "that when the monkey started to have babies, the babies looked just like the man. That's when they ran him out of town. Drowned him and his evil monkeys in the river."

The sisters gasped, and Buenaventura went on about the river. "It's the same river where some slaves once went swimming, and what do you think they found there? A treasure chest. The chest was only this big, no bigger than a footstool, but so filled with jewels and gold that it was too heavy to lift. It was inside a rotten boat, the wood so old it was practically not there anymore, just the ghost of a boat. But the chest was still perfect, not a scratch. It was still locked, and not a key to be found anywhere.

"Next to the chest they found a sword with the shape of a crown engraved on one side of the handle, and the shape of a cross on the other. And the strange part is, no one has ever opened that chest. Over a hundred years have passed, and there are many of us who know just where to find the chest, but not one who would dare open it, not one who wants the trouble it holds inside."

The fifteen sisters begged the maid to teach them how to carve baseballs from mahogany branches, how to swing a *machete*, how to sacrifice a rooster, how to sneak up on a shark or an alligator.

After they learned these skills, they then got it into their heads to learn every dance the old woman knew, and poor Buenaventura had to show them the same steps over and over.

"We may not be allowed to sing," they repeated every day, "but no one has said that we cannot dance."

So the old woman got up every morning and instead of polishing tables and mopping floors, she showed the sisters how to shuffle three steps forward, then rest.

"This is how the old Africans danced when they were chained together," she told the sisters. "In a long line, one, two, three, clunk, the chain falls. The chain was their drum."

The sisters found an old rope in the courtyard, and chained themselves together. One, two, three, shoosh. The sound of the rope was soft, but with it they were able to imagine dancing in the first *conga* line.

They danced past their mother in her chair, and past the barred windows where men could be spotted running in scattered groups, hurling rocks and bottles, singing defiant anthems.

When their father was home, they did not attempt to dance.

"Between dancing and singing," he said, "there is very little difference."

In the evenings the sisters cooked for Buenaventura and they served her and fanned her and made her tell them more stories.

"One very wealthy family," she told them, "always had a very dark secret. Long ago the patriarch of the family died without having married the mother of his children, a dance hall girl who ran away when she found that babies were too much for her.

"So when the patriarch died, all his grown sons and daughters propped the corpse up in its bed, and they went out and found a young woman who agreed to stand by the bedside and accept the dead man's hand in marriage. The priest who performed the ceremony was near-sighted to start with, and since the old man was obviously sick, the priest made a point of not looking too close, and that way no one ever knew the difference. The church was satisfied, and the sons and daughters became legitimate heirs of a married man, and each collected a share of the old man's fortune."

"That story," said the father of the fifteen sisters, "is better than any I have ever read to the girls at the cigar factory. If I could read them a story that good, they would give me a bonus and a few extra cigars as well."

The next day he left for work precisely at dawn as he always did, his black umbrella poised to defend himself against a whirl of rocks and *machetes*.

As the doors closed behind him, the din and furor of another day's fighting resumed. Through the barred windows all fifteen sisters heard and memorized the words of the new anthem.

"This," said the maid when she received her command, "is how you dance the *rumba*. The man puffs himself up, like this, very proud, and becomes a rooster in the barnyard. The woman is a coy hen. He ruffles his feathers and pursues her, like this. She dances away, dragging her tail, like this."

That morning not a single lace bedspread or embroidered tablecloth survived. Soon the sisters were wrapped in curtains and shawls, ruffles massed along their arms, fabric fluffed in back to make long tails resembling feathers.

It was very hard to dance without singing, but the sisters became masters of a silent *rumba*, no words, no clicking jawbone of a mule, no rattles or polished sticks or ceramic jugs or serrated gourds, no drums at all.

For more than a year they practiced this dance. Sometimes a rebel would pass close to the window, dodging from house to house, hugging the walls and singing about freedom.

If he happened to glance in the window, he would see a very fat, very old black woman swinging her hips, surrounded by fifteen wheat-colored girls all decorated with layers of lace and ruffles.

The rebel would rest his weapons and think how long it had been since he had seen so many smiles, such a shaking of hips and rolling of shoulders.

And he would wonder if he had grown deaf from the shooting and angry shouts, because certainly there was not a sound to be heard, not a trace of music, not a single enticing lyric.

Then the sound of approaching police would send him scurrying like some jungle creature, and soon the girls were dancing without any audience, just dancing for the joy of movement, for the freedom of being like chickens in a barnyard.

Most of the next two years were spent in preparation for the end of the rebellion, which, the girls had decided, must come sooner or later, just as all the previous rebellions against other tyrants had ended sooner or later.

"All year," the maid had explained, "we were slaves. But we always knew that one day out of every year would be Kings' Day, and we knew that every year on Kings' Day we would be released to dance in the carnival. Some of us would return to the *barracoons* after carnival, and some would not. So we spent every spare minute of every year making our costumes and practicing our steps. And when it came time for the *comparsas*, we were something to see! The masks we wore, the headdresses, the flowers and candelabras, the dances! How we could dance when there was only one chance in a year!

"Some of us would dress up as scorpions, others as *majá* snakes, with real snakes looped around our necks! The cane-cutters danced with their *machetes* flailing, and the washerwoman with their wooden tubs, and some of the dancers dressed as runaway *cimarrones*, and others as masters with whips and dogs. There were *Mambises* fighting against Spaniards, and Arabs who sold Africans, and Spanish aristocrats in velvet coats and powdered wigs, ladies with hooped skirts and black faces. There were gardener girls in short skirts, carrying baskets of flowers, and there I was too, the *Sultana*.

"This is how I sang," the old woman whispered. "Good-bye, Mamá, good-bye, Papá, I'm off to the harem, and I'll not be home until morning."

The fifteen sisters giggled so much that the maid was afraid their mother would emerge from her trance to discipline them, or the police would hear and carry them all away to the dungeons which were so many and so deep that surely they could never be filled.

"Shhh," the old woman warned, "the Spaniards are gone, but their prisons are still here."

There seemed no end to the rebellion. Riots one day, ambushes, battles, public executions, military displays, speeches, marches, notices posted on every door, and then the riots all over again, accompanied by the hilarity of forbidden singing.

None of the brothers ever returned.

The father found his way home by a different route every day; this way one day to avoid a barricade, another way the next day to bypass a burning warehouse, still another the third day to escape interrogation at a checkpoint manned by brutes armed with clubs and bayonets.

As abruptly as it had started, it was over. One day the streets were deserted, littered with corpses and the rubble of destruction. By dawn the next day people were emerging from their houses, singing a new anthem openly. They moved in groups of thousands and ten thousands, beating oil-can drums, shaking gourd rattles, old men clicking their canes against the cobblestone streets, women clattering their wooden cooking spoons against pots and pans.

And the sisters came out dancing. They came out wearing lace and feathers, ruffles and masks, headdresses and velvet, flounces and silver, satin and flowers, beads and shells.

Buenaventura danced with them, holding her silk fan in one hand and one of their father's best cigars in the other.

People watched them and said, "They dance as if they have been dreaming of this moment all their lives."

The fifteen sisters danced the way people dance when they know they will never be able to dance again. They matched their steps to the drumbeat of the new anthem, to the clacking of wild parrots in a long-ago jungle, to the rattle of cookware and the chanting of fire-eaters.

The crowd grew to a hundred thousand, then half a million, then a full million. Every soul on the island was in the streets singing, priests, rebels, children, prisoners emerging from the dungeons, police set free from their duties, housewives longing for the freedom to walk to market.

And in the crowd of one million, only Buenaventura could explain why the dance of the fifteen sisters was so enchanting and so wild.

Cimarrón

Benito was not the kind of slave who could stand at the head of the master's table during a meal, waving a palm frond to keep flies away from the food. He was not the type who could return to work after a vicious whipping.

He was a runaway from birth, *un cimarrón*, a man who could live alone in the forest for ten years at a stretch, without speaking, without a woman, without dancing, without playing at *monte* or *tejo*, without measuring the length of his penis against those of the others, without the freedom to whistle out loud for fear of being discovered by the *rancheadores* and their sniffing dogs.

He ate wild pigs and the smoked meat of *jutías*. His coffee was a brew of roasted *guanina* leaves, and his beer was *chanchanchara*, a drink of his own invention, a special mixture of wild honey and the cold water from a mountain stream. He rolled the leaves of the macaw-tree into tight little cigarettes. He cured his fevers with *cuajaní* berries, and cleansed his eyes with dew collected on *itamo* leaves.

He walked to pass the time. He walked all day, every day. He imagined himself whistling. He slept. He knew when it was mid-day, because he could hear distant *fotutos* from the *rancherías*, the calls of conch shell trumpets women used to bring their men home for dinner.

He missed the red scarves of the women, and their shiny black bodies, and the juice of sugarcane, and the sound of the *marímbula* which was like a voice from another world, and the drums and dances, the *yuka* dance, with its different sizes of drums, *caja*, *mula*, *cachimbo*, *catá*, the wild swooping movements of the women, who were like birds ready to fly.

He did not miss the *mayombé* with its evil *nganga*, the vast kettle where a slave could place the earth from beneath a master's footsteps and wait for vengeance, wait while the life of the master ebbed away. Only the Africans could get away with magic and not get caught. Only the old ones knew how to do it right. It was good to be away from the masters and the *chicherekú*, that little man with the big head who sneaked up on people and squealed like a rat. It was good to be away from the brawls between Lucumí and Congolese, but not from the palm-bark taverns. Sleeping in the cave, or out on the leaves, that was the way to sleep, not in the padlocked *barracoon* where all two hundred slaves slept in rows facing each other, haunted by fleas and ticks and witches, in a long room dreamed up in a master's nightmare, endless walls with no openings, mud floors just as bad in the dry season as in the rainy.

He never saw his mother, so young had he been sold away. But from the other women he knew that the ticks were the ghosts of Indians killed by the masters, ghosts which would never let go. The Chinese ghosts, on the other hand, abandoned the island as quickly as they could and returned to their own land. And the Congolese could come and go as they wished, dead or alive, because they could turn themselves into animals and move about unnoticed. The Canary Islanders could fly, and if they all decided to leave at once, a plantation might be left without any slaves at all.

Whenever Benito suspected that a witch might be loose in the forest, he dropped a mustard seed in its path. With so much as one little mustard seed on the ground, any passing witch would be rooted to the spot and would never move again.

Sometimes at night, when he was walking to pass the time, Benito would be followed by a devilish light. Sometimes a flame leaped from his right arm, but it did not frighten him too much because only a flame in the left arm meant certain death.

Benito refused to think. For ten years he refused to think. He walked, and when he was hungry, and the scent of African food hung along the edge of the forest, he did not let himself think about the food, or the drums, or the ceremonies. But the smell of the food was itself like a thought. It had form, *calalú* of okra, leaves of *guengeré, tamales* of *harina de amalá, masango* maize, *cheketé* of orange juice and vinegar, *ochinchín* of watercress, greens, almonds and prawns—food for the statues of the gods of the old ones.

Only an African could eat and still find his dinner intact in the pot when he was through. This was a trick the Congolese liked to play on Spaniards to make them furious. An African could not be starved.

Benito could not starve either. With wild pigs and *jutías* and *malanga* and yams and wild herbs and wild honey, there was always more food in the forest than one man could eat.

Of all the witches, only the barn-owl was Benito's friend. She flew in a ray of light, and when she passed, she called *chua chua, kui kui,* and Benito knew she was warning him that bounty hunters were entering the forest with their dogs.

He stayed near the mouth of the cave, and to him it was a real mouth, the black mouth of an animal.

In the mouth of the animal there were *majase* snakes which could knock you down with their breath. When you were asleep, a snake could suck out all your blood. The old ones said that when one of these snakes had lived a thousand years, suddenly it would turn into a sea creature and disappear into the ocean.

The bat droppings were soft to walk on, soft as the feather beds of the masters. The bats were free beings. No one would dare kill a bat. Bats always moved together, and in the darkness they had long conversations with each other. When they spoke the sound was *chui, chui, chui.*

The bats did not care if Benito lived or died. That is why he preferred the forest. When it was safe, he stayed in the forest, walking. He slept under a shelter of banana leaves, and the forest birds took care of him. Some of the birds were ghosts, but others were just birds. The *cotunto* was a cruel bird. It followed Benito about, repeating "you, you, you, you, you ate the cheese up".

The *sijú* only followed him at night; all it said to him was *cus, cus, cuuus.*

The sparrow, who was a Spaniard, followed him by day. Any slave who killed a sparrow would be whipped for harming a creature native to Spain.

The *tocororo* was green with a scarlet sash across its breast, just like the sash of the King of Spain. On a plantation the overseer would have whipped Benito just for looking at a *tocororo.* In the forest they were his companions, and the song of the King's messenger was Benito's favorite, a song which was like a secret, very short, *co, co, co, co, co.*

Only the *ciguapa* was intolerable. It whistled like a man, and every time it whistled, Benito was fooled, over and over. There was no telling the whistle of a *ciguapa* from the whistle of a hunter.

The trees also had their songs. The big white leaves of one would say *uch, uch, ui, ui, uch, uch,* and the soft green ones of another would say *shh, shh, shh, shh.* The prickly ones said *tut, tut, tut.*

The shadow of a tree was a safe place to hide in the daytime, but Benito knew better than to step on the shadow of a tree at night, because the shadow, to a tree, was like the soul to a man, and if you disturb a soul at night when the body is sleeping, the soul might not return to the body.

This was the way of sleep. The soul would wander far away from the body, to a place where it could be free. The soul did this to rest itself because, without rest, life would be unbearable.

When Benito allowed himself to stop walking, he would think about the soul, and he did not want to think. When thoughts about the color of a soul came, he shivered. The shivering was a warning from God. Take care of yourself, the shiver meant. Then Benito knew he needed to pray and leave the color of souls to God.

No human being could be trusted. Not even one's own heart could be trusted. One day it could stop pounding. Only the soul could be trusted, and the guardian angel who helped you decide the direction of your next step: this way toward the cave, or that way to the edge of the forest to smell the food.

Tuesdays were the most dreaded of days, but in the forest there was no way to tell whether it was Tuesday. If he heard the evil whistle of the *ciguapa*, Benito figured it was Tuesday.

When he had been alone for ten years, Benito suddenly heard shouting. The noise went on and on, and grew closer and faded, and took form.

He stepped out of the cave and followed the sun straight out of the forest, past the swamp where it was so easy to catch the suckling wild pigs.

He reached the road and stepped onto it. And on the road he saw an old African woman carrying two babies.

He followed the woman, and when he was close enough he asked, "Is it true?"

"Yes," she answered, "it is true," and she kept walking down the road, singing to the children.

Benito walked behind her, thinking. He was free now, to speak, to whistle, to be seen. He could kill a *tocororo*.

Later he would find that the masters refused to change and the whipping did not stop. He would fight in a war to free the Cubans from Spain, and after the war he would be treated the same as before.

Later he would live to be 105 years old and many wars would have come and gone, and he would still find himself laboring in the cane fields as before.

Later the young people of all colors would come to him and say, "Tell us what it was like," and they would invite him to speak at the University.

And he would do with them just what he did with the masters now, pass them walking on the road, refuse to answer their commands, and whistle as he tossed pebbles at the sparrows.

Photo © Copyright 1994 by Georgia McInnis

Paula María Espinosa

Paula María Espinosa was born into a family of German-Jewish and Sephardic origins. After attending Harvard University and receiving her B.S. degree in Comparative Literature from Columbia University, she lived in Paris where she met and married the Chilean writer and photographer Mario Espinosa Wellman. In Paris, she and Mario knew many members of the Latin American expatriate community. It is said that Julio Cortázar based his short story "Las babas del diablo" on Mario; this story in turn inspired Antonioni's film "Blow-up." Paula María's command of French resulted in a translation, with an introduction, of George Sand's *Lélia*, published by Indiana University Press in 1978. She later received her M.A. in Creative Writing from San Francisco State University, where for her thesis she submitted the manuscript for *Longing*. This novel, published in Berkeley in 1986, is semi-autobiographical and takes place on three continents. It is a brilliant yet disturbing novel of the tragedy of an ex-patriate who can no longer fit in with his former society nor function successfully in his new country. The Greek translation of *Longing* will appear in 1995. Espinosa's new provocative novel, *Dark Plums*, will be published in 1995 by Arte Público Press. In this novel, she captures the essence of distinctive communities in various parts of the United States, as her outer-directed heroine encounters the people who will affect the pattern of her life. In her fiction, Espinosa is concerned with human communication on a level that transcends the norms permitted by society. She lives in the San Francisco Bay Area with her husband and is presently working on a novel about *marranos* or hidden Jews in fifteenth-century Spain.

Three Day Flight

Paula María Espinosa

We were giving a party on Sunday after New Year's. Things were noisy and hectic when the phone rang, so I picked up the receiver in the bedroom. A man on the other end said, "I'm calling from Twenty-nine Palms about Antonio Ramírez..."

I knew immediately that Antonio had died.

It was the county coroner. He told me that Antonio's body had been found this morning, that he had been dead for several days, and that Isabel was next of kin. Antonio had evidently fallen on the kitchen floor and suffered a lot of internal bleeding. Blackish stools indicated liver disorder. Esther, who lived with him, found him like that when she returned from visiting relatives in Los Angeles.

The coroner wanted someone to pay for the burial costs. He said that, as there was apparently no will, Isabel would inherit what there was—a car, a little money in a bank account. He asked me to call Esther, who was very upset.

I called and told her that Isabel and I would come down to Twenty-nine Palms to sign the needed forms and take care of the burial. She said that she couldn't handle it, that she had no money. She repeated that Antonio's car was now legally Isabel's.

On Tuesday morning we flew down. It was cold, dark, and foggy in the suburb where we lived outside of San Francisco with Saul, my new husband, and with his two daughters. We left Saul's crowded, gloomy house, the windows tinted to keep in heat, the carpets with swirling patterns that I had not been able to persuade him to change. We left one of Saul's daughters on the phone, looking upset. Her mother called her daughters daily to rage at them. We left Saul's world where things are done brusquely and on schedule. In Saul's house I have stories to tell, but no one wants to listen to the stories of my life. Our needs are overshadowed by the immense needs of the children. Saul listens impassively, barely seeming to hear. He works hard as a research scientist. In his way he loves me. I feel closely bound with him. He lends me the money to fly down. When I become sentimental, Saul says, "What is this crap? The man raped his own daughter and never paid child support. It will be a hard trip for Isabel."

"I wish you were going, too. I need your common sense."

Despite what Antonio did to Isabel, I love him. I always did love him. I could not help it. I told Isabel that no one can dictate what we feel. I grieve over what he did to her. I grieve that it happened. I grieve for her and for him, and I love him. For the next three days I have crying jags and a splitting headache.

℘

The desert town was fifty or sixty miles out of Palm Springs. I rented a car at the airport and we drove for an hour, arriving at Esther's around one in the afternoon. She lived in a small stucco house off a dirt road. The desert stretched behind the house to the slope of a mountain. Here the sky was an intense blue, with no trace of smog, and the light was golden. Sandy earth was dotted with vegetation—small cactus plants, shrubs, and Joshua trees.

Esther was a few inches shorter than me, and attractive, despite the fact that her face was puffy from weeping. She had dark, wavy hair, dark eyes, olive skin, and she wore a long cotton robe with a sweater over it for warmth. "I have to go and teach in Riverside at four this afternoon, and I won't be home until Monday," she said.

"We need you here. We have to leave by Thursday. We've spent five-hundred dollars on plane tickets," I said.

Finally she agreed to stay, and she called up the school to say she would not be teaching that night.

She told us that drug users used to live here, before she and Antonio moved in. The walls had been painted in lurid colors, with drawings of dismembered bodies. However, just across the dirt road was an Indian burial ground with two stone-marked graves, and Antonio had felt the ground was holy. She and Antonio started to rebuild the house, but it was too much for them. So she got a HEW loan and called in professional builders. Nevertheless, she and Antonio did an enormous amount of work. "He put in a toilet that never worked right," she said.

I laughed. "When I was living with him, he put in a toilet that never worked right either."

They had installed new brick walls. New ceilings. Replastered. Rewired. Plumbed. Painted. It took them two years. They had struggled and worked. Time flowed on, with endless conversations, endless detours and delays, and Antonio's trips to the liquor store.

"He wanted to die," Esther said. "He wouldn't stop drinking. I tried to get him to stop. I tried to get him to a doctor. He wouldn't go. He had been sick a long time."

Esther's house was painted white and decorated with taste. There were was dark antique furniture—a wardrobe, a book case, a dining table. A mahogany chandelier hung over the table. Two couches faced each other in the narrow living room. The windows were hung with bamboo blinds, except in the bedroom, where Esther had sewn curtains out of pale flowered sheets.

At the center of the L-shaped house was the kitchen. The coroner said that Antonio had fallen onto the kitchen floor and hit his head, but there was no trace of blood on the white linoleum. No odor lingered.

"I cleaned and cleaned," said Esther.

In the studio hung a cardboard collage she had made. The background was blue wash streaked with gold. A postcard picturing palm trees and an actual roll of film were glued onto the cardboard. I asked to see her paintings, but she said she had none in the house and that she'd switched to photography a couple of years before. "Antonio liked my photography better."

She served us a lunch of cold cuts, bread, lettuce, tortilla chips, with our choice of wine or Seven-Up. Then she combed her hair, put on makeup, and changed into jeans, a hand-woven jacket, and high-heeled sandals. She looked elegant.

We drove in my rented car to the mortuary. The place stank of disinfectant. A man named Mr. Lowry was waiting for us in the front office, which had a rich purple carpet and gold lettering on the door. An impeccably folded white handkerchief protruded from the breast pocket of his dark suit.

"What was his occupation?" asked Mr. Lowry. "I need to put it down on the death certificate."

"He was a writer."

"No, a story teller," said Esther. "That's what he called himself."

Gravely, Mr. Lowry wrote this down. Then he asked what we wanted to do with the body.

We wanted cremation.

Mr. Lowry looked perturbed. First of all, the coroner's office required a routine autopsy. Then in order to cremate Antonio rather than bury him, the mortuary would need an order from a blood relative. But Isabel was a minor. Was there no one else? His only blood kin were in Chile. His body might stay in the San Bernardino Morgue until Isabel turned eighteen in three years, or until one of his more affluent family members, perhaps on vacation, decided to do something about the frozen corpse up in North America. Things were beginning to unroll as grotesquely as they might have in one of Antonio's own stories. To Mr. Lowry's astonishment, Esther and I burst into fits of laughter. I said the coroner had told me that the disposal of the body was up to Isabel. I kept insisting on this while Mr. Lowry hemmed and hawed.

"A dead body is just a dead body," said Isabel, who had been very quiet. "It doesn't matter."

At last Isabel and I both signed. The cremation would not take place for ten days.

Discreetly, Mr. Lowry handed me a sealed envelope. "The lock of hair you asked for, Ma'am." It was dark grey. I remembered it as chestnut.

Esther said she wanted to bury the ashes either at her place or at the Indian burial grounds. Isabel and I wanted some kind of service while we were still here, without the ashes.

"A funeral can be anything you want it to be. It doesn't have to be a certain way. The body doesn't have to be there," said Mr. Lowry. We looked at the mortuary chapel, but it was dark, small, and grim. So we decided to have the ceremony at Esther's.

Did we want a priest or minister?

"Antonio used to bike past the Assembly of God Church," said Esther. "He talked a few times to the minister...long, involved, theological discussions. Antonio liked the man."

I thought of him pedaling along the road, unshaven, dressed in the castoff shirts and trousers that he wore during those last years—a far cry from the impeccably dressed, serious young man who appeared in photographs taken of him long ago.

"How long ago?" asked Mr. Lowry.

"Maybe a year or so ago."

"A new minister just came in three months ago."

Mr. Lowry called the new minister, but he had never heard of Antonio. "He'd just as soon not do it."

℘

At dusk we drove to the beautiful little Catholic church nearby. The priest, a Father O'Brien, was out. We spoke to his secretary, a middle-aged woman with pursed lips, a beehive hairdo, and a lot of makeup. She drew us out with questions, and we found ourselves telling too much. We were Jewish, I said. But I used to pray to the Virgin in an old Catholic church in Paris when I was pregnant. Esther, I said, was his common-law wife. "No," hissed Esther. Later she was furious over this. "Companion," she said. "It could mess up the Social Security if they knew we lived together like that. We said he was the caretaker of my house."

"A pity he did not receive the Last Sacraments," said the woman. She talked about the apostolic succession, while I talked about Buddhist meditation. As we were about to leave, a sandy-haired man in levis and Western boots got out of his car and yelled out, "Howdy pardners." We wondered if he were the priest. Later we could not bring ourselves to phone him, as she had told us to.

Although Antonio had respected the Jesuit fathers who were his teachers at school, and he even dedicated a novel to them, the tone of this church seemed close to the blind orthodoxy he had hated.

We decided to perform the ceremony ourselves.

We ate dinner in a darkened bar at the motel. Afterwards we walked outside. Stars gleamed large and brilliant in the night sky, and I saw the flash of a shooting star. Esther came back with us to our room. We lit a fire and talked until almost midnight. She did not want to leave. I did not want her to. In her face I saw a quality of wonder, the quality of a child searching for a fairy tale. This seeking had drawn her to Antonio, just as something similar in me had sought him out long ago.

"He could see into the heart of a problem," Esther said. "He would present a solution somewhere from left field that I never would have thought about. He wanted to be a Pygmalion," she added. "I resented that."

"He wanted to be a Pygmalion with me, too," I said.

"He was enthusiastic about anyone who had a scrap of talent. He would build you up and then tear you down. He'd say things like, 'You're beautiful, but what have you done with your life?' I don't work well that way. I work better with praise than blame. He didn't understand that."

He blew up a car of hers, and he had totaled mine.

"I used to think that it was all my fault," I said. "My fault that he totaled the car."

"He gave away everything," she said. "One day I came home to find a couch gone. He'd given it to the neighbors, and I had to go and get it back. It was embarrassing!"

"Once he gave away my winter coat," I said. "He gave his own things away. If someone liked his jacket or his sweater or any of his books, he would give it to them. He gave the money that he inherited when his father died back to his mother. None of his brothers and sisters did."

While Esther and I talked in front of the fire, Isabel lay on her bed and made me a birthday card that said, "I love you very much and this is a hard time for me."

"I can't bear it. You and Esther are so sentimental," said Isabel when we were alone. "I never liked him much, after what he did to me."

ℰ𝒪

Late the next morning when we arrived at Esther's house, she was still in her robe. "I just woke up," she said. "I couldn't sleep. I was talking to you in my head all night, pacing up and down." Still grumpy with sleep, she made tea. "Antonio always said you were an early riser—up with the radio," she said. "It takes me a while to get started. Antonio and I were alike that way. We both liked to stay up late and sleep late."

John, who lived next door, shared Antonio's enthusiasm for growing plants in the desert. He had been the last person to see him alive. Had it been on December 29th or 30th? John couldn't remember. John was sixty-three, a kind, and sociable man with white hair. As we sipped tea in Esther's living room, he told us stories about his life. Time passed. There was no sense of hurry. He rambled on. One story would bring to mind another. We listened. There was the sunlight, the many windows, the quality of emotion in the house as we sat facing each other in the bright, narrow living room. I thought of how hurried everything was with Saul, of how there was no time or space for such conversations to flower, for sympathetic currents to build between people.

Saul is solid, grounded. With him my strength builds. Antonio tore me down until I was raw. However, he touched places of my emotions, intellect, spirit that no one else ever has.

Of what does love consist? Why do I love one person, and not another? I did not love his act of rape. I hated his hurting Isabel as he did. That last year he made frantic phone calls to us, but I refused to speak to him after I learned what had happened.

I believe that Antonio planned the rape. "Now your breasts will grow," he told her. "Now you will be able to get married and have children. You can tell your best friend, but don't tell your mother."

A disturbing memory plagued me. Years ago when she was a small child and we were still together, he had joked about doing this when she reached the age of thirteen in order to clear her of hangups. I had not imagined that he could be serious, but perhaps he had truly thought that in this way he would free her of the Oedipal bond.

Esther had been away on vacation when it happened. Why had I let Isabel visit? Why hadn't I made her wait until Esther came back? Isabel had been afraid to go, but I'd urged her, as I felt that Antonio did not have long to live. Isabel told me that afterwards she wanted to escape, but it was night. Outside it was cold and isolated, and she had nowhere to go.

ℰ𝒪

"He felt so isolated. Somewhere he lost the way," said a friend of his years earlier.

Antonio, I wish I understood you. I wish I could erase what you did to Isabel. Did you act out of rage? If you truly thought you were helping her, you were insane.

"Antonio loved his garden," said Esther. "At the end, that interested him more than anything else. He would order seed catalogues, and he would battle with the supply houses. The plants he wanted wouldn't grow in the desert. He insisted that they send them anyway. When the seeds didn't grow, he raised a big fuss, and the supply houses sent him more seeds... sixty or seventy dollars worth." She chuckled. "Antonio loved to screw people out of things."

"People even came out from the university at Irvine to see Antonio's jojoba plants. Luis Echeverría played a joke which made Antonio furious. He sent the editor of *Zig Zag* in Chile to visit us, telling him that Antonio was a jojoba expert, and he said nothing at all about Antonio being a writer."

John took Isabel and me over to his place. Large plastic containers, which he used for potting, were strewn around his yard. He showed us his mulberry, plum, and apricot trees, all covered with netting to protect them against storms and wild animals. He showed us aloe vera plants, fig trees and a prickly cactus with large flat leaves. The leaves could be boiled until the needle-filled skin slid off. Then candy and preserves could be made from its pulp. He showed us his carob tree and his jojoba plants.

Time passed.

We returned to Esther's house. By now she had showered and dressed. We ate toast, and drank more tea.

"We talked about getting married," she said. "We didn't, because it would have screwed up the SSI. If we had married, I would have gotten survivor's benefits."

Her hands trembled as she handed me Antonio's car papers, his savings book, his checkbook, and his safe deposit keys for the bank. Antonio's savings held $1,015. His checkbook held $496. Out of this we needed to pay burial costs, our plane tickets, and about $200 which Antonio owed Esther for food and rent. Isabel would inherit the rest.

His car was worth $1,500. It was a dusty blue 1974 Pinto with 84,000 miles on it. One door, said Esther, would not open, and another would not lock.

"He told everyone he was a writer, the fool," said Esther. "He screwed himself up with his big mouth. They didn't want to give him SSI, even though he was really sick. They thought he was faking so he could stay home and write."

We drove to the bank and talked with an effusive blonde woman named Lydia. I showed her Isabel's birth certificate and my passport. However, she wanted photographic proof, in the form of a passport or a driver's license, that Isabel was the person she claimed to be.

We lacked proof.

Lydia said she would have to consult with her supervisors. We went to lunch at the restaurant across the street. As I was biting into a sandwich, Lydia came in and tapped me on the shoulder. She told me that she could let us see the contents of the safe deposit box after all. But first, she, too, was going to lunch.

We waited a long time in the bank lobby, sitting on chairs like refugees. Esther was wearing a beige jumpsuit, while Isabel and I wore jeans and jogging shoes. With our casual dress, Esther's and my swarthy looks, and our indeterminate ages, we did not fit into this place at all. Isabel, in contrast, looked Nordic with her fair coloring and her clear blue eyes. I took out a barrette from my purse and tried to pin back my thick, dark hair.

Lydia was holding flurried conversations with other bank officials. They wanted the death certificate. I told her to call the mortuary. Finally she agreed to let Isabel and me open the safe deposit box. Esther held her head in her hands as Lydia led us away to the vault. We entered a room lined with metal boxes.

If we did not find a will, then Isabel would legally inherit everything.

Antonio's box was empty.

Esther rocked with hysterical laughter. "That bastard!"

ꕥ

We returned to Esther's for the ceremony. An elderly neighbor couple joined us, along with John. The six of us gathered in the back yard. We wanted to plant an aloe vera in Antonio's memory, but Esther could not decide where to put it. "This was not a good time to plant," said the neighbor man. "Why not just dig a symbolic shovel of earth and plant the aloe later in the spring, when she buried the ashes?"

We each spoke in front of the aloe vera plant in its five-gallon white plastic container. Tearfully, the woman said that she regretted that she slammed the door in Antonio's face the last time she saw him.

John mentioned how much Antonio had loved Isabel.

Isabel was silent.

The couple left. Then John led Esther and Isabel and me in a ritual. He recited a long chant, which ended with, "Antonio Ramírez, we wing thee on thy way towards the center of Eternal Light." On this chorus we all joined in as we circled around the plant, holding hands, and swooped in towards the middle. Again and again we repeated this chorus, circling and swooping.

Then a hush fell over us.

Afterwards, Isabel and I went out for dinner at an Italian restaurant. The food was heavy and made us feel a bit ill. We went back to the motel room. Isabel did homework, while I meditated.

The next day John gave Isabel a fig seedling to take home. Isabel handed Esther the papers for Antonio's car.

Esther showed me a poem she had written twenty years before about hot sand and a white pebble. "Antonio said we would get along," she said.

"We must be alike in some ways, or we wouldn't have chosen the same man."

"He played on our insecurities."

We left.

From Palm Springs we flew north. I looked through his last checking statements. Checks had been cashed almost daily until December 11th, but none after that date. Why? Probably he had been too ill. A few papers fell off the tray. I reached down and gathered them up.

Our plane was flying high over the desert. Next to the window, Isabel gave a long sigh. "I'm glad that's over with," she said.

"I loved him."

"How could you after what he did to me?" she asked, hesitating with the final words, her voice low and more than ever like a child's.

"I hate what he did to you, but I love *him*."

"Why?"

"I don't know. I wish I understood him. I wish I could undo what he did to you."

His death certificate came. He had died of massive internal hemorrhaging caused by a peptic ulcer. Advanced cirrhosis was a contributing cause. Cirrhosis makes a person age. In its advanced stages, it is not reversible.

"That last year he looked like an old man," Esther had said. "He aged so, you would not have recognized him."

Roberta Fernández

Roberta Fernández is a native of Laredo, Texas. She received a B.A. and an M.A. from the University of Texas, Austin, and a Ph. D. in Romance Languages and Literatures from the University of California, Berkeley. An arts advocate, she has worked at The Mexican Museum in San Francisco, directed a Bilingual Arts Program in the Oakland schools, and at Mills College founded *Prisma: A Multicultural, Multilingual Women's Literary Review* (1979-1982). Coordinating partnerships between academic and community groups, Fernández has directed two conferences with funding from state humanities councils: "The Cultural Roots of Chicana Literature, 1780-1980" (Mills College, 1981) and "Latinos in the United States: Cultural Roots and Present Diversity" (Brown University, 1985). Currently an editor at Arte Público Press, she also teaches in Modern and Classical Languages at the University of Houston, where in 1992 she curated "Twenty-Five Years of Hispanic Literature of the United States, 1975-1990," an exhibit selected by the Texas Humanities Resource Center for one of its traveling exhibits. A three-time resident at the MacDowell Colony, she was named in 1991 to the Texas Institute of Letters. Her work has appeared in many anthologies, among them *The Stories We Have Kept Secret: Tales of Women's Spiritual Development* (1986), *Short Fiction by Hispanic Writers of the United States.* (1993), and *Barrios and Borderlands: Cultures of Latinos and Latinas in the United States* (1994). Multicultural Publishers Exchanged selected her book, *Intaglio: A Novel in Six Stories,* about the transmission of women's cultural expressions on the Texas/Mexican border, as Best Fiction for 1991; her own Spanish version of *Intaglio* will be published in Mexico in the near future. Fernández has been awarded the 1974-75 post-doctoral fellowship sponsored by the center for Mexican-American Studies at the University of Texas in Austin.

Zulema

Roberta Fernández

I come from a long line of eloquent illiterates
whose history reveals what words don't say
Lorna Dee Cervantes

I.

The story Zulema heard that November morning in 1914 changed her forever, and for the rest of her life she had to deal with the consequences of what she was told on that long-ago Tuesday morning. All during the previous night she had listened to sporadic gunshots across the river where the Federales were shooting at the Villistas. The noise and the unfamiliar bed had made her wake up long before the bells of San Augustín Church pealed their daily calling to the faithful, and at six o'clock when the first sounds from the belfry echoed in the distance, Zulema got up, blessed herself, then knelt down to say her morning prayers. She heard her Aunt Mariana moving around in the next room and wondered if the disturbances in the night had also made her get up earlier than usual.

Mariana looked different that morning, puffy around the eyes and rather tense as she prepared the coffee and tortillas. Zulema sensed she had interrupted her aunt as she came into the kitchen, but Mariana instinctively left her comal to kiss the child. "I have a lot to tell you," Mariana whispered as she put her arms around Zulema's slender body. Then, as she moved back to the stove and stirred the chocolate she was preparing for the child, Mariana told her the story.

Her voice sounded a little forced and her face looked weary. Zulema would later try to recall the scene, but all she could remember was Mariana's pallor and the voice that had been pitched higher than normal. In this tone, Mariana had told her that her new brother had arrived during the night, tired from his journey but happy and fat and kicking with gusto.

The night had been full of activity, she continued, for not only had the new baby arrived and the shooting continued on the other side, but a messenger had also come from San Antonio. He had informed Zulema's mother that her other sister, Carmen, had come down with a serious case of pneumonia. Isabel had left right away with the messenger, leaving her new-born baby behind with the rest of the family. "Give my Zulemita and Miguelito a kiss and tell them I'll be home soon." Those had been her last words as she departed, Mariana said.

"You will stay with me for awhile," she continued. Miguel would stay with his father and his grandmother, and the baby would remain with Doña Julia who lived across the street and also had a small infant she was nursing. It had all been arranged.

II.

Thirty-five years later, sitting on some thick pillows Zulema had special-made for me, I heard many different versions of what I later realized was the same story. During my afternoon visits I listened to Zulema's calm, deep voice as she invented one tale after another with superbly eccentric characters who continued to dance and whirl about in my own accelerated imagination. Some of the stories were simple duplications of tales Mariana had told her, but most of the narratives were Zulema's own inventions. Often Mariana would join us, sitting on the rocking chair with her eyes closed as though she were reliving the episodes which Zulema was describing.

Now and then Mariana would open her eyes, then lean forward to listen more closely. Then, she would shake her head and correct Zulema. "No, no fue así," and she would turn to me with her own version of the story I had just heard. It was difficult for me to decide whose narrative I liked the most, for they each had their way with description and knew just when to pause for the maximum effect, but I suppose at that time I tended to think that Mariana's "bola de años," as she referred to her advancing age, gave her an edge over Zulema's rendition.

I soon learned that Zulema had a favorite story. It was the one about the camp follower Victoriana, who, at the height of the revolution, had crossed to this side to wait for her lover Joaquín. For a while people coming from her pueblo in Zacatecas confirmed her belief that Joaquín was still alive, but as the years passed, everyone simply forgot about Victoriana. She continued her vigil until that unexpected afternoon when the people had found her thirty years later, sitting in the same chair where she had first sat down to wait, covered with cobwebs and red dust but with a glowing expression on her face and her rusted rifle at her feet.

I never got tired of Zulema's cuento, for each time she'd recite it, she would pretend it was the first time she had confided to me about Victoriana and she would embellish the story with a few more details. The climax was always the same, though, as she'd describe how Victoriana was unable to recognize the man whose memory she had loved all those years, for when the newspapers had printed the story about her long wait, out of curiosity, Joaquín had come to see Victoriana and she had not singled him out from all the other visitors she had greeted that afternoon. No longer the campesino she had fallen in love with, but a very important businessman, Joaquín was alternately amused and mortified by all of the moths and butterflies entangled among the cobwebs in her silvered hair.

Zulema would conclude the story with Victoriana boarding the Ferrocarriles Nacionales Mexicanos, while the townspeople waved a sad farewell to the splendid and flamboyant figure who had enlivened their routine lives for a brief while. She, too, waved to the people as the train pulled away, taking her back to her pueblo where she hoped to locate some of the relatives she had last seen in Bachimba, claiming their rifles and riding off into the distance to be swept into the force of the revolution.

Unknown endings, unfinished lives. That was the subject of most of Zulema's narratives, but I cannot remember when I first began to notice this. On the day after my sixth birthday I sensed something different, for Zulema changed the story from fantasy to biography and for the first time mentioned Isabel to me. She took a photograph from her missal and passed the edge-worn picture to me. "Do you know who she is?"

Immediately, I recognized the photo as a copy of one my mother had. "Es tu mamá," I responded right away. "Mi abuelita Isabel."

I often opened the top drawer of my mother's dresser just to steal a peep at the young woman in the tucked, lace blouse who looked back at me with soft gentle eyes. No one had ever told me much about her except that she was my father's mother who had died when my uncle Luis was born. Each of the boys had been reared by different relatives who did not find it appropriate to talk to them about Isabel, possibly to spare the children from the memories the adults did not want them to have. Up to then I knew very little about her.

"She died when she was only twenty-four. I was six then," Zulema spoke very deliberately. "Mariana really pulled the wool over my eyes, telling me Mamá had gone away with Tía Carmen."

Zulema's shoulders began to rise up and down. Suddenly she started to sob uncontrollably, holding the photo to her breast. Through my own tears, I heard her describe how she had waited for days on end for her mother's return during that first winter when Isabel had gone away without a word to her. The minute she'd hear people pass by on the street, she'd run to the door on the chance her mother would be with them. The streetcar that clanged in front of the house seemed to sound especially for her, and every time she'd see Julia nursing the baby, she'd wonder if Luisito was hungry for his own mother. Feeling abandoned, she began to talk about her feelings; yet everyone maintained the story which Mariana had uttered. When, when, when she had asked her aunt, and Mariana had finally said, "When the war is over, she'll be back."

And so the eight-year old Zulema had become interested in the war. At night, whenever she heard gunshots or sirens, she'd cry herself to sleep. The bugles of the infantry across the river woke her up every morning and in the afternoons after class she'd go down to the river to look across its banks at the war-weary nation on the other side. Then she would wish the war away, praying with her eyes closed while she imagined her mother running towards her with outstretched arms. But Zulema could sense that Isabel would not be back for a long time, for every day she was aware of the dozens of people who crossed the bridge with their belongings in wheelbarrows or in suitcases of every sort. Some even had knapsacks slung across their back, looking tired and worn from the personal anxieties they too were experiencing. Sometimes her father would give work around the story or at the ranch to some of the people who had just arrived, and before they moved on farther north, Zulema would take advantage of their personal accounts to ask them questions about the war. No one had any idea when the fighting would end and many of them no longer cared about the revolution except for the manner in which it had altered the course of their lives. They were mostly preoccupied with the death and destruction over which they had absolutely no control.

With all the talk of death, Zulema soon became apprehensive. When the newly-arrived talked about the death of their loved ones, she began to associate their experiences with her own loss and slowly began to doubt the story about her mother's return. On her ninth birthday, in 1917, she had let everyone know she realized the war was supposed to be over and still her mother had not come back. "I know she is lost," she concluded. Then she looked directly at Mariana and stated in a tone of finality, "I no longer have a mother."

And that same day she had started to tell her own stories. She took Miguelito and Luisito to her room and sat them down on the floor while she lay on her bed looking up at the ceiling. "Les voy a contar un cuento de nunca acabar," she began, then started to narrate her own version of the Sleeping Beauty, who had been put under a spell by her wicked step-mother. Sleeping Beauty was supposed to be awakened by the kiss of a gorgeous prince, but that never really happened. She turned to her brothers and asked them if they knew why the prince had not found Sleeping Beauty. Then, without giving them a chance to answer, for this was supposed to be her very own story, she continued with melodramatic gestures.

The prince could not find Sleeping Beauty, she whispered, because a revolution broke out just as he was setting out on his journey. Word soon arrived that his white horse had been confiscated by Emiliano Zapata. So now the prince had to find his way around on foot, and not being accustomed to looking out for himself, he had no idea what direction he should take. Finally, he headed towards his castle, but when he got there he found that it had been blown to pieces and the revolutionaries had proclaimed that he could no longer be a prince. And so he was unable to complete his mission. Poor Sleeping Beauty was left forgotten in the woods, but since she could not live without the prince, for they needed each other to exist, she simply had no future and remained out there in the dark woods forever and ever. Pretty soon no one could remember, much less care, about the troubles of that poor little Sleeping Beauty, foolish enough to think she needed to live with a prince in a castle. So, without realizing what they had done, the revolutionaries got rid of all those charming princes and the silly, pampered Sleeping Beauties as well.

That afternoon, I listened for a long time as Zulema recited one such story after another. From the beginning, she said, her brothers did not like her plots because they considered her endings to be strange, even morbid at times. Once in a while she had tried to tell her stories to her father, but he did not seem the least bit interested in them. Mariana, who perhaps best understood what she was really trying to say, assumed she could change her endings. So, for lack of an audience, Zulema felt she had been fated to keep them to herself all those years. I was the only one who had let her tell the stories the way she wanted.

"Zulema, I like your stories," I reassured her as I undid her braids, then ran my small fingers through her hair.

I then looked at her in a whole new way. Unlike Mariana and the picture we had of Isabel, Zulema seemed quite ordinary, with her long hair parted in the middle and plaited into thick braids which she wore crisscrossed on top of her head. She did not look like my mother either, whose hair was swept up, away from her face and wrapped around a hair-piece that was pinned around her head in keeping with the fashion of the day. I much preferred Zulema's hair, which I loved to unbraid, then brushed out in waves which reached down to her waist.

That afternoon I gave her particular attention, weaving a red satin ribbon into her braids which made her look prettier than usual. Finally animated, she continued with the narrative that had gone unshared all those years. She skipped the elaboration she gave to her other tales and was direct and terse as she described the main event that had shaped her life. She really could not blame Mariana or her father, she said, for they had simply been trying to save her from the very pain they had inadvertently caused. By the time she was twelve she had given up altogether on her mother's return, although occasionally when she opened a door in her father's house, for an instant she felt she had caught a glimpse of her mother sitting there in her rocking chair. That was about the time she took to leaving all the doors in the house ajar. Gradually, she became fascinated with opening trunks and boxes as well.

One day while she was visiting her father and Amanda, she found herself alone in the room where he kept his papers. Slowly, she began to poke into his desk and in a drawer, underneath some photos, she uncovered the announcement which she unknowingly had been searching for all those months. She picked up the card, looked at its black borders, then read: ISABEL MENDOZA-DEL VALLE, esposa de José María Cárdenas—1890-1914. The rest of the announcement stated that Isabel was survived by three children—Zulema, Miguel and Luis.

Zulema put the card back where she had found it. After that she lost her interest in rummaging through boxes and drawers. She began to rise at six o'clock in order to attend daily mass where she remained until it was time for school. Gradually, she began to lose interest in her classes, and one day she decided to stay in church all day. For several weeks her memories and the candles she lit brightened the semi-darkness. Soon el Padre Salinas began to notice the disappearance of the candles. Concerned that almost no money was being left in the offering box to cover their cost, he staked out the various altars and shortly thereafter caught her sitting in the front pew facing the virgin and child. He watched as she lighted two or three candles at once, then when those burned down, he saw her light new ones.

Just about the time el Padre Salinas approached Mariana about the expense, the teacher paid José María a visit. José María did not take the trouble to discuss the matter with his daughter. Instead, he talked to Mariana, who related to Zulema that her father now wished to keep her at home, for she could no longer be trusted to go out on her own. From then on she would not be allowed to go anywhere without being accompanied either by one of the cousins or the aunts.

Zulema had not minded the restrictions at all. In fact, for the first time she felt she was the object of everyone's attention. Mariana taught her the secrets that went into cooking traditional dishes. For their mole de gallina, they would spend a good part of a day grinding sesame seeds, peanuts, and pastillas de chocolate on the metate. And once the ingredients for the sauce were ready, they would simmer it for hours. It was then that they would go to the chicken coop to pick out two or three chickens. At first Zulema was squeamish, but she soon learned to wring a chicken by the neck before chopping off its head with a machete. For dessert, she loved to make capirotada and leche quemada, and the first time she prepared the entire meal for a table of twelve, she relished all the compliments she got for her calabaza con puerco.

Doña Julia taught her to crochet—little squares at first, then larger items like tablecloths and bedspreads which she made as gifts for fiestas de quinceañeras, engagement showers and weddings. When she turned fifteen, she, too, was honored with a dance attended by all the relatives, their friends, and friends of her father. Everyone danced to the music of a local band until the early hours of the morning, and between dances they kept going back for more tamales and steaming cups of cinnamoned coffee. Before the night was over, all the spread on the table—barbacoa, guacamole, arroz, frijoles barrachos and freshly grilled gorditas—had been eaten up.

That was the first time she had met Carlos, who danced all evening with her. A few days later, he had called on her father, requesting permission to visit with her at home. Soon she began to be kidded about having a sweetheart, and when the comadres in Maríana's quilt-making group asked her about Carlos, Zulema smiled and pretended to be concentrating on her stitches. After a while, she filled her trunk with the essentials for her future life, and when she married Carlos, she brought to her new home all the exquisite handmade items that a seventeen-year-old bride needed. A few weeks after Zulema's and Carlos's first child was born, Mariana came to live with them, and for more than twenty years the three of them saw the family expand, then contract again, as the older sons went off to study at the university and the younger daughter married, at seventeen, like her mother.

Zulema had tried to get each one of her children interested in listening to her stories, but all four thought the stories were silly and repetitive. So, it wasn't until I started making requests for recitations about her extravagant characters that she began to ponder about this particular vacuum in her life.

Now, as the afternoon light softly faded, Zulema paused to reflect on everything she had told me. Finally, she sighed, "Telling stories. That's what I've enjoyed the most."

"Me, too," I smiled, tugging at her red ribbon.

Just then the door opened and my cousin Maruca turned on the light. Surprised, she asked, "How come you're sitting in the dark?"

Neither of us answered her. Then, she burst out, "Ay, Mamá, why are you wearing those silly ribbons? You look as if you were about to dance el jarabe tapatío."

"She looks great with her hair like this," I responded.

Maruca waved her hand as if to brush my comment aside. "You two live in your special little world, with all your cuentos. Come join us now. I've brought a big tray full of fried chicken and potato salad."

"We'll come in a minute," Zulema answered. "Just let us finish here."

As soon as we were alone again, Zulema looked at me very intently, tapping her index finger against her mouth. "Nenita, let's keep this to ourselves. Poor Mariana. It's been such a long time since mother died. There's no point in creating problems now. All this was just between you and me, okay?"

III.

Earlier that day, my sister Patricia had called to inform me about the heart attack. In my rush to the bus station I had forgotten my sunglasses and the bright light of the afternoon was now blinding me. Closing my eyes, I tried to sort out my feelings, but I couldn't focus on anything. Instead, I tried leafing through the magazine I had picked up at the Greyhound shop. News of Czechoslovakia, Viet Nam and Cambodia flashed by me. A picture of Joan Baez. Many anti-war demonstrators. Unable to concentrate, I set the magazine aside.

Leaning against the bus window, I stretched out my legs across the two seats and studied the passengers closest to me. Two rows up on my left was a woman with very teased hair. She reminded me of Florinda's Cuban mother whom I knew only through my sister's vivid description. I looked around at the other people, then fidgeted with the journal I had on my lap. Feeling its smooth leather cover, I remembered how pleased I had been the previous Christmas when Mariana and Zulema had given it to me. On its first page, they had inscribed: "Make this a memory book of your very own dreams and aspirations." It was the first thing I grabbed when I started to pack for this journey home, but at the moment I did not feel like looking at it.

I concentrated instead on the woman with the teased hair. Florinda's mother must have looked like that when she left Cuba ten years ago. In anticipation of the day when the family would leave the island, she had let her hair grow for more than a year. Then when the moment for their departure arrived, she had carefully teased her hair, then divided it into three layers. The first section had been twisted into a tight French roll fastened with pens encrusted with precious gems. A small fortune I was told. The tiny twist had been covered with a larger one held up by more jeweled hairpins. Finally, the top outer layer neatly covering the cache had been sprayed several times with a heavy lacquer. As if to mock fate, she had attached thin wires with pink and white gauze butterflies all over her hair. According to my sister, Florinda had said that her mother looked so outrageous no one bothered much with her and she had smuggled a sizeable sum which the family had used to set up a fabric store. Several years later, it was a thriving business.

For reasons I didn't quite understand, Florinda's mother's story always made me anxious. So, I lit a cigarette and watched the smoke whirl upwards. From the angle the sun was hitting me, the smoke resembled the tumultuous vapors in the film version of 'Pedro Páramo.' In that film, as Juan Preciado searched for his father, the vapors kept getting thicker and thicker the more he travelled inside the land of the dead.

"This is my favorite novel," I had pointed out to Zulema and Mariana on the previous Thanksgiving holiday. "But I'm sure there's a lot in this novel I don't understand," I had warned as I introduced them in the spirits, the espíritus, of Comala.

We had been reading from the paperback copies of Pedro Páramo that I had given to each of them. Mariana and I did most of the reading, although Zulema sometimes took her turn. Sipping Cuervo añejo, we had commented on the novel, pointing out the scenes we had particularly enjoyed. Mariana, especially, was enthralled with the characters at the Rancho Media Luna, for they were part of a period she still remembered well. And Zulema, as I had expected, identified with Susana, the character whose fate had also been shaped by the early death of her mother.

"The spirits always continue to influence those who live after them," Mariana had sighed. "Just right here, we have the example of Zulema, who suffered so much after the death of Isabel."

Zulema and I had glanced at one another. Fifty-five years after the death of her sister, Mariana was finally commenting on it.

"Why do you say that?" I had softly questioned.

"It's just that the murmurs get stronger by the day," she had answered, extending her hands on the armrest. She had closed her eyes, rocking herself back and forth to let us know the conversation had ended for the moment. Finally, she had murmured, "It is time now," and to our astonishment she said she would take us to Isabel's burial place.

As I drove to the cemetery in silence, my mind was full of questions. Like the rest of the family, I had succumbed to the story of Isabel's departure and had not even asked where she had been buried. For twenty years, since Zulema had told me her version of her mother's death, I had learned to think of Isabel as a spirit living the special life of the dead. I wondered if Zulema was as shocked as I was since she too had not uttered a word.

"Vamos por este camino." Mariana led us through the old part of the cemetery to an enclosed plot. There, a red tin can with a cluster of marigolds lay half-buried in front of a tombstone marked with the same inscription as on the death announcement which Zulema had read so long ago: ISABEL MENDOZA-DEL VALLE, 1890-1914.

I was stunned, realizing that for all these years Isabel had been within reach. Zulema's lower lip started to tremble and little whimpering sounds began to come out of her mouth. Mariana put her arm around Zulema's shoulder, then rested her head on it.

"I never knew how to remedy what had happened," Mariana said simply. It was obvious she finally wanted to break the silence surrounding Isabel, and in order to get her off her feet, we moved to a nearby bench.

For a while we sat quietly. Then Mariana began to tell us about the difficulty she had experienced in repeating the story the family had chosen for the children on the night Isabel had died. From the very beginning she had made adjustments in her life, for she had stayed home with Zulema while the rest of the family attended the novena for her sister. Later, when the child's suspicions were aroused, she had started to doubt the decision to protect Zulema from the truth.

Yet, after a few years they themselves had almost accepted the story as fact and tacitly believed it would be much more difficult to adjust to a new reality than to live with the pattern that had been set. "I didn't know what to do," Mariana repeated over and over.

Then she told us about her weekly visits to the cemetery and how she considered those visits her personal ritual in keeping the memory of Isabel alive. For years she had snuck away on the bus with her little bouquet of marigolds. But as she got older, her visits became more and more sporadic. Still, only a few days before, she had brought the flowers we had just seen.

I looked at Mariana's rheumatic limbs and wondered how she had managed to honor her sister for so long.

"Uno hace lo que tiene que hacer," she affirmed as we headed back to the car. I repeated those words to myself, "One simply does what one has to do."

For the rest of the day I tried to fit together all the pieces of the story and started to write long entries about Mariana, Isabel and Zulema in a loose-leaf journal. When I got back to my apartment, I continued writing, and one day in early December I stuffed my notes into an envelope and mailed it off to them with instructions to save the pages for me. A few weeks after that they gave me my blue leather-bound book as a present.

I reached over to feel it, then opened my eyes. We had arrived. As soon as we pulled into the terminal, I saw my sister Patricia waiting for me.

"How is she doing?" I asked.

"She's been hanging on, but she won't last much longer. Late this morning she had another heart attack, and the doctor does not think she'll pull through this time."

IV.

As I opened the door, I heard Father Murphy reciting the prayers of Extreme Unction and saw him blessing the small body on the hospital bed. My mother leaned towards me and whispered as she put her arm around me, "I'm so sorry. She died about fifteen minutes ago."

I felt everyone's eyes on me as I walked up to the bed. As tears streamed down my face, I kissed the smooth sallow cheeks, then looked at the body for a long time without saying anything. It was useless for me to remain there, I thought, and slowly I began to envision what it was I had to do.

In my sister's car, I drove across the border to the church by the first plaza, then walked towards the adjacent small shop which sold religious articles. As I had hoped, its window display was full of saints with tin milagros for sale in many different shapes, sizes and materials. Immediately, I by-passed the larger ones and the gold ones which I could not afford. Looking at the half-inch tin offerings, I carefully selected from those in the shape of human profiles, hearts, and tongues of fire. The volunteer at the shop seemed surprised when I said I wanted five dozen of each, then waited patiently while I made my selection. Eventually, she divided the offerings into small plastic bags.

With the milagros on my lap, I drove a few blocks to the flower market. There I purchased bunches of marigolds and asked the vendor to divide them up into small bouquets which he tied together with white ribbons. They took up most of the back seat, making the custom inspector remark on my collection of flores para los muertos. My next stop was the stationery shop where I bought a small box of red cinnamon-scented candles. Then, on my way to the funeral parlor I passed a record shop. Slamming on the brakes, I double-parked and ran in to inquire if they sold small 45's that were blank. The clerk thought they had three such records left over from an old special order. As soon as he found them, I rushed back to the car and made my way to the funeral parlor. The administrator listened rather dubiously to my plans, then reluctantly gave me permission to do as I wished.

I went home to rest for a while, then at the agreed-upon hour I returned to the funeral parlor and for the next three hours carried out my task. My back hurt from being bent for so long as, between tears, I carefully sewed the milagros on the white satin which lined the inside cover of the casket. Applying three stitches through the tiny hole on each tin sculpture, I made a design of three arcs—the faces were on the outer row, the tongues in the middle, and the hearts on the inner row. Once I finished with the milagros, I stepped back to get a better view. Seeing how pretty they looked, each with its accompanying tiny red ribbon, I cried once more, yet felt a little relief from my sorrow knowing that when the lid was closed, the milagros would be a lovely sight to behold from inside. Then, with the marigolds, I created a halo effect on the space above the corpse, hoping its spirit could savor the smell of the flowers. I arranged the candles in a row in front of the casket and felt myself tremble as I placed the three records on the left side of the body. "Llénalos con tus cuentos favoritos," I whispered. "Fill them with your favorite stories."

For a long time I sat in the semi-darkness, mesmerized by the smell of the flowers and the perfumed glow of the candles. Recalling the many cuentos which had inspired my youthful imagination, I felt I could stay there forever. But I knew I did not want to see anyone tonight, and soon someone would be coming to sit out the early morning vigil.

Slowly, I got up and walked to the coffin once again. The milagros and the flowers looked splendid, but I wondered what the rest of the family would say when they saw them. I touched the dear figure for the last time, then walked out into the night knowing I would not be going to the burial ceremony the next afternoon.

Instead, I went home and immediately began to write in my journal. For two days I wrote, filling all its pages. Then I gave my thick blue book to Patricia so she should read what I had just finished.

She started reading right away and did not move from her chair for hours. At times, I would see her shake her head and make almost audible sounds. Finally, when she finished she closed the book, but kept her hand on its cover.

"No," she asked. "No fue así." A stern expression crossed her face. "It's not been at all the way you've presented it. You've mixed up some of the stories Mariana and Zulema have told you, which might not even be true in the first place. I've heard other versions from Tía Carmen and, in fact, from Zulema herself. Mariana will never even recognize herself if you ever show this to her."

"I'm not sure what you are trying to do," Patricia continued, "but what you have here is not at all what really happened."

"Lo que tienes aquí no es lo que pasó."

Linda Feyder

Linda Feyder grew up in California and is of French, German and Mexican descent. She received her B.A. from Loyola Marymount University and her M.A. in Creative Writing from the University of Houston. Her story, "Maria del Angel," won *Hispanic Magazine*'s 1991 fiction contest. While in Houston, she worked as an assistant editor at Arte Público Press and edited the anthology, *Shattering the Myth: Plays by Hispanic Women,* with compilation by Denise Chávez. Feyder has taught English at Houston Community College and Sacred Heart University in Connecticut, as well as creative writing to primary school children. She lives in New York City with her husband and son, and is currently working on a collection of short stories.

Marta del Ángel

Linda Feyder

My name is Marta de Ángel. It's a pretty name; I am named after my father's dead sister. In California they call me Mar*tha* with a tongue stuck to their top front teeth when they come to the "*t*." It sounds different here, like they are going to spit.

I married an American man I met in a supermarket parking lot. He worked in construction, and when I met him he was sitting in his truck swallowing beer. I fell in love with his arms; they were golden from the sun and a thin film of dust glistened on his blonde hairs. These are the things of love, my father once told me. "*Cuídese, mi hija*. It only takes one thing."

We rented an apartment in Oxnard not far from the water. I could hear the bells from the dock and at times a foghorn. The home, I kept it spotless, and my husband never had to wait for his dinner. These are the lessons of my mother, and her kitchen had been my classroom where I learned many things. I woke up with the roosters to make fresh cheese for my brothers. My mother tested the coffee before serving it to my father.

The second summer of the marriage, my husband said he had a construction job in Arizona and he never came back. I kept his dinner in the freezer, and on lonely nights I would go to the boats and stare out across the ocean, where on a clear day I could see the dark outlines of the Channel Islands. I liked to think the heavy shapes resting on the ocean were the shores of Mexico and the foghorn's bellow was the once tired sounds of an old aunt I listened to.

My American girlfriend told me he was probably just working hard. "He'll come home," she said. I wanted to say to her, "You *gringas*, you are too stupid about men." But I also wanted to believe her. She took me to the movies. I made her *tortas* when she came to visit me on her lunch break. I liked her. She wore large, dangling earrings that looked like coins strung together, and I never met a woman who could fix her hair in so many different shapes. We talked about many things, but mostly about men. She was dating a boy three years younger than herself, and he kept telling her he didn't want to get married until he was "settled." *Mentiras*, the liar. She said, "You see how mature he is." She kept saying this as if she was trying to convince me. *Pobrecita*, I thought, you believe what the men tell you.

I sat up nights and embroidered anything I could get my hands on. I didn't embroider the pretty roses and curling leaves my mother taught me to embroider; I now had skeletons and dark-winged birds on my dish towels and bed sheets. I stitched and wondered why I had come here, why I was the one out of my mother's seven daughters to follow her five sons across the border because I didn't want to stay behind and embroider table covers for the next wedding. I wanted more than dry, sleepy afternoons preparing *tamales* with *las señoras*. Making cheese. Watching *novelas*. I didn't want to be like the other girls in Ramblas, waiting for Christmas or Mother's Day or *el Día de los Muertos* when the boys returned home for a visit puffed with pride and American dollars. I fixed my hair for them, decided for weeks what to wear to the dances that celebrated them, after they had left me with *los ninos* and our suffering mother who longed for them.

I said to Carol, my American friend, "Have you ever had a Mexican man?"

We sat on the steps leading to my apartment and watched Mrs. Hidalgo's pantyhose swing on a clothesline.

"A Brazilian," she said, "but it wasn't all it's cracked up to be. I don't know, I think he intimidated me. You know, all that stuff you hear. I wasn't sure if I was up to it."

Carol bit into an orange slice and juice squirted from her mouth. Her hair was held off her face by a tie-dye scarf and she braided the rest into two big loops.

"Why?" she asked. "Are they worth it?"

"I don't know," I said. "I never slept with anyone before I married my husband."

In the mornings, I looked into my husband's sock drawer or closet and counted the number of shirts and rolled knee-highs he left behind. I always woke up with renewed hope and thought maybe Carol was right. I counted these things because I thought he wouldn't leave so many behind. There were too many.

Sometimes I called my mother in Mexico and she was usually watching a *novela* with my little sister. I didn't tell her my husband left me. It was hard to keep her attention for very long. She'd start to weep on the phone and I'd say, "What happened, *mamá*?" and she'd say, "Oh, *m'hija*, the lady on the television looks just like you."

M'hija. My daughter. I called when I knew my father wasn't home. I thought about the deal I made with my papi after his last son finished school and left for the border. My father was standing beneath a tree, *un pino triste*, with his low mustache, his long gaze, and his cowboy hat lowered to cover the knot above his right eye. I knew I was his favorite daughter. I said, "Papi, let me finish school." None of his daughters completed more than three grades. "I can still do my chores," I told him. "Pay for me to finish school."

He dug his boot into the dry earth, *la tierra de Guanajuato*, the state he never left in his entire life. But he was still the smartest man in Ramblas. He read books about Egypt and he knew how to handwrite, unlike my mother who never had an education.

"Why do you want to return to school?" he said, lowering his eyes on me. "So you can meet a man, marry, and quit? You want me to pay for that?"

"No, Papi," I said. "I won't marry in school and I promise I'll graduate."

The wind whistled through the tree. My father saw a fisherman with a pole bent over the ledge of *la presa*, his thin shoulders hunched as if the small anchor pulled them. I said urgently, "Papi," and I almost grabbed his thick, brown wrist. He would stop and talk to any stranger, my father, no matter what he was doing. On dusty back roads in the hills or walking a dried riverbed, he would sense, like a dog smells a buried bone, a stranger to talk to. His eyes would look over the horizon, squinting in concentration, but never on the stranger's face. He would talk about the harvest, the weather, the latest family to lose sons to *el norte*, but mostly he would listen.

He turned and stepped onto the stone dam, making his way to the lone fisherman. I followed behind him in open-toed sandals, carefully picking my steps. I knew I had lost his attention and I searched around me for something to fill the time I would spend waiting. But there was nothing and nobody. How often my brothers, sisters, and I wished he would meet strangers in town. If he met them in a crowded bus station or near the *zócalo*, we could occupy ourselves easily. But he never did. In those places he walked as the stranger, with a stone face and rigid posture; he would say he had to get back to the ranch by noon.

"*Buenos días*," my father said to the fisherman.

I found a smooth stone jutting out of the dam and took my seat ten-feet from them. I picked up a gray rock and threw it at a bird searching for something to eat between the stones. Father stood with his hands clasped on his hips, his dusty leather jacket open and rising above his stomach. They stared across the lake. I could hear them talking about *la bruja de Aguascalientes*. The fisherman said he had a deaf friend and this witch, she made it so that he could hear again. Their voices droned on and blended with the wind until I wasn't aware of their talking and I daydreamed.

"Marta, *venga*," my father called to me. The fisherman looked in my direction, his eyes crinkled in a smile but his mouth remained turned down.

I lifted myself from the stone and shuffled toward them.

"Marta," my father said, "I have asked Don Tomás what he thinks about your promise."

I stared at the fisherman, this stranger, with his empty fishnet and slack, orange pole and then back to my father with wide eyes.

"I told him about *tu promesa de quedarte soltera*, and he tells me, '*Déjala*—let her go.'"

The fisherman looked down at his worn canvas shoes. "If you want it," he said to the wet stone beneath his feet.

Carol took me to a pet shop to buy me a bird. We picked out a green one with yellow cheeks; the man behind the counter showed us three different types of bird seed. I said to him, "Will it talk?"

"Not unless you give him vocal cords," he said, laughing.

To Carol I said under my breath, "Too bad. I would teach it to say *pendejo*."

Carol laughed out loud and her earrings jangled. She liked it when I cursed in Spanish.

At home I watched the bird eat his seed. I tried to see if he swallowed. This bird, I liked to watch him bathe. He would flutter into himself, burying his face into his feathers. And he had such courage, my bird. He flew head first into my window panes without a second thought. The next day he would do the same thing. He sang clear and beautiful. It didn't matter that he was without vocal cords.

I thought about the fisherman with his pole and no fish. My father called him "*un testigo*," the witness to my promise. I was father's only daughter to complete a high school education and the only one to leave *la casa de mi padre, soltera*. Unmarried.

I remembered my father's face on the day of my graduation. He had become drunk after toasting my achievement in a *pulquería* full of strangers. He sat straight and glassy-eyed in a small cluster of waving parents. I remembered thinking his strangers had been my teachers. If I hadn't had *un testigo*, would I have finished school? I watch Papi remove his hat, something he did only in churches and the few moments before laying his crop-weary body to bed. The lump above his brow shone brightly against the old adobe walls.

"Carol," I said one afternoon, watching her pick the green peppers from her rice, "do you still think he'll come home?"

She looked at me with a long face. She was sad and quiet on this day. Her young boyfriend had left her for a girl with straight teeth, and I asked her this question to remind her that her problem was nothing.

She brought a pink fingernail to her temple and tapped it there. "You know," she said, "I didn't know how to say this to you, but I'm not so sure anymore."

She brought her legs up on the chair and wrapped her arms around her knees. I felt sad now because I didn't expect her to finally tell me the truth. I looked at the bird in his cage. I had tied bows of red ribbon on the bars and the one he pecked rested loose on the floor. I watched him clean his feathers. His beak worked rapidly.

Carol said, "From now on I may sleep with younger men, but I'll never picture them at the altar, Martha. I swear it."

In the morning, I walked to the water and my steps made the wood dock creak. I read the names of the boats: Treasure Chest, Whimsy, Dolores. Who was Dolores? I passed two guys with skin like my own sitting with their legs dangling over the edge of the dock. One of them hissed, "*Chi, chi, chi,*" and I kept staring at the boats. I thought about Carol. I wondered about me. We needed *testigos*, she and I, a face off the street.

I passed an old woman with a paper sack, but she didn't see me. I remembered my father bought three fish, but the fisherman had no change, so he kept the money and Papi chose two more. They were the only fish he caught all day. They were silver and yellow in the sunshine and they flopped around the stone dam. I stood next to my father and watched the fisherman take a buck knife and slit their stomachs while they still sucked for breath. I watched the red life drain out of them.

The fisherman took them down to the water and rinsed them off. My father said to him, "I think we will have rain tomorrow."

Alicia Gaspar de Alba

Alicia Gaspar de Alba was born in El Paso, Texas, just a few miles from the Córdoba bridge which connects the United States and Mexico. She received her B.A. and M.A. in English and Creative Writing from the University of Texas at El Paso, and her Ph.D. in American Studies from the University of New Mexico. She has taught at the University of Massachusetts in Boston, and in 1989 she received a Massachusetts Artists Foundation award in poetry. Presently, she lives in Southern California. In her personal essay, "Literary Wetback" (*The Massachusetts Review*, XXIX: 2, 1988), Gaspar de Alba identifies as a *fronteriza* who experienced "cultural schizophrenia" as she was growing up. In her writing, she considers the role played by boundaries between sexes, lovers, cultures and generations, and allows her characters to defy and celebrate those boundaries. One of three poets whose work is featured in *Three Times a Woman* (1989), she is also the author of a collection of poetry, *Beggar on the Córdoba Bridge* (1989), and a collection of short fiction, *The Mystery of Survival and Other Stories* (1993). Her novel-in-progress, *Athena among Calalillies,* is based on the life and times of Sor Juana Inés de la Cruz, the Mexican nun who was the foremost intellectual of the seventeenth-century Hispanic world, and a proto-feminist writer who serves as a role model for contemporary Latina writers. "Cimarrona" is from another working manuscript entitled *Thankful Sea Graves: A Chicana Gothic*. Her work has been published in numerous journals and anthologies, including, most recently, *Growing Up Chicano* (1993), *Infinite Divisions* (1993), and *After Aztlán: Latino Poets in the '90s* (1992).

Cimarrona*

Alicia Gaspar de Alba

I.

"Laaaand fall!"

Captain Laurens de Graaf opened his spyglass and looked out. Yes, there it was, the dreary, foggy New England coast. The Puritan merchants had commissioned him back in January to bring sugar, rum, and slaves to the Bay Colony. Back then, the Captain had not been rich, as he was now. He had not yet plundered Vera Cruz. At the time he had signed the agreement with the English merchants, the siege of Vera Cruz had been only a dare that Van Horn had thrown in the Captain's face during a night of Christmas feasting in Port Royale. If the Captain had known back in January that Van Horn's outlandish plan would work so well, that they would pull off the siege of Vera Cruz with the Spanish colors flying from the masts of their buccaneer ships while the Spanish Fleet sat in the harbor, he would never have agreed to do business with the Puritans. This foggy, gloomy wilderness, which the Puritans referred to as the city built upon a hill for the chosen children of God, always gave Captain de Graaf nightmares. More and more he had come to despise his annual visit to the Boston port; having to return twice in one year was enough to depress him until Christmas.

"Pedro!" the Captain called to his Spanish matelot. "Lay out my wig and greatcoat, and don't forget the wool stockings. We'll be putting into harbor soon. Tell Cook to get the punch ready."

Though Dutch by nationality, the Captain had learned Castilian during his long service in the Spanish navy. And he could speak French as well, having picked it up from the corsairs who ten years earlier had captured his Spanish vessel and then invited him to join their company. Not one to bite the hand of opportunity, Captain de Graaf had become a buc-

a run-away slave

caneer and now commanded two ships, his favorite of which was the *Neptune*. Though he had some French sailors on board, his crew on the *Neptune* was composed mainly of Englishmen. So Captain de Graaf had had to learn English, too. The only Castilian among them was Pedro, loyal to the Captain ever since his Spanish navy days.

Pedro went below deck, and the Captain watched the crew scrambling on deck, taking in the sails, uncoiling the anchor ropes, loading one of the cannons to announce their arrival, and shouting and slapping each other on the back in anticipation of going ashore. The Captain yelled for the first mate and told him to inform the crew that nobody was to leave the ship. They would send out the longboat to bring the English merchants aboard, dispose of the cargo, and sail the same day for Virginia. It was early enough still, and a good wind would find them once they left the cold shadow of the Boston port. Captain de Graaf was a superstitious man. The New England coast reminded him too much of the English dungeon where he'd been imprisoned back at the beginning of his buccaneer fame. He heard the cannon go off. Out of a habit he had never managed to suppress, he blessed himself with the triple sign of the cross.

"She made a mess in your cabin again, *mi Capitán*," Pedro said when he returned to the poop.

"Not another fire, Pedro!"

"Looks like she got into your logbook this time, sir. There's hen-scratching all over the pages."

"Damn the louse!" said the Captain, snapping his spyglass shut. "Why did we let her loose again, Pedro?"

Pedro followed the Captain down the ladder, his lips pursed tightly. *You've been craving bitch meat ever since she came on board*, he wanted to say, but *el capitán* de Graaf, the infamous Lorencillo, scourge of the Spanish Main, took to insolence the way he took to the pox. "You wanted her last night, *mi Capitán*." Pedro tried to keep the edge of jealousy out of his voice. "You know she always pays you back in some way."

"Damn her! I should've left her in Tortuga. What am I doing with this crazy wench!"

Mexican half-breed bitch, thought Pedro, but again he kept his mouth shut.

In his cabin, the Captain threw his arms up in anger. The captive had spilled the inkhorn on the floor and smeared ink all over the bedclothes. The written pages of his log were torn in half, the other pages... The Captain dragged the lamp across the desk to see his logbook better. "By your life, Pedro!" he said under his breath. "This is no hen-scratching , man!"

On one page the girl had written the name *Jerónima* over and over, and on the other pages a long verse, in a penmanship so elegant and curlicued it confirmed his suspicion that the halfbreed he'd been sporting with for the past six weeks had been educated in a monastery. How she'd gotten mixed in with the Negroes, he didn't know. It wasn't common buccaneer practice to take Indians or halfbreeds for slaves, but the girl was attached to one of the Negro girls in his share of the plunder they'd captured in Vera Cruz, and had pleaded with him to take her along, had actually knelt at his feet and kissed his groin, promising to do whatever he wanted in exchange for coming on the *Neptune*. Captain de Graaf had a weakness for brave women. Besides, he had never bedded a wench that had eyes of different colors: one dark as Jamaican rum, the other green as French chartreuse.

At first the girl was dutiful and obedient, though she was a virgin, and wept each time he took her. But then the Negro girl who was her friend caught the pox from some of the slaves they'd picked up in Havana, and his men had thrown them all overboard to keep the rest of the cargo from getting infected. Ever since then, the halfbreed wandered through the decks, calling for her friend, wailing like a madwoman.

In the mornings and in the evenings, when the slaves were brought up to the light to eat and exercise, the girl served their food, chanting the "*Ave María*" with such sorrow that the slaves and some of the French sailors broke into sobbing. Cook said that when the girl helped him in the galley, she talked to a black figure that she carried in a pouch hanging from her neck. She could stand for hours in the stern, staring at the water, ignoring the sailors pinching and fondling, holding an invisible rosary between her hands, her lips moving in silent prayer. When the Captain brought her to his bed, she stared at him with crazed, terrified eyes and shouted a rhymed verse to him—until he finished. The Captain thought the girl had lost her wits completely, but this writing on the page showed him that he was wrong, that there was still hope of getting rid of her at a good price.

"*Hombres necios que acusaís a la sin razón, sin ver que sois la ocasión de lo mismo que culpais,*" the Captain read the beginning of the verse aloud. "Pedro. Go find her, quick! I have to talk to her before the merchants get here."

When Pedro left, the Captain sat down at his desk and drew up a bill of sale, dipping the pen into the puddle of ink soaking into the floor.

I, Captain Laurens-Cornille de Graaf, commander of the buccaneer frigate, the Neptune, hereby sell this halfbreed wench, captured in war on the coast of New Spain and subject to servitude. Her name is Jeronima. She is approximately twenty years old, has all her teeth and is immune to the pox. For her sturdy health and her knowledge of letters, her price is 50 sterling pounds.

21 June 1683

The Captain signed the bill, sprinkled sand over the ink, then poured himself a generous shot of Spanish brandy to celebrate his fortune. If there was one friendly thing he could say about the Puritans, it was that they knew how to appreciate fine penmanship, even in a wench. He heard the cannons go off in the harbor and knew that the ghosts of New England were just up ahead.

II.

She could not remember how long the journey had taken. After Aléndula's disappearance, she had stopped counting the days since the pirates' ship had left Vera Cruz. She had stopped listening to the wailing of the slaves and to the strange sounds of the pirates' language. She heard only water, the flapping of sails, the night wind howling through the portholes. In the mornings, when she had to mash the horse beans for the slaves' breakfast, the stench of it brought her momentarily out of the numbness that had grown around her like a silkworm's case. In that slit of time, she would notice where she was, and remember what had happened to Aléndula. She would see the swollen boards of the kitchen floor where every night, except those she spent with the white-haired man who spoke her language, the cook rolled her over and pumped her from behind. She would hear the clank of chains on the ladders and know that the slaves were being shuffled up to the upper deck for their morning rations of horse beans and water. After they ate, one of the pirates would pound stupidly on a drum, and the other pirates would prod or whip the slaves to dance to the rhythmless drum beats, their chains rattling, their moans strung in a perverse harmony. It was this, more than being shackled to the lower deck, more than breathing the fumes of excrement and vomit, more than hearing the constant keening of the other slaves; it was this denigrating dance in the open air that had most poisoned Aléndula's soul until finally she could not stand up any longer, and could not climb the ladder to the upper deck, and the little water she drank convulsed her body.

She remembered saying, "I don't know where we're going, Aléndula, and you're making this more difficult for us. Why don't you eat? Look at you! You'll die down here without any air. Please try to get up!"

But Aléndula was delirious at that point, her mind still traveling to the village of San Lorenzo that they had never reached because they had gone to Vera Cruz first. It had taken them all of April and half of May to cross the mountains and come in sight of Vera Cruz. From the foothills they could see the big ships anchored by the fort, the Spanish colors waving in the hot wind. Aléndula said it was the *Flota* and they ran down to the port to watch the spectacle of seasick *señoras* and dizzy *hidalgos* and water-logged priests descending from the Spanish Fleet, unloading the wondrous treasures they had brought from across the sea. Instead of the Spaniards, they had found pirates. The flyblown air of Vera Cruz burned with the screams of women being forced, of men being tortured, of Negroes and mulattoes falling to the sword or to the musket or to the clanking coffle of slaves.

What had happened then? How had she gotten on the same ship with Aléndula? There were so many ships. So many pirates. All she remembered was sneaking down to the deck where the Negroes were chained to great iron rings on the floor, having to crawl over their bodies, no space between them, no room in which to stand. And Aléndula weeping constantly.

"My mother's a free woman. Tell them that, Concepción. If my mother's free, I'm free. Don't they know that? I'm not a slave. They can't make me a slave! I'm from San Lorenzo!

One morning Aléndula refused to dance with the others on the top deck, and the pirate beating the drum came up and kicked her in the belly. Aléndula's eyes rolled back in her head and she started screaming *"Eleggua! Eleggua!"* Her voice was like the cry of a rabid cat. The pirate kicked Aléndula again and again until she stopped screaming, blood and the gray foam of bean mash dribbling from her mouth.

She had watched Aléndula's beating with a hatred so pure it felt like a blessing, like a bath in holy water that purified her spirit. Her mission was clear. She had to kill somebody. She would stab the Captain with his own sword the next time he rammed himself inside her. But that night, after the Captain had used her, he was called to the top deck and left her alone in his cabin. She would have to do something else. Break everything in the room. Or better still, set the cabin on fire. She took the lamp and smashed it on the floor, watched the oily puddle grow blue then explode into flames, felt the smoke in her eyes as the flames tunneled into the Captain's chair and caught on the leather. Somehow Pedro stopped the fire, and the Captain had her locked up in a storeroom in the lowest deck. With no pirates defiling her, nothing but the rocking of the ship and the continual slap of the sea to distract her, she was able to sleep and remember.

At first the memories were only sounds: hushed voices, a trill of birdsong, footsteps, the keening chords of an instrument. Gradually the sounds collected weight. Like magnets, they drew pieces of images to their core, became shadows and then figures that moved like puppets on a makeshift stage. There were two central players: Aléndula and a woman called *Madre,* whose face was hidden under a black veil. There was a garden, and a shack in the garden where Aléndula lived in chains.

There was a great house with many rooms, and many mysteries within the rooms, and many footsteps. She looked for herself in the garden and in the house, but neither was her place. In a corner of the stage stood a birdcage and it was here she found the shadow that belonged to her, and a voice that said, *"We are all slaves to our destinies, Concepción. Destiny is the cage each woman is born with."* Another figure appeared, dressed in sackcloth, her white-gloved hands pushing a broom.

III.

Madre. The word tumbled in her sleep like a dry weed, thorny stems scratching behind her eyes. *Madre.* A woman in a white tunic and a long black veil, an angel pinned to her chest, a quill in her hand, a woman with ink-stained fingers. *Madre,* Concépcion had called her, though her own mother had been a Zapotec and had died at Concepción's birth. Why did she call that woman *Madre*?

Awake, she pressed her fingers against her eyelids, pressed hard until she saw lights and rows of tiny squares, her pupils throbbing under her fingertips and dark shapes swirling into focus. A great patio with five fountains. Grapefruit and lemon trees. Birdcages hanging from the branches. It was the place where she had lived, a house full of women dressed like *Madre,* bells tolling seven times a day. The house of San Jerónimo.

Madre had been her mistress, her teacher. *Madre* had trained her to take dictation, to read Latin and play chess, to copy manuscripts in the calligraphy of Benedictine monks.

She remembered Madre's voice singing a sad song about a fallen apple. *"Señora Santana, ¿por qué llora la niña? Por una manzana que se le ha caído..."* She had been so little then. Concepción remembered another woman, much older than *Madre,* who had said to her, *"In here, I am not your father's mother. Never call me grandmother. Never forget your place. You are here only because I am the Mother Superior of this house and because my son felt pity for you and didn't want to put you out into the street."*

She eased the pressure on her eyes and wept into her palms.

ꙮ

She had dreamed of leaving the convent only to ride the canoes among the floating gardens of Xochimilco, or to take the yearly pilgrimage to the holy hills of Tepeyac to see the bullfights and the *teatros de corrales,* to wear a costume and dance in the *mascaradas.* It had never occurred to Concepción to leave the convent forever or to run away from the place of her birth. But Aléndula had told her stories of the village of San Lorenzo where free Negroes ruled like kings. She spoke of ceremonies that startled Concepción. Of moon mothers and river goddesses and altars piled with coconuts, oranges, and bones. Of old women who smoked cinnamon bark to see the future and sacrificed roosters to talk to the dead.

"You have to see it, Concepción. *Please* come with me to San Lorenzo! It won't be the same to go without you."

"But I'm not a *cimarrona*. I don't belong there."

"I'm not a *cimarrona* either, not anymore. I wouldn't be a prisoner in a convent if I hadn't failed as a *cimarrona*."

It wasn't your fault, Aléndula. There were spies all over the city. Everyone knew about the insurrection."

"I should have been hung. A *cimarrón* must live free or die. That's the law of San Lorenzo. I should have been hung like my *papi*."

"I'm glad they didn't hang you, Aléndula. You're the only friend I've ever had. My mistress says I shouldn't associate with the maids, but the boarders won't talk to me either."

"It was so horrible, Chica, the way they quartered him, the dogs snarling over his entrails. But he didn't bleed, not a drop of blood. He took all of his *ashé* with him to *Olorum*. I know he's ashamed of me, locked up here for three years, never even attempting to escape. I have to get out of here. I have to be free. You can get me out of here. I know you can. Even if you free just one person, you'll be a *cimarrona*, and then you can go with me to San Lorenzo and we'll both be free."

"I'm not a slave, Aléndula, *nor* a prisoner. I don't need to go to San Lorenzo to be free."

"You don't know anything," Aléndula said, sinking back into the swamp-thick shadows of her prison shed. "To live without a mistress, to listen to your own head, to make your own destiny. You don't know what any of that is, Concepción."

"*Madre*, what's the difference between freedom and destiny?"

"Freedom is the opposite of destiny," *Madre* said.

"What's destiny?"

"Look up, Concepción. Look around you. What do you see?"

Concepción's eyes roamed over the bookshelves and the cluttered tables of *Madre*'s study. "Your cell," she answered.

"You see a cage. Destiny is the cage that each of us is born with, and we can't ever leave that cage, Concepción. We are all slaves to our destinies."

"But you told me that being a *mestiza* made me free."

Madre twisted three handfuls of Concepción's hair into a tight braid. "No, you're not free," she said.

"Didn't you say I could leave here if I wanted to?"

"That's not what I mean, Concepción. I'm not talking about physical freedom. You can leave the convent if you want to, but that won't make you free. Look at yourself." She handed Concepción the mirror. "What kind of face do you see?"

"I don't know, *Madre*. *My* face."

"A *woman's* face," said *Madre*. "A woman who will never be allowed to be the kind of person she wants to be."

"Because I'm a *mestiza*?"

"Because you're a woman. That's the cage we're both born with, Concepción. It doesn't matter that you're a *mestiza* or a *criolla* or a servant or a nun. If your destiny is to be a woman, you will never know what it means to fly."

"Did I make you angry, *Madre*?"

"I'm angry at *them*."

"At who, *Madre*?"

"*Men*. Bullheaded men who won't allow women to live according to our natures."

"I thought destiny came from God."

"God made man in his own image; that's what we're taught, isn't it, Concepción?"

ꟹ

She smelled pineapples and boiled beef, garlic, starch and wax. The smells of the kitchen in *Madre's* cell, and of Jane, *Madre's* slave, stirring the pots. Jane of the *metate* and the broom, of the long tongue and the shifty eyes and the voice strident as a *verdulera*'s.

"I know all about your plan, *mestiza*. Think I don't have ears? Think I haven't seen you sneaking around the prisoner every chance you get? Spying on the gatekeeper to see where she hides the keys to that shack. I know exactly what you two are up to. That's why I figured I better talk to you before you and your prisoner friend jump the fence."

"You stopped at a *pulqueria* when you went to the market today, didn't you, Jane? How can you go there? How can you drink that slime? Aren't you worried she's going to smell it on you?"

"I can tell you a secret, Concepción, and you'll be thanking me the rest of your days, wondering what you would've done without me teaching you this secret about men."

"Leave me alone. I don't want to hear your vulgar stories. I have to finish this work before she gets back from prayers."

"Now, don't go acting like you're as pure as the Immaculate Conception. Even if that *is* your name, you're nothing but a halfbreed and halfbreeds ain't never been immaculately conceived."

"Shut your mouth, Jane!"

"Listen to this, *mestiza*! She don't know anything about men, and even if she did, she'd never do you the favor of telling you how they are. Men are everywhere out there, and they can smell you when you're green and ignorant, the way you are. Just remember this: men got one weakness, and it's always hanging in the same place. He'll do anything for that weakness. First time he uses it on you it'll hurt like the devil's tearing into you with his hot fork. But don't let him know how much it hurts, or he'll hurt you more. Only way to heal the wound is to rub gunpowder into it. Good thing about gunpowder is it kills his seed. Bad thing is it'll nearly kill you, too, if you use too much, or if you do it when the moon is full."

The brisk, dark morning air had made her teeth chatter; dread had prowled in her veins.

"Aléndula! *Despierta!* We're leaving!" she whispered, trying to find the keyhole of the toolshed in the darkness. She heard Aléndula stirring inside, her heavy chains rattling.

"Concepción?"

"I've got the keys, Aléndula."

"Hurry up, Chica!"

Concepción felt the key slip into the chamber. She crossed herself quickly. The lock clicked. Aléndula yanked on the door.

"My hands! Free my hands!"

Concepción fumbled in the darkness with the manacles on Aléndula's wrists. She felt a cry swelling in her throat. Her fingers were moving so slowly! *Help me, Santa Lucía,* she prayed in silence. She felt the shackles open. Again, she crossed herself.

"Hold this!" She gave Aléndula the basket that she carried on her arm. Inside were the clothes she had brought for her, as well as a blanket and the scissors she had taken from *Madre*'s desk. The pouch of coins that *Madre* had given her the night before hung between her breasts. She squatted to free Aléndula's ankles, her head pounding as though she had woodpeckers trapped in her skull.

"Santísima Virgen de Guadalupe, Angel de la guardia, ayúdenme!" she prayed aloud. Her hands were trembling so hard she couldn't find the keyhole and she dropped the keys.

"Por tu vida, Concepción," muttered Aléndula. "You're looking in the wrong place. It's on the inside of my other foot."

"Don't talk to me, Aléndula! I'm too scared." She turned the key.

"They're off!" cried Aléndula, stepping out of the fetters. "Let's get out of here!"

But the door hinges squeaked. The sound of breathing filled the dark shack. Aléndula's hand clamped around Concepción's arm. The cry in Concepción's throat leaked out.

"Is that you, Jane?" Concepción managed to say. She heard whining. The dogs had followed her. She crossed herself a third time, nearly wetting her pants with relief. *"Son los perros,"* she said as the dogs encircled them and sniffed at their knees. Holding hands, they inched out the door, Aléndula closing the door of the shed behind them. Startled birds flapped out of the bushes.

By the time they reached the mulberry grove at the back of the garden, the sky had turned from black to indigo.

"Take off those rags," Concepción said. She handed Aléndula the extra skirt and *huipil* and *huaraches* that she had bundled up in her *rebozo*. The clear, high voices of the nuns at *matins* rose from the open windows of the choir.

"Put these on, Aléndula. I'm going to cut some carnations. That way, when we leave the city we can look like we're selling flowers."

"You're going with me, after all?"

"I guess so."

For a moment, Aléndula held her tightly and kissed both her cheeks. "I owe you my life for freeing me, Concepción."

"We have to wait until it's lighter so that we can see what we're doing," said Concepción, "and then we'll climb the tree and drop down to the street at first light. We can't go anywhere until the night watchmen go away."

"Don't be a fool, Concepción. What are we waiting for? We'll be safer in the dark!"

"If I'm such a fool, I don't know why you want me to go with you. Can you see anything? Do you know there's broken glass on the wall that'll tear your skin off? Go ahead! Jump over!"

"Don't get angry, Chica. I'm scared, that's all. I know you know what you're doing."

"Just get dressed," said Concepción. "The *huaraches* will probably be too big for you, but that's all I have." She took the scissors and ran to the field of carnations, their smell of damp cloves spicing the cold air.

They waited up in the mulberry tree until the bells of all the churches and all the monasteries of the city announced morning Mass, and then they let themselves drop to the cobbled street. Carrying the basket of carnations between them, they tried not to run to the causeway southeast of the Plaza Mayor. At that early hour the causeway was crowded with merchants, muleteers, gypsies, Indians, beggars, and mounted soldiers patrolling the lake of bodies moving into and out of Mexico City.

IV.

"Hungry, bitch? Here, bitch." The pirate named Pedro lured her out of confinement with a piece of roasted turtle meat dangling from a stick. The smell of the meat turned her mouth into a saliva pit, but she knew that right behind Pedro was the cook with his net. They had played this game before. They would not catch her again. She let them think they had baited her, and then just as the net swooped down, Concepción kicked her way out of Pedro's grasp and ran to the slave deck.

Nearly half the Negroes had died already on the journey. The ones who remained didn't speak to each other anymore. Curled into balls, they whimpered and moaned and waited. Concepción found Aléndula feverish and reeking of urine. Her teeth were loose and her gums bled. Concepción grabbed Aléndula's hand and pinched what was left of the ash-gray skin.

"Aléndula! Wake up! What's happened to you?"

The crust around Aléndula's eyes cracked open. "Concepción? Where have you been, Chica? I thought you went back to that convent."

"I wish I could go back. This is like purgatory, worse than purgatory because we're not even dead. What have you done to yourself, Aléndula? Why aren't you getting better? I can't take care of you all the time."

"I'm happy, Concepción. I know the way now."

"I'm so afraid, Aléndula. I think I'm losing my mind. I can't remember *Madre's* name. I can't remember what happened between Mexico and Vera Cruz. Tell me about the journey, Aléndula. What did we do?"

"I dreamt the alligator again." Aléndula said, her breath rank as sour dough. "It was a long dream, Concepción. I was walking with my *papi to* the swamp and it was very bright and windy. My *papi*'s voice kept getting lost in the wind, but I know that he is telling me to call Eleggua, that Eleggua would meet me at the crossroads if I made my *ashé* burn." She paused to lick the cracked leather of her lips.

"What are you saying, Aléndula? You know I don't understand this *ashé* business."

"At the edge of the swamp under the ceiba tree," Aléndula continued, "my papi danced Eleggua's dance and then he rolled on the ground and his body changed into an alligator and he swam away into the swamp. He wants me to follow him. Don't you see my papi wants to free me? I'll be free in the water. Yemayá will take me to Eleggua."

Concepción shook the bones of Aléndula's shoulders. "Stop it! You're babbling like a fool. I'm going to get you some water now, and you're going to drink it, and then I'm going to give you some bread, and I'm going to wash you, and your fever's going to go away."

"I have to make my *ashé* burn, Chica. I'll be free in the water."

Concepción felt her hand slapping the hot flesh of Aléndula's cheek. "Does this look like freedom to you? *Cimarrona?* Is that what you are? You and your stupid freedom!"

The slaves had started to wail again, and the smell of Aléndula's body made Concepción want to retch. She crawled through the open spaces and climbed to the upper deck to wash herself in the night air.

The next morning Pedro told her that Aléndula had caught the pestilence of the Havana slaves, that she had been thrown into the sea in the middle of the night along with the others, and Concepción knew that Aléndula had been making herself weak on purpose, that whoever Eleggua was, Aléndula had wanted him to come and claim her. And suddenly she hated Aléndula—her cowardice, her stupid beliefs. Hated her so much she would black out from hoping with all her strength that Aléndula would be torn apart by every creature in the deep. It was Aléndula's fault that she was here, alone, sodomized and violated by pirates, trapped in a floating prison heading God knows where on the rocking nightmare of the open sea. She had lost everything, and for that she cursed Aléndula to eternal bleeding at the bottom of the ocean.

May the ocean turn red with your blood. May you never stop bleeding. May your blood feed all the fishes and all the monsters and all the spirits of the sea.

Suddenly she was empty. She remembered nothing except Aléndula, her ghost twitching from the rigging of the ship, flapping on the sails, howling with the wind. Her own name shriveled on her tongue and vanished. And then the singing started. A singing filled with a knowledge that punched her throat but did not surface from the darkness. The words of the singing ululated through her vocal cords in a language that was not her own. *Sancta Maria mater dei, salve mater misericordia, mea culpa, mea culpa, Ave Maria, Alleluia, mea culpa.* She would find herself gazing at the ocean, waiting for Aléndula to rise with the moon, and the words would flow out of her like blood. A rosary of jade beads would appear in her hands. And above her, the ship's sails would become women in white tunics and black veils bending down to kiss her.

Other times, with the Captain moving on top of her, she would see a woman in the background, sitting at the Captain's desk, dipping the quill into the ink, writing, dipping, writing, and in the doorway, the shadow of a cloaked man holding a long, hooked staff.

Peeling yams or kneading dough in the ship's kitchen, she would suddenly take the black queen out of her pouch and stroke her and kiss her, knowing the black queen had a name that she could no longer recall.

One day just before dawn, standing at her vigil for Aléndula, she noticed a briskness in the air and white birds perched on the rigging. She saw something moving in the water. Something dark and heavy and huge nearly rubbing up against the side of the ship, arching out of the water and sinking again, soaking her in the heavy splash of its gray-black tail. She had seen other ocean creatures on the journey, but none had stirred her as this one, none had showed her the dark and massive weight of her own solitude. In that moment, with the creature suspended just above the water, the name came to her, the name of the black queen: *Jerónima*. She rushed down to the Captain's desk and wrote it down on the only parchment she could find. *Jerónima,* over and over so that she would not forget it again. And as she wrote, a body of words surged like the creature out of the dark water.

She saw a stack of pages scribbled in an almost illegible hand. A magnifying glass appeared, and through the glass she could discern that the writing formed a long poem which she had to copy:

Hombres necios que acusáis
a la mujer sin razón,
sin ver que sois la ocasión
de lo mismo que culpáis:

She inked the pen again, and the pen became the goose quill she had always held. The horn of the inkpot turned to silver.

si con ansia sin igual
solicitáis su desdén
¿por qué queréis que obren bien
si las incitáis al mal?

She saw the range of green mountains that she and Aléndula had trekked, the waterfalls in which they bathed, the fish Aléndula yanked from the streams, the caves they slept in where at sunrise swarms of bats returned to claim their darkness. She remembered resting in the shade of cypresses and weeping willows, counting the dried carcasses of cicadas that still clung to the bark of the trees.

...¿cuál es más de culpar,
aunque cualquiera mal haga:
la que peca por la paga,
o el que paga por pecar?

She saw the pass between the volcanoes, Popocateptl and Ixtaccihuatl, their white crests more luminous than clouds in the turquoise twilight, the torches of Mexico City lighting the valley of Anahuac behind them.

V.

A chessboard. Bells tolling in the distance. Two voices whispering as though in a confessional.

"Maybe it's a good idea for you to leave."

"*Madre,* I'm afraid to go. What if we get lost or if we're attacked by some wild animal."

"I think you will be much safer than I in that wilderness. In here, there are more wild animals than you know."

"I thought you would beg me to stay, *Madre.* I thought I meant more to you."

"You have been invaluable to me, Concepción. But the new archbishop is not my friend. He is not any woman's friend. the rumor is he's cleaning out the convents of all particular friendships, and if Mother Superior gets her way, you'll be the first to be taken away from here. Who knows where they'd send you. It's much better if you choose your own path. You're eighteen now."

"I didn't know I was your friend, *Madre;* I thought I was just your assistant."

"I know this is a difficult choice, *cariño.* Long ago I had to decide whether I wanted to sign my life away to the convent, and guess what helped me make my decision? I played a chess game with la Marquesa and decided if I lost I had to leave."

"But I always lose, *Madre.*"

"Not always, *cariño.* Let's play one last game. I'll be black tonight, so that you can begin."

The pieces moved across the board, the white side losing quickly, until the queens faced each other across the same rank and file. It was

Madre's move, but instead of taking the white queen, she picked up the black queen and turned the piece slowly between her ink-stained fingers.

"You can start your life over, Concepción. You can shed everything but death. Even if you'll never be as free as you want to be, at least you can say you *own* this decision; that's as close as you can get to owning your own life."

And then *Madre* got to her feet and stepped out from behind the chess table. They stood face to face like the black queen and the white queen. And suddenly they were embracing. They were the same height, their bodies so close that Concepción could feel the bindings on *Madre*'s breasts, could smell the castile soap that *Madre* had lathered in her bath. *Madre* gazed at her strangely, and for an instant Concepción felt her belly quivering and a small thing opening and closing inside her, the meaning in *Madre*'s eyes transparent as the moon's reflection in a fountain.

"Write to me, *cariño*. Sign your letters with the name *Jerónima*, that way the Abbess won't know it's you, and the name will remind you of this place."

"I could never forget this place. That would be like forgetting you, *Madre*."

Madre handed her the black queen. "I want you to take this to remember me by, Concepción, to remember the eleven years we spent together and all the work we did."

"I'll name her *Jerónima*," Concepción said, and pressed the onyx queen to her lips.

Madre's gaze rested for a moment on Concepción's mouth. Then she shook her head slightly and stepped away, turning her back to Concepción.

VI.

The cannon boom startled her. She smelled sulfur. The ship had slowed down. Feet pounding the upper deck. The squeak of rigging and masts. The weight of the anchors dragging the ship to a heavy stop. She climbed on the berth, and through the porthole she saw green islets floating in a teal-blue bay, thick mist in the distance. The white birds she had seen earlier circled in and out of the mist, screeching like birds of doom. They had arrived wherever they were going. They would be looking for her, she knew. They would be leaving her here.

She ran out of the cabin and down to her hiding place behind the cannon balls, clutching Jerónima. If they didn't find her, maybe the pirate ship would take her back to Mexico.

VII.

Pedro knocked on the Captain's door and came in, dragging the half-breed. The girl had her hands crossed and was mumbling into her fingers like a lunatic.

"*¿Os escribisteis esto?*" asked the Captain, pointing to the page.

The girl glanced at the logbook and shook her head.

"*¿Sois Jerónima?*"

At the sound of the name, the girl pressed her sooty hands to her chest.

"*¿Sois Jerónima?*" the Captain repeated.

The girl shook her head again. "Concepción," she mumbled.

"*¿Concepción?*" said the Captain. "*Ese nombre es muy difícil.* The people here will find that name too difficult to say, and they'll baptize you with a name of their own. You've written *Jerónima* all over my book. That name will be easier for these English tongues. I've called you Jeronima on this bill of sale."

The girl's eyes turned to water. "Bill of sale?" she managed to ask.

"What did you think?" the Captain said in his own language. "I'm a man of business. I didn't bring you all the way to New England to let you off without paying for your trip."

The girl had pressed her eyes shut, and the tears streaked the grime on her gaunt, brown cheeks.

"*Este lugar se llama Boston. ¿Podéis decir Boston?*" The Captain found himself explaining. "*Es otro colonia. Nueva Inglaterra. Vinimos de Nueva España.* These people are English. They like discipline and hard work. They don't know your language. If you want to survive among them, you must learn their language right away. They will not tolerate your speaking in a language they don't understand. Most important, you must never pray or sing or let your wits go out of control as you've done on the *Neptune*. Do you understand what I'm saying, Jeronima?"

The girl opened her eyes and looked at him. Yes, he could definitely see the intelligence in there, a clear space under the dark layer of madness. But it wasn't madness, after all. The girl, he realized, was full of rage, a rage so bitter it had changed her face, made her seem as wild as the Arawak boy who had stowed away on his ship so many years ago. To think he had actually slept in her presence! The wench could have slit his throat or pumped him full of powder. The thought made his groin jump, and he wanted to take her one last time, slide between her skinny thighs and tame her wildness.

"I want to go back to Mexico," the girl said, the first clear sentence she had spoken in six weeks.

"No, Jeronima. You begged me to bring you aboard the *Neptune*. Remember that. I would have left you on that island. Now, you must forget Mexico. This is where you will live from now on."

The Captain tore the pages of the girl's writing out of his logbook and stitched them to the tattered embroidery of her blouse. Then he pulled the girl's *rebozo* up over her shorn head.

"The English don't like women walking around with their naked heads showing," he said. He looked down at what was left of the girl's sandals. "They don't like the feet to show either, but we can't do anything about that. Pedro! Bring a towel and clean Jeronima's face!"

The girl did not take her eyes off the black wick of the lamp as Pedro scrubbed her face with the wet cloth, mumbling insults to her under his breath. The Captain buckled on his cutlass and instructed Pedro to take the girl to the poop deck and stand her away from the Negroes. This one would not be auctioned. This one had a *precio fijo*.

VIII.

Precio fijo. Fixed price. She was aware of something cold and hard clamping around her rib cage, an iron fist battering at her chest. Her body felt like a dried carcass still clinging to the bark of life.

I'll be free in the water, she heard Aléndula say as she climbed the ladder with the pirate behind her. An auction block had been set up on the deck, and the Negroes were already being paraded in front of white-wigged men in velvet coats and black hats. The pirate led her to the other end of the deck where a short man and a tall man stood beside a table, looking impatient.

IX.

"And who is this, Captain?" said the merchant who had commissioned him. "Have you taken a wife?"

"I have brought you something most unusual, Mr. Shrimpton," said the Captain. "This halfbreed wanted to escape the Papists of New Spain and begged me to bring her along. She is a diligent maid, but also an accomplished scribe, as you can see for yourself." The Captain handed the bill of sale to Shrimpton's assistant, the cross-eyed Mr. Adder.

"It says fifty pounds for the wench," said Adder.

"Fifty pounds for a cursed wench?" said Shrimpton.

"Why say you she is cursed?" asked the Captain.

"She has the eyes of a devil, Captain. I would not take her even if she were free," said Shrimpton. "Now, what about the sugar?"

"She is not a devil. She is a halfbreed," said the Captain.

"Tell me, Captain, is there a difference?" said Shrimpton. "Adder, are you seriously contemplating the purchase of this heathen?"

Adder was bending over the pages that the Captain had sewed to the girl's blouse, scrutinizing the writing through a pair of spectacles.

"I've got a chicken farm and a lame father-in-law that need tending to," said Adder. "I'll give you thirty pounds, Captain."

"Yet you'd pay twenty for a simple-minded slave," said Captain de Graaf. "Her price is fixed, Mr. Adder. If you don't want her, I'm sure some gentleman in Virginia will."

"Captain? You did bring the sugar, I trust?" asked Shrimpton, looking around the deck.

"Can she count?" asked Adder.

"Her education is impeccable, as you can see, Sir. Surely she was not spared the knowledge of numbers." To Shrimpton the Captain said, "We've brought you thirty barrels of raw sugar and eighteen barrels of rum."

"Captain de Graaf, our agreement stated—"

From the corner of his eye, the Captain was watching Adder poke the end of his knife handle into the girl's mouth.

"Yes, Mr. Shrimpton, our agreement stated that we would provide you with fifty barrels of sugar and twenty-five barrels of rum, but you see, it's been a dry season in the West Indies, and there aren't enough buccaneers doing business in sugar anymore."

Now Adder was prodding the girl's sandals with the toe of his buckled shoe. The girl's eyes were like smoldering coal under the sparse line of her brows. Her gaze fixed on the sea.

"It's easier to procure silver than sugar these days," the Captain continued. "We're lucky we brought this much. We did, however, bring you double the slaves you asked for; of course, the pox and the fever always take their toll. Nothing we can do about that."

Adder straightened up and flicked the girl's *rebozo* off with the back of his knuckles. "What happened to her hair?"

"Six weeks among slaves," the Captain implied. But seeing that neither of them understood, he added, "Lice. But she's clean now."

Adder read and reread the bill of sale, then looked into the girl's eyes. "You ought to be thankful that the Captain brought you here among God's chosen in the new Zion. We shall name you Thankful Breed." He set the bill of sale on the table, took the pen, and scratched out *Jeronima*.

"Thankful Breed," he said aloud as he wrote in the girl's new name.

X.

The man's hands and face were as white as limestone, his eyes like blue flames burning her skin. She turned her head and watched the Negroes being auctioned and appraised, each one trapped in the cage of her own and his own destiny. *We are all slaves to our destinies, Madre* had said, and now she understood, finally, why Aléndula had let the pestilence take her.

I'll be free in the water.
Fixed price.

She felt her legs running. Her *rebozo* sliding off her shoulders. She heard shouting behind her. Felt the hard thump of her knees hitting the side of the ship. Her hands gripping the rail, the muscles wrenching in her shoulders, and her body swinging down, suspended for an instant and then sinking, sinking as fast and heavy as the huge creature who had surfaced to show her the way.

The water, like thousands of needles, pierced her bones. She had never known so much cold. Her veins grew numb. She opened her eyes, and they stung from the salt. She saw nothing above her but clear gray water, black shapes in the depths below. Her sandals slipped off. The pouch that held Jeronima floated away. Her skirt clung to her like a shroud. A current of joy heaved through her chest. She was free. She had escaped the cage of her destiny and was sinking, now, to the depths of the sea to join Aléndula.

And suddenly the air stopped bubbling from her mouth. Her ears popped. Something drifted past her face. Something pale and phosphorescent swirling in the water, coiling and uncoiling like a snake. *You can shed everything but death*. She saw the mouth opening, the fangs long and luminous. She gasped, and her stomach bloated with saltwater. In the wild kicking of her heart, she knew she needed air. She *wanted* air. She needed to cough, to breathe. Her arms and legs pumped like windmills in the water, but her body continued to sink. She was sobbing, now, choking on the humors of the sea, fighting the currents like a netted fish until at last she felt her head break through the surface, and her face came up and she swallowed air.

Nora Glickman

Nora Glickman is a professor of Spanish at Queens College, City University of New York. She was born in La Pampa, Argentina, and studied in Israel, England, and the United States, where she has lived for many years. Glickman has written two books of short stories: *Uno de sus Juanes* (1983) and *Mujeres, memorias, malogros* (1991), as well as other fictional pieces which have appeared in many journals and anthologies, and have been translated into English, Hebrew and Portuguese. Her play, "Noticias de suburbio," received dramatic readings both here and abroad. Glickman has written extensively on contemporary Latin American literature, with special emphasis on Argentine theatre and narrative. Her research towards her doctoral dissertation on "The Jewish Image in Brazilian and Argentine Literature" (1972) led to further critical studies, including her book on the white slave trade, *La trata de blancas en la literatura latinoamericana,* and a translation from Yiddish of Leib Malach's play "Regeneración" (1984). She has edited two volumes of *Modern Jewish Studies* (1993) devoted to Argentine fiction and criticism, and co-edited, with Robert Di Antonio, a volume of critical essays entitled *Tradition and Innovation: Jewish Issues in Latin American Writings* (1993). Her present work includes a book on the narrative of Jewish women in Latin America, and a third collection of short stories, *Clavel temprano.* She is co-editing a bilingual anthology of Latin American Women Dramatists with Flora Schiminovich, and a critical anthology on Argentine dramatists. "A Day in New York" is an example of her short fiction written in English.

A Day in New York

Nora Glickman

How's New York these days? — is the most frequent question asked of me every time I visit my country. I try to go down to South America every year or two, to keep in touch with family and friends. My friends, mostly professional and business people, come to the U.S. whenever they save a few dollars, to get a healthy dose of shopping, musicals and museums. But no matter how much they walk the streets of Manhattan, they want to hear of the real New York from someone like them, a Latin American, who actually lives and works here. They don't realize that one is never a citizen of this city. At most, one is an inhabitant, a sharer of the space and the experience. Nevertheless, I tell them about a typical day:

I leave the house at 8:00 a.m. and drive the children to their respective schools. After that I park my car in front of a tranquil pond, sharing the landscape with shrieking, unkempt geese. There I do some stretching exercises to warm up, then run three miles, passing through shady streets and trying to avoid nasty dogs. Then I check my pulse, walk about one block, and check it again after I've cooled down and got my breath back. Today, Friday, while running, I notice a long line of cars around one corner, a sign that a tag-sale is nearby, and can't resist the temptation to go in, even for just a few minutes, before returning home for a shower, to be ready for work before 10 a.m. I am still sweating, and my red jogging suit seems too heavy for this warm day. The door of the house is open and there is a crowd inside. I go directly to the living room and look around at the furniture, unsure as to what I'll find. I can leave the place with an old ladle, a picture frame, a thimble, or a sofa-bed; I never know in advance. I notice now that there are no price tags on the books and no price lists on the wall. People are busy chatting. They are wearing dark clothes - too sober, it seems to me, for a tag-sale. I walk to the adjoining room and come upon a long coffin where the body of an old man is lying. I back up a few steps, like a robot, without looking at the mourners, and only turn when I reach the front door and go out running.

I drive to my college listening to a recorded tape borrowed from the library. This time it is Voltaire's *Candide*. In the time it takes to get from Westchester to Queens, I hear more than one side of a tape.

> Cunégonde dropped her handkerchief, and Candide picked it up. She quite innocently took his hand; he as innocently kissed hers with singular grace and ardour. Their lips met, their eyes flashed, their knees trembled, and their hands would not keep still. Baron Thunder-ten-tronckh, happening to pass the screen at that moment, noticed both cause and effect, and drove Candide from the house with powerful kicks on the backside. Cunégonde fainted, and on recovering her senses was boxed on the ears by the Baroness. Thus consternation reigned in the most beautiful of all possible mansions.

After teaching two classes, I use my lunch break to go to the local bakery and buy a cake for Dorothy's celebration on Sunday. Each of her friends will bring something different: ice cream, balloons, potato chips, and potted flowers that Dorothy will plant in her garden after the party is over. Robbie and his band will provide the music. Not his usual "heavy metal," I hope. Dorothy adores the boy. Her daughter Melissa introduced them to her at her high-school graduation ceremony, and they took to each other.

So this Sunday Dorothy and her five children, with Bobby and his band and her many friends, will celebrate with wine and cheese, cakes and balloons.

"How would you like this cake decorated, Miss?" the baker asks me.

"Pink, green and purple flowers would be fine."

"What should I write on the cake?"

"In big letters, please write: HAPPY DIVORCE, DOROTHY!"

I pay for the cake and rush to Barnes and Noble to buy a book for Michael's wedding the following Sunday. Michael, Rabbi Goldman's son, is marrying Paul, who is Episcopalian. They'll celebrate their wedding in the chapel of Columbia University, where Paul is a student, because it is an ecumenical chapel, and no questions are asked, provided you supply your own minister. Everyone agrees the two boys are great. Their fathers, however, will not attend. The mothers are more sensible on such occasions. They feel relieved that at least for now, amidst the AIDS epidemic, their boys are safe from the plague. Promiscuity is a killer, they know, so it's reassuring that Paul and Michael are a steady couple; they love each other, and they even swear that they'll honor and obey each other for as long as they do love.

I manage to return on time to my office to see some students, to attend a boring committee meeting, and to pick up a couple of books from the library. Such is the pleasure of the routine: it allows me to get on with my life outside work, without putting any strain on my mind. When I'm finished with work at the college, I call home to check on the kids, see that they're back home from their afternoon activities, and make sure that the baby-sitter makes them go to bed on time. Then I drive to Forest Hills to give a public lecture.

> A proposal was then made to Don Issachar that he should surrender me to His Eminence. Don Issachar, who is a Court banker, and therefore a man of some standing, would not hear of the proposition, until the Inquisitor threatened him with an auto-de-fé. This forced the Jew's hand, but he made a bargain by which this house and I should belong to both of them in common, to the Jew on Mondays, Wednesdays, and Sabbath days, and to the Inquisitor the other days of the week. This agreement has now lasted for some six months. There has been some quarreling, as they cannot decide whether Saturday night belongs to the old law or to the new. For my part I have resisted both of them so far, and I think that this is why they love me still.

At the Jewish Center I talk about the immigration waves from the Old World into Latin America at the turn of the century. The average age of the audience is seventy. Among the various groups of immigrants, I mention a notorious minority: the white slave traffickers and their merchandise—the innocent young girls who they prostituted. Some of the people in my audience first knew of the existence of a ring of prostitution in Latin America, operated by Jews, mostly from rumors they heard at home from their parents. I also recall the piteous lies that the Jewish victims wrote to their parents back in Poland: "I'm married now...my husband adores me...we keep a *kosher* home...I purify myself at the *mikveh* every month...the gentiles are kind people over here...gold is within the reach of everyone..."

An old woman interrupts me to say that back in those days, in Poland, she used to read to the parents the letters in Yiddish that the girls wrote from Argentina.

"We knew something was wrong, but we didn't know for sure. I didn't fall into that trap. I got out of Poland as soon as my American relatives sent me a ticket. To this America, I mean."

When my talk is over, I stay to have a cup of coffee with the woman, Golda. Her chiseled features have the mark of age and suffering. She has a chalky complexion; her hair is held up by a scarf. You can see the thick veins of her legs through the heavy stockings she wears, in spite of the hot weather. She tells me of her arrival at Ellis Island, and of her three months' internment for tuberculosis.

"How did you manage to enter if you still had T.B.?"

"By pinching my cheeks till they hurt a lot, lowering my head into my legs to make the blood rush up, learning to hold in my cough when I had to. Here my rich relatives—a curse on them!—promised they'd help me bring my parents and brothers if I worked for them. I slaved for years...years of misery those were...And what did they pay me? *Kaduches!* Not a penny did I get from them. I was their maid, their serf. But my people..."

She pauses, and seeing that I do not react, she adds:

"My people are alive. They are here, you know... in this very place, under this very floor."

Golda gets up, and so do I, uncertain as to what to do next.

"Come with me," she says. She takes me to the basement of the building, where she opens a metal door and enters an art studio, crammed with clay busts and statues. At the back, there is a large oven.

"You see? This is my family," Golda says, as she introduces each one to me. "My mother, my father, my brothers Leib and Itzik, my *rebbe*, my grandmother Reizel. And I am here in the center, always with them."

"What are all these nails sticking out?"

"Barbed wire. From Auschwitz."

"And who are all these people over here? Why are they headless?"

"They are all *soneyudim*, that's why."

"*Soneyudim?* What's that?"

"What kind of a Jew are you? Don't you know? *Soneyudim*...Jew haters."

I didn't know.

"And this group of people, in the boat?"

"This is the Ship of Death that carries them all...and I am here in the center too, can you recognize me? I am dead, along with my people."

"What are you saying, Golda! You are outside the boat, you are here, with me, today, in New York. And you are a great artist. You've given life to all these people through your sculpture. It's remarkable. You are an artist. Truly, your work is astonishing!"

She gives me a sidelong look; I can't tell if she feels sorry for me, or pleased.

"I'm not alive. I am dead. I am a living corpse. You are the one who's deceiving yourself, *professoreske*. You and all these people who are as dead as I am...We're all corpses, lost and wandering through this city..."

I drive Golda back to her apartment in Flushing, promising to visit her soon. I eat my sandwich and drink my coffee from a thermos on my way to Manhattan, as the trip to the theatre takes over an hour, and I can't be late.

> Candide made off as quickly as he could to another village. This was in Bulgar territory, and had been treated in the same way by Abar heroes. Candide walked through the ruins over heaps of writhing bodies and at last left the theatre of war behind him. He had some food in his knapsack and his thoughts still ran upon Lady Cunégonde.

My friends and Leo are awaiting me in Soho, a neighborhood in which misery and bohemia compete with each other. Here the chic boutiques share the sidewalk with abandoned buildings, infested with rats and roaches. The streets are filled with motorists, cyclists, skaters, and pedestrians who stop to look at the wares of Pakistani and African salesmen displaying exotic necklaces, leathers and spices. The homeless walk the street pushing supermarket carriages. They stake out their space on sheets of cardboard, huddled beneath ragged coats. Some sleep clutching a plastic bag containing a few empty cans, for redemption at a market, in exchange for a few cents.

We are used to this scene, so Peggy and Howard, and Leo and I walk past and look away, pretending not to see, and go inside the theatre. The lights go down in a few minutes. A beggar walks down the aisle, jingling coins in a plastic cup. Nobody gives him anything, although people ask how the man managed to slip inside. Let him go back to the street if he wants to beg. Finally—either to get rid of him, or out of pity—someone gives him a few cents, and the beggar shouts, at the top of his voice:

"Dirty bastard! You give me a quarter when you just paid over fifty bucks a seat! Can't you spare at least a dollar?"

We are disconcerted. A few more beggars followed the first, armed with knives and sticks. Now it is turning ugly. These don't ask; they demand. Some of us beg them to take our money and leave us alone. This is *our* place. We're relieved to see that they are not drugged, nor about to rape or torture anybody. Once they've filled up their pockets they'll leave us alone. This is the price one has to pay for coming to Soho these days... As soon as their job is done, the first beggar tells us we've just witnessed a new Soho "happening" and that in fact the purpose of the dramatization was to raise our consciousness; to teach us to better appreciate the tragedy of the homeless, the anguish of the dispossessed. They are willing to return our money unless we choose to donate it to a charity to help the homeless. Some of the people don't want their money back; others snatch it away, furious. And as they help us recompose ourselves, they ask us not to reveal the beginning of the play because it would take away the desired suspense.

The rest of the show, of preachy social content, is not as dramatic as the surprise beginning. After the performance, Peggy and Howard go for a bite at a Vietnamese restaurant nearby. Leo and I prefer to wait for them at Rizzoli bookstore, browsing. They return sooner than expected. Peggy is sobbing; Howard looks pale and frightened.

"I just asked some loudmouthed jerks who were sitting next to us to lower their voices, and they did..."

"Oh, yes, they did! You saw what happened after they left," shouted Peggy hysterically."

"We're not sure those were the same guys. They were covered with masks and had weird hats."

"And they scared the hell out of us!"

"So what happened?" I asked.

"They walked toward us with rubber bats in their hands. Then started laughing and turned round and walked away."

"Sure! Nothing happened! Just look at us, shaking like a leaf..."

I suggested they wait at the bookstore while Leo and I brought the car over.

"How do you know you'll find the car where you left it? How do you know they won't come back? I'm not waiting. Sorry! I'm going to get a taxi."

Peggy was too upset. So we walked them to their cab.

From time to time Pangloss would say to Candide:

> "There is a chain of events in this best of all possible worlds; for if you had not been turned out of a beautiful mansion at the point of a jackbox for the love of Lady Cunégonde, and if you had not been involved in the Inquisition, and had not wandered over America on foot, and had not struck the Baron with your sword, and lost all those sheep you brought from Eldorado, you would not be here eating candied fruit and pistachio nuts."
>
> That's true enough, said Candide, "but we must go and work in the garden."

Upon our return to the suburbs, I drop Leo off at our house, but I want to take advantage of the Western Beef supermarket, open 24 hours a day, and shop now that it's empty. I'm exhausted, but tomorrow we're supposed to attend the school's picnic, and my fridge is almost bare. This Western Beef is located in a fast-changing neighborhood; its population varies according to the immigrants who come through Kennedy or across the Rio Grande, according to the foreign wars, and the degree of misery other countries are suffering; here you can find Palestinians, Syrians, Pakistanis, Poles, Salvadorans, Dominicans, Cypriots, Kuwaitis, Russians. As it's late and I'm very cold, I hasten to fill my cart with enough fruits, vegetables, meats, fish, and drinks to last us a couple of weeks at least. I select the food by the sales of the day rather than by the quality of the products, trying to check that the fruit is not rotten, and that the meat is not discolored. The variety and excess of food at the stalls is staggering.

At the corner I recognize the familiar voices of *Latinos* who were sweeping the floor or unloading the vegetables when I came in. Now they are smoking and laughing. My heavy cart pulls me down the ramp at full speed. When I reach the front, where the cashiers should be, it turns out there is no one there.

Some guards are putting the registers away into an armored truck. The policeman who was pacing up and down flinging his billy club is now standing here on guard.

The men look at me half-amused, half-condescending. It probably isn't the first time they've watched someone fill up her cart to the brim while they were closing. Now I see the winter hours posted on the wall: "7:00 a.m. to 2:00 a.m." But I only carry a watch for decoration. Other people's faces and occasional clocks set my hours.

"Wait! Wait for me! Don't take them away yet, I haven't paid for my food!"

The Doberman Pinschers drool impatiently, anticipating their release as soon as the metal curtain drops. Then comes the alarm system directly connected with the police station. So much fuss for apples and cabbages.

I leave in utter disgust, cursing them. It doesn't even console me to think that tomorrow some poor nobody will have to replace all my food in the stalls, that some of the meat and fish will have rotted by then.

As I pull out, one of the men runs towards my car holding a cutting of a tomato plant that he took from the store.

"Para su jardín, doña."

I drive home in silence.

Photo by Linda Haas

Aurora Levins Morales

Aurora Levins Morales was born in Indiera Baja, Puerto Rico, to Rosario, a Puerto Rican born in Spanish Harlem, and Richard, a Russian Jew born in Brooklyn. Both of her parents were political activists. Levins Morales spent most of her childhood in Indiera, a coffee-farming community in the western mountains of Puerto Rico. When she was thirteen, her family moved to Chicago. She started writing as a young child; then, as a teenager, reeling from the culture shock of urban Chicago, she began writing journals about her life. She attended college in northern New Hampshire, and in 1976 moved to the San Francisco Bay Area. Presently, she lives in Berkeley with her daughter. In 1994 she received a Ph.D. in Women's Studies and Puerto Rican history from The Union Institute. Her early essays and short fiction appeared in *Revista Chicano-Riqueña, This Bridge Called My Back* (1981), and *Cuentos: Stories by Latinas* (1983). In 1986 she and her mother, Rosario Morales, published *Getting Home Alive,* a collection of poetry and prose, hailed by critic Efraín Barradas as "the most important book to come out of the Puerto Rican diaspora in a generation." Her recent fiction has appeared in *Ms Magazine, The American Voice* and *Puerto Rican Writers at Home in the USA* (1991). She has just completed a second collection of fiction, *A Remedy for Heartburn and Other Medicine Stories,* and *Remedios: Lives of Puerto Rican Women,* a retelling of Puerto Rican history through prose-poetry stories of the lives of women. She is a frequent contributor to *The Women's Review of Books* and *Bridges: A Journal for Jewish Feminists and Our Friends.* With Rosario Morales, she is gathering material for an anthology: *Malascrianzas: Voices of the Puerto Rican Diaspora.*

A Remedy for Heartburn

Aurora Levins Morales

In Memory of Doña Gina Torres of Bartolo

Our people have always been good at digesting even the most indigestible items on life's menu. Insults that would give a *conquistador* a heart attack—we have learned to wipe them off our faces and put on the handkerchief away for later consideration. Sometimes our pockets bulge with insults, and personally, I have a little red leather coin purse that I had to quit using because it wouldn't close anymore. There were so many insults and so few coins that I was always turning up something nasty whenever I dug around for a subway token. When you run out of storage space, sometimes a hiss or a sneer or some offhand and cheerful piece of disrespect goes down your throat and your stomach has to deal with it. It's not easy. It gives you heartburn like you wouldn't believe, but we can do it. All of us are experts.

As for this jaw-breaking language that gets pushed into our mouths every time we ask for a piece of bread, we're the best there is at digesting that. We roll it around in our sweet tropical saliva and spit it back, sweeter and sharper and altogether more *sabroso.* Everything they dish out to us, we soften and satirize with our acrobatic tongues. We wash with *Palmolíveh* and brush with super-white *Colgáteh.* We rub Vicks *Vaporú* on our chests when we get a cold, and halfway through each day of hard work and boredom, we stop and have some *lonche.* Not at home on weekends. We never have *lonche* at home. But weekdays when we step into some hallway with a counter and six red stools and order a *sánguich*—that's *lonche.*

That's hard to digest, too — tasteless white bread, a smear of mayonnaise, a few wrinkled slices of ham or old-shoe beef, a square of what these people actually were not embarrassed to call American cheese, and some kind of a pale green leaf. But our people have hard stomachs. Hunger makes people more like goats. I've known old men who lived for months on end on nothing but the *malanga* they dug out of other people's land. The USDA surplus lunches they served at our grade school *comedor* were excellent training for the immigrant eater's *lonche* break. The kids used to say the beans tasted of *cucaracha*, they'd been sitting in some warehouse so long. As for the lukewarm powdered milk we gagged on, it was what each of us was told to be grateful for—it would make us strong and healthy—and, if we got good grades and had respect for our elders, it would make us worthy of our citizenship in that great nation, *los Estados Unidos*, where everything good came from.

At home, there was a lot to swallow, too. The men swallowed the bad price of coffee and pocket-size bottles of rum, and the women swallowed hunger and fear for their children and the mean language and hard hands of their drunk husbands. There was boredom enough to make you go crazy looking for something to gossip about. Petty feuds between hard-up people who had to find someplace to put all the grief and desperation of watching poverty carve furrows in their lives as deep as the rain did in the hillsides. If you lacked the staying power for neighborly backbiting, you could join a religion, one of those fervent, severe, evangelical sects that were always holy-rolling through the mountains in search of depressed and lonely people ready to try anything. Or you could drown yourself in illicit love affairs and star in your own *novela*, playing hourly in the patios and kitchens of your scandalized *vecinas*. Or if you were lucky, you had the gift of humor and could laugh hard and long at each of the slaps and *cocotazos* life dealt you.

I said before that hunger makes people more like goats, able to swallow tin cans and get something like nourishment from them. But sometimes hunger makes people fierce, like those wild dogs left to starve by the humans that go hunting in packs, stealing chickens and small pets and sometimes mauling people. Every so often, when they all band together, they do manage to maul some people. That kind of anger was hard to lay hands on where I grew up. Discouragement left us numb.

My mother said I was a very hungry child, always wanting more, which there wasn't much of because Papi would usually take his pay to the store and drink a few *palitos* and a few more before he turned the leftovers over to Mami. Then he would stay up all night giving crazy orders, like no-one could sleep as long as he was awake. He would play the TV and the radio at the same time, and turn on all the lights, and go from room to room, banging pots together and dragging us out of bed to keep him company in his drunkard's nightmare. The rest of the time he was a sweet enough guy, affectionate and funny. But as for me, I was always hungry and bad-tempered.

Not Mami. At least not that anyone could tell. Everyone called her a saint. You know that way that Puerto Rican country women can look at a woman's suffering and turn it into a kind of special attention from God?

My mother was that kind of a saint. She worked twice as hard as Papi, in the house and on the farm; longer and harder than anyone else I knew. Her house was ramshackle, but spotless, her food was exquisite, her garden plot was in order, and she always knew where a sweet orange tree was ready for picking, or when a bunch of the best cooking bananas had gotten big enough to cut. She was the one everyone asked for sprigs of oregano and bits of geranium to plant. She was good-humored and generous, and several times a month my father threw her and all of us kids out of doors, tore up her meager belongings, raged and cursed at her, and hit her a few clumsy blows across the back and shoulders. Although she yelled at him to leave the kids alone, she never complained about his treatment of her. So they called her a saint.

The only thing to my knowledge that she actually longed for was a good house with a nice kitchen. But every day of her life she contrived and conspired for her children, and especially for me, her ravenous little goat. She saw to it that I stayed in high school by doing the extra work I would have done, and she picked coffee for *don* Luis three years in a row to send me to secretarial school in the city. I stayed with a cousin of hers who gave me room and board for helping out with the house and kids, and learned to type and answer telephones and memorize all the correct formats for business letters.

I got a job in an office with some nice people, and at first having even that small salary belong to me, in my own name, was enough to please me. After a while, seeing how little it really could buy made it less of a thrill, but sending some of it home to Mami, secretly, so Papi couldn't turn it into Palo Viejo, was satisfying.

After a couple of years I met Papo, and in not too long I married him and we went back to New York, where he'd been working the year before. He was a good dancer and a hard worker and had to be because it turned out he was keeping three separate families of his own. One was a woman with two kids who lived in the Bronx. She was under the impression that he'd been visiting a sick mother on the island, and at the very moment that *Doña Justa* was kicking up her heels at my wedding, this woman, Sara, was lighting candles for her preservation from some kind of kidney disease. The other was Cindy (her mother had named her Lucinda), an eighteen-year old girl he started in on about six months after we moved into our place in Brooklyn. By the time I found out about her, she was very pregnant. She also lived only a block away from us, which was convenient for him. As soon as I had some steady work, I left him to his other families and moved in with my cousin Tinita. I had never mentioned to Papo that a little outpatient surgery I'd had done a few years back had insured that I would not end up like Cindy or Sara. Then again, he had never asked.

Well, about then I signed up for a class at City College. This girlfriend of mine at my job, Julia, told me about it. It was a class about history, our history. The man who taught it was smart. Puerto Rican, but brought up in *los Nueva Yores*. I love that expression. It's one of the ways we take something too big to swallow—a country as big as a continent, and all full of *americanos*—and make it bite-size. New York is about the limit of what we want to think about, so we wave a vague hand north, south and west of it and call it all *los Nueva Yores*. I think this fellow grew up in Chicago.

Anyway, we learned all about the Conquistadores and the Taínos and the African slaves. We learned about the Spanish governors who ran Puerto Rico like an army camp, and about Betances and his buddies trying to get a fight going to kick them out, and then the way the U.S. just helped themselves when Spain got old and weak and tired. Ricardo, that's our teacher, told us about the big strikes they had for better work and pay, and about this woman who went around reading speeches to the tobacco workers while the bosses thought she was reading them novels, and writing her own magazine called *La Mujer* where she said that marriage was nothing but a pain and women should love whoever they wanted without any scandal, and leave them when they were ready to, without any fuss. I thought about that for a long time, and I finally told Julia maybe she wore boots and smoked cigars, but this Luisa Capetillo was right about one thing anyway. Marriage had not been set up for the benefit of any woman I had ever heard of. Taking this class was making me very hungry indeed. Not goat-hungry. The wild-dog kind. The kind where you only swallow what tastes good to you and spit the rest out, snarling.

I thought about Mami's life. I had been expecting for years to hear that Papi had driven the jeep over a cliff on his way home from the store, but by some kind of miracle, Papi had suddenly decided not to drink anymore. He had given the old house to my brother Paquito and his family, and had finally built Mami the house she always wanted. It was made of cement, with nothing a termite might fancy to eat. The rain stayed out and so did the rats. It had a real kitchen with a Kenmore stove and a Whirlpool refrigerator. It even had a water heater, and with fifteen or twenty minutes notice, it was possible to have a hot shower, something my mother had never had before in her long life of cold water bucket baths at noon.

Then one day I got a letter from Paquito's wife, Migdalia. Mami had been saying lately that food just didn't agree with her. "You know how Mamá is—she never complains." But finally she had mentioned that her stomach hurt, and one day Migdalia found her vomiting. They took her to the doctor in Ponce, and the whole way she kept telling them it was silly, she just had a flu—it was from the cold weather lately. But when they took some pictures, it turned out she had so much cancer in her stomach that nothing else fit. They said they had to operate immediately, then, when they had her open, they decided not to bother because there wasn't any good stomach left. So they sewed her up and sent her home with some pain pills, and three days later she died.

Now cancer isn't something that happens overnight. It must have been secretly growing in her, a thwarted appetite for flesh, for a long time. I've been sitting here thinking and I believe it was hunger that killed Mami. Not the times there wasn't enough to eat, because Mami always found ways to stretch a little *bacalao* a long way. I think it was the wild-dog hunger in her that never had anything to eat but the insults she swallowed, and those English brand names all full of corners, and the vicious retorts she never made to my father's abuse. Migdalia says they offered to drive to the *farmácia* and call me, but she wouldn't let them. She didn't send any special message, no last words for me, but I've been piecing together the clues.

The kind of hunger that ate Mami's stomach can't be kept in. It isn't house-broken, tame. It can go years looking like a farm animal, hauling water, carrying wood, cooking and digging and trying to stretch a handful of change into a living. It can even be hit with a stick and cursed for its lameness, but watch out. Sooner or later it gnaws at the rope that binds it, and if that rope is your own life, you die. That's the message she sent me. Her hungriest daughter. The one she managed to send away. I imagine her showing me her cancer-eaten belly, holding up the tumors the way she used to show me the *yautia* she pulled out of the ground. If you swallow bitterness, she says, you eat death.

Recently, I don't eat death anymore, and I've been doing my piece to change the national diet of Puerto Rico. *Death al escabeche, death al fricasé, death frito and death con habichuelas.* I've learned a lot of history by now, and I know that at least since Colón, we've always been hungry and dying. Some of us have gotten fierce enough to attack the ones who starve us, but mostly the wild-dog kind just maul their neighbors and themselves. And the rest of us, we're good farm animals. We get milked all our lives, and then butchered for soup.

Instead of swallowing bitterness, I've been spitting it up. In a way it was Luisa Capetillo who gave me the idea. I got home from Mami's funeral and that Monday after work I began this book. Now its done. It's a kind of cookbook I wrote for Mami. A different set of recipes than the ones she lived her life by, those poisonous brews of resignation and regret, those soups of monotony and neighborly malice that only give you gas. Each recipe has a piece of what she gave me though, nourishing as *ñame*, floating in a rich broth. It starts this way: My mother taught me to cook. The name of the first dish was *dutiful daughter*, but she had a special way with it, so it turned out different from what her neighbors made. There are recipes for *Amores a la Capetillo* (subtitled "for Papo"), and a *Medianoche* full of all my mother never screamed at my father. There's one called *Secretarial Lonche* that calls for a good stiff pinch of union wage. But my favorite recipe is the one at the very end. *Remedy For Heartburn*. This is the most challenging recipe in my book, *comadres*. The ingredients? You already have them. In your pockets, in your purses, in your bellies and your bedrooms. For this kind of broth, there can't be too many cooks. Get together. Stir the stuff around. Listen to your hunger. Get ready. Get organized.

Graciela Limón

Graciela Limón was born in East Los Angeles of Mexican immigrant parents. Her father, Jesús Limón, was born in the state of Sonora, and her mother, Altagracia Gómez, was from Jalisco. Limón received a B.A. in Spanish from Marymount College in Palos Verdes, California, an M.A. from the University of the Americas in Mexico City, and a Ph.D. from the University of California in Los Angeles. A specialist in contemporary Latin-American literature, Limón is currently the Chair of the Department of Modern Languages at Loyola Marymount University in Los Angeles. In 1990, she went to El Salvador as part of a delegation to investigate the murder of the Jesuit priests on the first anniversary of their deaths. The result was *In Search of Bernabé* (1993), her stark, resonant first novel which follows the lives of several characters, most notably a mother and her two sons caught up in El Salvador's bloody civil war. Against incredible odds, Luz Delcano is determined to find her son Bernabé, from whom she gets separated in the chaos that follows the assassination of Archbishop Romero. Her odyssey takes her through Mexico and into Southern California, then back again to El Salvador. There, the pieces of this postmodernist novel come together in breathtaking final scenes. *In Search of Bernabé*, a family saga that has repercussions of biblical dimension and resonates with international intrigue, was selected as one of the "Notable Books of the Year" by the *The New York Times Book Review*. Excerpted here are the first two chapters of Part I of this absorbing novel. Limón has published two other novels: *The Memories of Ana Calderón* (1994) and *María de Belén, the Autobiography of an Indian Woman* (1990).

from *In Search of Bernabé*

Graciela Limón

I.

San Salvador—March 1980

Even though the size of the crowd was immense, a strange silence prevailed. Only the hushed shuffling of the mourners' feet and that of their intermittent prayers broke the stillness. The streets surrounding the cathedral were clogged with people who had come from every sector of the city, and from beyond San Salvador. There were those who had left kitchens, factories, and schoolrooms. Campesinos had walked distances from valleys and volcanoes, from coffee plantations and cotton fields. They all came to accompany their Archbishop on his last pilgrimage through the city. Most of them wept, crouching close to one another, some in grief and others in fear. They pressed and pushed against one another hoping to see something, anything that might give them a sense of direction. They were nervous, knowing that every doorway could be a sniper's hiding place.

From the Basilica of the Sacred Heart, where the Archbishop had lain in state, the grievers filed toward the steps of the cathedral's crypt. The murmur of whispered prayers and stifled sobs rose, crashing against the shell-pocked walls, swirling and tumbling in mid-air.

"Padre nuestro, que estás en el cielo, santificado sea tu nombre..."

Bernabé Delcano struggled with the crucifix he had been assigned to carry in the funeral procession. He was holding the cross high above his head, even though its weight made his forearms ache. His hands, which clutched the cross tightly, were stiff and white around the knuckles and fingertips. The young man, like his fellow seminarians, was dressed in a cassock which slowed down his movements. The intense heat made his head throb, and the public speakers that blared the prayers of the Mass only increased his discomfort.

He continually looked back into the crowd, making sure that his mother was not far from him. Bernabé felt assured each time he saw

Luz's round face returning his glances, knowing that she, too, was keeping her eyes on him. Once, he held on to the crucifix with one hand and quickly waved at her with the other, but he didn't attempt that again, since the gesture almost made him drop the cross. Sweat formed on his neck and trickled down the inside of his shirt to his waist. He looked around him, seeing his mother's face again, but now the interference of faces and bodies made it impossible for him to get a sense of her feelings.

He looked at the faces of the other seminarians, hoping to catch a glimpse or a look that would indicate that their confusion was like his. Instead he saw blank, expressionless eyes. Only their lips moved in automatic response to the Our Fathers and Hail Marys mumbled by the priests at the head of the funeral procession. Bernabé looked beyond the faces of his classmates to those of the people. Some were lining the streets, but the majority walked behind the priests and the nuns, the seminarians and the altar boys. Looking at those faces, he was suddenly reminded of a painting. Once he had taken an art class in which his professor had dismissed the unit on cubism with one word: excrement. Yet, Bernabé had been fascinated by the pictures and examples shown in the textbook, and had spent hours in the library of the seminary reflecting on them. One of the selections had been entitled "Guernica," and the caption beneath the picture had identified it as the work of Pablo Picasso. Bernabé knew little regarding the artist, except that people argued as to whether he was a Spaniard or a Frenchman. What mattered to Bernabé, though, was the painting.

In it were fragments of human beings. The portrait showed incongruously shaped heads, rigid outstretched arms, dilated eyes, twisted lips, jagged profiles, all scattered without apparent meaning. It also showed parts of an animal, the face of a horse. Bernabé had noticed that the animal bore the look of terrified human beings. Or was it, he had wondered, that the reverse was true, and that human faces looked like animals when they sensed their slaughter was near. The odd thing, he had thought at the time, was that those broken pieces of human beings could not be brought together again, even though he had attempted to imagine a head attached to some arms as he tried to piece together a human figure.

Now, as Bernabé marched in the cortege, he realized that these people around him were really fragmented: faces, eyes, cheeks, and arms. They were broken pieces just like in Picasso's disjointed painting.

"Ave María, llena eres de gracia..."

The cortege wound through the streets, past the indifferent eyes of the wealthy, and past those who pretended to be wealthy. Their tight lips betrayed a feeling of disgust. It was a pity, those faces said to Bernabé, that the Archbishop had not heeded his finer instincts, his better judgment. Their eyes betrayed their beliefs that priests had best stay out of politics and confine themselves to Mass and to forgiving.

"Gloria al Padre, y al Hijo, y al Espíritu Santo..."

Bernabé began to feel fatigued; faces blurred in front of him. The endless prayers droned monotonously in his ears. The cross seemed heavier with each minute. As he moved along with the rest of the mourners, he began to stumble on the wet pavement. His fingers went numb and his perspiration made the cross slip in his clutching fists. Suddenly, he dropped the cross and fell on his knees. His cassock got entangled around his ankles and the press of people from behind kept him down, forcing him to crawl on his hands and knees.

Bernabé jerked his head right and left. Unexpectedly, a loud blast shook the ground under his hands. A grenade exploded in the midst of the surging crowd at the edge of Plaza Barrios facing the cathedral. The blast was followed by machine gun fire and rifle shots that came from several directions making the mass of people panic. Hastily, the Archbishop's body was picked up and taken into the church by four bishops. Most of the mourners, however, were unable to reach the sanctuary of the cathedral, and could not find shelter anywhere. They swerved and lunged in every direction, screaming hysterically.

Mothers crouched wherever they could in an attempt to protect their babies. Men and women pressed against the Cathedral walls hoping to find cover behind a corner or a sharp angle. Young men, mostly guerrillas, pulled out hand guns, then fired indiscriminately into the crowd in an attempt to hit members of the death squads with their random bullets. Uniformed soldiers suddenly appeared, also firing automatic weapons into the crowd.

The plaza was soon littered with bodies of the dead and the dying. People pushed and trampled each other in a frenzy to survive. No one thought. No one reasoned. Everyone acted out of instinct, pieces and fragments of tormented beasts driven by a compelling desire to live. All the time, the blasting and the firing of weapons and grenades continued.

Bernabé, crawling on the asphalt, was caught unaware by the first blast. The shifting weight of bodies pressing above and around him made it impossible for him to rise. Then bodies began crashing in on him, pinning him down. Suddenly, he felt intolerable pain as someone stepped on his hand, grinding the bones of his fingers against the pavement. He screamed as he attempted to defend himself with his other hand, but it was to no avail. The boot swiveled in the other direction, stepping on Bernabé's hand with an even greater force. The crowd dragged him back and forth, finally smashing him against a wall. Managing to pick himself up with his left hand, he leaned against the stone wall and looked at the bobbing heads and twisted limbs. The panic was at its peak.

"¡Mama-á-á-á-á!"

Bernabé's scream was hoarse and choked; it emanated from his guts, not from his throat. He didn't know what to do, where to go. His wailing rose above the howling of those around him, and he continued screaming for his mother.

The pain in Bernabé's arm was intense, forcing him to remain against the wall despite his urge to run. He remained motionless, feet planted on the bloodied concrete. His body was bathed in sweat and his face, neck, and hair were caked with grime, dirt, and blood. Bernabé began to sob, crying inconsolably even though he was a man of twenty years. He screamed because he feared he was going to die, and he didn't feel shame, nor did he care what anyone might think.

Suddenly the thought that his mother was also in danger cut short his panic. Bernabé lunged into the crowd, kicking and thrashing against the bodies that pushed him in different directions. He screamed out his mother's name, using his able arm to raise himself on whatever shoulder or object he could find, trying to get a glimpse of her. But his mother was nowhere in sight.

Bernabé was able to get away from the plaza, slipping through a break in the encircling cordon of soldiers. He ran around the fringes of the square several times. He rushed up and down streets, and into doorways, shouting her name, but his voice was drowned out by the din of sirens, the horrified screams of people, and the blasts of machine guns. Bernabé shouted out his mother's name until his voice grew hoarse and his throat began to make wheezing, gasping sounds.

He suddenly thought that she might have gotten out of the plaza and run home. So he scrambled toward his house, hoping that he would find her waiting for him, but when he arrived there the door was locked. With his good hand, he beat on the door. When his fingers became numb with pain, he banged with his forehead until he felt blood dripping down his cheeks.

Suddenly, a brutal shove sent Bernabé sprawling on the pavement. When he looked up he saw an armed soldier standing over him. "What are you doing here, Faggot? Better pick up your skirt and find a church to hide along with the other women. If you don't get your ass out of here, your brains are going to be shit splattered all over these walls. You have until the count of five. Uno, dos, tres..."

Bernabé sprang to his feet and ran. He kept running even though his breath began to give out, even though the pain in his arm was intolerable, even though he knew his mother needed him. Panic gripped at his guts and his brain. He knew he had to keep on running.

After the horror had spent itself in the plaza, stunned men and women searched in the lingering blue haze for a son, or a wife, or even an entire family. Among them was Luz Delcano. She called out her son's name, her soft weeping joining that of others, like the rotting moss that clung to the stone walls of the buildings surrounding the square. Luz Delcano went from one body to the next, taking the face of this one in her hands, turning over the body of another one. Desperation began to overcome her. In her fears she remembered the loss of her first son Lucio. Now Bernabé, her second born, was also gone.

Government troops had taken control of the area. They ordered all stragglers to go home and not to return. Luz Delcano had no choice but to follow the orders.

II.

The day was ending, and Bernabé was too fatigued to continue running. His lungs felt as if they were about to rupture, and he was forced to stop abruptly, gasping through his open mouth. The plaza was behind him, but he didn't know what to do next, so he followed three men who were leaving the city, heading in a northern direction toward the Volcán de Guazapa. As he followed, Bernabé tripped over his torn cassock several times, each time hurting his broken hand. He tried to tear off the long garment, but it was impossible for him to undo the front buttons with only one hand.

As they moved closer to the volcano, Bernabé realized that there were others besides him heading up the same path. Without asking, he knew that they were going up into the mountains, to the guerrilla's stronghold. He saw the crowd growing. People appeared from everywhere, trickling into the group from behind the trees, from under shaded awnings, from the entrances of houses and huts. There were people of all shapes and ages. Men walked side by side with grandmothers. Children and adolescents as well as old men mingled with the crowd. Young women, many of them pregnant, others with babies and older children at their side, walked, taking short, rapid steps.

Bernabé saw that they were mostly field workers, men and women with hardened hands and leathery faces. As he looked around him, he saw people whose eyes were small from squinting in the harsh sunlight. Their lips had tightened against pain and humiliation, against suffering. Most of them were dressed in tattered clothing. The women covered their heads with faded shawls, and the men wore ragged trousers and threadbare shirts, their heads covered with frayed sombreros, yellowed and stained by years of sweat. Their feet, some clad in rough sandals, others bare and toughened, pounded the volcanic earth which rose in dusty gusts. The evening air was tinted with hues of yellow and gold, and the shadows of those men and women lengthened in the setting sun.

Bernabé was bewildered by what was happening to him. He looked at the unknown faces swirling around him, trying to understand the events of that day. He was afraid, but not knowing what to do, he continued walking as if in a daze, caught in the press of bodies that pushed him forward.

The crowd continued its trek up the skirt of the volcano, but came to a sudden stop when another group, armed men and women, appeared from behind a ridge in the mountain. They rushed forward embracing as many of the newcomers as possible. Bernabé suddenly found himself surrounded by a cluster of smiling, laughing, jubilant men, women and children. He felt as if he had stumbled onto a carnival or a fiesta; there was handshaking, hugging, and back-slapping. He turned in circles, looking in every direction, thinking that perhaps he was the only stranger among them, when unexpectedly two arms encircled him from behind. Bernabé turned and looked into a face that seemed friendly. He returned the warmth of the embrace.

"Me llamo Nestor Solís."

"Yo soy Bernabé Delcano."

Nestor Solís was more or less Bernabé's age. He was dressed in faded pants and a coarse white shirt that was half-buttoned, exposing his bronzed chest. He wore heavy boots. A straw sombrero shaded his eyes. Like his compañeros, he was armed with a weapon which he wore strapped across his chest. As he spoke, Nestor's eyes were bright with exhilaration at the wave of new recruits joining the ranks of the guerrillas. When he smiled, Bernabé saw that several of Nestor's front teeth were missing.

"Are you a priest?" Nestor asked.

"No, not yet, and I suppose I never will be now."

Bernabé heard his words and he was shocked by what he had just uttered. The thought of not returning had not crossed his mind. When he spoke again, his words were hesitant.

"I, well, I think God has other plans for me. I suppose. Someone else will have to be a priest in my place. Maybe I'll have to stay with you." As he said these words, Bernabé lifted his arm in a broad curve to include the guerrilla force. Even though he had used his able arm, the motion had caused him to flinch.

"You're hurt. Is it bad?"

"No, Señor. It'll soon pass."

Bernabé lied, for his hand was hurting more than ever. He momentarily forgot his pain though when an armed, powerfully built man called for the attention of the crowd.

"¡Bienvenidos, compañeros y compañeras! Soy el Capitán Gato. I'm here to welcome all of you, and to let you know that you're safe. Up there, beyond that mountain, you'll find shelter and protection. You might want to return to where you came from but, on the other hand, you might want to join us. You'll have time to find out for yourselves."

He paused, as if expecting someone to ask a question, but there was silence, interrupted only by the sound of wind sliding off the volcano's side. Capitán Gato had more to say to the crowd.

"We're still a long way from the end of our road. We must march past Presa Embalse, then up the mountains of Chalatenango to where our other brothers and sisters are waiting for us. It's going to be difficult, so you need to help one another."

After a brief rest, the exodus of men, women, and children resumed the journey. Nestor kept close to Bernabé as they moved forward. He pointed out the trails used by the guerrillas and explained what he knew of life in the mountains.

"Listen, compañero, don't assume that I know everything just because I can show you a thing or two. In fact, I haven't been up here for too long. I'm really a campesino. I was born on a small piece of land where I lived all my life with my mother, my father, and my two sisters. The two girls are younger than I am."

Bernabé was listening to Nestor with interest. He glanced at him as they walked. When Nestor stopped talking, Bernabé questioned him. "Why did you join the guerrillas if you're a campesino?

Nestor licked his lips as he concentrated on his answer. "Not so long ago, just last January, one evening when we were eating our dinner, four soldiers broke into our house. It happened so suddenly that none of us could do anything. My father's ankle had been broken in an accident he had with the mule, so he couldn't even stand up. When I tried to defend my mother and my sisters, I got smashed in the mouth with a rifle butt."

Nestor was again quiet; he seemed to be brooding. Bernabé decided not to ask any more questions, but his companion suddenly began to speak again.

"They wanted something to drink, so my mother gave them water. Then they said they were hungry, so we shared what we were eating."

When Nestor paused, Bernabé looked at him and saw that the vein in his neck had swollen, and that he was swallowing rapidly. Not knowing what to say, Bernabé kept quiet.

"Then one of the pigs began to laugh, and he said that he was hungry, but not for the maize we were eating. He was looking at my sisters, and I knew what he was saying. I'll tell you, compañero, I hope you never feel what I felt at that moment. I was afraid, but at the same time I felt rage pulling at my hair.

"I jumped at the pig, and grabbed his filthy throat. Then everything went black. One of them hit me on the head with a rifle. But the blackness lasted just a few minutes, because when I opened my eyes I saw that my father had crawled to one of the mierdas and had taken hold of his ankle. The animal shot my father in the head. When my mother tried to reach my father, the soldier shoved her so hard that she fell to the floor."

"Por favor, compañero, don't tell me anymore. Let's just keep quiet while we're walking."

"No, no, I need to tell you what happened. ¡Esos marranos! It was easy for them. While one aimed his gun at me and my mother, the others did what they wanted with my sisters. They forced them to take their clothes off in front of us. They were laughing and making filthy noises with their teeth. The girls fought. They kicked and scratched, but that only excited the shit-eaters more. They took turns making my sisters kneel down in front of them. They forced them to suck their pinga, all the time yelling '¡Más! más!'"

Then they took the next step. They raped them. When the filthy pigs were tired, like animals, they went over to the table and ate what was there. Then they left."

Nestor began to choke, but he regained his voice in a few moments. "Sometimes I feel bad because I left my mother and sisters to come here, but I couldn't think of any other way to make those animals pay for what they did to us. Here I have the opportunity to look for the pigs. Each time the compañeros capture a handful, I am the first one who looks at them. You think it's impossible for me to find those soldiers, don't you? Well, compañero, I'll tell you, you're wrong. I remember that one of them had a scar that crossed his face from his ear to his nose. I'll recognize that one's face even at midnight! Sooner or later he'll show up."

In the two days it took the group to arrive at the guerrilla headquarters in the Chalatenango Mountains, Nestor and Bernabé continued talking. Travel had been slow because of the number of the group and the scarcity of food, but when they arrived they were happy in spite of their fatigue and hunger. As they walked through the center of a small, makeshift village, Bernabé was surprised by the dwellings he saw. Houses, shed and shelters had been carved out of the lush mountain forest, and even though the shacks were tiny, they were sturdy, and they provided shelter and safety.

Bernabé now felt less pain in his hand. Still wearing his torn, mud-caked cassock, he walked with the rest of the group as they were noisily welcomed by the guerrillas who had been expecting them. Men and women waved their hands, calling out, "¡Bienvenidos, bienvenidos!" There were women outside of each hut, their cooking gear in place. Bernabé, who was famished, saw griddles placed over inviting fires with pupusas and other appetizing foods piled on them. He noticed with even more interest that the women were armed, and that each woman had a weapon which was leaning carefully against a rusty tub, or a tree stump, or some other place nearby. He also saw that each woman, regardless of age, was wearing a bandolier stuffed with ammunition.

Bernabé thought of his mother, and he tried to imagine her dressed like those women. To his surprise he found it easy to picture her among the other women.

"You would be right there, Madre, welcoming me and the other new people. Your legs would be spread apart, planted in the dirt. You'd be wearing one of those big sombreros, and you'd like the ammunition belt that everyone wears here. Your arms would be folded over your chest as if to let everyone know that you were capable of being a dangerous person. Sí, mamá. You would be a good guerrilla!"

He caught himself smiling at his thoughts. But when he looked around, he felt confusion and fear gripping him. When night approached, Bernabé was shown where he was to sleep. There, a young man pointed to the cot that would be for his use. He told Bernabé that he would be leaving soon, but that in the meantime he would be happy to help him. Bernabé welcomed the man's friendliness, and asked him his name.

"Arturo Escutia," was the brief response.

The following morning when Bernabé awoke, he noticed that the young man was gone. He wondered why Arturo Escutia had not asked him for his own name, then did not give the young man another thought.

Photo by Cindy Grossman

Nicholasa Mohr

Nicholasa Mohr has the distinction of being the only Latina writer of the United States with a continuous success as a writer published by mainstream presses. Her semi-autobiographical *Nilda* (1973), a novel about a Puerto Rican girl coming of age in New York during World War II, received the American Book Award and was National Book Award finalist. Through this novel of formation, Mohr offers a cultural critique of her young protagonist's struggle against poverty and stereotypical expectations of what it is to be Hispanic and female. *Nilda* received numerous awards, among them selections as one of the Best Books of 1973 by the *School Library Journal* and *The New York Times*. Mohr is the author of several children's books, as well as two collections of short stories, *El Bronx Remembered* and *In Nueva York*, selected by *The New York Times* as one of the Ten Best new and noteworthy paperbacks for 1979. In 1985, she published *Rituals of Survival: A Woman's Portfolio*, stories that are testimonies to women struggling with (and surviving) racism and sexism. "Happy Birthday" is a story from this collection. Mohr received an honorary Doctor of Letters degree from the State University of New York, Albany campus. A distinguished Visiting Professor at Queens College for several years, she has also held writer residencies at numerous universities and cultural centers, among them the University of San Francisco, the Smithsonian Institution and at the Center for American Culture Studies at Columbia University. Mohr's fiction has been widely anthologized. She is undoubtedly the best known Puerto Rican writer in the United States and is certainly one of the most celebrated authors of children's/young adult literature in the country.

"Happy Birthday"

Nicholasa Mohr

Welfare Island, 1954

Lucía lay in her hospital bed and waited anxiously. She tried to get the nurse's attention. She wanted someone to prop her bed up, so that she could have a better view of the entrance into the ward. Lucía saw one of the nurses at the far end of the ward and waited patiently. She knew better than to press the service button located near the side wall of her bed. That only irritated the nurses, and if one did come to do what she asked, there might be hell to pay later. It all depended on the nurse and her mood at the time. Often, after Lucía complained or insisted that some small favor be done, she found her dinner would be ice cold that evening, or her dessert missing. Simple and small everyday requests, such as more water or the need for a bedpan, might be ignored. Once, when she was very weak and cried out for service, Lucía had to wait several days before she could get a change of bedclothes and a sponge bath. By now, she had learned how to wait, and how to be very patient and very polite.

The nurse was examining several bed charts and when she finished, she walked toward Lucía's part of the ward. Slowly, and with effort, Lucía pushed herself forward and with her free hand, waved to the nurse. The nurse saw her and nodded, then turned and went in the other direction. After several moments, the nurse approached her.

"What do you want?"

"Please, raise the bed, nurse; on top here."

Without looking at her, the nurse cranked up the bed, raising the upper part of Lucía's body, so that she was now in a comfortable elevated position.

"Enough?"

"Yes. Thank you very much, Miss Nurse Heller."

Lucía sighed, feeling better; now she had a good view of the entrance. There were thirty-six beds in this large ward. Eighteen beds were places against opposite walls, creating a center aisle fourteen feet wide and over one hundred feet long. All the patients in this ward were chronically ill. Most of them had terminal cancer, except for a few like Lucía; they had advanced cases of tuberculosis.

"Hemoptysis and cavities," the doctor had told her. She had not taken proper care of herself and now would have to face being "a terminal case with severe progression and hemorrhaging." Lucía had listened and thanked him for all his help and for all the staff was doing for her. She had no family and so the doctor had been frank and honest.

Lucía's bed was placed closer to the end wall near the huge window which overlooked the grounds and shrubbery of Welfare Island, the murky waters of the East River, and part of the concrete gray silhouette of Manhattan's upper East Side. Lucía turned from the window and looked around at the other women. Most of them were quiet, either napping, reading or just resting. The small clock on top of her side table showed the time to be 12:30. Today was Sunday and lunch had been served early so that visiting hours could be extended for an additional hour. Of course, Lucía reminded herself, everyone's resting after lunch. Visiting hours were usually from two to three in the afternoon, and from seven to eight in the evening. Today, the hours were from one to three in the afternoon and from seven to nine in the evening. Except for the new patient being admitted and accompanied by a friend or relation, or the vigil of relatives over a dying patient, there was no contact with the outside world during the week. But Sundays, the ward was lively with visitors and most of the women were in much better spirits.

Lucía glanced at the woman to the right of her. She lay back with her eyes shut and her mouth partially open, emitting a soft and even snore. Today was a happy day for her; her husband and daughter were sure to come. They never missed a Sunday, just like clockwork. Lucía turned to Roxanne, her other neighbor on the left, who had her back to her. Roxanne's hair had come untied and was sticking out of her head like puffs of black cotton. Her dark brown arm was thrown casually over her hip, contrasting against the whiteness of the sheets. Lucía smiled. Roxanne was always in a good mood. But she lived for Sundays, when her family brought her lots of food. "Girl, when the powers that be give me a reprieve, I'm gonna eat good every day of my life!" Roxanne believed she would get well. She was a devout Evangelist, and on Sundays, after she had eaten, her family would join in prayer for most of the visits. "Believe in Him, Lucía. You got to have faith...faith in Him, Lucía. For He shall save you if you trust and believe." Everyday Roxanne preached and proselytized to the other patients. Few listened, except for Lucía, and so they had become friends.

Lucía looked up at the large unit that held the clear intravenous liquid and watched the fluid rhythmically bubbling as it went through the thin plastic tube and into the needle taped securely in her left forearm. With her free hand, she reached over to the bedside cabinet and opened a small drawer. She found her comb, brush, make-up kit, hand mirror, and small bottle of Tabu perfume. She still had time to freshen her make-up and make sure she looked her best for *him*. Lucía was positive he would be here today, for today was special.

She rolled her tray stand toward her, set up her hand mirror. Carefully she combed and brushed her hair, applied a light film of soft powder over her rouged cheeks before putting on some more lipstick. Lucía looked at her image and bit her lip with disappointment. The make-up didn't hide the shallow tone of her dark skin which appeared ashen in spots. The dark circles under her light hazel eyes made them look so transparent and sunken that it seemed to her if she touched the back of her head, she would feel her eye sockets. Lucía closed her eyes. God, she was so very thin. Had she lost that much weight? She placed her hand on her chest, pressing the small gold medal of the Immaculate Conception that hung on a thin chain around her neck. Lucía felt the hardness of her collar bone as it protruded through her hospital bedgown, then she felt her breasts. They were like two pieces of tissue paper, limp and lifeless. She removed the top of her perfume bottle and dabbed the scent sparingly behind her ears and on her throat. What a sight he's gonna see today...if he comes. Lucía shook her head. I'm not even gonna think like that. He'll be here. "By the time your birthday comes around, I'll be out to see you, baby. You get yourself well again, okay? You got to get looking better, *mami*, and we'll celebrate your next birthday together," Eddie had promised. She had written countless long, passionate letters to him. Most had been returned and there had been no response to the few he might have received.

Lucía wished she could have stayed in the city. It had been easier for people to visit her when she had been in Manhattan. At the beginning, the girls had come from time to time, and Eddie's mother had been to see her once. Since Lucía had been transferred to Welfare Island, no one had been out to see her.

She felt very tired and thirsty. She put her personal things away and picked up the glass of water that was on the table. It was warm and tasted of chlorine. She searched for a nurse, hoping to get some fresh water, but it was very quiet and no one was about. She put the glass back and decided to nap for a few minutes. She checked the clock; it was twenty minutes to one.

Lucía leaned back against the pillow and looked over at the large window. It was divided into many small window panes; exactly thirty-six, one for each bed, she had decided, as she counted them over and over again. First vertically, then horizontally, obliquely and from every angle she could discover. It was a freezing cold February day and ice had formed on the panes, developing into delicate shapes that appeared like leaves, flowers and lace patterns. The ice sparkled like diamonds as the long beams of the bright winter sunlight passed through the windows and splashed into the ward, creating large shadowy areas on the gray-green walls. Lucía smiled. How beautiful it all was. She realized that if she concentrated on the sparkling panes and shadows, she could separate herself from the ward.

She felt a warmth and happiness that reminded her of the beautiful riverbed in her mountain village in Sierra de Luquillo where as a little girl she used to bathe and play with her brother. That part of the river was tucked safely into the side of a steep mountain and was partially shaded by ferns, shrubs, and wild flowers. She used to sit for hours just watching the tiny darting fish and tadpoles, the bobbing twigs and dry leaves as the tropical sun bounced on the water making them sparkle like jewels. Lucía felt mesmerized by the movement of all those tiny things being transported through the sluices of shallow water that had been formed by the rocks and fallen branches. She had loved that part of the river. It had all been magical and wonderful, and belonged to her, until the day she began to bleed in the water.

At first she and her little brother thought leeches had gotten into her skin. Then they thought she had been cut by something. But the blood seemed to be coming from inside her body and for no reason at all. Frightened, she and her little brother ran all the way home. Confused and bewildered, Lucía had listened to her mother who forbade her to bathe or swim at that end of the river. From that day on she had to go in at the side of the river with the other women. Her grandmother had put her arms gently around her, rocking her and from time to time stroking her hair, as she whispered in a soft voice, "My little brand new virgin...Lucía, my sweet little precious virgin...just born, my little virgin." Lucía, perplexed, had not understood until later, much later, when she gave herself freely and openly to Manuel, just before the departure. Afterward, she had cried and Manuel vowed that he would always respect her and someday they would be legally husband and wife.

Lucía's eyes were almost completely shut as she concentrated on the dark shadows spread across the walls of the ward. She remembered her departure. She went into service as a domestic. Early that day, her new employers arrived. Being in such a great hurry, they had remained in the car. The wife had explained that they were in the process of closing their home in San Juan because, in two weeks time, they would be leaving for New York City. Lucía barely had time to say goodbye to her parents, to her grandmother and her little brother. The man and his wife sat in the front seat of the black limousine, and she had sat in the back. She had wanted to open the window and say something, to wave or shout, but she had no idea how to do it, and she had been afraid to touch anything in that splendid car. Lucía had gripped the twine tied tightly around the cardboard box that occupied the seat next to hers. Her clothes and possessions had been neatly packed in the box by her mother. The last glimpse of her family and of Manuel, standing by the side of the road wearing his best clothes as he waved goodbye, was forever etched in her memory.

The car had sped quickly out of her village and her fright had intensified as she saw the capital city for the first time. Cars, trucks, large buildings and people were as abundant as the flies that swarmed around the pigpen. Lucía remembered the cold shiver that had passed right through her when she realized that she was going even farther away in two weeks and that she might never again see the trees and foliage of the quiet mountain region which had been the only world she had ever known.

"Ssst...sst...Lucía." She opened her eyes and saw him. His large dark eyes were staring at her. "How are you? How are you feeling, Lucía?"

Somehow he looked different and he sounded different. "Lucía, ¿cómo estás?" Doña Nora was smiling at her. Reaching over, Doña Nora patted Lucía's hand. "Are you all right, child?"

"Yes..." Lucía blinked. "Doña Nora, I thought...I thought at first," she hesitated.

"Thought what?"

"That it might be Eddie. Eddie was supposed to come today."

"Today? You heard from him, then? Did he say he was coming?"

"No. Bueno...not exactly."

"Then, what..."

"He promised me when I left, you know, when I got sick, that he would come...that he would see me before today was over."

"Child, that was more than six months ago. Nobody has seen that son of mine and nobody knows where he is. When I saw you last time, in the hospital back in the city, I told you he had left New York. He was in trouble again. You know how Eddie is. Lucía, by now you should know."

"But he's different with me, Doña Nora." Lucía's voice had a sharpness as she continued, "I never was like the rest!"

"I know..." Doña Nora answered in a soft voice. She stared at Lucía for a moment, as if today she were really seeing her for the first time. "I know you were not like the rest. We all knew and know that, Lucía."

"All right then," Lucía nodded at Doña Nora. "I only did what I had to...until, until Eddie could get the money he needed to set up a business. There were a lot of sacrifices we had to go through. But we were gonna get married. That was our goal, Eddie's and mine. It still is... someday...I..."

"Of course," Doña Nora interrupted her, speaking quickly. "Look, look what I brought for you, Lucía." She lifted a large shopping bag and placed it on a chair. "See, all homemade, eh? I just finished it this morning. Chicken broth with a nice piece of white meat. Here, I have some viandas: platanos, malanga, yautia, batata, and a piece of..."

Lucía watched Doña Nora and smiled as she took out jars and plastic bowls filled with things to eat. "That's so much food. You are still the same, Doña Nora, thank you. You shouldn't have gone to such trouble."

"Nonsense, it's not so much. Anyway, I have to cook for my family. Besides, all of this will help you get well faster. You'll see."

"I don't know, Doña Nora. I don't think I'm getting well again."

"What a thing to say! Not getting well? Shame! Don't talk like that!" Doña Nora shook her head. "Of course you're gonna get well! Good as new again. You're young, child, and the young heal quickly."

"I'm not young no more..." Lucía looked at Doña Nora. "And I don't heal fast."

"What? What are you saying? Why, how old can you be? Twenty-four or twenty-five at the most. Eh?

"Twenty. Today I'm twenty years old, Doña Nora."

"Twenty?"

"Yes, today is my birthday, Doña Nora."

"Well, there, you see? Had I known, I would have gotten you a present..." Doña Nora's voice faded and she found that she could not look at Lucía. Quickly, she turned her head and looked around at the other patients. "My, look at how busy it is in here today. Lots of people visiting."

"All I wanted for today, Doña Nora, was to see him. That's all. Once before I die."

"Die? Stop that, you are not going to die; you'll get well. But, you must stop talking like that. Think of the future, of what's ahead of you. You have your whole life before you. Lucía, don't talk about... talk about living."

"You know, Vickie and Carmen used to come to see me when I was in City Hospital, and I told them just how I felt. They had left Eddie by then, but anyway, they understood. Maybe, because we were all so close. They knew I was different from them. They always told me so. With them it was just a business because if it wasn't Eddie, it would be somebody else. But with me, there was never nobody else but him." Lucía stopped speaking and lowered her voice, continuing almost in a whisper. "When I was with other men, well...I never got used to it, and I never liked it." Lucía turned her head away and shut her eyes. "I hope you believe me, Doña Nora."

"Why do you think I'm here today, Lucía? Because I know you are different from those other women. They are professionals. Whores in that kind of business! But, not you, I know it was because of Eddie you got into that life. I even remember when he first brought you to see us. You were so shy and respectful. I knew then you were different. He even said to me, 'Ma, she's different! This one's a good girl.' And I was happy. I thought he was going to settle down and stop what he was doing. But...instead, Dios mio, I don't understand Eddie. He's my son, but he's not like the rest of my children. God! I don't know why he's that way. So ruthless and uncaring. I don't know what I did or maybe what I didn't do. Could be that he was the oldest and had too much responsibility for the rest of the kids. And, he never got along with his stepfather..."

Doña Nora hesitated and waited a moment for Lucía to respond. Lucía remained perfectly still, her head turned away and her eyes closed.

"Oh, my God, Lucía, what did I do to have such a son that he can do this to you? Look, I'm trying to make it up to you in some way. Let me help you, Lucía, let me try to help you. Look at you, you're so young...don't do this. Bendito, Lucía, don't give up like this. Please." Doña Nora's voice began to quiver and she cried quietly.

After a moment she wiped her eyes and drew a deep breath. "I don't know where he is. I never know where he is. Sometimes, the police come for him. Sometimes, there's some strange woman, a prostitute, or some man who's after him. I don't know how long I can love my son. There are times I hate him! I hate him so much I want to see him dead." She held back the tears and, with effort, continued, "Not just because of you, but because of all he's put me and the family through. Did you know he hid drugs in our house? That he gave his younger brother a gun to hide? A loaded pistol! Dear Virgin Mary, I can't cope with him no more. Right now, I never want to see him again. I think his being alive is more of a torture to me than if he were dead!" Doña Nora broke into sobs and covered her face with her hands.

"Doña Nora." Lucía reached over and gently touched the older woman's arm. "Don't! You see, he didn't force me. Don't think that. I knew what it was all about. He told me how it was. I did what I did because I wanted to. I'm not sorry about loving Eddie, you know, only about some of the things I did."

Doña Nora wiped her eyes and face and looked silently at Lucía. After a moment, she spoke in a calm voice. "Ay, Lucía...you can still love him? You didn't hear what I said? You don't see, do you?"

"I see. But with me, he's different. He was really changing with me. Perhaps, if I hadn't gotten so sick, things would be better with him. I understood Eddie and what he wanted."

"All right, Lucía, let me help you. Let me contact your family. I can write to them. They will want to know where you are and what is happening to you."

"No..." Lucía hesitated, "I don't want them to know."

"But, child, why?"

"Please, Doña Nora, I don't want to talk about them. Look, I appreciate your coming to see me and whatever you do for me, but...I don't want to talk about my family."

"You are being foolish not to let your people know."

"It's better like this."

"How can you say that? They are your family after all, and your parents should know where and how you are."

"No."

"I don't agree, Lucía."

"Doña Nora, it's better like this. Like you, with Eddie, I don't want them to wish me dead!"

"Oh! That was cruel," Doña Nora gasped. "I'm surprised at you!"

"Let's leave things as they are."

Both women looked at each other silently. Doña Nora was the first to turn away.

"I'm sorry, I forgot to ask about the kids. How are they, Doña Nora? And, Don Luis, is he better?"

"Yes, he's a little better with his asthma. It's hard when he's not working, because they dock his pay. You know, there's just so many sick days allowed. And the kids are fine. Frankie is graduating and Gilberto is doing good, too. Linda is getting all grown up. In fact, I have to keep a sharp eye out in her direction. She just got her first period."

The two women continued speaking politely and quietly until the loudspeaker interrupted them.

"VISITING HOURS ARE OVER. VISITORS, PLEASE LEAVE THE HOSPITAL. VISITING HOURS ARE..."

"Do you need anything, Lucía?" Doña Nora opened her purse and took out three dollars. "Here…"

"No, thank you, you've done enough."

"It's okay. Take it. You were very kind to my kids. Giving them presents and all. Go on, take it."

"Thank you." Lucía took the money and put it in the drawer of her bedside table. "I could use some toothpaste and talc."

Doña Nora picked up her empty shopping bag and carefully folded it. "If you need anything else, let us know."

"I will. Thank you for coming and for the things you brought me."

"VISITING HOURS ARE OVER. VISITORS, PLEASE LEAVE..."

"Well, I better go, it's a long trip back to Brooklyn from here."

"Doña Nora?"

"Yes?"

"Don't hate him. Don't hate Eddie, please."

"It's all right, Lucía. I don't hate Eddie. I only hate what he's become. I just don't know if I still have a son, that's all. Bueno...never mind all that. You try to get well."

"Thank you."

"Goodbye, Lucía."

"Goodbye, Doña Nora."

"Oh...Lucía,"

"Yes?"

"Happy Birthday."

Lucía nodded and smiled as she watched the older woman walk toward the large open doorway and disappear. She checked the time once more. It was twenty minutes past three. There's still tonight, and it's still my birthday, she thought. She looked at all the food Doña Nora had brought. Later she would try to eat some. Right now she was tired.

Lucía closed her eyes. Lately, Eddie and Manuel had been getting all mixed up in her mind. She could not really separate them. Even their features blended together until they appeared as one person. It was too confusing and she was too exhausted to think about all that; instead she would go back and bathe in the riverbed. Lucía concentrated once more and saw the clear, transparent water and the swift movement of her hand as she tried to grab a tadpole. The cool water splashed her face, running down her neck and body. She stepped into the river and felt the water envelop her. She turned and swam toward the deeper part. Slowly, and without any resistance, Lucía let the current take her downstream and she drifted with the river into a journey of quiet bliss.

Judith Ortiz Cofer

Judith Ortiz Cofer was born in Puerto Rico, the daughter of a Navy man who, in the 1960s, moved his family to Paterson, N.J., where she lived as a bicultural, bilingual child. She received her B.A. in English from Augusta College. A fellow of the English Speaking Union of America, she studied at the Summer Graduate School at Oxford University, then completed her M.A. in English at Florida Atlantic University. Ortiz Cofer is the author of *The Line of the Sun* (1989), the first original novel published by the University of Georgia Press, which also published her collection of prose and poetry, *The Latin Deli* (1993). In addition, she has published a collection of personal essays and poems, *Silent Dancing* (1990), two collections of poetry, *Terms of Survival* (1987) and *Reaching for the Mainland* (1987), as well as *Peregrina* (1986), a winning manuscript in the Riverstone International Chapbook Competition. Ortiz Cofer has published in numerous national reviews, including *Prairie Schooner, The Kenyon Review, Antioch Review* and *The Southern Review. Silent Dancing* was awarded a PEN American/Albrand Special Citation in the category of best non-fiction by an American author in 1991. Its title essay was selected by Joyce Carol Oates for inclusion in *The Best American Essays 1991. Silent Dancing* was also chosen as one of the Best Books for the Teen Age by the New York City Public Library, which in 1989 selected *The Line of the Sun* as one of the "25 Books to Remember." Ortiz Cofer is on the associate teaching staff at the Bread Loaf Writers' Conference. She teaches English and Creative Writing at the University of Georgia.

Monologue of the Spanish Gentleman

Judith Ortiz Cofer

Women and blood. There is no separating them. They are an open wound. That's the way God made them. Of course I know what they call me in this town—the women, that is—*la bestia*. I am a monster because I am a man. But, I tell you something, Señor, I would rather be hated than humiliated by a woman. My wife hates me. My lovely Minerva fears me—she is a saint—she doesn't know how to hate. The other women look at me as if I had a dagger between my legs and not the most vulnerable organ in my body. They are fools, all of them. But I have loved some women. I will confess to you because we are talking man to man that I loved my mother, may she be frying in hot grease up to her eyeballs in hell—don't look so shocked—sit down, let me explain. My mother was more beautiful than my daughter Minerva—you find that hard to believe? It's true. My father, Don Juan José de la Luz, had to fight off an army of suitors back in Madrid to win her heart. She never forgave him for bringing her to Puerto Rico, or this savage place, as she always called it. But once married, a woman has to do what her man says, and Don Juan made a fortune as an agent for the Spanish Crown. She had all the fine clothes a woman could ever want, and all the luxuries, but no place to show off her beauty. Her name was Prudencia, did I mention that? What irony, that woman lacked many virtues, but the one that did her in was the very same she was named after. My old man had to be away from our hacienda much of the time, and Doña Prudencia began to find ways to fill her hours of leisure, which were twenty-four a day. Her three sons were looked after by servants. Until the age of three I thought my mother was a black woman we called Mosca, because she was tiny and black as a housefly but full of buzzing energy. It was to her I went with my problems and childish fears. She was the first woman I loved, but she died in childbirth (Don Juan's bastard killed her I found out later, the baby was too big to come out, my half-brother tore her apart). We then turned for love to this stranger we were supposed to call *Madre*. But she had no interest in us. By then she had developed certain habits that accounted for the sudden silences we provoked on entering any room in any house in the county. She was taking young men to her bed. Not men of her class—she was sleeping with the natives, you might say. The reverse of cannibalism—she was the missionary consuming the savages. Her sexual appetite was tremendous (you smile, perhaps thinking that my own legendary prowess can be explained by inheritance, but what is a gift in a man may be a curse for a woman). By the time I was old enough to understand the nature of the scandal, it was too late to save her, even if I had wanted to. Where it may have started out as a diversion—it was characteristic of her to seek revenge in the most pleasurable way possible—it turned into a vice and an obsession. My last image of her is of a dried up rose. Her lust consumed her.

I remember as a young boy listening to the muffled sounds of love-making, hiding behind a staircase late one night when even the indefatigable Mosca was snoring on her pallet on the nursery floor. Yes, I recognized them at an early age, you don't grow up around animals and servants and miss nature's first lesson—it was mostly her voice I heard, pleading, demanding, and then the sweeping of her lace gown as she led the boy, not much older than myself, out of her room. I watched that boy come down the stairs with the knife of cold hatred twisting through my chest. I looked at his bare back. It was streaked with blood from scratches that could have only been her signature. She used them and marked them for life. Like the bulls on our farms we branded with a cross. I wanted to kill that black bastard; now that I say it, he could have been another of my black half-brothers—my father left his mark in his own way—perhaps all the *café con leche* children born at that finca were his offspring. Who knows? I am not judging him. I myself have a taste for brown skin. But let me continue. I wanted to kill her and her lovers. But I was too young to kill. I did the next best thing. I exposed her infamy. Yes, *hombre*, somebody had to do it, and even then, I had the balls to do what other men will not do. I didn't betray a mother; I told on a whore. Not that I ever believed that my father was ignorant of her dissolute ways, but I have already explained that no man could resist her charms. She was the Duchess of Alba to him, his mistress and his most treasured possession. His jealousy was boundless—I finally understood that his desire to keep her to himself only was the main reason he had taken her away from the glittering social circles of Spain and secluded her in this "savage place." But he was put in an untenable situation when she started taking black lovers—to confront her would be to admit that she preferred the bestial company of servant boys to his exalted presence. Pride was Don Juan's tragic flaw. Or perhaps he was a blind fool. Women have their sinister ways of undermining a man. Their minds work differently from ours; they live by guile and deceit, and so it is entirely possible that she seduced him into believing that she was as pure as the white lace gowns she wore. She wore them to seduce her lovers, too, out of a perverse pleasure in the contrast of her whiteness to their blackness. I am just guessing, but it would have been like her to think of such a demonic detail.

Yet, I love her. I was a lonely child. My brothers were already involved in farm business, and they accompanied my father to Spain most of the time. I resembled her—this pale skin is her inheritance—I've been ridiculed for burning in the sun like a damsel. And so in my solitude I would have given anything to come near this woman who wasted her caresses on those wretched black boys who were no more than beasts of burden to us.

Yes, I'm getting to that part. What I did was this: I purloined a letter from my father announcing his unscheduled arrival on the island—due to political conflict brewing between Spain and the United States. I intercepted the messenger he had paid to come by horseback from Ponce, the harbor to the south of the island where he always disembarked. I was about thirteen years old then. Time had passed since that night when I saw the nail prints on that boy's back—a bloody map that charted our destiny, but my surveillance of her despicable activities had become the obsession of my life. I had gathered evidence and lined up witnesses—there were plenty of envious people in that province who would enjoy seeing one of the mighty fall. I read his letter, written in the elegant script of his own hand, telling his beloved Prudencia that they would soon be reunited. He talked briefly of dangerous seas and the American threat of war with Spain. Even I could see that he was trying not to alarm my delicate mother with the rumors of an invasion of the island by the Americans. I had spent my time devising an escape if there should be a war. The six months that Don Juan was away I had traveled with messengers over the *cordillera*, the mountain range that divides the island, taking routes only these men knew. I was getting old enough so that no one questioned my decisions, and my mother kept to her rooms most of the days, afraid that the relentless Puerto Rican sun would stain her tender flesh, or afraid that she would have to face me; I liked to think that she feared me as much as I hated her.

Anyway, I was thrilled with the idea of a war. I knew the Spanish would smash the United States invaders like a hand swatting a mosquito. Of course, I was ignorant of the real power of the Northerners. All I knew was what my royalist family taught us—that Spain was the most civilized and powerful nation on the earth. In our outpost in the center of a half-settled colony, we got news of the world only through our traveling father, and to him the center of the universe was Madrid. But I am wandering away from my story again, am I not? But only a little, for what I have just told you, about my knowledge of the island's terrain, played a big part in the final chapter of my story.

It so happened that my father arrived on the island the day the American ships reached our shores. He and my brothers rode furiously on horseback towards home, warning the Spanish patriots along the way of the invasion. I heard about his mad ride much later, for I was on one of my scouting trips at the time in the mountains. They say that when the weary, dust-covered Don Juan dismounted at his front door, no one was there to greet him. Since I had intercepted his letter, nobody knew that he was on his way. So, instead of his usual formal and dignified entrance into his home, Don Juan rushed up the stairs to his beloved Prudencia's room. He wanted to play her rescuer, to sweep her in his manly arms and tell her that soon she would be back home in Spain. Don Juan's plan was to send his wife and youngest son back to Europe while he stayed home to organize an army of gentlemen who would quickly repel the Yankee invaders. It was a grand plan that he had worked out during his rough ride through the island. What he found in his wife's room that day changed everything. All was forgotten in the chaos that followed. There were gunshots and blood, and the hasty departure of the whole family, accompanied by a few loyal servants. When I returned to the farm, I found only our cook waiting for me in the deserted house. She had an envelope with my name scribbled on it, and a note from one of my brothers telling me that I was to make my way to Ponce where money had been left for me at the house of my father's friend, a man too old to travel, who would help me get to Spain where I would rejoin my family.

I had to pry the rest of the story from the loyal servant whose horror at what she had witnessed had left her in shock. She urged me to leave at once for Ponce, for she had heard that the Northerners were making their way around the island. She herself was planning to return to her home village of Río Seco. She had only stayed to give me the envelope. But I had no intention of following them anywhere. So I stayed at the hacienda with Cocinera and a few other workers, declaring myself the new master of the place. In time I learned the whole story. I can only summarize it for you, Compadre.

You want to know if he killed her? I would have, I can tell you that. But that old fool couldn't bring himself to believe his eyes. He called it a rape and shot the boy. Then he dragged her along with his trunks of gold and silver back to Spain where she ended up crazy, locked in an attic. Though I never answered his letters, I read them. My old father used the last of his money to buy a house in the center of Madrid where Mother always wanted to live. Then he declared her insane and locked her up until her death a few years later—of consumption, I heard. He's dead now, too, and I haven't heard from my brothers for years.

So, what do you think of my story, *hombre*? Of course it is all true. Yes, I had to give up the farm. It was too much for a boy to run. I sold what I could from the house, and the land is still in my family's name, though I haven't done anything with it. That year of the Americans' arrival, I made a little fortune acting as a guide for both sides. I knew the mountain paths as well as the natives, and I led many a frightened Spaniard to the port in Ponce—for a price, of course. And when the Americans decided to plant their flag on our soil, they found me waiting by the seashore, ready to offer my services as a guide—they paid well. Soon, I had made enough money that I was able to follow my destiny here, to this nothing town, a place my dear mother would have hated. Río Seco, the dry river—I liked the paradox in the name—the challenge of it. You know the rest. I own most of these shacks we can see from my veranda. One thing I learned from my old man: if you have the biggest house in the region, make sure everybody knows it. That is why I built my *casa* on this hill. I am the overseer, and I see everything.

But listen. Are those the church bells I hear? Tonight begins the novena for the Black Virgin. No, Compadre, of course I am not going. But, I have to go home and make sure that my Minerva and her mother do not forget that I paid for several of these masses, and they have to be there to represent me. I don't want that scoundrel priest to skip over my name in the offering, as I know he will unless he sees my family in church. He hates me, that old ninny. I think we would all be better off if women were the keepers at the temples as they were in pagan times. They are much better at housekeeping—and even God's house needs a good sweeping now and then, don't you agree?

Hasta luego. Tomorrow we will continue our domino game. Yes, I will tell you in detail how the beautiful Prudencia turned into a hag in the mansion my father bought for her in the middle of Madrid. It is a fascinating story and worth recounting. People always want to know what happens to beautiful women who go wrong. I understand. Personally, I prefer tales with happy endings like the adventures of Odyseo, the mariner. Now there was a real man, and his Penelope waited faithfully at home for his return, while her man did what a macho is born to do.

Photo by Yvon Douran

Mary Helen Ponce

Mary Helen Ponce was born in Pacoima, California. After high school, she married and raised four children before she enrolled at California State University at Northridge, where she received two degrees, a B.A. in anthropology—she graduated Magna Cum Laude—and an M.A. in Chicano Studies and anthropology. The recipient of a Danforth Fellowship and the Chicana Dissertation Fellowship at the University of California at Santa Barbara, Ponce is earning her Ph.D. in American Studies at the University of New Mexico. She is the author of a collection of short fiction, *Taking Control* (1985) and a novel, *The Wedding* (1989), in which she displays a fine ear for dialogue, a characteristic which is also well demonstrated in her contribution (a chapter from *Raising Albuquerque*, a novel-in-progress) to this anthology. In 1993, the University of New Mexico Press published her *Hoyt Street*, the first contemporary Chicana autobiography. In *The Nation* (June 7, 1993), Ray González states that "Ponce's reputation as a fine fiction writer will be enhanced by this hypnotic journey into her childhood in Pacoima, California...one of the famous enclaves of Chicano culture.... Her ability to create detailed descriptions of the language, clothes, houses and food Mexican-Americans embraced during World War II and the fifties becomes a priceless portrait of how tradition builds and sustains all cultures." Ponce is now working on a biography of the New Mexican writer, Fabiola Cabeza de Vaca. Through a 1993 grant from the Mexico Fund for Culture, she pursued her work on biographies of several Mexican women writers. Ponce has recently returned home to the San Fernando Valley.

"Green? or Red?"

Mary Helen Ponce

I'm hungry again! My only frying pan and my blue pot-with-a-lid-double-boiler lie soaking in the sink, and I'm out of paper dishes. Which means I have to leave my comfy apartment in Greenwood Village and find a cheap place to eat. I swore I'd never return to the Ponderosa, where I've been hanging out since my arrival in Albuquerque. But, it's late and my stomach is growling. I grab my down coat, twist two scarves across my neck, bolt the door and leave.

The restaurant is crowded, chock full of folks encased in denim jeans and cowboy boots. Students in corduroy jackets and high-top boots, canvas backpacks slung across their stooped shoulders, dash in for a quick bite between classes. They congregate in the back where they spread then review the class notes written earlier in haste. No one bothers them here and, provided they order coffee, they can remain late into the night.

The leather booths and chrome tables of lime green and sick-gray reek of the 1950s, as does the jukebox now blaring in a far corner. Randy Travis is belting out his new hit, about an ex-wife in Texas, but no one appears to be paying attention to the music. The cooks behind the counter, most of whom shout to each other in Spanish, work hard for minimum wage. Their brown faces are shiny from working so close to the grill that spews grease and smoke. They slap bowls of chile stew, hot tortillas, and an occasional hamburger on the shiny counter with practiced skill.

It's coupon night at the Ponderosa Restaurant, a popular eatery on Central Avenue, directly across from the University of New Mexico. Each Tuesday and Thursday, The Lobo—UNM's student paper—offers discount coupons, which accounts for today's huge crowd. It's almost certain that customers are here to scarf on the 'chile special' billed as "the hottest chile west of the Pecos." Served with a big scoop of beans and a hot tortilla with butter, the Ponderosa's chile stew is said to be the best in town.

My first time in the Ponderosa was for a quick coffee. I sat next to the window from where I looked out at the traffic on Central, and across to the university. In an attempt to memorize the campus—I had just driven in from California—I scanned the map before me and the buildings across the way. Although the campus of adobe-like buildings is unique, and students willingly pointed out classrooms, I still got lost when I mistook the Humanities Building for Ortega Hall...and vice-versa.

One cold day on my way to Kinko's I saw a group of hippies standing near the Ponderosa. The men wore headbands, torn jeans, suede fringe vests, and cowboy boots. The women with long, stringy hair wore full skirts, gauze tops and love beads in bright colors. "Look, they're making a movie," I said to Jenny, my new friend. "Those must be the extras."

We turned the corner, paid for an assigned reader at Kinko's, then traced our steps back toward campus. Curious as to when the action was to begin, I turned to stare at *los hippies,* now drinking coffee and talking among themselves.

"I'll bet it's a 60s movie," I announced to Jenny, "but where are the lights? And the cameras?"

I'm no stranger to movie-making. When in my home state, I saw three movies filmed at the local high school where the Spanish architecture of the school buildings was the lure. Later I saw a documentary filmed at the San Fernando Mission. Men smeared with dark makeup and dressed as Plains Indians paid homage to a tall, slender man representing Father Junipero Serra. It's gotten so I can spot a camera crew in minutes, what with all the cables they sling across the way. That day a reluctant Jenny and I waited for the camera crew to arrive. The next day the hippies were back. This was no movie, I realized, only folks in their forties dressed like in their prime.

New Mexico is the chile capitol of the Southwest...and perhaps of the entire nation, I have since learned. People here take their chile seriously. Brawls have been fought over chile, wedding postponed for lack of chile, and each summer, chile contests are held in parks throughout the city. Whereas other states hold beauty and surfing contests, New Mexico competes for the hottest and tastiest chile based on recipes passed down from ancestors now resting in Fairview Cemetery and points north.

"Folks who eat chile live longer," claimed a famous nutritionist in *Chile Peppers Magazine,* a publication that sells like hotcakes. As a recent convert to chile, the editor-as-expert spends his spare time judging chile contest throughout the southwest. He's hated by Texans because he never finds in their favor. Still, he knows his product, and can name every type of chile grown: *serranos, manzana, piquant, Mirasol.* At least twenty species. "Studies show that if eaten once a day, chile can cure a sinus condition," he wrote in the premier issue of the magazine. I believe him. It has been my experience that New Mexican chile not only cures sinus, but also unplugs eardrums and activates sweat glands.

It's in the low 30s outside, and getting colder by the minute. At the Ponderosa the atmosphere is decidedly cheery. At tables sit students, university professors, and those who simply want a hot, cheap meal. Everyone meets here. Open 24 hours a day, the restaurant is packed to the gills each night and, according to advertisements, has sold over 50 tons of chile!

Inside the Ponderosa, everyone looks warm and happy, anticipating the red chile—complete with pods—that burns not only the tongue and lips, but also kills bacteria and one's appetite for at least an hour. Or perhaps folks want to try the chile stew, as they call the green chile strips mixed with diced potatoes and blobs of beef. Fresh cooked beans are also popular, and in rare cases, eaten to dilute the chile. But often they too are hot or, as folks around here say, "spiced."

I want to try the chile stew, but am not sure this is wise. The first time I ate chile at this place, I ended up ordering two sides of beans, which did not help a bit. I then ordered thick tortillas, gobbled them up, and followed this with a pitcher of ice water. But all that gave me was a buzz. In desperation I ordered the house specialty: hot cider made with whole cinnamon cloves. I took one sip, then another, until the cup was empty. All it did was to turn up the heat centered in my mouth. I walked home with a strange buzzing in my ears.

Now, as I wait in line, a couple walks in and heads for the order counter.

"Can't make et without ma chile," grins the burly man to his companion, a stout woman stuffed into what resembles a parka. On her feet are the cowboy boots I recently saw at Kmart: purple with black trim and tassels that twirl as she moves. A bright scarf is wound around her wide neck and head. She peruses the menu with care.

"And don't I know et," she finally responds, wiping her nose with a red handkerchief. She is almost salivating, anticipating the treat that will probably exhaust her kerchief and tissue supply.

"Green? Or red?" The man turns to her, then removes a wallet stenciled with the word *Mexico* from his back pocket.

"Make it red this time, honey." The woman takes a toothpick, works it inside her generous mouth, then plunks herself down on an empty booth.

When I first arrived in Albuquerque in January, in time for the Spring semester—and the movers had not yet delivered my belongings, which included my two pots and frying pan—I ate here every day. One blustery day I ordered the daily special: hamburger, fries and coke. When the counter-person asked: "Green? Or red?" I grinned and said, "Surprise me," confident he meant pickles. Once seated at a booth I saw that the hamburger bun was not California crispy, but New Mexico wet. Green chile, pods and all, oozed from the sides and bottom. I was about to return the soggy sandwich when I saw a woman sopping up what looked like red gravy with her hamburger bun. Now and then she stopped to lick her fingers, then once more, her mouth open like that of a healthy fish, she closed in on the chile-saturated bun as the red stuff dripped down her chin. Thoroughly disgusted, I picked at the fries that had escaped *el chile*, bolted a glass of water, then once at home chowed-down a peanut butter and jelly sandwich.

In the following weeks I perused the Ponderosa's menu with care, caution even, and paid close attention to what others ordered—and ate. The favorite choices seemed to be their chile specials. "Green? Or red?" "Red? Or green?" the question was academic. I dared not order eggs, as I saw that most folks ate theirs slathered with gobs and gobs of chile. Fried eggs swam between rivers of red chile; scrambled eggs poked through strips of green chile, and eggs over-easy perched atop mounds of red or green pods. Each meat dish was served con chile: pork and chile, ribs and chile, steak and chile. Not even the meat loaf was immune. Like their Texan neighbors to the east, *nuevomexicanos* pepper their steaks with mounds and mounds of chile.

To some, the Ponderosa is the town's best steak house. Two favorites are the Porterhouse and T-Bone steaks cooked in one of two ways: near raw, or charred. The few Californians I know of who do eat meat stick to steak tartare and London broil, but folks here like their meat raw—and their chile hot. At the Ponderosa, the all-American pot pies with a thick crust are served with a bowl of jalapeños, Hatch chiles, and the chiles *güeritos*, a mild chile with tiny seeds that are more tasty than hot. The cooks here rarely bother with a garnish. I have yet to spot a radish or parsley sprig atop a mound of chile.

One cold day, fed up with my swollen lip and tired of chewing on Rolaids, I walked up Central towards the Double Rainbow, my California stomach crying out for relief. I needed whole-wheat bread, organic lettuce and tomatoes, alfalfa sprouts, and Grey Poupon. As I staggered up the street with my down coat brushing against my knees, I spotted a cozy restaurant up ahead. A worn menu was pasted in the window. I pushed my way in, unwrapped my weary body from coat and scarf, removed my thick mittens, then read the menu. I was shocked to see no mention of chile. I questioned the waitress, a shy young woman who was also the cook, then ordered the house specialty: buttermilk pancakes (sans chile). The next day I ate French waffles. On the following days I pigged out on oatmeal served with English scones and imported marmalade, *baklava* that dripped honey, and meaty turnovers that weighed a ton. Not until my jeans refused to zip—and my daughter announced her impending visit—did I think about chile.

She flew in from LAX on a warm Thursday (read 40 degrees) before Christmas, visibly tired from a trip that had started at nine o'clock that evening and, after numerous delays, ended at two in the morning in Albuquerque. Not wanting to be late, I stationed myself near the Southwest terminal and waited, and waited. The building was half-empty; the cleaning women were long gone. Only the guards and a porter were working. My daughter's was the last flight in. We groped our way through the icy night to the empty parking lot, then headed to my apartment in Greenwood Village.

The first few days we played tourist: visited the holy shrine at Chimayó, a small village north of Santa Fe. From afar, *el santuario* beckoned all pilgrims; an array of Christmas lights were strung across its gate. We made our way to the ancient church—our feet gripping the uneven tile floor that seemed to dip in the middle—and to the altar of carved wood. The *santos*, dressed in thin garments, cast shadows on the white adobe walls. Once inside the small room where the miraculous earth lay, my daughter chided me for wanting to pinch some "holy" dirt to take home. She read with interest the numerous petitions—in Spanish and English—pinned on the tiny altars. Many were petitions, while others were a response to prayers answered. When I added my *notita* to the pile, my daughter appeared to frown, but when she thought I wasn't looking, she lit a votive candle at the altar rail.

Another day we took the tram to Sandia Peak, sampled hot toddies inside the glassed coffee shop as low clouds drifted by, then went for a short hike across the trail that cut through the mountains. Above us stood majestic trees of pine and aspen, and the common scrub pine. Once back on track, we headed for Acoma Pueblo, where a bus took us right to the top. On the way home we ate at a soup and salad place on Central.

One cold night we toured Old Town in Albuquerque. I wanted my daughter to see the *farolitos* that during the Nativity season decorate the old Mission church and adjacent homes. I explained what I knew of this New Mexican tradition and, although it was extremely cold, suggested we circle the plaza to admire the pretty sight and the *farolitos*.

"Mother," she hissed, pulling tight her coat, "you see one burning lunch bag—and you see them all!"

"Cómo?"

"That's what they are, see?" She pointed to the *farolitos* that stood alongside the darkened buildings, then stomped off, her leather boots scraping the sidewalk. Appalled at this lack of respect for Hispanic traditions—and tired of her California flip, I stomped off after her. Later that week, at Isleta Pueblo, I was almost furious when she first refused to remain outdoors to watch the Indian dances. We both stomped our feet to keep warm while the half-clad dancers in Native gear went through their paces. It was cold. Just as the dancers went by, my daughter marched off to take refuge inside the car. "So what if it's 10 degrees and dropping," I screeched to her retreating back, "you'll never see this in California."

We saved Santa Fe for last. On Christmas morning we got up early, opened presents, sipped tea, and prepared to leave. By now I knew enough to allow at two hours for the daily shampoo and blow-dry routine that was *de rigor* for my daughter. "I live in Hollywood, mother," she often reminded me, "and have to look good."

We left Albuquerque at ten, and, although it was terribly chilly and the car windows kept fogging up, once in the city we strolled around the plaza, now teeming with well-heeled *turistas*, many of them dressed to the teeth: *high leather boots, gorgeous wool coats, and imported hand knit scarves*. We priced weavings made in a former commune in Penasco, now home to Hispanic entrepreneurs who raise the sheep that produces the organic wool found in their blankets. At an exclusive shop above a bookstore that reeked of money, my daughter tried on a conch belt of solid silver that the clerk insisted was a bargain at $600.00. At a frame shop we admired the artwork waiting to be set inside a frame of one's choice, then toured the basket shop where tortilla baskets made in Taiwan sold for $2.99.

In an effort to instill a respect for Spanish Colonial history in my daughter, I steered her towards a large building near the plaza.

"See this building?" I pointed to the oldest structure in the state—the country perhaps—and began to recite the names and dates of early settlers when my daughter pulled me towards the silver jewelry displayed in the window of an adjacent restaurant. Thinking she might be hungry, I joined her, only to see that while she did appear interested in silver bracelets, she was sizing up the handsome waiter inside.

He was slender, about five-ten, *moreno*, with dark, limpid eyes and a black ponytail that bounded as he moved. A turquoise earring dangled from one slender earlobe, a conch belt encircled his waist. His firm buttocks were encased in hand-stitched leather pants. He twirled in-between the tables, absorbed in his job, totally aware of his charms.

"Are you hungry?" I asked my daughter, certain she would be delighted with her first taste of sopaipillas with honey.

"I sure am," she snickered, staring at the waiter now giving *her* the once-over.

Thoroughly disgusted, I yanked her by the arm and marched her to Tía María's, a Mexican restaurant on Galisteo Street. We found a seat near the window, then settled down. She scanned the menu, then asked about a meat dish. "Does it come with tofu?"

"I'll have coffee first," I told our waitress, "then I'll order." I then sat back and unwrapped the wool scarf that was about to choke me.

"I'll have the chicken fajitas," my daughter announced, staring at a young dude in tight jeans and cowboy boots just then walking in, "...and herb tea with a slice of lemon." She settled back, fluffed her dark hair toward the ceiling, then checked her lipstick.

"Green? Or red? asked the waitress, eyeing my daughter's black mini-skirt—and the pale flesh that was beginning to protrude.

"Uhhh, let me see!" I felt like a judge at a chile contest; I wanted to pass for a *real* connoisseur. I stuck what my friend calls my "arrogant California pose," sniffed the air, and looked with disdain at folks around me now sporting runny noses.

"What does she mean?" my daughter inquired, "Red, or green what?" She checked her skirt, now crawling dangerously towards her hips, then she sipped tea and glanced across the room.

"Chile," I answered, trying to curb my impatience. I started to describe the importance of chile to New Mexicans and suggested we might visit Hatch, a town near Las Cruces, that grows a type of chile unmatched in the state. She listened for a minute, toying with her fork, then her attention shifted to a couple swaddled in furs who were now entering the restaurant.

"Neat," she exclaimed, tossing back her dark mane.

"Neat?"

"Yeah. I like guys who are into fur. Y'know, like Mick Jagger. He wore a mink coat to the floor at his last concert...and really got mobbed!"

"By crazies?"

"He was mobbed by environmentalists, mother. Y' know, people out to protect animals."

Just then the waitress came back with my coffee. Clearly impatient, she plunked the cup on the table, then arranged cream and sugar on the table.

"I'll have a large bowl of CHILE," I said, as I smoothed my down jacket. Already I felt warm.

"Red? Or green?" she asked in the now familiar sing-song. She balanced an order-pad on her generous hip and turned to smile at the cowboy now scoping my daughter, then walked off to the kitchen.

The restaurant was crowded. There was a festive feeling in the air. Holiday wreaths braided with scarlet ribbons and red berries hung from each wall. Fragrant pine branches—with tiny cones still attached—decorated the front counter where the owner, decked out in a Santa hat, presided. At each table sat red and green candles; they exuded the smell of pine. I'm glad we came here, I thought to myself, it's a nice place to be.

"Ummm," gushed my daughter, rolling her dark eyes, "I'd sure like to order him for lunch!" Once more she sneaked a look across the room, then straightened her leather skirt.

"You are beginning to disgust me," I whispered, trying to keep from shouting. "Is this what I've taught you?"

"Yup," she grinned, then pulled at her skirt and eased out of the seat. She sauntered towards the bathroom, making sure she passed by the cute cowboy, who stared after her with glazed eyes.

Once she was out of earshot I was tempted to call the waitress back to order the Christmas special...just in case, but I knew the chile would warm me up. I sipped my coffee and waited.

Our order arrived just as my daughter exited the women's bathroom, a layer of purple eye-shadow on her eyelids. She all but shimmied as she came down the aisle; her black curls swirled in wild abandon. I waited to see if she'd dropped a hankie—or whatever it is young women drop today—but all she did was glide by the cowboy who blushed, dropped his fork, then leaned over to pick it up, all the while staring at my daughter's behind.

We attacked our food with gusto. I cut a tortilla in thirds, lathered it with butter, then nibbled at it. I was eating around the stew! I stared at the abundance of green swimming in the bowl, wiped my soup spoon on a napkin, then slowly dipped it in the chile stew.

"Why aren't you eating?" My daughter asked between mouthfuls of fajitas.

"I'm waiting for it to cool down."

The chile was hot, hot. I felt my throat constrict, my nose expand. Damn! It was hotter than cajun and the curry I once braved when trying to impress my friend from India. Even the *chiles güeritos* straight from the jar were not this spicy. I held the bits of meat and chile in my rapidly swelling mouth, then pushed them from one side to the other with my feverish tongue. Afraid of gagging on a pod and having it go up my nose, I sipped water and avoided my daughter's gaze, thankful for the cowboy who held her attention. Undaunted—and determined not to act *como una turista*—I neutralized the stew with bits of flour tortillas, and once more dug in.

"Good?" asked my daughter, squeezing lemon juice into her tea. "Is it what you wanted?"

"Ummmm."

My mouth was on fire and my ears, as if invaded by a swarm of bees, were beginning to buzz. The heat traveled to my throat, then returned to its place of origin. I'm going to die, I thought, and ruin my daughter's visit. And all because I had to have the damn chile. I bent over, sipped water, then turned aside to blow my plugged-up nose.

"And how is everything?" asked the waitress, chewing furiously on a wad of gum. "Hot enough for ya?"

I looked daggers at her. "It *is* a bit hot," I managed to whisper, my voice all but gone.

"It's the house recipe," she grinned, "extra hot. Ya know, for real aficionados like yerself."

"Ahhhhhhh"

I felt betrayed, not unlike the time I went to Palmillas. For some time my friends at the university had insisted I try the food at Palmillas, a family-owned restaurant on Girard. Its Thursday night specials of carne asada and spinach (*espinaca* in Spanish) was said to be the best in town. Better yet, the place was close to my apartment. During Lent, I feasted on their *lentejas al estilo nuevomexicano*. I soon became hooked on their homemade tortillas. "You haven't lived until you've tasted their spinach special," my friends had insisted. One Thursday evening I did—and barely lived to tell about it.

But that is past history. This is now, I conceded, as I prepared to take another spoonful of chile.

"You don't have to eat it, you know," intoned my daughter, wise beyond her years. "Order something else."

"But I'm now a New Mexican," I insisted. "Everyone here eats chile. Everyone." I dabbed at my eyes, trying not to stare at the tortillas scattered on the table.

"Everyone but you, mother."

"Ready for dessert?" The waitress was back. She took one look at my eyes, then trotted back to the kitchen, and returned with a bowl of plain beans. "These are on the house, she explained, then cleaned the mess on the table.

I mixed the beans with the chile, then took another sip. It was worse! About to gag, I swallowed a chunk of chile, pods and all. My head began to pound; I couldn't breathe! I began to cough, as around me customers tittered. In desperation I buttered a fresh tortilla and crammed it into my mouth.

"You don't have to impress me, mother," my daughter offered, smiling at the cowboy who had ordered another Dos Equis. "Just leave it," she commanded.

But I was determined. As a legal resident of New Mexico (I had a new driver's license and the red and yellow license plates with a Zia), I would not give up. No longer the health-conscious Californian who once lived on tuna, tofu and sprouts, I was committed to scarfing chile with the best of then, or die trying. I spooned another portion of *chile verde*, intent on not repeating the adventure of the previous week.

The week before, as part of a Women Studies search committee, I interviewed an applicant for a position in that department. My colleagues and I met at El Pavo restaurant. Our assignment was to get to know Nancy S., a finalist for the job, in an informal setting. Nancy was a pale, blond woman from an Eastern college with exquisite manners, classy clothes, and a Ph.D. from Cornell. Reservations were made; we ordered individual dinners and drinks. Nancy ordered carne adobada, meat marinated in red chile—the house specialty—and Carta Blanca beer. I wanted to warn Nancy about the chile that once was *almost* my undoing, but my job was to observe, not dictate. Besides, Nancy was busy charming the departmental chairperson. *Pobrecita.* Within minutes, she began to gasp for air; her eyes watered and her nose turned red. I munched on chiles rellenos, unaware of the pods under the melted cheese. Suddenly, I too began to gasp. Across from me, Nancy sipped her cold beer, then gamely ate some more. When able to breathe—and talk—she bragged about eating chile all the time. "I'm into Cajun," she told the group, her nose a bulbous red, "but this stuff is the berries." She killed another beer, then recovered with Kahlua and coffee dotted with whipped cream and cinnamon. Needless to say, she did not get the job.

But that was Nancy and not me, I thought, as I waited for my daughter to polish off the fajitas. As dessert, she ordered a second serving of sopaipillas, hooked on the fried bread that tasted like Mexican *churros*. Earlier, I explained how sopaipillas were part of the meal as are tortillas—and not dessert, but she ignored me. She slathered honey on a large hunk, then silently handed it to me.

Success! The honey stuck to my palate, the inside of my mouth, and my Mick Jagger lips. Within minutes I was able to breath normally, and to once more make light conversation.

It was early evening when we exited the restaurant and headed for the parking lot. Across the way the cluster of adobes that make up La Fonda—a ritzy hotel—glowed pink in the setting sun; the cobalt sky was empty of clouds.

"So, mother, still feel like a New Mexican?" my daughter teased.

"When you come this summer, let's go to Los Altos for enchiladas verdes," I suggested. "Or we could try the home-made chile at ..."

"Better stick to Bob's," my daughter quipped as she gave me a quick hug.

Estela Portillo Trambley

Estela Portillo Trambley is a native of El Paso. After receiving her B.A. and M.A. from the University of Texas at El Paso, she became a high-school administrator and teacher; since 1977, she has been affiliated with the Department of Special Services of the El Paso Public Schools. Since the early 1970s, she has had a distinguished career as a writer. In 1972 she was honored with the Quinto Sol Literary Prize for her play, *The Day of the Swallows,* and for three of the stories that had appeared in *El Grito*, the first journal associated with the Chicano movement. She guest-edited the September, 1973, milestone issue of *El Grito*, which included the first contemporary collection of works written by Chicana authors. With *Rain of Scorpions* (1975), a collection of short stories, she became the first successful Chicana writer in a field then dominated by patriarchal standards. Among her other works are the theatrical pieces *Sun Images* (1979) and *Sor Juana Inés and Other Plays* (1983); a collection of Haiku, *Impressions of a Chicana* (1974); and the novel *Trini* (1986). In 1993, Bilingual Press re-issued the new *Rain of Scorpions and Other Stories*, with most of Portillo Trambley's early fiction rewritten. Recently, she completed a novel, *Mafiani*, based on the original Aztec legend of La Llorona. Well-received by critics and scholars, her work is the subject of many studies; in fact, Patricia Hopkins's "Bibliography of Works By and About Estela Portillo Trambley" (included in the 1993 edition of *Rain of Scorpions*) lists seventy-four entries. Her women are strong and take center stage. Portillo Trambley's work continues to forge new images of female representation and to challenge our own unconscious stereotyping of Latinos and their culture.

The Burning

Estela Portillo Trambley

The women of the barrio, the ones pockmarked by life, sat in council. Their minds were a dark, narrow tunnel that had long ago withered their souls. They had gathered in this heath all as one to condemn an enemy, to accuse her, to punish her. One old woman added fuel to the fire of hate. "This Lela changes light into darkness. I've seen her with my very own eyes!"

"You know the caves outside the town?" A woman dressed in black added to the fuel. "At night, when she stays in the caves, she goes through their open mouths into the long darkness and stays there days on end. When she's there I have seen lights appear like fireflies. It's her black magic! She's working some evil against us."

One with wild eyes nodded her head in affirmation. "She makes this potion. She says it's medicine for the sick. I say that it's the bitterness of good; I think she makes it for herself. What could it be but the red honey milk of evil?"

A cadaverous old woman pointed to the darkened sky. "I hear thunder. Lightning is not far."

A murmur rose in unison. "We could use some rain, but rain will not cleanse her evil."

The oldest one among them, one with dirty claws, stood up with arms outstretched to the sky, sniffing the sky of night as lightning flashed. Her voice was harsh and came from ages past. "She must burn! She's a witch! A witch!"

As the women circled the heath, a cloud, black and tortured, dug into the sky. Each pair of eyes looked into another pair—were they all in agreement? There were only grating sounds of frenzy, tight and straining. Thunder was riding the lightning now, directly over their heads. But still no signs of blistering words to justify the deed to come. Some women found their voices; anger, heavy like the cloud, crouched and waited for further accusations. Another soul took up the dirge. "The Devil's pawn! On nights like this, when the air is heavy like thick blood, she sings among the dead, preferring them to the living. I have seen her chase the dead back to their graves."

A feverish assent from another member of the group: "She stays and stays with those who die, like one possessed. You know what I think? I think she catches the fleeing souls of the dead and turns them into flies. She doesn't want them to find heaven."

They chorused, "A plague!"

Another clap of thunder reaffirmed. An old one, with nervous, clutching, spidery hands, made the most grievous charge, the cause for the meeting. With bony gestures the old woman shaped the anger in her heart. "She's the enemy of God! She put her obscenities on each doorstep. She wants us Christians as accomplices. She has committed sacrilege against the holy church!"

The fervor rose like a tide. "Burn her! Burn her! Burn her!"

The council howled that she must burn that very night. The sentence given could only have been born of night. Fear takes the disguise of outrage at night. The craved human sacrifice. The accused, a woman called Lela, was the eye of the storm. She must be erased from the world to make them whole when the earth turned to light. It was a tempest grown in narrow margins where slavish minds punish the free. "Lela! Lela! Lela must burn!"

Lela had crossed the blue mountain to their pueblo many years before. It was one ranging south in La Barranca de Cobre. She had walked into San Angelo a bloody, ragged girl. In her apron she had carried some shining sand. She had hesitated on the outskirts of the pueblo, like a frightened fawn, to be asked into the village. The people gathered around her, wondering where she had come from. She had fallen to the ground in exhaustion. The people of the town did not take to strangers, especially to barranca Indians, los descalzos, for they were thought to be savage and uncivilized. She was a frightened child, hungry and lost, but she was a human being needing help. They took her in reluctantly. She remained a stranger to them, all that time. She refused baptism and never attended the Catholic church. She said her pagan prayers and shaped little pagan gods from clay. She sang songs to her nature gods in her dialect and kept her native tongue, learning just enough Spanish to make herself understood. The pueblo knew she was a Tarahumara from Batopilas, but it was her refusal to convert to Christianity that made people suspicious and hostile toward her.

She was kind and gentle and hard working, and she was able to cure the sick with her miracle sand. She was able to cure people with skin diseases, sores, or open wounds. Some wondered if the sand was the evil magic of her gods, but the results of the cure were sure and clean, so she became their curandera, outside their Christian lives.

She became the potter's helper since that had been her mother's trade. The potter was old, and some years after her arrival, he died. She now made beautiful things with clay for the village and surrounding villages. She became the favorite healer for many villages; her life was a busy one. But there were no suitors and few friends. Besides curing with medicinal herbs, she learned to set bones with great success; still, she was never invited to a baptism or wedding. Certainly never to a dance or a village festival. The role of outcast could have been hard and unacceptable to her, but she was in tune to the cycles of the universe, and her imagination and her beliefs sang the song of stars and seasons. She knew down deep that life simply passes unto life. Each of her days had a pattern of firmed senses and feelings. A current flowed through her from the earth, thus she intuitively knew the close mystery of her source. And the loneliness in her life, the emptiness, was filled with a steadiness and grace for necessary things. In time the loneliness became a silent love for the people of the village. Were they not miracles? She would listen to the silence, the nothingness and the allness of which life was made, learning to live happily in the oneness of herself. Many times she made plans to go back to Batopilas, but there was always someone who needed her. The welfare of the people came first.

Each day she lived the memories of her faith and that was what gave her the greatest joy. Her mother and father, and all her family before her, circling the centuries, had been the magic potters for the holy temples. They were endowed with a spirit that ran through their fingers, a spirit transferred to the clay figures of the little gods. Now they could hear the prayers and supplications of the people. Her mother and father had taught her how to shape the little gods, the household gods that shared family blessings and family problems. The stone images of the greater god, like the awesome Tecuat, who commanded silence and obedience, were sculpted by the holy artists, the elder wise. The greater gods were ritual gods that never got close to the people. They were the Lords Above and existed mostly to punish the weak and sinful.

She remembered as a child going to the rituals in honor of Tecuat. She would make her offering in front of the forbidding figure, then run off with a sigh of relief. But the little gods! Ah! They did everything human beings did: laugh, sing, dance, make love, enjoy and she learned to mold them in the manner of the act. Each home had its little god. He lived with members of the family as a friend, a confidant and a comforter. They did not rule or demand obedience but were a source of hope, companions to the people. Little gods, born of river, sky, fire, seed, birds and butterflies, were hidden in small niches in the woods, in the hills, along the river, in the caves, and in the natural grottoes behind the waterfall.

When she was growing up, Lela would often go god-hunting in the woods and hills and river paths. She would find a god in a cave or in a hidden niche overgrown with vines. A special, holy time, a time of prayer and meditation, and of talk. The little god, smiling at her, would accept her prayers and her simple offering. She would sit cross-legged, her eye level to his, and confide her dreams and fears. Both dreams and fears were intertwined in the mind of the young girl. She dreamed of venturing out beyond her village to discover new worlds, to learn new things, but she feared leaving her parents and her friends. Her longing to leave frightened her because she dreamed about it every day; she was ashamed of telling anyone she was restless and desiring new things to learn and do.

One day she walked too far toward the pines, too far toward a roar that spoke of rushing life. She followed a butterfly that must also have heard the command of dreams. It flitted toward the lake; she followed, looking for little gods in the glint of the sun and in the open branches that pierced that absoluteness of the sky. The soft breath of the wind was the breath of little gods, and the crystal shine of rocks, polished by wind and water, was their winking language.

When she reached the lake, Lela stepped into the water, feeling the cool mud against her open toes. She gently touched the ripples of the broken surface with her fingertips, ever so lightly. After awhile her feet felt no more bottom, so she cut through the water with smooth, clean strokes, swimming out to the pearly green rocks that hid the roar. She floated for awhile, looking up at the light filtering through eternal trees. The silence spoke of other than itself; it spoke in colors born of water, plant and sun. She swam all the way to the turn that led to the cradle of the roar, the waterfall.

This became her favorite place until the day god-hunting became a child's game. She was no longer a child, and the dream of going beyond her world possessed her every thought. She could think of nothing else. So one day she went beyond the waterfall without telling any one, beyond the purple trees that led to the mountain that hid the other worlds outside of Batopilas.

If she could cross the desert, she would find another village, other people, other ways. In her innocence she never realized that people could be different from her. The spirits of the little gods protected her. Feeling safe in their protection, she journeyed one whole day, the piercing sun beating down mercilessly. She lost all sense of direction; the terrain was all new to her, so she made her way toward the horizon. At dusk her dry, parched skin welcomed the coldness of the night wind. But not for long, for the wind grew cold and was just as merciless as the sun had been. She found a clump of mesquite behind some giant saguaros. This became her shelter for the night. Cold and hungry, she curled up and gazed into the garden of stars which comforted her until she fell asleep.

At first light she awakened and quickly resumed her journey. She was halfway up the mountain by noon. She rested for awhile, then set out again. Her mouth felt like sand and her stomach gnawed as she followed a path made narrow by a blanket of desert brush. Thorns tore the flesh of her legs and feet as she made her way up, up to the top. But before she reached it, climbing became a torture—no sure footing until the path lost itself in a cleavage of rocks. Night again, but she was not afraid, for the sky was full of blinking little gods.

Making her way along a zigzagging path, she lost her footing, falling down, down into a crevice between two huge boulders. As she fell, her lungs filled with air, then her body hit soft sand. On the edge of her foot she felt the cutting sharpness of a stone. She lay stunned for awhile, feeling a sharp pain on the side of her foot. Somewhat dizzy, she managed to sit up to look at it. It was bleeding profusely, blood soaking the soft sand. The huge boulders loomed upward, rebuking her helplessness. She began to cry. She quickly dried her tears and set about stanching the blood. She tore off a piece of her skirt to use as a bandage. While wrapping her foot, she noticed the sand. It was crystalline and loose, shining in the light of a rising moon. Lela took a handful of the sand and let it spill from her fingers, fascinated by the flow of silver grains.

"The sand of little gods," she whispered to herself. She took some sand and rubbed it on the wound before she wrapped it. Burning with fever she tried to sleep. The fever filtered into dreams of delirium. But as the night went on, she dreamed of the sand becoming the faces of happy little gods. She slept until dawn passed over her head.

The Indian girl rested, then awakened feeling well. She had no fever. She examined the wound, and to her amazement, there was no swelling or infection, only a healthy scab. If it had healed normally, it would have taken weeks to reach that stage of healing. She stood and felt no pain when she put weight on her foot. She kneeled and kissed the shining sands. The sand was too precious to leave behind. It could cure many wounds. She would take as much of the miracle as she could. She took off her apron and filled it with sand, securing it before climbing up the crevice. When she reached the top, she circled the crevice for miles, finally ending up on the other side of the mountain. Below her was another world. She made her way down, fatigued and half-starved, into the arms of strangers.

This place was to be her home for a lifetime. The indifference of the people, their coldness, grew into a long loneliness. One day while exploring the caves on the side of a mountain, she found an entrance where feldspar and black tourmaline formed adventures of light which filtered through the narrow opening to the sky, a ladder of light where little gods danced a skein of colors. Here she found the warmth of a lost sun. Here she wove the delicate dreams of loneliness. But weaving dreams was not enough. She brought clay and dyes to the cave to shape and mold her little gods.

Years flew by, she was old now and her body must give way. One day her little gods, the many kept on shelves in her little house, sang a song of truth, of a long life lived well—a song of returning back to Batopilas, to her origin. For the cold of the snake had never touched her heart; she knew it was the price she had to pay for not giving up her faith, the way of her people. Soon the journey began, a journey to discover the Oneness of herself and the Allness of living things. They told her to race back to the waterfall. Yes! Yes! Of course she would go back with her little gods, but first she had to leave something behind to show the people of the village how much they meant to her as human beings, even if they had shunned her for a lifetime. I must let them know I love them, she decided. An answer came: she would give them a part of herself, something holy, something happy. She would shape a little god for each of them and leave it on their doorstep.

In the cave, she happily shaped a little god for each family, and when she was done, by the light of the moon, she reverently placed one on each doorstep. When the act of love was finished she went back to her house to await the journey back to where water laughed and the earth smiled. It would be a life-giving road back to her origin.

ℌ

And the women who sat in council? They were caught in a fearful sweep of hate. Spiderlike, apelike, toadlike, in their smallness, they were tortured minions. They could not be stopped now. The scurrying creatures gathered firewood in the gloom. With antlike intentions, they hurried back and forth carrying wood to build the fire that would burn Lela, the witch. They piled the wood in a circle around her house, singing their brittle song, "Burn her! Burn her! Tonight! Tonight!"

"The circle of fire will drain her powers!" shouted the old one with claws. She and the others were piling wood when the parish priest came running from the church. He commanded with raised arms as he ran among them.

"Stop! Stop this madness!" The thunder and lightning seemed to ask, What is evil? No evil—only the vacuum of good. What is good? The empty ones turned a deaf ear to their priest. They were deadwood themselves. "Burn! Burn! Burn!"

The priest pleaded with one woman, then another, begging until his voice was raw, taking the wood from their hands. He tried to reason. "All is forgiven, my children. She only made some figures of clay."

There was a hush. The old woman with claws came up to the priest and spit the condemnation in his face. "Only figures of clay! She took our holy saints, so pure, that pray and look up to heaven, she took our Joseph, our Mary, and so many more and made them obscene. How can you defend the right hand of the Devil? She left them undressed, fornicating, drinking, winking, singing, dancing. Can you forgive that? Can anyone forgive it?"

"All of you," the priest said simply, without hope. What the women saw in those figures was the filth of humankind, the celebrating of sin itself! They could not believe their ears. The priest that blessed them with holy water wanted to forgive the rape of their holy saints who knew not sin or lust, whose eyes saw only heaven. Why did he contradict his own teachings? The old one with claws said triumphantly, "She turned our holy Christian saints into pagan devils!"

The priest shook his head, realizing the futility of the struggle. "They are not sinful in her beliefs. She did not sin."

They all turned their backs on the priest and continued piling the wood. Soon the pile would be high enough to set a match to it. Soon it would burn the sin and the sinner.

There was no thought, there was no dream in Lela's dying body. She was waiting for another wave of pain. She was savoring the calm before the pain's return. She fell asleep. A brief sleep, because the pain took over, and she writhed upon the bed, the sheet clinging to her body, her face dripping with perspiration. A moan funneled from her throat; when would the body give way? Give way, give way, she begged in torment. After a long struggle, the pain broke into a blackness. She tried to use her mind against the pain. Memories came, bright and real—the waterfall! She was back in the grotto behind the waterfall, the song of the cascading water filling her with happiness...her hermitage of dreams about new worlds. She did not regret; alone, always alone, she had found the Oneness of herself. Life had knitted all the little gods inside, within her being. She had found a wholeness with the earth itself.

New pain tore her body in two. She gripped the edge of the bed to withstand the pain. In her half-consciousness, white blurs whirled into black, black into white, again and again, until another interval of peace returned. She looked at the shelf above her bed holding rows of smiling little gods, humble and human like herself. Their eyes wore a fierceness for life, a wonder for having life. They were guardians over their maker. She whispered, "Is it time? Is it time to go back to the waterfall?" Their smiles said yes.

As the women outside the house lit the fire, another roll of pain took Lela's body; it rolled, rolled, rolled itself into a fiery redness. Between pain and breath, she saw the kind face of the goddess Ta Te, born of the union of clean rock and blue flowers. She was beckoning, "Come, child, come home..."

Lela saw the little gods becoming whirls of light, like falling silver sand. The body was giving way now; still, there was one wish, her dying breath. "Oh, find me a clean burning, a dying by fire, give my ashes to the wind, the destiny of all my fathers..."

The little gods were racing to the waterfall.

Bessy Reyna

Bessy Reyna was born in Cuba and resided in Panama until 1968, when she came to the United States. She has a B.A. in Psychology from Mt. Holyoke College, an M.A. in Child Development and Family Relations from the University of Connecticut, and has a J.D. from the School of Law at the University of Connecticut. Currently she is working for the Judicial Department of the State of Connecticut. Her poems, short stories and essays have been published in newspapers and literary magazines in the United States and in Latin America, including the *Women's Review of Books, When New Flowers Bloomed: Women Writers of Costa Rica and Panama* (1992), *Twentieth Century African and Latin American Poetry* (1989), *Breaking Boundaries: Latina Writing and Critical Readings* (1989) and *The Defiant Muse: Hispanic Feminist Poems from the Middle Ages to the Present* (1986). She was an invited participant as a Convenor at "Conclave Cultural," a conference by and for Latino artists in Massachusetts and New England, which took place in Boston in 1987. Reyna has been the producer and organizer of numerous literary events, including "Sisters of the Americas," a reading by five award-winning poets held at the Wadsworth Atheneum in conjunction with a traveling exhibit of Women in the Arts. She has served as editor of *El Taller Literario*, the first Connecticut-based Hispanic arts and literature magazine and has been on the board of producers of "Adelante," WVIT-30, a bi-weekly television program in Spanish seen in Hartford, Connecticut.

And This Blue Surrounding Me Again

Bessy Reyna

At times, the simplest of things become even simpler. Like calling someone who lives far away, just to say "I miss you." Simple gestures, like opening a door and entering a room we have been in so many times before. Like the night I went back to her house and entered that blue room for the first time in five years. It was hot and the clothes I was wearing, long-sleeve shirt and heavy pants, made it so much worse. She opened the door, wearing a tank-top and baggy shorts. I walked in pretending not to be uncomfortable, and we sat making small talk, looking at each other and trying to guess if we really had become immune to one another. Without a word, she got up and walked away. I sat, listening to the jazz record she had been playing when I walked in. "Here, why don't you change into these clothes, you will be more comfortable," she said, handing me a pair of old shorts and a T-shirt. A simple gesture. The simple gestures of this person I once loved who was now handing me clothes, her hand touching mine when I reached for the clothes, as if nothing had happened. As if time had not been. As if the years in between never existed.

I wanted to believe it was the simple gesture of her love surfacing when she smiled. Me, wanted again, years later in this room where I now sat surveying my surroundings making an inventory of things replaced, remembering lying here on the same worn-out blue carpet, blue light, blue furniture. I never really paid attention then to how blue this room was. Even the paintings hanging on the walls are done in blues. The wallpaper used to be light blue, but now, covered with water stains, it's mostly peeling pieces of blue. The moonlight coming in from two sides makes the room look even bluer.

I want to stop all the memories flashing in front of me, aware of how this room is affecting me, merging with my mood, infecting me. Can I fight this? She probably wants me here tonight because there is no one else around. What has she done in the last five years? I found clues in her bedroom when I went to change my clothes: new faces smiling from elaborate picture frames. I found myself smiling back at me from one of them, each frame carefully placed like those in a gallery. Did she love them?

I had thought the night I left her bedroom, five years ago, that it would be the last time I would be in that room. Did she plan for the hate? For the dryness of her sex? Lifting her body abruptly in the middle of making love, she looked amused, "You think for a moment that I enjoy sex with you? You must be kidding!" Her face was so full of contempt. "I am fed up with you. I have someone else now," she shouted at me. "You are just like nothing to me now," she kept saying while I was still panting from make-believe love-making that a short time back had seemed like caring. After that, every movement hurt me. Getting dressed and leaving seemed to take place in slow motion.

Earlier that day, we had gone to visit some friends for dinner, only I didn't know I was supposed to be the chef. They had bought lobsters. "We hear you are a great cook," they told me, daring me. "Sure! just give me a cookbook and I can do anything!" I never believed they would take me seriously. I had never cooked a lobster before, and this one was alive. I chose the fanciest French recipe I could find, one with cognac, hoping they wouldn't have the ingredients I needed, but they did. We were all impressed when I lit the sauce at the table. The meal was a great success, but I just couldn't eat it, not after cleaning it and letting all the gunk spill out into my hands. I didn't even taste it.

After dinner we sat talking to each other, the way people do when they get together, not wanting to sound too controversial or too boring. She got up from the living room, went to make a phone call and stayed away for the longest time. Who was she whispering to on the phone? I sat pretending to enjoy my after-dinner drink. "Sorry it took so long," she said casually, trying to smile, sitting next to me, touching me. I resisted her touch wondering who it was at the other end of the phone. Was I so jealous because I recognized the signs?

It was not the first time we broke up. This time it took longer for me to return, that's all. We like pretending it was entirely the other's fault. Can I hate and keep on wanting? (She was right, these clothes are more comfortable.) The simplest gestures making the hurt come back.

It is so still outside. I turned off the light and sat in the darkest corner. She will probably notice my absence after a while and will try to talk me into returning to her bed. I can't, not tonight. Tonight I want to be part of this blue room which my mind converts into a stage set where, at the end of the play, one character moves away to another city.

I didn't hear her walk into the blue room. Next thing I know her hands were caressing me and our fingers were searching and I couldn't stop this need from developing inside of me once again as if nothing else mattered, as if I had stopped caring about anything but feeling her touch. On-again, off-again love, like changing radio stations when you don't like the music. Only it was me this time, me being changed. Does it really matter, here in this blue room? Fingers not daring to rush, to be too obvious, to get too carried away, centering on each touch, because nothing else matters but the blue warmth surrounding us and the room encouraging us to touch and to forget having left it, to forget I now have someone else who loves me, and who I am loving most of the time, except for this one moment when all this blueness surrounds me and I must find out why she left me, and why she hurt me so much and she is not going to tell me, just like before, and it does not matter because in this blue room nothing matters but her touch and the warmth around us.

She had carefully orchestrated my return, planning how to get me back. She searched for me, found me and brought me back. A message left on an answering machine, reaching out, "I had to talk to you, no one else would understand, you are the only one who understands, I have to see you." The past skillfully avoided, coming back to entice me.

She glides expertly next to me, as if she owns the space I occupy, her body surrounds me, overcomes me and I follow her rhythms losing myself for an instant and then I struggle to recapture my body as if it had been invaded. But it wasn't really; I let it happen. She was giving me something I wanted but didn't want to have, because I was used to knowing how it felt when I didn't have it and now I wish I didn't know how it feels having it again. But now I do.

I had to find out. No, didn't have to, simply wanted to.

Photo © Copyright by Georgia McInnis

Helena María Viramontes

Helena María Viramontes was born and grew up in East Los Angeles, which provides the setting for her fiction. She received her B.A. from Immaculate Heart College and her M.F.A. in Creative Writing from the University of California at Irving. Viramontes has been very active in the Latino arts scene in Los Angeles, where she has served as coordinator of the Los Angeles Latino Writers Association, Literary Editor of *XhismeArte*, and co-founder of Latino Writers and Filmmakers. Her short fiction has received awards from *Statement Magazine* (the literary journal of California State University in Los Angeles) and from the Chicano Literary Contest at the University of California, Irvine, a contest which, in recent years, she has helped to coordinate and to judge. Viramontes has received a Creative Writing fellowship from the National Endowment for the Arts, and was selected as a participant in a screen-writing workshop directed by Gabriel García Márquez at the Sundance Institute. Presently, she is a member of Women Behind the Camera, a Los Angeles professional organization of Latinas who work on various aspects of filmmaking. Her short-story collection, *The Moths and Other Stories* (1985), focused on East Los Angeles women of various ages struggling against the restraints placed on them by a patriarchal Latino society. With María Herrera-Sobek, Viramontes co-edited the anthology, *Chicana Creativity and Criticism: Charting New Frontiers in American Literature* (1988). She is presently working on her second collection of short stories, *Paris Rats in East Los Angeles.*

from *The Moths*

Helena María Viramontes

Growing

The two walked down First Street hand in reluctant hand. The smaller one wore a thick, red sweater which had a desperately loose button that swung like a pendulum. She carried her crayons, humming "Jesus loves little boys and girls" to the speeding echo of the Saturday morning traffic, and was totally oblivious to her older sister's wrath.

"My eye!" Naomi ground out the words from between her teeth. She turned to her youngest sister who seemed unconcerned and quite delighted at the prospect of another adventure. "Chaperone," she said with great disdain. "My EYE!" Lucía was chosen by Apá to be Naomi's chaperone. Infuriated, Naomi dragged her along impatiently, pulling and jerking at almost every step. She was 14, almost 15, the idea of having to be watched by a young snot like Lucía was insulting to her maturity. She flicked her hair over her shoulder. "Goddammit," she murmured, making sure that the words were soft enough so that both God and Lucía could not hear them.

There seemed to be no way out of the custom. Her arguments were always the same and always turned into pleas. This morning was no different. Amá, Naomi said, exasperated but determined not to cower out of this one, Amá, the United States is different. Here girls don't need chaperones. Parents trust their daughters. As usual Amá turned to the kitchen sink or the ice box, shrugged her shoulders and said: "You have to ask your father." Naomi's nostrils flexed in fury as she pleaded, but, Amá, it's embarrassing. I'm too old for that. I am an adult. And as usual, Apá felt different, and in his house she had absolutely no other choice but to drag Lucía to a sock hop or church carnival or anywhere Apá was sure a social interaction was inevitable and Lucía came along as a spy, a gnat, a pain in the neck.

Well, Naomi debated with herself, it wasn't Lucía's fault, really. She suddenly felt sympathy for the humming little girl who scrambled to keep up with her as they crossed the freeway overpass. She stopped and tugged Lucía's shorts up, and although her shoelaces were tied, Naomi retied them. No, it wasn't her fault after all, Naomi thought, and she patted her sister's soft light brown almost blondish hair; it was Apá's. She slowed her pace as they continued their journey to Jorge's house. It was Apá who refused to trust her and she could not understand what she had done to make him so distrustful. *TÚ ERES MUJER,* he thundered like a great voice above the heavens, and that was the end of any argument, any question, because he said those words not as truth, but as a verdict, and she could almost see the clouds parting, the thunderbolts breaking the tranquility of her sex. Naomi tightened her grasp with the thought, shaking her head in disbelief.

"So what's wrong with being a mujer," she asked herself out loud.

"Wait up. Wait," Lucía said, rushing behind her.

"Well, would you hurry. Would you?" Naomi reconsidered: Lucía did have some fault in the matter after all, and she became irritated at once at Lucía's smile and the way her chaperone had of taking and holding her hand. As they passed El Gallo, Lucía began fussing, hanging on to her older sister's waist for reassurance.

"Stop it. Would you stop it?" She unglued her sister's grasp and continued pulling her along. "What's wrong with you?" she asked Lucía. I'll tell you what's wrong with you, she thought, as they waited at the corner of an intersection for the light to change: You have a big mouth. That's it. If it wasn't for Lucía's willingness to tattle, she would not have been grounded for three months. Three months, twelve Saturday nights and two church bazaars later, Naomi still hadn't forgiven her youngest sister. When they crossed the street, a homely young man with a face full of acne honked at her tight purple pedal pushers. The two were startled by the honk.

"Go to hell," she yelled at the man in the blue and white Chevy. She indignantly continued her walk.

"Don' be mad, my little baby," he said, his car crawling across the street, then speeding off leaving tracks on the pavement. "You make me ache," he yelled, and he was gone.

"GO TO HELL, goddamn you!" she screamed at the top of her lungs, forgetting for a moment that Lucía told everything to Apá. What a big mouth her youngest sister had, for chrissakes. Three months.

Naomi stewed in anger when she thought of the Salesian Carnival and how she first met a Letterman Senior whose eyes, she remembered with a soft smile, sparkled like crystals of brown sugar. She sighed deeply as she recalled the excitement she experiences when she first became aware that he was following them from booth to booth. Joe's hair was greased back and his dimples were deep. When he finally handed her a stuffed rabbit he had won pitching dimes, she knew she wanted him.

As they continued walking, Lucía waved to the Fruit Man. He slipped off his teeth and, again, she was bewildered.

"Would you hurry up!" Naomi told Lucía as she told her that same night at the carnival. Joe walked beside them and he took out a whole roll of tickets, trying to convince her to leave her youngest sister on the ferris wheel. "You could watch her from behind the gym," he had told her, and his eyes smiled pleasure. "Come on," he said, "have a little fun." They waited in the ferris-wheel line of people.

"Stay on the ride," she finally instructed Lucía, making sure her sweater was buttoned. "And when it stops again, just give the man another ticket, okay?" Lucía said okay, excited at the prospect of heights and dips and her stomach wheezing in between. After Naomi saw her go up for the first time, she waved to her, then slipped away into the darkness and joined the other hungry couples behind the gym. Occasionally, she would open her eyes to see the lights of the ferris wheel spinning in the air with dizzy speed.

When Naomi returned to the ferris wheel, her hair undone, her lips still tingling from his newly stubbled cheeks, Lucía walked off and vomited. She vomited the popcorn, a hot dog, some chocolate raisins, and a candied apple, and all Naomi knew was that she was definitely in trouble.

"It was the ferris wheel," Lucía said to Apá. "The wheel going like this over and over again." She circled her arms in the air and vomited again at the thought of it.

"Where was you sister?" Apá had asked, his voice raising.

"I don't know," Lucía replied, and Naomi knew she had just committed a major offense, and Joe would never wait until her prison sentence was completed.

"Owwww," Lucía said. "You're pulling too hard."

"You're a slow poke, that's why," Naomi snarled back. They crossed the street and passed the rows of junk yards and the shells of cars which looked like abandoned skull heads. They passed Señora Núñuz's neat, wooden house and Naomi saw her peeking through the curtains of her window. They passed the Tú y Yo, the one-room dirt pit of a liquor store where the men bought their beers and sat outside on the curb drinking quietly. When they reached Fourth Street, Naomi spotted the neighborhood kids playing stickball with a broomstick and a ball. Naomi recognized them right away and Tina waved to her from the pitcher's mound.

"Wanna play?" Lourdes yelled from center field. "Come on, have some fun."

"Can't," Naomi replied. "I can't." Kids, kids, she thought. My, my. It wasn't more than a few years ago that she played baseball with Eloy and the rest of them. But she was in high school now, too old now, and it was unbecoming of her. She was an adult.

"I'm tired," Lucía said. "I wanna ice cream."

"You got money?"

"No."

"Then shut up." Lucía sat on the curb, hot and tired, and began removing her sweater. Naomi decided to sit down next to her for a few minutes and watch the game. Anyway, she wasn't really that much in a hurry to get to Jorge's. A few minutes wouldn't make much difference to someone who spent most of his time listening to the radio.

She counted them by names. They were all there. Fifteen of them and their ages varied just as much as their clothes. They dressed in an assortment of colors, and looked like confetti thrown out in the street. Pants, skirts, shorts were always too big and had to be tugged up constantly, and shirt sleeves rolled and unrolled, or socks colorfully mismatched with shoes that did not fit. But the way they dressed presented no obstacle for scoring or yelling foul and she enjoyed the abandonment with which they played. She knew that the only decision these kids made was what to play next, and for a moment she wished to return to those days.

Chano's team was up. The teams were oddly numbered. Chano had nine on his team because everybody wanted to be on a winning team. It was an unwritten law of stickball that anyone who wanted to play joined in on whatever team they preferred. Tina's team had the family faithful 6. Of course numbers determined nothing. Naomi remembered once playing with Eloy and three of her cousins against ten players, and still winning by three points.

Chano was at bat and everybody fanned out far and wide. He was a power hitter and Tina's team prepared for him. They could not afford a home run now because Piri was on second, legs apart, waiting to rush home and score. And Piri wanted to score at all costs. It was important for him because his father sat outside the liquor store with a couple of his uncles and a couple of malt liquors watching the game.

"Steal the base," his father yelled. "Run, menso." But Piri hesitated. He was too afraid to take the risk. Tina pitched and Chano swung, missed, strike one.

"Batter, batter, swing," Naomi yelled from the curb. She stood to watch the action better.

"I wanna ice cream," Lucía said.

"Come on, Chano," Piri yelled, bending his knees and resting his hands on them like a true baseball player. He spat, clapped his hands. "Come on."

"Ah, shut up, sissy." This came from Lourdes, Tina's younger sister. Naomi smiled at the rivals. "Can't you see you're making the pitcher nervous?" She pushed him hard between the shoulder blades, then returned to her position in the outfield, holding her hand over her eyes to shield them from the sun. "Strike the batter out," she screamed at the top of her lungs. "Come on, strike the menso out!" Tina delivered another pitch, but not before going through the motions of a professional preparing for the perfect pitch. Naomi knew she was a much better pitcher than Tina. Strike two. Maybe not. Lourdes let out such a cry of joy that Piri's father called her a dog.

Chano was angry now, nervous and upset. He put his bat down, spat in his hands and rubbed them together, wiped the sides of his jeans, kicked the dirt for perfect footing.

"Get on with the game," Naomi shouted impatiently. Chano tested his swing. He swung so hard that he caused Juan, Tina's brother and devoted catcher, to jump back.

"Hey, baboso, watch out," Juan said. "You almost hit my coco." And he pointed to his forehead.

"Well, don't be so stupid," Chano replied, positioning himself once again. "Next time back off when I come to bat."

"Baboso," Juan repeated.

"Say it to my face," Chano said, breaking his stance and turning to Juan. "Say it again so I can break this bat over your head."

"Ah, come on," Kiki, the shortstop yelled, "I gotta go home pretty soon."

"Let up," Tina demanded.

"Shut up, marrana," Piri said, turning to his father to make sure he heard. "Tinasana, cola de marrana. Tinasana, cola de marrana." Tina became so infuriated that she threw the ball directly at his stomach. Piri folded over in pain.

"No! No!" Sylvia yelled. "Don't get off the base or she'll tag you out."

"It's a trick," Miguel yelled from behind home plate.

"That's what you get!" This came from Lourdes. Piri did not move, and although Naomi felt sorry for him, she giggled at the scene just the same.

"I heard the ice cream man," Lucía said.

"You're all right, Tina," Naomi yelled, laughing, "You're A-O-K." And with that compliment, Tina took a bow for her performance until everyone began shouting and booing. Tina was prepared. She pitched and Chano made the connection quick, hard, the ball rising high and flying over Piri's, Lourdes', Naomi's and Lucía's head and landing inside the Chinese Cemetery.

"DON'T JUST STAND THERE!!" Tina screamed to Lourdes. "Go get it, stupid." After Lourdes broke out of her trance, she ran to the tall, chain link fence which surrounded the cemetery, jumped on it with great urgency and crawled up like a scrambling spider. When she jumped over the top of the fence, her dress tore with a rip-roar.

"We saw your calzones, we saw your calzones," Lucía sang.

"Go! Lourdes, go!" Naomi jumped up and down in excitement, feeling like a player who so much wanted to help her team win, but was benched on the sidelines for good. The kids blended into one huge noise, like an untuned orchestra, screaming and shouting, Get the ball, Run in, Piri, Go Lourdes, Go, Throw the ball, Chano pick up your feetthrowtheballrunrunrunthrow the ball. "*THROW* the ball to me!!" Naomi waved and waved her arms. She was no longer concerned with her age, her menstruations, her breasts that bounced with every jump. All she wanted was an out at home plate. To hell with being benched. "Throw it to me," she yelled.

In the meantime, Lourdes searched frantically for the ball, tip-toeing across the graves saying, excuse me, please excuse me, excuse me, until she found the ball peacefully buried behind a huge gray marble stone, and she yelled to no one particular, CATCH IT, SOMEONE CATCH IT. She threw the ball up and over the fence and it landed near Lucia. Lucía was about to reach for it when Naomi picked it off the ground and threw it straight to Tina. Tina caught the ball, dropped it, picked it up, and was about to throw it to Juan at home plate when she realized that Juan had picked up the home plate and run, zigzagging across the street, while Piri and Chano ran after him. Chano was a much faster runner, but Piri insisted that he be the first to touch the base.

"I gotta touch it first," he kept repeating between pants. "I gotta."

The kids on both teams grew wild with anger and encouragement. Seeing an opportunity, Tina ran as fast as her stocky legs could take her. Because Chano slowed down to let Piri touch the base first, Tina was able to reach him, and with one quick blow, she thundered OUT! She made one last desperate throw to Juan so that he could tag Piri out, but she threw it so hard that it struck Piri right in the back of his head, and the blow forced him to stumble just within reach of Juan and home plate.

"You're out!!" Tina said, out of breath. "O-U-T, out."

"No fair!" Piri immediately screamed. "NO FAIR!!" He stomped his feet in rage. "You marrana, you marrana."

"Don't be such a baby. Take it like a man," Piri's father said as he opened another malt liquor with a can opener. But Piri continued stomping and screaming until his shouts were buried by the honk of an oncoming car and the kids obediently opened up like a zipper to let the car pass.

Naomi felt like a victor. She had helped once again. Delighted, she giggled, laughed, laughed harder, suppressed her laughter into chuckles, then laughed again. Lucía sat quietly, to her surprise, and her eyes were heavy with sleep. She wiped them, looked at Naomi. "Vamos," Naomi said, offering her hand. By the end of the block, she lifted Lucía and laid her head on her shoulder. As Lucía fell asleep, Naomi wondered why things were always so complicated once you became older. Funny how the old want to be young and the young want to be old. She was guilty of that. Now that she was older, her obligations became heavier both at home and at school. There were too many expectations, and no one instructed her on how to fulfill them, and wasn't it crazy? She cradled Lucía gently, kissed her cheek. They were almost at Jorge's now, and reading to him was just one more thing she dreaded, and one more thing she had no control over: it was another one of Apá's thunderous commands.

When she was Lucía's age, she hunted for lizards and played stickball with her cousins. When her body began to bleed at twelve, Eloy saw her in a different light. Under the house, he sucked her swelling nipples and became jealous when she spoke to other boys. He no longer wanted to throw rocks at the cars on the freeway with her and she began to act differently because everyone began treating her differently and wasn't it crazy? She could no longer be herself and her father could no longer trust her, because she was a woman. Jorge's gate hung on a hinge and she was almost afraid it would fall off when she opened it. She felt Lucía's warm, deep breath on her neck and it tickled her.

"Tomorrow," she whispered lovingly to her sister as she entered the yard. "Tomorrow I'll buy you all the ice creams you want."

The Moths

I was fourteen years old when Abuelita requested my help. And it only seemed fair. Abuelita had pulled me through the rages of scarlet fever by placing, removing, and replacing potato slices on the temples of my forehead; she had seen me through several whippings, an arm broken by a dare jump off Tío Enrique's tool shed, puberty, and my first lie. Really, I told Amá, it was only fair.

Not that I was her favorite granddaughter or anything special. I wasn't even pretty or nice like my older sisters, and I just couldn't do the girl things they could do. My hands were too big to handle the fineries of crocheting or embroidery, and I always pricked my fingers or knotted my colored threads time and time again while my sisters laughed and called me bull hands with their cute waterlike voices. So I began keeping a piece of jagged brick in my sock to bash my sisters or anyone who called me bull hands. Once, while we all sat in the bedroom, I hit Teresa on the forehead, right above her eyebrow, and she ran to Amá with her mouth open, her hand over her eye while the blood seeped between her fingers. I was used to the whippings by then.

I wasn't respectful either. I even went so far as to doubt the power of Abuelita's slices, the slices she said absorbed my fever. "You're still alive, aren't you?" Abuelita snapped back, her pasty-gray eye beaming at me and burning holes in my suspicions. Regretful that I had let secret questions drop out of my mouth, I couldn't look into her eyes. My hands began to fan out, grow like a liar's nose until they hung by my side like low weights. Abuelita made a balm out of dried moth wings and Vicks and rubbed my hands, shaped them back to size, and it was the strangest feeling. Like bones melting. Like sun shining through the darkness of your eyelids. I didn't mind helping Abuelita after that, so Amá would always send me over to her.

In the early afternoon Amá would push her hair back, hand me my sweater and shoes, and tell me to go to Mamá Luna's. This was to avoid another fight and another whipping, I knew. I would deliver one last direct shot on Marisela's arm and jump out of our house, the slam of the screen door burying her cries of anger, and I'd gladly go help Abuelita plant her wild lilies or jasmine or heliotrope or cilantro or hierbabuena in red Hills Brothers' coffee cans. Abuelita would wait for me at the top step of her porch, holding a hammer and nail and empty coffee cans. And although we hardly spoke, hardly looked at each other as we worked over root transplants, I always felt her gray eye on me. It made me feel, in a strange sort of way, safe and guarded and not alone. Like God was supposed to make you feel.

On Abuelita's porch, I would puncture holes in the bottom of the coffee cans with a nail and a precise hit of a hammer. This completed, my job was to fill them with red clay mud from beneath her rose bushes, packing it softly, then making a perfect hole, four fingers round, to nest a sprouting avocado pit, or the spidery sweet potatoes that Abuelita rooted in mayonnaise jars with toothpicks and daily water, or prickly chayotes that produced vines that twisted and wound all over her porch pillars, crawling to the roof, up and over the roof, and down the other side, making her small brick house look like it was cradled within the vines that grew pear-shaped squashes ready for the pick, ready to be steamed with onions and cheese and butter. The roots would burst out of the rusted coffee cans and search for a place to connect. I would then feed the seedlings with water.

But this was a different kind of help, Amá said, because Abuelita was dying. Looking into her gray eye, then into her brown one, the doctor said it was only a matter of days. And so it seemed only fair that these hands she had melted and formed found use in rubbing her caving body with alcohol and marihuana, rubbing her arms and legs, turning her face to the window so she could watch the Bird of Paradise blooming or smell the scent of clove in the air. I toweled her face frequently and held her hand for hours. Her gray wiry hair hung over the mattress. Since I could remember, she'd kept her long hair in braids. Her mouth was vacant and when she slept, her eyelids never closed all the way. Up close, you could see her gray eye beaming out the window, staring hard as if to remember everything. I never kissed her. I left the window open when I went to the market.

Across the street from Jay's Market there was a chapel. I never knew its denomination, but I went in just the same to search for candles. I sat down on one of the pews because there were none. After I cleaned my fingernails, I looked up at the high ceiling. I had forgotten the vastness of these places, the coolness of the marble pillars and the frozen statues with blank eyes. I was alone. I knew why I had never returned.

That was one of Apá's biggest complaints. He would pound his hands on the table, rocking the sugar dish or spilling a cup of coffee and scream that if I didn't go to mass every Sunday to save my goddamn sinning soul, then I had no reason to go out of the house, period. Punto final. He would grab my arm and dig his nails into me to make sure I understood the importance of catechism. Did he make himself clear? Then he strategically directed his anger at Amá for her lousy ways of bringing up daughters, being disrespectful and unbelieving, and my older sisters would pull me aside and tell me if I didn't get to mass right this minute, they were all going to kick the holy shit out of me. Why am I so selfish? Can't you see what it's doing to Amá, you idiot? So I would wash my feet and stuff them in my black Easter shoes that shone with Vaseline, grab a *missal* and veil, and wave good-bye to Amá.

I would walk slowly down Lorena to First to Evergreen, counting the cracks on the cement. On Evergreen I would turn left and walk to Abuelita's. I liked her porch because it was shielded by the vines of the chayotes and I could get a good look at the people and car traffic on Evergreen without them knowing. I would jump up the porch steps, knock on the screen door as I wiped my feet and call Abuelita? Mi Abuelita? As I opened the door and stuck my head in, I would catch the gagging scent of toasting chile on the placa. When I entered the sala, she would greet me from the kitchen, wringing her hands in her apron. I'd sit at the corner of the table to keep from being in her way. The chiles made my eyes water. Am I crying? No, Mamá Luna, I'm sure I'm not crying. I don't like going to mass, but my eyes watered anyway, the tears dropping on the tablecloth like candle wax. Abuelita lifted the burnt chiles from the fire and sprinkled water on them until the skins began to separate. Placing them in front of me, she turned to check the menudo. I peeled the skins off and put the flimsy, limp looking green and yellow chiles in the molcajete and began to crush and crush and twist and crush the heart out of the tomato, the clove of garlic, the stupid chiles that made me cry, crushed them until they turned into liquid under my bull hand. With a wooden spoon, I scraped hard to destroy the guilt, and my tears were gone. I put the bowl of chile next to a vase filled with freshly cut roses. Abuelita touched my hand and pointed to the bowl of menudo that steamed in front of me. I spooned some chile into the menudo and rolled a corn tortilla thin with the palms of my hands. As I ate, a fine Sunday breeze entered the kitchen and a rose petal calmly feathered down to the table.

I left the chapel without blessing myself and walked to Jay's. Most of the time Jay didn't have much of anything. The tomatoes were always soft and the cans of Campbell soups had rusted spots on them. There was dust on the tops of cereal boxes. I picked up what I needed: rubbing alcohol, five cans of chicken broth, a big bottle of Pine Sol. At first Jay got mad because I thought I had forgotten the money. But it was there all the time, in my back pocket.

When I returned from the market, I heard Amá crying in Abuelita's kitchen. She looked up at me with puffy eyes. I placed the bags of groceries on the table and began putting the cans of soup away. Amá sobbed quietly. I never kissed her. After a while, I patted her on the back for comfort. Finally: "¿Y mi Amá?" she asked in a whisper, then choked again and cried into her apron.

Abuelita fell off the bed twice yesterday, I said, knowing that I shouldn't have said it and wondering why I wanted to say it because it only made Amá cry harder. I guess I became angry and just so tired of the quarrels and beatings and unanswered prayers and my hands just there hanging helplessly by my side. Amá looked at me again, confused, angry, and her eyes were filled with sorrow. I went outside and sat on the porch swing and watched the people pass. I sat there until she left. I dozed off repeating the words to myself like rosary prayers: when do you stop giving when do you stop giving when do you... and when my hands fell from my lap, I awoke to catch them. The sun was setting, an orange glow, and I knew Abuelita was hungry.

There comes a time when the sun is defiant. Just about the time when moods change, inevitable seasons of a day, transitions from one color to another, that hour or minute or second when the sun is finally defeated, finally sinks into the realization that it cannot with all its power to heal or burn, exist forever, there comes an illumination where the sun and earth meet, a final burst of burning red orange fury reminding us that although endings are inevitable, they are necessary for rebirths, and when that time came, just when I switched on the light in the kitchen to open Abuelita's can of soup, it was probably then that she died.

The room smelled of Pine Sol and vomit and Abuelita had defecated the remains of her cancerous stomach. She had turned to the window and tried to speak, but her mouth remained open and speechless. I heard you, Abuelita, I said, stroking her cheek, I heard you. I opened the windows of the house and let the soup simmer and overboil on the stove. I turned the stove off and poured the soup down the sink. From the cabinet I got a tin basin, filled it with lukewarm water and carried it carefully to the room. I went to the linen closet and took out some modest bleached white towels. With the sacredness of a priest preparing his vestments, I unfolded the towels one by one on my shoulders. I removed the sheets and blankets from her bed and peeled off her thick flannel nightgown. I toweled her puzzled face, stretching out the wrinkles, removing the coils of her neck, toweled her shoulders and her breasts. Then I changed the water. I returned to towel the creases of her stretch-marked stomach, her sporadic vaginal hairs, and her sagging thighs. I removed the lint from between her toes and noticed a mapped birthmark on the fold of her buttock. The scars on her back, which were as thin as the life lines on the palms of her hands, made me realize how little I really knew of Abuelita. I covered her with a thin blanket and went into the bathroom. I washed my hands, and turned on the tub faucets and watched the water pour into the tub with vitality and steam. When it was full, I turned off the water and undressed. Then, I went to get Abuelita.

She was not as heavy as I thought, and when I carried her in my arms, her body fell into a V, and yet my legs were tired, shaky, and I felt as if the distance between the bedroom and bathroom was miles and years away. Amá, where are you?

I stepped into the bathtub one leg first, then the other. I bent my knees slowly to descend into the water slowly so I wouldn't scald her skin. There, there, Abuelita, I said, cradling her, smoothing her as we descended, I heard you. Her hair fell back and spread across the water like eagle's wings. The water in the tub overflowed and poured onto the tile of the floor. Then the moths came. Small, gray ones that came from her soul and out through her mouth fluttering to light, circling the single dull light bulb of the bathroom. Dying is lonely and I wanted to go where the moths were, stay with her and plant chayotes whose vines would crawl up her fingers and into the clouds; I wanted to rest my head on her chest with her stroking my hair, telling me about the moths that lay within the soul and slowly eat the spirit up; I wanted to return to the waters of the womb with her so that we would never be alone again. I wanted. I wanted my Amá. I removed a few strands of hair from Abuelita's face and held her small light head within the hollow of my neck. The bathroom was filled with moths, and for the first time in a long time I cried, rocking us, crying for her, for me, for Amá, the sobs emerging from the depths of anguish, the misery of feeling half-born, sobbing until finally the sobs rippled into circles and circles of sadness and relief. There, there, I said to Abuelita, rocking us gently, there, there.

Part Four: Drama

Photo by Rita Prats

Dolores Prida

Dolores Prida is ranked among the most important playwrights of the contemporary Latino theater in the United States. Together with the highly talented María Irene Fornés and Ana María Simó, Prida has helped to develop contemporary Cuban theater in this country. Prida incorporates various techniques into her plays, from realistic musical theater to the nonrealistic theater of the absurd. She is preoccupied with both national and sexual identity, and explores what it means to be a woman. Prida was born in Cuba and came to this country as a child. She has written for the stage and television, and has taught playwriting techniques in New York. The director of the Association of Hispanic Artists, and editor of its newsletter, *AHA!*, Prida has been a Playwright-in-Residence at INTAR in New York City. She is a recipient of the CAPS Playwriting Fellowship and the CINTAS Literature Fellowship. In 1989 she received an Honorary Doctorate Degree from Mount Holyoke College. Prida has published a collection of five plays, *Beautiful Señoritas and Other Plays* (1991) in which she has mapped the urban landscape and covered most of the important topics of her generation. Like her fellow playwrights, she writes in English, in Spanish, and bilingually to reflect the biculturalism she explores so incisively. "Beautiful Señoritas" is a musical satire of women's roles and images in Latino culture. Prida's love of both the American musical and the strong Cuban-Spanish tradition of the musical comedy is expressed in a theatricality closely associated with her work. Referring to the humor in this play, Judith Weiss says that it is the insider's knowledge of the music which empowers Prida to turn it into a weapon against the dominant ideology.

Beautiful Señoritas

A Play with Music, 1977

Dolores Prida

Characters

Four BEAUTIFUL SEÑORITAS who also play assorted characters: Catch Women, Martyrs, Saints and just women.

The MIDWIFE, who also plays the Mother

The MAN, who plays all the male roles

The GIRL, who grows up before our eyes

Set

The set is an open space or a series of platforms and a ramp, which become the various playing areas as each scene flows into the next.

Beautiful Señoritas was first performed at Duo Theater in New York City on November 25, 1977 with the following cast:

THE BEAUTIFUL SEÑORITAS....................................Vira Colorado,
María Norman Lourdes Ramírez and Lucy Vega
THE MIDWIFE ....Sol Echeverría
THE GIRL ....Viridiana Villaverde
THE MAN ....Manuel Yesckas

It was directed by Gloria Zelaya. Music by Tania León and Victoria Ruiz. Musical direction, Lydia Rivera. Choreography by Lourdes Ramírez.

Beautiful Señoritas opened on the West Coast April 6, 1979 at the Inner City Cultural Center's Stormy Weather Cafe in Los Angeles with the following cast:

THE BEAUTIFUL SEÑORITAS............................Roseanna Campos,
Jeannie Linero Rosa María Márquez and Ilka Tanya Payán
THE MIDWIFE...Peggy Hutcherson
THE GIRL..Gabrielle Gazón
THE MAN...Ron Godines

It was codirected by Educardo Machado and Ilka Tanya Payán. Musical direction by Bob Zeigler. Choreography by Joanne Figueras.

ACT I

As lights go up DON JOSÉ *paces nervously back and forth. He smokes a big cigar, talking to himself.*

DON JOSÉ: Come on, woman. Hurry up. I have waited long enough for this child. Come on, a son. Give me a son…I will start training him right away. To ride horses. To shoot. To drink. As soon as he is old enough I'll take him to La Casa de Luisa. There they'll teach him what to do to women. Ha, ha, ha! If he's anything like his father, in twenty years everyone in this town will be related to each other! Ha, ha, ha! My name will never die. My son will see to that…

MIDWIFE: (MIDWIFE *enters running, excited.*) Don José! Don José!

DON JOSÉ: ¡Al fin! ¿Qué? Dígame, ¿todo está bien?

MIDWIFE: Yes, everything is fine, Don José. Your wife just gave birth to a healthy…

DON JOSÉ: …(*Interrupting excitedly*). Ha, ha, I knew it! A healthy son!

MIDWIFE: …It is a girl, Don José…

DON JOSÉ: (*Disappointment and disbelief creep onto his face. Then anger. He throws the cigar on the floor with force, then steps on it.*) A girl! ¡No puede ser! ¡Imposible! What do you mean a girl! ¡Cómo puede pasarme esto a mí? The first child that will bear my name and it is a…girl! ¡Una chancleta! ¡Carajo! (*He storms away, muttering under his breath.*)

MIDWIFE: (*Looks at* DON JOSÉ *as he exits, then addresses the audience. At some point during the following monologue the Girl will appear. She looks at everything as if seeing the world for the first time.*) He's off to drown his disappointment in rum because another woman is born into this world. The same woman another man's son will covet and pursue and try to rape at the first opportunity. The same woman whose virginity he will protect with a gun. Another woman is born into this world. In Managua, in San Juan, in an Andres' mountain town. She'll be put on a pedestal and trampled upon at the same time. She will be made a saint and a whore, crowned queen and exploited and adored. No, she's not just any woman. She will be called upon to…(*The* MIDWIFE *is interrupted by offstage voices.*)

BEAUTIFUL SEÑORITA 1: ¡Cuchi cuchi chi-a-boom!

BEAUTIFUL SEÑORITA 2: ¡Mira caramba oye!

BEAUTIFUL SEÑORITA 3: ¡Rumba pachanga mambo!

BEAUTIFUL SEÑORITA 4: Oye papito, ay ayayaiiii!

Immediately a rumba is heard. The four BEAUTIFUL SEÑORITAS *enter dancing. They dress as Carmen Miranda, Iris Chacón, Charo and María la O. They sing:*

"THE BEAUTIFUL SEÑORITAS' SONG"

WE BEAUTIFUL SEÑORITAS
WITH MARACAS IN OUR SOULS
MIRA PAPI AY CARIÑO
ALWAYS READY FOR AMOR

WE BEAUTIFUL SEÑORITAS
MUCHA SALSA AND SABOR
CUCHI CUCHI LATIN BOMBAS
ALWAYS READY FOR AMOR

AY CARAMBA MIRA OYE
DANCE THE TANGO ALL NIGHT LONG
GUACAMOLE LATIN LOVER
ALWAYS READY FOR AMOR

ONE PAYAYA ONE BANANA
AY SÍ SÍ SÍ SÍ SEÑOR
SIMPÁTICAS MUCHACHITAS
ALWAYS READY FOR AMOR

PIÑA PLÁTANOS CHIQUITAS
OF THE RAINBOW EL COLOR
CUCARACHAS MUY BONITAS
ALWAYS READY FOR AMOR

WE BEAUTIFUL SEÑORITAS
WITH MARACAS IN OUR SOULS
MIRA PAPI AY CARIÑO
ALWAYS READY FOR AMOR

AY SÍ SÍ SÍ SÍ SEÑOR
ALWAYS READY FOR AMOR
AY SÍ SÍ SÍ SÍ SEÑOR
ALWAYS READY FOR AMOR
AY SÍ SÍ SÍ SÍ SEÑOR

The SEÑORITAS *bow and exit.* MARÍA LA O *returns and takes more bows.*

MARÍA LA O *bows for the last time. Goes to her dressing room. Sits down and removes her shoes.*

MARÍA LA O: My feet are killing me. These juanetes get worse by the minute. (*She rubs her feet. She appears older and tired, all the glamour gone out of her. She takes her false eyelashes off, examines her face carefully in the mirror, begins to remove makeup.*) Two hundred lousy bucks a week for all that tit-shaking. But I need the extra money. What am I going to do? A job is a job. And with my artistic inclinations...well...But look at this joint! A dressing room. They have the nerve to call this a dressing room. I have to be careful not to step on a rat. They squeak too loud. The patrons out there may hear, you know. Anyway, I sort of liked dancing since I was a kid. But this! I meant dancing like Alicia Alonso, Margot Fonteyn...and I end up as a cheap Iris Chacón. At least she shook her behind in Radio City Music Hall. Ha! That's one up on the Rockettes!

BEAUTY QUEEN: (*She enters, wearing a beauty contest bathing suit.*) María la O, you still here? I thought everyone was gone. You always run after the show.

MARÍA LA O: No, not tonight. Somebody is taking care of the kid. I'm so tired that I don't feel like moving from here. Estoy muerta, m'ija. (*Looks* BEAUTY QUEEN *up and down.*) And where are *you* going?

BEAUTY QUEEN: To a beauty contest, of course.

MARÍA LA O: Don't you get tired of that, mujer!

BEAUTY QUEEN: Never. I was born to be a beauty queen. I have been a beauty queen ever since I was born. "La reinecita" they used to call me. My mother entered me in my first contest at the age of two. Then, it was one contest after the other. I have been in a bathing suit ever since. I save a lot in clothes...Anyway, my mother used to read all those womens' magazines—*Vanidades, Cosmopolitan, Claudia, Buenhogar*—where everyone is so beautiful and happy. She, of course, wanted me to be like them...(*Examines herself in the mirror.*) I have won hundreds of contests, you know. I have been Queen of Los Hijos Ausentes Club; Reina El Diario-La Prensa; Queen of Plátano Chips; Queen of the Hispanic Hairdressers Association; Reina de la Alcapurria; Miss Caribbean Sunshine; Señorita Turismo de Staten Island; Queen of the Texas Enchilada...and now, of course, I am Miss Banana Republic!

MARÍA LA O: Muchacha, I bet you don't have time for anything else!

BEAUTY QUEEN: Oh, I sure do. I wax my legs every day. I keep in shape. I practice my smile. Because one day, in one of those beauty contests, someone will come up to me and say...

MARÍA LA O: You're on Candid Camera?

BEAUTY QUEEN: ...Where have you been all my life! I'll be discovered, become a movie star, a millionaire, appear on the cover of *People Magazine*...and anyway, even if I don't win, I still make some money.

MARÍA LA O: Money? How much money?

BEAUTY QUEEN: Five hundred. A thousand. A trip here. A trip there. Depends on the contest.

MARÍA LA O: I could sure use some extra chavos...Hey, do you think I could win, be discovered by a movie producer or something...

BEAUTY QUEEN: Weeell...I don't know. They've just re-made "King Kong"...ha, ha!

MARÍA LA O: (MARÍA LA O *doesn't pay attention. She's busily thinking about the money.* BEAUTY QUEEN *turns to go.*) Even if I am only third, I still make some extra money. I can send Johnny home for summer. He's never seen his grandparents. Ya ni habla español. (MARÍA LA O *quickly tries to put eyelashes back on. Grabs her shoes and runs after* BEAUTY QUEEN.) Wait, wait for me! ¡Espérame! I'll go with you to the beauty contest! (*She exits. The* MIDWIFE *enters immediately. She calls after* MARÍA LA O.)

MIDWIFE: And don't forget to smile! Give them your brightest smile! As if your life depended on it!

The GIRL *enters and sits at* MARÍA LA O's *dressing table. During the following monologue, the* GIRL *will play with the makeup, slowly applying lipstick, mascara, and eye shadow in a very serious, concentrated manner.*

MIDWIFE: Yes. You have to smile to win. A girl with a serious face has no future. But what can you do when a butterfly is trapped in your insides and you cannot smile? How can you smile with a butterfly condemned to beat its ever-changing wings in the pit of your stomach? There it is. Now a flutter. Now a storm. Carried by the winds of emotion, this butterfly transforms the shape, the color, the texture of its wings; the speed and range of its flight. Now it becomes a stained-glass butterfly, light shining through its yellow-colored wings, which move ever so slowly, up and down, up and down, sometimes remaining still for a second too long. Then the world stops and takes a plunge, becoming a brief black hole in space. A burned-out star wandering through the galaxies is like a smile meant, but not delivered. And I am so full of undelivered smiles! So pregnant with undetected laughter! Sonrisas, sonrisas, who would exchange a butterfly for a permanent smile! Hear, hear, this butterfly will keep you alive and running, awake and on your toes, speeding along the herd of wild horses stampeding through the heart! This butterfly is magic. It changes its size. It becomes big and small. Who will take this wondrous butterfly and give me a simple, lasting smile! A smile for a day and night, winter and fall. A smile for all occaisions. A smile to survive... (*With the last line, the* MIDWIFE *turns to the* GIRL, *who by now has her face made up like a clown. They look at each other. The* GIRL *faces the audience. She is not smiling. They freeze. Black out.)*

In the dark we hear a fanfare. Lights go up on the MC. He wears a velvet tuxedo with a pink ruffled skirt. He combs his hair, twirls his moustache, adjusts his bow tie and smiles. He wields a microphone with a flourish.

MC: Ladies and gentlemen. Señoras y señores. Tonight. Esta noche. Right here. Aquí mismo. You will have the opportunity to see the most exquisite, sexy, exotic, sandungueras, jacarandosas and most beautiful señoritas of all. You will be the judge of the contest, where beauty will compete with belleza; where women of the tropical Caribbean will battle the señoritas of South America. Ladies and gentlemen, the poets have said it. The composers of boleros have said it. Latin women are the most beautiful, the most passionate, the most virtuous, the best housewives and cooks. And they all know how to dance to salsa, and to the hustle, the mambo, the guaguancó...And they are always ready for amor, señores! What treasures! See for yourselves!...Ladies and gentlemen, señoras y señores...from the sandy beaches of Florida, esbelta as a palm tree, please welcome Miss Little Havana! (*Music from "Cuando salí de Cuba" is heard. Miss Little Havana enters. She wears a bathing suit, sun glasses and a string of pearls. She sings.*)

CUANDO SALÍ DE CUBA
DEJÉ MI CASA, DEJÉ MI AVIÓN
CUANDO SALÍ DE CUBA
DEJÉ ENTERRADO MEDIO MILLÓN

MC: Oye, chica, what's your name?

MISS LITTLE HAVANA: Fina de la Garza del Vedado y Miramar. From the best families of the Cuba de Ayer.

MC: (*To the audience.*) As you can see, ladies and gentlemen, Fina es muy fina. Really fine, he, he, he. Tell the judges, Fina, what are your best assets?

MISS LITTLE HAVANA: Well, back in Cuba of Yesterday, I had a house with ten rooms and fifty maids, two cars, un avión and a sugar mill. But Fidel took everything away. So, here in the U.S. of A. my only assets are 36-28-42.

MC: Hmmm! That's what I call a positive attitude. Miss Fina, some day you'll get it all back. Un aplauso for Fina, ladies and gentlemen! (MISS LITTLE HAVANA *steps back and freezes into a doll-like posture, with a fixed smile on her face.*)

MC: Now, from South of the Border, ladies and gentlemen—hold on to your tacos, because here she is...Miss Chili Tamale! (*Music begins: "Allá en el Rancho Grande."*) Please, un aplauso! Welcome, welcome chaparrita! (MISS CHILI TAMALE *enters. She also wears a bathing suit and a sarape over her shoulder. She sings.*)

ALLÁ EN EL RANCHO GRANDE
ALLA DONDE VIVÍA
YO ERA UNA FLACA MORENITA
QUE TRISTE SE QUEJABA
QUE TRISTE SE QUEJAABAAA
NO TENGO NI UN PAR DE CALZONES
NI SIN REMIENDOS DE CUERO
NI DOS HUEVOS RANCHEROS
Y LAS TORTILLAS QUEMADAS

MC: Your name, beautiful señorita?

MISS CHILI TAMALE: Lupe Lupita Guadalupe Viva Zapata y Enchilada, para servirle.

MC: What good manners! Tell us, what's your most fervent desire?

MISS CHILI TAMALE: My most fervent desire is to marry a big, handsome, very rich americano.

MC: Aha! What have we here! You mean you prefer gringos instead of Latin men?

MISS CHILI TAMALE: Oh no, no, no. But, you see, I need my green card. La migra is after me.

MC: (*Nervously, the* MC *looks around, then pushes* MISS TAMALE *back. She joins* MISS LITTLE HAVANA *in her doll-like pose.*) Ahem, ahem. Now ladies and gentlemen, the dream girl of every American male, the most beautiful señorita of all. Created by Madison Avenue exclusively for the United Fruit Company...ladies and gentlemen, please welcome Miss Conchita Banana! ("*Chiquita Banana music begins.* MISS CONCHITA BANANA *enters. She wears plastic bananas on her head and holds two real ones in her hands. She sings.*)

I'M CONCHITA BANANA
AND I'M HERE TO SAY
THAT BANANAS TASTE THE BEST
IN A CERTAIN WAY
YOU CAN PUT'EM IN YOUR HUM HUM
YOU CAN SLICE'EM IN YOUR HA HA
ANYWAY YOU WANT TO EAT'EM
IT'S IMPOSSIBLE TO BEAT'EM
BUT NEVER, NEVER, NEVER
PUT BANANAS IN THE REFRIGERATOR
NO, NO, NO, NO!

(*She throws the two real bananas to the audience.*)

MC: Brava, bravissima, Miss Banana! Do you realize you have made our humble fruit, el plátano, very very famous all over the world?

MISS CONCHITA BANANA: Yes, I know. That has been the goal of my whole life.

MC: And we are proud of you, Conchita. But, come here, just between the two of us…tell me the truth, do you really like bananas?

MISS CONCHITA BANANA: Of course I do! I eat them all the time. My motto is: a banana a day keeps the doctor away!

MC: (*Motioning to audience to applaud.*) What intelligence! What insight! Un aplauso, ladies and gentlemen…(MISS CONCHITA BANANA *bows and steps back, joining the other doll-like contestants. As each woman says the following lines, she becomes human again. The MC moves to one side and freezes.*)

WOMAN 1: (*Previously* MISS LITTLE HAVANA.) No one knows me. They see me passing by, but they don't know me. They don't see me. They hear my accent but not my words. If anyone wants to find me, I'll be sitting by the beach.

WOMAN 2: (*Previously* MISS CHILI TAMALE.) My mother, my grandmother, and her mother before her walked the land with barefeet, as I have done, too. We have given birth to our daughters on the bare soil. We have seen them grow and go to market. Now we need permits to walk the land—our land.

WOMAN 3: (*Previously* MISS CONCHITA BANANA.) I have been invented for a photograph. Sometimes I wish to be a person, to exist for my own sake, to stop dancing, to stop smiling. One day I think I will want to cry.

MC: (*We hear a fanfare. The* MC *unfreezes. The contestants become dolls again.*) Ladies and gentlemen…don't go away, because we still have more for you! Now, señoras y señores, from la Isla del Encanto, please welcome Miss Commonwealth! Un aplauso, please! (*We hear music from "Cortaron a Elena."* MISS COMMONWEALTH *enters, giggling and waving. She sings.*)

CORTARON EL BUDGET
CORTARON EL BUDGET
CORTARON EL BUDGET
Y NOS QUEDAMOS
SIN FOOD STAMPS
CORTARON A ELENA
CORTARON A JUANA
CORTARON A LOLA
Y NOS QUEDAMOS
SIN NA' PA' NA'

MC: ¡Qué sabor! Tell us your name, beautiful jibarita...

MISS COMMONWEALTH: Lucy Wisteria Rivera (*Giggles.*)

MC: Let me ask you, what do you think of the political status of the island?

MISS COMMONWEALTH: (*Giggles.*) Oh, I don't know about that. La belleza y la política no se mezclan. Beauty and politics do not mix. (*Giggles.*)

MC: True, true, preciosa-por-ser-un-encanto-por-ser-un-edén. Tell me, what is your goal in life?

MISS COMMONWEALTH: I want to find a boyfriend and get married. I will be a great housewife, cook and mother. I will only live for my husband and my children. (*Giggles.*)

MC: Ave María, nena! You are a tesoro! Well, Miss Commonwealth, finding a boyfriend should not be difficult for you. You have everything a man wants right there up front. (*Points to her breasts with the microphone.*) I am sure you already have several novios, no?

MISS COMMONWEALTH: Oh no, I don't have a boyfriend yet. My father doesn't let me. And besides, it isn't as easy as you think. To catch a man you must know the rules of the game, the technique, the tricks, the know-how, the how-to, the expertise, the go-get-it, the...works! Let me show you. (*The* MC *stands to one side and freezes. The doll-like contestants in the back exit.* MISS COMMONWEALTH *begins to exit. She runs into the* GIRL *as she enters.* MISS COMMONWEALTH'*s crown falls to the floor. She looks at the girl who seems to remind her of something far away.*)

WOMAN 4: (*Previously* MISS COMMONWEALTH.) The girl who had never seen the ocean decided one day to see it. Just one startled footprint on the sand and the sea came roaring at her. A thousand waves, an infinite horizon, a storm of salt and two diving birds thrusted themselves furiously into her eyes. Today she walks blindly through the smog and the dust of cities and villages. But she travels with a smile, because she carries the ocean in her eyes. (WOMAN 4 *exits. Spot on the* GIRL. *She picks up the crown from the floor and places it on her head. Spot closes in on the crown.*)

As lights go up, the MAN *enters with a chair and places it center stage. He sits on it. The* GIRL *sits on the floor with her back to the audience. The* CATCH WOMEN *enter and take their places around the man. Each* WOMAN *addresses the* GIRL, *as a teacher would.)*

CATCH WOMAN 1: There are many ways to catch a man. Watch... (*Walks over to the* MAN.) Hypnotize him. Be a good listener. (*She sits on his knees.*) Laugh at his jokes, even if you heard them before.

(*To* MAN.) Honey, tell them the one about the two bartenders...(*The* MAN *mouths words as if telling a joke. She listens and laughs loudly. Gets up.*) Cuá, cuá, cuá! Isn't he a riot! (*She begins to walk away, turns and addresses the* GIRL.) Ah, and don't forget to move your hips.

CATCH WOMAN 2: (CATCH WOMAN 1 *walks moving her hips back to her place.* CATCH WOMAN 2 *steps forward and addresses the* GIRL.) Women can't be too intellectual. He will get bored. (*To* MAN, *in earnest.*) Honey, don't you think nuclear disarmament is our only hope for survival? (*The* MAN *yawns. To* GIRL.) See? When a man goes out with a woman he wants to relax, to have fun, to feel good. He doesn't want to talk about heavy stuff, know what I mean? (CATCH WOMAN 2 *walks back to her place. She flirts with her boa, wrapping it around the man's head. Teasing.*) Toro, toro, torito!

CATCH WOMAN 3: (*The* MAN *charges after* CATCH WOMAN 2. CATCH WOMAN 3 *stops him with a hypnotic look. He sits down again.* CATCH WOMAN 3 *addresses the* GIRL.) Looks are a very powerful weapon. Use your eyes, honey. Look at him now and then. Directly. Sideways. Through your eyelashes. From the corner of your eyes. Over your sunglasses. Look at him up and down. But not with too much insistence. And never ever look directly at his crotch. (*She walks away, dropping her handkerchief. The* MAN *stops to pick it up.* CATCH WOMAN 4 *places her foot on it. Pushes the* MAN *away.*) Make him suffer. Make him jealous. (*Waves to someone offstage, flirting.*) Hi, Johnny! (*To* GIRL.) They like it. It gives them a good excuse to get drunk. Tease him. Find out what he likes. (*To* MAN.) Un masajito, papi? I'll make you a burrito de machaca con huevo, sí? (*She massages his neck.*) Keep him in suspense. (*To* MAN.) I love you. I don't love you. To quiero. No te quiero. I love you. I don't love you...(*She walks away.*)

ALL: (*All four* CATCH WOMEN *come forward.*) We do it all for him!

MAN: They do it all for me! (MAN *raps the song, while the* CATCH WOMEN *parade around him.*)

"THEY DO IT ALL FOR ME."

(*Wolf whistles.*)

MIRA MAMI, PSST, COSA LINDA!
OYE MUÑECA, DAME UN POQUITO
AY, MIREN ESO
LO QUE DIOS HA HECHO
PARA NOSOTROS LOS PECADORES
AY MAMÁ, DON'T WALK LIKE THAT
DON'T MOVE LIKE THAT

DON'T LOOK LIKE THAT
'CAUSE YOU GONNA GIVE ME
A HEART ATTACK
THEY DO IT ALL FOR ME
WHAT THEY LEARN IN A MAGAZINE
THEY DO IT ALL FOR ME
'CAUSE YOU KNOW WHAT THEY WANT
AY MAMÁ, TAN PRECIOSA TAN HERMOSA
GIVE ME A PIECE OF THAT
'CAUSE I KNOW YOU DO IT ALL FOR ME
DON'T YOU DON'T YOU
DON'T YOU DO IT ALL FOR ME

(CATCH WOMAN 2 *throws her boa around his neck, ropes in the* MAN *and exits with him in tow.*)

CATCH WOMAN 1: ¡Mira, esa mosquita muerta ya agarró uno!
CATCH WOMAN 3: Look at that, she caught him!
CATCH WOMAN 4: Pero, ¡qué tiene ella que no tengo yo! (*All exit. The* GIRL *stands up, picks up the handkerchief from the floor. Mimes imitations of some of the* WOMEN'*s moves, flirting, listening to jokes, giggling, moving her hips, etc. Church music comes on.*

The NUN *enters carrying a bouquet or roses cradled in her arms. She stands in the back and looks up bathed in a sacred light. Her lips move as if praying. She lowers her eyes and sees the* GIRL *imitating more sexy moves. The* NUN'*s eyes widen in disbelief.*

NUN: What are you doing, creature? That is sinful! A woman must be recatada, saintly. Thoughts of the flesh must be banished from your head and your heart. Close your eyes and your pores to desire. The only love there is is the love of the Lord. The Lord is the only lover! (*The* GIRL *stops, thoroughly confused. The* NUN *strikes her with the bouquet or roses.*) ¡Arrodíllate! Kneel down on these roses! Let your blood erase your sinful thoughts! You may still be saved. Pray, pray! (*The* GIRL *kneels on the roses, grimacing with pain. The* PRIEST *enters, makes the sign of the cross on the scene. The* NUN *kneels in front of the* PRIEST.) Father, forgive me, for I have sinned...

The SEÑORITAS *enter with her lines. They wear mantillas and peinetas, holding Spanish fans in their hands, a red carnation between their teeth.*

SEÑORITA 1: Me too, father!
SEÑORITA 2: ¡Y yo también!
SEÑORITA 3: And me!

SEÑORITA 4: Me too! (*A tango begins. The following lines are integrated into the choreography.*)

SEÑORITA 1: Father, it has been two weeks since my last confession…

PRIEST: Speak, hija mía.

SEÑORITA 2: Padre, my boyfriend used to kiss me on the lips…but it's all over now.

PRIEST: Lord, oh Lord!

SEÑORITA 3: Forgive me father, but I have masturbated three times. Twice mentally, once physically.

PRIEST: Ave María Purísima, sin pecado concebida…

SEÑORITA 4: I have sinned, santo padre. Last night I had wet dreams.

PRIEST: Socorro espiritual, Dios mío. Help these lost souls!

SEÑORITA 1: He said, fellatio…I said, cunnilingus!

PRIEST: No, not in a beautiful señorita's mouth! Such evil words, Señor, oh Lord!

SEÑORITA 2: Father, listen. I have sinned. I have really really sinned. I did it, I did it! All the way I did it! (*All the* SEÑORITAS *and the* NUN *turn to* SEÑORITA 2 *and make the sign of the cross. They point at her with the fans.*)

SEÑORITAS 1, 3, 4: She's done it, Dios mío, she's done it! Santísima Virgen, she's done it!

PRIEST: She's done it! She's done it!

SEÑORITA 2: (*Tangoing backwards.*) I did it. Yes. Lo hice. I did it, father. Forgive me, for I have fornicated!

PRIEST: She's done it! She's done it! (*The* NUN *faints in the* PRIEST'*s arms.*)

SEÑORITAS 1, 3, 4: Fornication! Copulation! Indigestion! ¡Qué pecado y que horror! ¡Culpable! ¡Culpable! ¡Culpable! (*They exit tangoing. The* PRIEST, *with the fainted* NUN *in his arms, looks at the audience bewildered.*)

PRIEST: (*To audience.*) Intermission!

Black out

ACT II

In the dark we hear a fanfare. Spotlight on MC.

MC: Welcome back, ladies and gentlemen, señoras y señores. There's more, much much more yet to come. For, you see, our contestants are not only beautiful, but also very talented señoritas. For the benefit of the judges they will sing, they will dance, they will perform the most daring acts on the flying trapeze!

Spotlight on WOMAN 3 *swinging on a swing center stage. She sings:*

"BOLERO TRAICIONERO"

TAKE ME IN YOUR ARMS
LET'S DANCE AWAY THE NIGHT
WHISPER IN MY EARS
THE SWEETEST WORDS OF LOVE

I'M THE WOMAN IN YOUR LIFE
SAY YOU DIE EVERY TIME
YOU ARE AWAY FROM ME
AND WHISPER IN MY EAR
THE SWEETEST WORDS OF LOVE

PROMISE ME THE SKY
GET ME THE MOON, THE STARS
IF IT IS A LIE
WHISPER IN MY EAR
THE SWEETEST WORDS OF LOVE

DARLING IN A DREAM OF FLOWERS
WE ARE PLAYING ALL THE GREATEST GAMES
LIE TO ME WITH ROMANCE AGAIN
TRAICIÓNAME ASÍ, TRAICIÓNAME MÁS

(*Bis*)

PROMISE ME THE SKY…

During the song, lights go up to reveal the other women sitting in various poses waiting to be asked to dance. The GIRL *is also there, closely watched by the* CHAPERONE, *who also keeps an eye on all the other women. The* MAN *enters wearing a white tuxedo and a Zorro mask. He dances with each one. Gives each a flower, which he pulls out of his pocket like a magician. The* GIRL *wants to dance, the* MAN *comes and asks her, but the* CHAPERONE *doesn't let her. The* MAN *asks another woman to dance. They dance very close. The* CHAPERONE *comes and taps the woman on the shoulder. They stop dancing. The* MAN *goes to the woman singing, pushes the swing back and forth. At the end of the song, the singer leaves with the* MAN. *The other women follow them with their eyes.*

SEÑORITA 2: I swear I only did it for love! He sang in my ear the sweetest words, the most romantic boleros. Saturdays and Sundays he sat at the bar across the street drinking beer. He kept playing the same record on the juke box over and over. It was a pasodoble about being as lonely as a stray dog. He would send me flowers and candies with the shoeshine boy. My father and brother had sworn to kill him if they ever saw him near me. But he insisted. He kept saying how much he loved me and he kept getting drunk right at my doorsteps. He serenaded me every weekend. He said I was the most decent woman in the world. Only his mother was more saintly…he said.

SEÑORITA 3: He said the same thing to me. Then he said the same thing to my sister and then to her best friend. My sister was heartbroken. She was so young. She had given him her virginity and he would not marry her. Then three days before Christmas she set herself on fire. She poured gasoline on her dress, put a match to it and then started to run. She ran like a vision of hell through the streets of the town. Her screams awoke all the dead lovers for miles around. Her long hair, her flowing dress were like a banner of fire calling followers to battle. She ran down Main Street—the street that leads directly to the sea. I ran after her trying to catch her to embrace her, to smother the flames with my own body. I ran after her, yelling not to go into the water. She couldn't, she wouldn't hear. She ran into the sea like thunder…Such drama, such fiery spectacle, such pain…It all ended with a half-silent hiss and a thin column of smoke rising up from the water, near the beach where we played as children…(*We hear the sound of drums. The women join in making mournful sounds.*)

The mournful sounds slowly turn into the "Wedding Song."

"THE WEDDING SONG"
("Where Have All the Women Gone")

WOMAN:
THERE, THERE'S JUANA
SEE JUANA JUMP
SEE HOW SHE JUMPS
WHEN HE DOES CALL
THERE, THERE'S ROSA
SEE ROSA CRY
SHE HOW SHE CRIES
WHEN HE DOESN'T CALL

CHORUS:
WHERE HAVE ALL
THE WOMEN GONE

WOMAN:
JUANA ROSA CARMEN GO
NOT WITH A BANG
BUT WITH A WHIMPER
WHERE HAVE THEY GONE
LEAVING THEIR DREAMS
BEHIND
LEAVING THEIR DREAMS
LETTING THEIR LIVES
UNDONE

CHORUS:
(Wedding March Music)
LOOK HOW THEY GO
LOOK AT THEM GO
SIGHING AND CRYING
LOOK AT THEM GO

Towards the end of the song the women will form a line before the CHAPERONE *who is holding a big basket. From it she takes and gives each woman a wig with hair rollers on it. Assisted by the* GIRL, *each woman will put her wig on. Once the song ends, each woman will start miming various housecleaning chores: sweeping, ironing, washing, etc. The* MOTHER *sews. The* GIRL *watches.*

MARTYR 1: Cry my child. Las mujeres nacimos para sufrir. There's no other way but to cry. One is born awake and crying. That's the way God meant it. And who are we to question the ways of the Lord?

MARTYR 2: I don't live for myself. I live for my husband and my children. A woman's work is never done: what to make for lunch, cook the beans, start the rice, and then again, what to make for supper, and the fact that Juanito needs new shoes for school. (*She holds her side in pain.*)

MARTYR 3: What's wrong with you?

MARTYR 2: I have female problems.

MARTYR 3: The menstruation again?

MARTYR 2: No, my husband beat me up again last night. (*The* GIRL *covers her ears, then covers her eyes and begins to play "Put the Tail on the Donkey" all by herself.*)

MARTYR 3: I know what you mean, m'ija. We women were born to suffer. I sacrifice myself for my children. But, do they appreciate it?

No. Someday, someday when I'm gone they'll remember me and all I did for them. But then it will be too late. Too late.

MOTHER: Such metaphysics. Women should not worry about philosophical matters. That's for men. (*She returns to her sewing, humming a song of oblivion.*)

MARTYR 3: The Virgin Mary never worried about forced sterilization or torture in Argentina or minimum wages. True, she had housing problems, but I'm sure there was never a quarrel as to who washed the dishes or fed that burro.

MAMA: Such heretic thoughts will not lead to anything good, I tell you. It is better not to have many thoughts. When you do the ironing or the cooking or set your hair in rollers, it is better not to think too much. I know what I'm saying. I know…(*Continues her sewing and humming.*)

MARTYR 1: And this headache. We're born with migraine. And with the nerves on edge. It is so, I know. I remember my mother and her mother before her. They always had jaquecas. I inherited the pain and tazas de tilo, the Valiums and the Libriums…

MAMA: You don't keep busy enough. While your hands are busy…

MARTYR 2: …And your mouth is busy, while your run from bed to stove to shop to work to sink to bed to mirror no one notices the little light shining in your eyes. It is better that way…because I…I don't live for myself. I live for my husband and my children, and it is better that they don't notice that flash in my eyes, that sparkle of a threat, that flickering death wish…(*The* GIRL *tears off the cloth covering her eyes. Looks at the women expecting some action. Mumbling and complaining under their breath, the women go back to their chores. The* GUERRILLERA *enters. She is self-assured and full of energy. The* GIRL *gives her all her attention.*)

GUERRILLERA: Stop your laments, sisters!

MARTYR 1: Who's she?

GUERRILLERA: Complaining and whining won't help!

MARTYR 3: That's true!

GUERRILLERA: We can change the world and then our lot will improve!

MARTYR 3: It's about time!

GUERRILLERA: Let's fight oppression!

MARTYR 3: I'm ready! Let's go!

MARTYR 2: I ain't going nowhere. I think she's a lesbian.

GUERRILLERA: We, as third world women…

MARTYR 1: Third world?…I'm from Michoacán…

GUERRILLERA: …Are triply oppressed, so we have to fight three times as hard!

MARTYR 3: That's right!
GUERRILLERA: Come to the meetings!
MARTYR 3: Where? Where? When?
GUERRILLERA: ...Have your consciousness raised!
MARTYR 2: What's consciousness?
MARTYR 1: I don't know, but I'm keeping my legs crossed...(*Holds her skirt down on her knees.*)
GUERRILLERA: Come with me and help make the revolution!
MARTYR 3: Let's go, kill'em, kill'em!
GUERRILLERA: Good things will come to pass. Come with me and rebel!
MARTYR 3: Let's go! (*To the others.*) Come on!
MARTYR 2: All right, let's go!
MARTYR 1: Bueno...
ALL: Let's go, vamos! ¡Sí! ¡Arriba! ¡Vamos! Come on, come on!

MARTYR 3 *picks up a broom and rests it on her shoulder like a rifle. The others follow suit. All sing.*

SI ADELITA SE FUERA CON OTRO
LA SEGUIRÍA POR TIERRA Y POR MAR
SI POR MAR EN UN BUQUE DE GUERRA
SI POR TIERRA EN UN TREN MILITAR

GUERRILLERA: But first...hold it, hold it...but first...we must peel the potatoes, cook the rice, make the menudo and sweep the hall...(*The* WOMEN *groan and lose enthusiasm.*)...because there's gonna be a fund-raiser tonight!

Music begins. The GUERRILLERA *and* WOMEN *sing.*

GUERRILLERA:
THERE'S GONNA BE A FUND-RAISER
THE BROTHERS WILL SPEAK OF CHANGE

CHORUS:
WE GONNA HAVE BANANA SURPRISE
WE GONNA CUT YAUTÍAS IN SLICE
THERE'S GONNA BE A FUND-RAISER
BUT THEY'LL ASK US TO PEEL AND FRY

GUERRILLERA:
WE SAY OKAY
WE WILL FIGHT NOT CLEAN
BUT THEY SAY GO DEAR
AND TYPE THE SPEECH

ANITA IS GONNA MAKE IT
SHE'S GONNA MAKE IT

CHORUS:
MARÍA WILL SWEEP THE FLOOR
JUANITA IS FAT AND PREGNANT
PREGNANT FOR WHAT
NO MATTER IF WE'RE TIRED
AS LONG LONG LONG LONG
AS LONG AS THEY'RE NOT

TONIGHT TONIGHT
TONIGHT TONIGHT
TONIGHT TONIGHT
TONIGHT TONIGHT

GUERRILLERA:

WON'T BE JUST ANY NIGHT

CHORUS:
TONIGHT TONIGHT
TONIGHT TONIGHT
TONIGHT TONIGHT
TONIGHT TONIGHT

GUERRILLERA:
WE'LL BE NO MORE HARASSED

CHORUS:
TONIGHT TONIGHT
TONIGHT TONIGHT
TONIGHT TONIGHT
TONIGHT TONIGHT

GUERRILLERA:
I'LL HAVE SOMETHING TO SAY

CHORUS:
TONIGHT TONIGHT

GUERRILLERA:
FOR US A NEW DAY WILL START

CHORUS:
TODAY THE WOMEN
WANT THE HOURS

GUERRILLERA:
HOURS TO BE LOVING

CHORUS:
TODAY THE WOMEN
WANT THE HOURS

GUERRILLERA:
AND STILL THE TIME TO FIGHT
TO MAKE THIS ENDLESS
BORING BORING BORING
BORING BORING BORING
FLIGHT!

CHORUS:
BORING BORING
BORING BORING
BORING BORING
BORING BORING
FLIGHT!

All end the song with mops and brooms upraised. A voices is heard offstage.

MAN: (*Offstage.*) Is dinner ready! (*The* WOMEN *drop their "weapons" and run away.*)

WOMAN 1: ¡Ay, se me quema el arroz!

WOMAN 2: ¡Bendito, las habichuelas!

WOMAN 3: ¡Ay, Virgen de Guadalupe, las enchiladas! (*They exit.*)

GUERRILLERA: (*Exiting after them.*) Wait! Wait! What about the revolution!…(*Black out.*)

As the lights go up, the MAN *enters dressed as a campesino, with poncho and sombrero. The* SOCIAL RESEARCHER *enters right behind. She holds a notebook and a pencil.*

RESEARCHER: (*With an accent.*) Excuse me señor…buenas tardes. Me llamo Miss Smith. I'm from the Peaceful Corps. Could you be so kind to answer some questions for me—for our research study?

MAN: Bueno.

RESEARCHER: Have you many children?

MAN: God has not been good to me. Of sixteen children born, only nine live.

RESEARCHER: Does your wife work?

MAN: No. She stays at home.

RESEARCHER: I see. How does she spend the day?

MAN: (*Scratching his head.*) Well, she gets up at four in the morning, fetches water and wood, makes the fire and cooks breakfast. Then she goes to the river and washes the clothes. After that she goes to town to get the corn ground and buy what we need in the market. Then she cooks the midday meal.

RESEARCHER: You come home at midday?

MAN: No, no, she brings the meal to me in the field—about three kilometers from home.

RESEARCHER: And after that?

MAN: Well, she takes care of the hens and the pigs…and of course, she looks after the children all day…then she prepares supper so it is ready when I come home.

RESEARCHER: Does she go to bed after supper?

MAN: No, I do. She has things to do around the house until about ten o'clock.

RESEARCHER: But, señor, you said your wife doesn't work…

MAN: Of course, she doesn't work. I told you, she stays home!

RESEARCHER: (*Closing notebook.*) Thank you, señor. You have been very helpful. Adiós. (*She exits. The* MAN *follows her.*)

MAN: Hey, psst, señorita…my wife goes to bed at ten o'clock. I can answer more questions for you later…(*Black out.*)

In the dark we hear the beginning of "Dolphins by the Beach." The DAUGHTER 1 *and the* GIRL *enter. They dance to the music. This dance portrays the fantasies of a young woman. It is a dance of freedom and self-realization. A fanfare is heard, breaking the spell. They run away. The* MC *enters.*

MC: Ladies and gentlemen, señoras y señores…the show goes on and on and on and ON! The beauty, the talent, the endurance of these contestants is, you have to agree, OVERWHELMING. They have gone beyond the call of duty in pursuit of their goal. They have performed unselfishly. They have given their all. And will give even more, for, ladies and gentlemen, señoras y señores, the contest is not over yet. As the excitement mounts—I can feel it in the air!—the question burning in everyone's mind is: who will be the winner? (*As soap opera narrator.*) Who will wear that crown on that pretty little head? What will she do? Will she laugh? Will she cry? Will she faint in my arms?…Stay tuned for the last chapter of Reina for Day! (MC *exits. All the women enter.*)

DAUGHTER 1: Mamá, may I go out and play? It is such a beautiful day and the tree is full of mangoes. May I get some? Let me go out to the top of the hill. Please. I just want to sit there and look ahead, far away. If I squint my eyes real hard, I think I can see the ocean. Mami, please, may I, may I go out?

MOTHER: Niña, what nonsense. Your head is always in the clouds. I can't give you permission to go out. Wait until your father comes home and ask him. (*Father enters.*)

DAUGHTER 1: Papá, please, may I go out and play? It is such a beautiful day and…

FATHER: No. Stay home with your mother. Girls belong at home. You are becoming too much of a tomboy. Why don't you learn to cook, to sew, to mend my sock…

WIFE: Husband, I would like to buy some flowers for the windows, and that vase I saw yesterday at the shop…

HUSBAND: Flowers, flowers, vases. What luxury! Instead of such fuss about the house, why don't you do something about having a child? I want a son. We've been married two years now and I am tired of waiting. What's the matter with you? People are already talking. It's me they suspect…

MOTHER: Son, I have placed all my hopes on you. I hope you will be better than your father and take care of me…

SON: I'm going off to the war. I have been called to play the game of death. I must leave you now. I must go and kill…

WIDOW: He gave his life for the country in a far-away land, killing people he didn't know, people who didn't speak his language. I'm with child. His child. I hope it's a son…he wanted a son so much…

DAUGHTER 2: Mother, I'm pregnant. He doesn't want to get married. I don't want to get married. I don't even know whether I want this child…

MOTHER: Hija…how can you do this to me?! How is it possible. That's not what I taught you! I…your father…your brother…the neighbors…what would people say?

BROTHER: I'll kill him. I know who did it. I'll wring his neck. He'll pay for this! Abusador sin escrúpulos…Dishonoring decent girls…And I thought he was my friend. He'll pay dearly for my sister's virginity. ¡Lo pagará con sangre!

DAUGHTER 1: But I read it in *Cosmopolitan*. It said everyone is doing it! And the TV commercials…and…

MOTHER: Hijo, what's the matter? You look worried…

SON: Mother, my girlfriend is having a baby. My baby. I want to bring her here. You know, I don't have a job, and well, her parents kicked her out of the house…

MOTHER: Just like his father! So young and already spilling his seed around like a generous spring shower. Bring her. Bring your woman to me. I hope she has wide hips and gives you many healthy sons. (MOTHER *and* SON *exit.*)

The WOMEN *make moaning sounds, moving around, grouping and regrouping. Loud Latin music bursts on. The* WOMEN *dance frenetically, then suddenly the music stops.*

WOMAN 1: Sometimes, while I dance, I hear—behind the rhythmically shuffling feet—the roar of the water cascading down the mountain, thrown against the cliffs by an enraged ocean.

WOMAN 2: …I hear the sound of water in a shower, splattering against the tiles where a woman lies dead. I hear noises beyond the water, and sometimes they frighten me.

WOMAN 3: Behind the beat of the drums I hear the thud of a young woman's body thrown from a roof. I hear the screeching of wheels from a speeding car and the stifled cries of a young girl lying on the street.

WOMAN 4: Muffled by the brass section, I sometimes hear in the distance desperate cries of help from elevators, parking lots and apartment buildings. I hear the echoes in a forest: "please... no...don't..." of a child whimpering.

WOMAN 1: I think I hear my sister cry while we dance.

WOMAN 2: I hear screams. I hear the terrorized sounds of a young girl running naked along the highway.

WOMAN 3: The string section seems to murmur names...

WOMAN 4: To remind me that the woman, the girl who at this very moment is being beaten...

WOMAN 1: raped...

WOMAN 2: murdered...

WOMAN 3: is my sister...

WOMAN 4: my daughter...

WOMAN 1: my mother...

ALL: myself...

The WOMEN *remain on stage, backs turned to the audience. We hear a fanfare. The* MC *enters.*

MC: Ladies and gentlemen, the choice has been made, the votes have been counted, the results are in...and the winner is...señoras y señores: the queen of queens, Miss Señorita Mañana! There she is...(*Music from Miss America's "There She is...." The* GIRL *enters followed by Mamá. The* GIRL *is wearing all the items she has picked from previous scenes: the tinsel crown, the flowers, a mantilla, etc. Her face is still made up as a clown. The* WOMEN *turn around to look. The* GIRL *looks upset, restless with all the manipulation she has endured. The* WOMEN *are distressed by what they see. They surround the* GIRL.)

WOMAN 1: This is not what I meant at all...

WOMAN 2: I meant...

WOMAN 3: I don't know what I meant.

WOMAN 4: I think we goofed. She's a mess. (*They look at Mamá reproachfully. Mamá looks apologetic.*)

MAMÁ: I only wanted...

WOMAN 1: (*Pointing to the* MC.) It's all his fault!

MC: Me? I only wanted to make her a queen! Can we go on with the contest? This is a waste of time...

WOMAN 2: You and your fff...contest!

WOMAN 3: Cálmate, chica. Wait.

WOMAN 4: (*To* MC.) Look, we have to discuss this by ourselves. Give us a break, okay?

MC: (*Mumbling as he exits.*) What do they want? What's the matter with them?...

WOMAN 1: (*To* GIRL.) Ven acá, m'ija. (*The* WOMEN *take off, one by one, all the various items, clean her face, etc.*)

WOMAN 2: Honey, this is not what it is about…
WOMAN 3: I'm not sure yet what it's all about…
WOMAN 4: It is about what really makes you a woman.
WOMAN 1: It is not the clothes.
WOMAN 2: Or the hair.
WOMAN 3: Or the lipstick.
WOMAN 4: Or the cooking.
WOMAN 3: But…what is it about?
WOMAN 4: Well…I was thirteen when the blood first arrived. My mother locked herself in the bathroom with me and recited the facts of life, and right then and there, very solemnly, she declared me a woman.
WOMAN 1: I was eighteen when, amid pain and pleasure, my virginity floated away in a sea of blood. He held me tight and said, "now I have made you a woman."
WOMAN 2: Then, from my insides a child burst forth…crying, bathed in blood and other personal substances. And then someone whispered in my ear: "Now you are a real, real woman."
WOMAN 3: In their songs they have given me the body of a mermaid, of a palm tree, of an ample-hipped guitar. In the movies I see myself as a whore, a nymphomaniac, a dumb servant or a third-rate dancer. I look for myself and I can't find me. I only find someone else's idea of me.
MAMÁ: But think…what a dangerous, deadly adventure being a woman is! The harassment of being a woman…So many parts to be played, so many parts to be stifled and denied. But look at so many wild, free young things crying, like the fox in the story: "tame me, tame me and I'll be yours!"
WOMAN 1: But I'm tired of stories!
WOMAN 2: Yes, enough of "be this," "do it!"
WOMAN 3: "Look like that!" Mira, mira!
WOMAN 4: "Buy this product!"
WOMAN 1: "Lose ten pounds!"
MAMÁ: Wait, wait some more, and maybe, just maybe…
WOMAN 1: Tell my daughter that I love her…
WOMAN 2: Tell my daughter I wish I had really taught her the facts of life…
WOMAN 3: Tell my daughter that still there are mysteries…
WOMAN 4: …that the life I gave her doesn't have to be like mine.
THE GIRL: …that there are possibilities. That women who go crazy in the night, that women who die alone and frustrated, that women who exist only in the mind, are only half of the story, because a woman is…

WOMAN 1: A fountain of fire!
WOMAN 2: A river of love!
WOMAN 3: An ocean of strength!
WOMAN 4: Mirror, mirror on the wall…

They look at each other as images on a mirror, discovering themselves in each other. The GIRL *is now one of them. She steps out and sings:*

"DON'T DENY US THE MUSIC"

WOMAN IS A FOUNTAIN OF FIRE
WOMAN IS A RIVER OF LOVE
A LATIN WOMAN IS JUST A WOMAN
WITH THE MUSIC INSIDE

DON'T DENY US THE MUSIC
DON'T IMAGINE MY FACE
I'VE FOUGHT MANY BATTLES
I'VE SUNG MANY SONGS
I AM JUST A WOMAN
WITH THE MUSIC INSIDE

I AM JUST A WOMAN BREAKING
THE LINKS OF A CHAIN
I AM JUST A WOMAN
WITH THE MUSIC INSIDE

FREE THE BUTTERFLY
LET THE OCEANS ROLL IN
FREE THE BUTTERFLY
LET THE OCEANS ROLL IN
I AM ONLY A WOMAN
WITH THE MUSIC INSIDE

Black out

The End

A Selected Bibliography of Latina Literature of the United States

Compiled by Roberta Fernández

Literature by Latinas

Acosta, Teresa Palomo. *Nile and Other Poems: A 1985-1994 Notebook.* Austin: Privately published, 1994. (Poetry)

_____. *Passing Time.* Austin: Privately published, 1984. (Poetry)

Agosín, Marjorie. *Brujas y algo más/Witches and Other Things.* Translated by Cola Franzen. Pittsbury: Latin American Review Press, 1986. (Poetry)

_____. *Chile: Gemidos y Cantares.* Santiago de Chile: Editorial El Observador, 1977. (Poetry)

_____. *Conchali.* Montclair, N.J.: Senda Nueva de Ediciones, 1980. (Poetry)

_____. *Circles of Madness: Mothers of the Plaza de Mayo.* Translated by Celeste Kostupulos-Cooperman. (With photographs by Alicia D'Amico and Alicia Sanguinetti.) Fredonia, N.Y.: While Pine Press, 1992. (Poetry & photography)

_____. *La felicidad.* Santiago de Chile: Editorial Cuarto Propio, 1991. (Short fiction)

_____. *Happiness.* Translated by Elizabeth Horan. Fredonia, N.Y.: White Pine Press, 1993. (Short fiction)

_____. *Hogueras.* Santiago de Chile: Editorial Universitaria, 1986. (Poetry)

_____. *Hogueras/Bonfires.* Translated by Naomi Lindstrom. Tempe, AZ: Bilingual Press, 1990. (Poetry)

_____. *Mujeres de humo.* Madrid: Ediciones Torremozas, 1987.

_____. *Sargazo/Sargasso.* Translated by Cola Franzen. Fredonia, N.Y.: While Pine Press, 1993. (Poetry)

_____. *Women of Smoke.* Translated by Janice Molloy. Lawrenceville, N.Y.: Red Sea Press, 1989.

_____. *Zones of Pain.* Translated by Cola Franzen. Fredonia, N.Y.: White Pine Press, 1988. (Poetry)

Alvárez, Julia. *How the García Girls Lost Their Accents.* New York: Plume, 1992. (Fiction)

Alvárez, Gloria Enedina. *La Excusa/The Excuse.* Los Angeles: Ediciones El Juglar, 1991. (Poetry)

Anzaldúa, Gloria. *Borderlands/La Frontera: The New Mestiza.* San Francisco: Spinsters/Aunt Lute Book Company, 1987. (Essay, fiction, poetry)

_____. *Prietita Has A Friend/Prietita tiene un amigo.* Children's Book Press, 1991. (Children's fiction)

Behar, Ruth. *Translated Woman: Crossing the Border with Esperanza's Story.* Boston: Beacon Press, 1993. (Testimonial literature)

Beltrán Hernández, Irene. *Across the Great River.* Houston: Arte Público Press, 1990. (Young Adult Fiction)

_____. *Heartbeat Drumbeat.* Houston: Arte Público Press, 1992. (Young Adult Fiction)

Brinson Curiel, Barbara. *Speak to Me from Dreams.* Berkeley: Third Woman Press, 1989. (Poetry)

Candelaria, Cordelia. *Ojo de la Cueva/Cave Springs.* Colorado Springs: Maize Press, 1984. (Poetry)

Castedo, Elena. *Paradise.* NY: Grove Weidenfeld, 1990. (Fiction)

Castillo, Ana. *The Mixquiahuala Letters.* Binghamton, N.Y.: Bilingual Press, 1986. (Fiction)

_____. *My Father Was A Toltec.* Albuquerque: West End Press, 1988. (Poetry)

_____. *Sapogonia.* Tempe, AZ: Bilingual Press, 1990. (Fiction)

_____. *So Far from God.* N.Y.: W.W. Norton & Co., 1993. (Fiction)

_____. *Women Are Not Roses.* Houston: Arte Público Press, 1984. (Poetry)

Catacalos, Rosemary. *Again for the First Time.* Santa Fe: Tooth of Time Books, 1984. (Poetry) [Out of print]

Cervantes, Lorna Dee. *Emplumada.* Pittsburg: U of Pittsburg Press, 1981. (Poetry)

_____. *From the Cables of Genocide: Poems of Love and Hunger.* Houston: Arte Público Press, 1991. (Poetry)

Chávez, Denise. *The Last of the Menu Girls.* Houston: Arte Público Press, 1986. (Fiction)

Cisneros, Sandra. *The House on Mango Street.* Houston: Arte Público Press, 1985. 2nd ed. New York: Vintage Books, 1991. (Fiction)

_____. *Loose Woman.* NY: Knopf, 1994. (Poetry)

_____. *Woman Hollering Creek and Other Stories*. NY: Random House, 1991. (Short fiction)

_____. *My Wicked, Wicked Ways*. Bloomington: Third Woman Press, 1987. (Poetry)

Corpi, Lucha. *Delia's Song*. Houston: Arte Público Press, 1988. (Fiction)

_____. *Eulogy for a Brown Angel*. Houston: Arte Público Press, 1992. (Fiction)

_____. *Noon Words/Palabras de Mediodía*. Translated by Catherine Rodríguez-Nieto. Berkeley: El Fuego de Aztlán Publications, 1980. (Poetry)[Out of print]

_____. *Variaciones sobre una tempestad/Variations on a Storm*, Translated by Catherine Rodríguez-Nieto. Berkeley: Third Woman Press, 1990. (Poetry)

Cota-Cárdenas, Margarita. *Noches despertando in/conciencias*. Tucson: Scorpion Press, 1975. (Poetry)

_____. *Puppet: A Chicano Novella*. Austin: Relámpago Books Press, 1985.

de Hoyos, Angela. *Arise, Chicano! and Other Poems*. Translated into Spanish by Mireya Robles. Bloomington, Indiana: Backstage Books, 1975. 2nd ed., San Antonio: M & A Editions, 1976.

_____. *Chicano Poems: For the Barrio*. Bloomington: Backstage Books, 1975. 2nd ed., San Antonio: M & A editions, 1976.

_____. *Selected Poems/Selecciones*. Translated into Spanish by Mireya Robles. Xalapa, Veracruz: Universidad Veracruzana, 1975. 2nd ed., San Antonio: Dezkalzo Press/ M & A Editions, 1989.

_____. *Woman, Woman*. Houston: Arte Público Press, 1985. (Poetry)

de Monteflores, Carmen. *Singing Softly/Cantando Bajito*. San Francisco: Spinsters/Aute Lute, 1990.

de Vallbona, Rima. *Cosecha de pecadores*. San José, Costa Rica: Editorial Costa Rica, 1988. (Fiction)

_____. *Mujeres y agonías*. Houston: Arte Público Press, 1981. (Fiction)

_____. *Mundo, mujer y demonio*. Houston: Arte Público Press, 1991. (Fiction)

_____. *Noche en vela*. Houston: Arte Público Press, 1982. (Fiction)

_____. *Polvo del camino*. Houston: Arte Público Press, 1985. (Fiction)

_____. *Las sombras que perseguimos*. Houston: Arte Público Press, 1983. (Fiction)

Engle, Margarita. *Singing to Cuba*. Houston: Arte Público Press, 1993. (Fiction)

Espaillat, Rhina. *Lapsing to Grace*. East Lansing: Bennett & Kitchel, 199[illegible] (Poetry & line drawings)

Espinosa, Paula María. *Dark Plums*. Houston: Arte Público Press, 1995. (Fiction)

_____. *Longing*. Berkeley: Cayuse Press, 1986. (Fiction) [Out of print]

_____. *Night Music*. Sausalito, CA: The Tides, 1969. (Poetry)

Esteves, Sandra María. *Bluestown Mockingbird Mambo*. Houston: Arte Público Press, 1990. (Poetry)

_____. *Tropical Rains: A Bilingual Downpour*. Bonx, New York: African Caribbean Poetry Theater, 1984. (Poetry)

_____. *Yerbabuena*. Greenfield, New York: Greenfield Review Press, 1980. (Poetry)

Fernández, Carol. *Sleep of the Innocent*. Houston: Arte Público Press, 1991. (Fiction)

Fernández, Roberta. *Intaglio: A Novel in Six Stories*. Houston: Arte Público Press, 1990. (Fiction)

Galliano, Alina. *La geometría de lo incandescente*. Miami: U of Miami, Iberian Studies Institute, 1990. (Poetry)

García, Cristina. *Singing to Cuba*. New York: Knopf, 1992. (Fiction)

Gaspar de Alba, Alicia. *The Mystery of Survival and Other Stories*. Tempe, Az: Bilingual Press, 1993. (Short fiction)

Gaspar de Alba, Alicia, María Herrera-Sobek and Demetria Martínez. *Three Times a Woman*. Tempe, Az: Bilingual Press, 1989.

Gil, Lourdes. *Blanca aldaba preludia*. Madrid: Betania, 1989. (Poetry)

_____. *Empieza la ciudad*. Coral Gables, Florida: La Torre de Papel, 1993. (Poetry)

_____. *Neumas*. Montclair, N.J.: Senda Nueva de Ediciones, 1977. (Poetry)

_____. *Vencido el fuego de la especie*. New Brunswick: Editorial Slusa, 1983. (Poetry)

Glickman, Nora. *Mujeres, memorias, malogros*. Buenos Aires: Editorial Mila, 1991. (Short fiction)

_____. *Uno de sus Juanes y otros cuentos*. Buenos Aires: Ediciones de la Flor, 1983. (Short fiction)

Gómez-Vega, Ibis. *Send My Roots Rain*. San Francisco: Aunt Lute, 1991. (Fiction)

Gonzales-Berry, Erlinda. *Paletitas de guayaba*. Albuquerque: Academia/El Norte Publications, 1991. (Fiction)

Hernández, Inés. *Con razón corazón*. San Antonio: Caracol, 1977. 2nd ed., San Antonio: M & A Editions, 1987. (Poetry)

Islas, Maya. *Merla*. Madrid: Editorial Betania, 1971. (Poetry)

Iturralde, Iraida. *Hubo la viola*. Montclair, N.J.: Ediciones Contra Viento y Marea, 1979. (Poetry)

_____. *El libro de Josefat/The Book of Josephat*. Guttenberg, N.J.: Giralt Editorial, 1983. (Poetry)

_____. *Tropel de espejos*. Madrid: Editorial Betania, 1989. (Poetry)

Levins Morales, Aurora and Rosario Morales. *Getting Home Alive*. Ithaca, N.Y.: Firebrand Press, 1986. (Personal Essays)

Limón, Graciela. *In Search of Bernabé*. Houston: Arte Público Press, 1993. (Fiction)

_____. *María de Belén, the Autobiography of an Indian Woman*. N.Y.: Vantage Press, 1990. (Fiction)

_____. *The Memories of Ana Calderón*. Houston: Arte Público Press, 1994. (Fiction)

Mattei, Olga Elena. *Cosmoagonía: Misa Cósmica*. Medellín: Sunday Literary Supplement to *El Colombiano* [April 17, 1994].

_____. *Cosmofonía*. Medellín: Secretaría de Educación Municipal, 1975.

_____. *La Gente*. Bogotá: Instituto Colombiano de Cultura, 1974.

_____. *Sílabas de Arena*. Medellín: Colección La Tertulia, 1962.

Mohr, Nicholasa. *El Bronx Remembered*. New York: Harper & Row, 1976. (Short fiction)

_____. *Felita*. New York: Dial Press, 1979. (Short fiction)

_____. *Going Home*. New York: Dial Books for Young Readers, 1986. (Short fiction)

_____. *In Nueva York*. New York: Dial Press, 1977. 2nd ed. Houston: Arte Público Press, 1993. (Short fiction)

_____. *Nilda*. New York: Harper & Row, 1973. 2nd ed. Houston: Arte Público Press, 1986. (Fiction)

_____. *Rituals of Survival: A Woman's Portfolio*. Houston: Arte Público Press, 1985. (Short fiction)

Mora, Pat. *A Birthday Basket for Tía*. New York: Macmillan, 1992. (Children's fiction)

_____. *Borders*. Houston: Arte Público Press, 1986. (Poetry)

_____. *Chants*. Houston: Arte Público Press, 1984. (Poetry)

_____. *Communion*. Houston: Arte Público Press, 1991. (Poetry)

_____. *The Desert Is My Mother*. Houston: Arte Público Press, 1994. (Children's fiction)

__________. *Nepantla*. Albuquerque: U of New Mexiso Press, 1993. (Personal essays)

Moraga, Cherríe. *Giving Up the Ghost: Teatro in Two Acts*. Los Angeles: West End Press, 1986.

_____. *The Last Generation*. Boston: South End Press, 1993. (Essay, fiction, poetry)
_____. *Loving in the War Years*. Boston: South End Press, 1983. (Essay, ficiton, poetry)

Moreno, Dorinda. *La mujer es la tierra*. San Francisco: Casa Editorial, 1975. (Poetry)

Ortiz Cofer, Judith. *The Latin Deli*. Athens, Georgia: U of Georgia Press, 1993. (Poetry, fiction, essay)
_____. *The Line of the Sun*. Athens, Georgia: U of Georgia Press, 1989. (Fiction)
_____. *Silent Dancing: A Partial Remembrance of a Puerto Rican Childhood*. Houston: Arte Público Press, 1990. (Personal essay & Poetry)
_____. *Terms of Survival*. Houston: Arte Público Press, 1987. (Poetry)

Pineda, Cecile. *Face*. New York: Viking-Penguin, 1985. (Fiction)
_____. *Frieze*. New York: Viking-Penquin, 1986. (Fiction)
_____. *The Love Queen of the Amazon*. Boston: Little, Brown and Company, 1992. (Fiction)

Ponce, Mary Helen. *Hoyt Street: An Autobiography*. Albuquerque: U of New Mexico Press, 1993.
_____. *Taking Control*. Houston: Arte Público Press, 1987. (Fiction)
_____. *The Wedding*. Houston: Arte Público Press, 1989. (Fiction)

Portillo Trambley, Estela. *The Day of the Swallows*. In *Contemporary Chicano Theater* edited by Roberto Garza. Notre Dame: Notre Dame University Press, 1976.
_____. *Rain of Scorpions and Other Writings*. Berkeley: Tonatiuh International, 1975. 2nd ed. *Rain of Scorpions and Other Stories*. Tempe, Arizona: Bilingual Press, 1993. (Short fiction)
_____. *Sor Juana Inés and Other Plays*. Ypsilanti, Michigan: Bilingual Press, 1983.
_____. *Trini*. Binghamton, N.Y.: Bilingual Press, 1986. (Novel)

Prida, Dolores. *Beautiful Señoritas and Other Plays*. Houston: Arte Público Press, 1991.

Pursifull, Carmen M. *Elsewhere in a Parallel Universe*. Urbana, IL: The Red Herring Press, 19

Quiñónez, Naomi. *Sueño de Colibrí/Hummingbird Dream*. Los Angeles: West End Press, 1985. (Poetry) [Out of print]

Serrano, Nina. *Heart Songs: The Collected Poems of Nina Serrano (1969-1979)*. San Francisco: Editorial Pocho Che, 1980. [Out of print]

Ríos, Isabel. *Victuum*. Ventura, California: Diana Etna, 1976. (Fiction)

Rivero, Eliana. *Cuerpos breves*. Tucson: Scorpion Press, 1977. (Poetry)

_____. *De cal y arena*. Sevilla: Aldebarán, 1975. (Poetry)

Romero, Lin. *Happy Songs, Bleeding Hearts*. San Diego: Toltecas en Aztlán Publications, 1974. (Poetry)

Tafolla, Carmen. *Curandera*. San Antonio: M & A Publications, 1983. (Poetry)

_____. *To Split a Human: Mitos, Machos y la Mujer Chicana*. San Antonio: Mexican-American Cultural Center, 1985. (Poetry)

_____. *Sonnets to Human Beings and Other Selected Works*. Santa Monica: Lalo Press, 1993. (Poetry)

Tafolla, Carmen, Cecilio García-Camarillo, and Reyes Cárdenas. *Get Your Tortillas Together*. San Antonio: M & A Publications, 1976. (Poetry)

Umpierre, Luz María. *El país de las maravillas*. Bloomington: Third Woman Press, 1985. (Poetry)

_____. *The Margarita Poems*. Bloomington: Third Woman Press.

_____. *Una puertorriqueña en Penna*. San Juan, Puerto Rico: P. R. Masters, 1979. (Poetry)

_____. *Y otras desgracias/And Other Misfortunes*. Bloomington: Third Woman Press, 1985. (Poetry)

Valdés, Gina. *There Are No Madmen Here*. San Diego: Maize Press, 1981. (Poetry)

Vando, Gloria. *Promesas: Geography of the Impossible*. Houston: Arte Público Press, 1993. (Poetry)

Vélez-Mitchell, Anita. *Primavida*. Bilingual edition, with translations by the author. Río Piedras, Puerto Rico: Ediciones Mairena, 1978. (Poetry)

Vicuña, Cecilia. *Palabrarmás*. Buenos Aires: Ediciones El Imaginero, 1984. (Poetry)

_____. *Precario/Precarious*. Translated by Anne Twitty. New York: Tanam Press, 1983. (Poetry)

_____. *Sabor a mí*. Translated by Filipe Ehrenberg with the author. London: Beau Geste Press, 1973. (Poetry)

_____. *Unravelling Words and the Weaving of Water*, Eliot Weinberger, ed. Translated by Eliot Weinberger and Suzanne Jill Levine. Saint Paul, MN: Graywolf Press, 1992. (Poetry)

_____. *La Wik'uña*. Santiago de Chile: Francisco Zegers Editorial, 1990. (Poetry)

Vigil-Piñón, Evangelina. *The Computer is Down*. Houston: Arte Público Press, 1987. (Poetry)

_____. *Nade y Nade*. San Antonio: M. & A. Editions, 1978. (Poetry)
_____. *Thirty an' Seen a Lot*. Houston: Arte Público Press, 1982. (Poetry)

Villanueva, Alma Luz. *Bloodroot*. Austin: Place of Herons Press, 1977. (Poetry)
_____. *La Chingada*. Binghamton, N.Y.: Bilingual Press, 1985. (Poetry)
_____. *Life Span*. Austin: Place of Herons Press, 1985. (Poetry)
_____. *Mother, May I?* Pittsburgh: Motheroot Publications, 1978. (Poetry)
_____. *Naked Ladies*. Tempe, Az: Bilingual Press, 1994. (Fiction)
_____. *Planet and Mother, May I ?*. Tempe, Az: Bilingual Press, 1993. (Poetry)
_____. *Poems: Third Chicano Literary Prize*. University of California, Irvine, 1977.
_____. *The Ultraviolet Sky*. Tempe, Az: Bilingual Press, 1988. (Fiction)
_____. *Weeping Woman/La Llorona and Other Stories*. Tempe, Az: Bilingual Press, 1994. (Short fiction)

Viramontes, Helena María. *The Moths and Other Stories*. Houston: Arte Público Press, 1985. (Short fiction)

Zamora, Bernice. *Releasing Serpents*. Tempe, Az: Bilingual Press, 1994. (Poetry)
_____. *Restless Serpents*. Menlo Park, CA: Diseños Literarios, 1976. (Poetry)

Anthologies

Alarcón, Norma, Ana Castillo and Cherríe Moraga, eds. *Third Woman: The Sexuality of Latinas*. Berkeley: Third Woman Press, 1989.

Alurista et. al., eds. *Festival de flor y canto: An Anthology of Chicano Literature*. Los Angeles: U of Southern California Press, 1976.

Anzaldúa, Gloria, ed. *Making Faces, Making Soul/Haciendo Caras: Creative and Critical Perspectives by Women of Color*. San Francisco: Aunt Lute Foundation Books, 1990.

Aponixk, Kathleen et. al., ed. *Poetry, Merrimack: A Poetry Anthology*, Lowell, MA: Loom Press, 1992.

Augenbraum, Harold and Illán Stavans, eds. *Growing Up Latino: Memoirs and Stories*. New York: Houghton Mifflin, 1993.

Babín, María Teresa and Stan Steiner, eds. *Borinquen: An Anthology of Puerto Rican Literature*. New York: Knopf, 1974.

Bornstein-Somoza, Mirian, Maya Islas, Inés Hernández Tovar, Eliana Rivero, Margarita Cota Cárdenas, Mireya Robles and Lucía Sol, eds. *Siete poetas*. Tucson: Scorpion, 1978.

Boza, María del Carmen, Beverly Silva and Carmen Valle, eds. *Nosotras: Latina Literature Today*. Binghamton, N.Y.: Bilingual Press, 1986.

Bruchac, Carol, Linda Hogan and Judith McDaniel, eds. *The Stories We Hold Secret: Tales of Women's Spiritual Development*. Greenfield, New York: Greenfield Review Press, 1986.

Daydé Tolson, Santiago, ed. *Five Poets of Aztlán*. Binghamton, New York: Bilingual Press, 1985.

Daly Heyck, Denis Lynn, ed. *Barrios and Borderlands: Cultures of Latinos and Latinas in the United States*. New York: Routledge, 1994.

Durán, Roberto, ed. *Reaching for the Mainland*. Tempe, Az: Bilingual Press, 1987.

Fernández, Roberta, ed. *In Other Words: Literature by Latinas of the United States*. Houston: Arte Público Press, 1994.

Feyder, Linda, ed. *Shattering the Myth: Plays by Hispanic Women*. Selected by Denise Chávez. Houston: Arte Público Press, 1991.

Finch, Annie, ed. *A Formal Feeling Comes: Poems in Form by Contemporary Women*. Brownsville, Oregon: Story Line, 1994.

Fisher, Dexter, ed. *The Third Woman: Minority Women Writers of the United States*. Boston: Houghton, 1980.

Gómez, Alma, Cherríe Moraga and Mariana Carmona-Romo, eds. *Cuentos: Stories by Latinas*. Lathan, NY: Kitchen Table Women of Color Press, 1983.

González, Ray, ed. *After Aztlán: Latino Poets of the Nineties*. Boston: Godine, 1992.

_____. *Mirrors Beneath the Earth*. Willimantic, CT: Curbstone Press, 1992.

_____. *Without Discovery: A Native Response to Columbus*. Seattle: Broken Moon Press, 1992.

Herrera-Sobek, María and Helena María Viramontes, eds. *Chicana Creativity and Criticism: Charting New Frontiers in American Literature*. Houston: Arte Público Press, 1988.

Hospital, Carolina, ed. *Cuban American Writers: Los Atrevidos*. Princeton, N.J.: Ediciones Ellas/Linden Lane Press, 1988.

Kanellos, Nicolás, ed. *Short Fiction by Hispanic Writers of the United States*. Houston: Arte Público Press, 1993.

Keenan, Deborah and Roseann Lloyd, eds. *Looking for Home: Women Writing about Exile*. Minneapolis,: Milkweed Editions, 1990.

Lázaro, Felipe, ed. *Poetas cubanas en Nueva York/Cuban Women Poets in New York: A Brief Anthology*. Madrid: Editorial Betania, 1991.

Marzán, Julio, ed. *Inventing a Word: An Anthology of Twentieth-Century Puerto Rican Poetry*. New York: Columbia U Press, 1980.

Minnesota Humanities Commission, comp. *Braided Lives: An Anthology of Multicultural Writing*. St. Paul: Minnesota Humanities Commision, 1992.

Milligan, Bryce, ed. *Linking Roots: Writing by Six Women with Distinct Ethnic Heritages*. San Antonio, TX: M & A Editions, 1993.

Moraga, Cherríe and Gloria Anzaldúa, eds. *This Bridge Called My Back: Writings by Radical Women of Color*. Boston: Persephone Press, 1991. 2nd ed. Lathan, N.Y.: Kitchen Table Women of Color Press, 1983.

Moraga, Cherríe and Ana Castillo, eds. *Esta puente, mi espalda*. [Spanish ed. of *This Bridge Called My Back*] San Francisco: 1988.

Olivares, Julián, ed. *Cuentos hispanos de los Estados Unidos*. Houston: Arte Público Press, 1993.

Olivares, Julián and Evangelina Vigil-Pinón, eds. *Decade II: A Twentieth Anniversary Anthology*. Houston: Arte Público Press, 1993.

Osborn, M. Elizabeth, ed. *On New Ground: Contemporary Hispanic-American Plays*. New York: Theatre Communications Group, 1987.

Parera, Isabel. *Houghton Mifflin English*. Boston: MA.

Partnoy, Alicia, ed. *You Can't Drown the Fire: Latin American Women Writing in Exile*. Pittsburgh: Cleis Press, 1988.

Poey, Delia and Virgil Suárez, eds. *Iguana Dreams: New Latino Fiction*. NY: HarperPerennial, 1992.

Quiñónez, Naomi, ed. *Invocation L.A.: Urban Multicultural Poetry*. West End Press, 1989.

Ramos, Juanita, ed. *Compañeras: Latina Lesbians*. New York: Latina Women's Educational Resources, 1987.

Rebolledo, Tey Diana and Eliana Rivero, eds. *Infinite Divisions: An Anthology of Chicana Literature*. Tucson: U of Arizona Press, 1993.

Rebolledo, Tey Diana, Erlinda Gonzales-Berry, and Teresa Márquez, eds. *Las Mujeres Hablan: An Anthology of Nuevo Mexicana Writers*. Albuquerque: El Norte Publications, 1988.

Reed, Ismael, Kathryn Trueblood and Shawn Wong, eds. *The Before Columbus Foundation Fiction Anthology: Selections from the American Book Awards, 1980-1900*. New York: W.W. Norton & Company, 1992.

Sánchez, Rosaura. *Requisa 32*. San Diego: UCSD Chicano Research Publications, 1979.

Soto, Gary, ed. *Pieces of the Heart: New Chicano Fiction*. San Francisco: Chronicle Books, 1993.

Tatum, Charles, M., ed. *New Chicana/Chicano Writing*. Vol. 1. Tucson: U of Arizona Press, 1991.

_____, ed. *New Chicana/Chicano Writing*. Vol. 2. Tucson: U of Arizona Press, 1992.

_____, ed. *New Chicana/Chicano Writing*. Vol. 3, Tucson: U of Arizona Press, 1993.

Third World Communications Women's Collective. *Third World Women*. San Francisco: Third World Communications, 1972.

Trujillo, Carla, ed. *Chicana Lesbians: The Girls Our Mothers Warned Us About*. Berkeley: Third Woman Press, 1991.

Vélez, Diana, ed. *Reclaiming Medusa: Short Stories by Contemporary Puerto Rican Women*. San Francisco: Spinsters/Aunt Lute, 1988.

Vigil-Piñón, Evangelina, ed. *Woman of Her Word: Hispanic Women Write*. Houston: Arte Público Press, 1983.

Wenkart, Henny, ed. *Sarah's Daughters Sing: A Sampler of Poems by Jewish Women*. Hoboken, N.J., KTAV Publishing House, 1990.

Criticism

Acosta-Belén, Edna, ed. *The Puerto Rican Woman: Perspectives on Culture, History and Society*. New York: Praeger, 1986.

Aguilar-Henson, Marcella. *The Multi-faceted Poetic World of Angela de Hoyos*. Austin: Relámpago Books Press, 1985.

Burunat, Silvia and Ofelia García, eds. *Veinte años de literatura cubano-americana: Antología 1962-1982*. Tempe, AZ: Bilingual Press, 1988.

Calderón, Héctor and José David Saldívar, eds. *Criticism in the Borderlands: Studies in Chicano Literature, Culture and Ideology*. Durham, North Carolina: Duke University Press, 1991.

Candelaria, Cordelia. *Chicano Poetry: A Critical Introduction*. Westport, Connecticut: Greenwood Press, 1986.

Chabran, Angie and Rosalinda Fregoso, eds. *Chicana/o Cultural Representations: Reframing Critical Discourses*. Special issue of *Cultural Studies* 4, no. 3 (1900).

Córdova, Teresa, Norma Cantú, Gilberto Cárdenas, Juan García and Christine M. Sierra, eds. *Chicana Voices: Intersections of Class, Race, and Gender*. Austin: Center for Mexican American Studies, 1986. [Proceedings of the National Association of Chicano Studies Annual Meeting, Austin, Texas, 1984]

Cotera, Marta. *The Chicana Feminist.* Austin: International Systems Development, 1977.

Fernández, Roberta. *Twenty-five Years of Hispanic Literature in the United States, 1965-1990.* [Catalogue accompanying an exhibit] Houston: University of Houston Libraries, 1992.

Gonzales-Berry, Erlinda, ed. *Pasó por Aquí: Critical Essays on the New Mexican Literary Tradition 1542-1988.* Albuquerque: U of New Mexico Press, 1989.

Herrera-Sobek, María, ed. *Beyond Stereotypes: The Critical Analysis of Chicana Literature.* Binghamton, N.Y.: Bilingual Press, 1985.

Herrera-Sobek, María and Helena María Viramontes. *Chicana Creativity and Criticism: Charting New Frontiers in American Literature.* Houston: Arte Público Press, 1988.

Horno-Delgado, Asunción, Eliana Ortega, Nina M. Scott and Nancy Saporta-Sternbach, eds. *Breaking Boundaries: Latina Writings and Critical Readings.* Amherst: U of Massachusetts Press, 1989.

López-González, Amelia Malagamba, and Elena Urrutia, eds. *Mujer y literatura mexicana y chicana: Culturas en contacto.* Tijuana: El Colegio de la Frontera Norte, 1988.

Miller, Beth, ed. *Women in Hispanic Literature: Icons and Fallen Idols.* Berkeley: U of California Press, 1983.

Mora, Magdalena and Adelaida R. del Castillo, eds. *Mexican Women in the United States: Struggles Past and Present.* Los Angeles: UCLA Chicano Studies Center, 1980.

Ramos, Luis Arturo. *Angela de Hoyos: A Critical Look.* Albuquerque: Pajarito Publications, 1979.

Romo, Ricardo, ed. *Chicana Voices: Intersections of Class, Race and Gender.* Austin: Center for Mexican American Studies Publications, 1986.

Saldívar, Ramón. *Chicano Narrative: The Dialectics of Difference.* Madison: U of Wisconsin Press, 1990.

Sánchez, Marta Sánchez. *Contemporary Chicana Poetry: A Critical Approach to An Emerging Literature.* Berkeley: University of California Press, 1985.

Sánchez, Rosaura. *Chicano Discourse: Socio-historic Perspectives.* Rowley, Mass.: Newbury House, 1983. 2nd ed. Houston: Arte Público Press, 1994.

_____. *Essays on La Mujer*. Los Angeles: UCLA Chicano Studies Center Publication, 1977.

Presses

ARTE PÚBLICO PRESS
University of Houston
Houston, TX 77204-2090
Tel: (713) 743-2841
FAX: (713) 743-2847

AUNT LUTE BOOKS
P.O. Box 410687
San Francisco, CA 94141
Tel: (415) 558-8116

BACKSTAGE PRESS
Div. of Billboard Publications
1515 Broadway, N.Y. 10036
Tel: 1-800-451-1741

BEACON PRESS
25 Beacon St.
Boston, MA 02108-2892

BILINGUAL REVIEW/PRESS
Hispanic Research Center
Arizona State University
Tempe, Arizona 85287
Tel: (602) 965-3867

BENNET & KITCHEL
P.O. Box 4422
East Lansing, Michigan 48826

BROKEN MOON PRESS
P.O. Box 24585
Seattle, Washington 98124-0585
Tel: (206) 548-1340

CHICANO STUDIES RESEARCH CENTER PUBLICATIONS
University of California
405 Hilgard Ave
Los Angeles, CA 90024

CURBSTONE PRESS
321 Jackson St.
Willimantic, CT 06226
Tel: 423-9190

EDICIONES DE LA FLOR
Anchoris 27
1280 Buenos Aires
Argentina

EDICIONES TORREMOZAS
Apartado 19.032
Madrid
Tel: 250-50-27

EDITORIAL BETANIA
Apartado de Correos 50 767
28080 Madrid
España

EDITORIAL COSTA RICA
Apartado Postal 10.010-1.000
San José, Costa Rica

EDITORIAL CUARTO PROPIO
Keller 1175
Providencia, Santiago
Chile
Tel: 2047645
FAX: 2047622

EDITORIAL MILA
Pasteur 633-1ero Piso (1028)
Buenos Aires
Argentina

EL NORTE PUBLICATIONS
P.O. Box 7266
Albuquerque, New Mexico 87194

FIREBRAND BOOKS
141 The Commons
Ithaca, N.Y. 14850
Tel: (607) 272-0000

GRAYWOLF PRESS
P.O. Box 75006
Saint Paul, MN 55175

GREENFIELD REVIEW PRESS
R.D. #1 Box 80
Greenfield Center, N.Y. 12833
Tel: (518) 584-1728

GROVE WEIDENFELD
841 Broadway
New York, NY 10003-4793

KITCHEN TABLE WOMEN OF COLOR PRESS
P.O. Box 908
Lathan, N.Y. 12110

LA TORRE DE PAPEL
29 Santilane Ave, Suite 1
Coral Gables, Florida 33134

LINDEN LANE PRESS
P.O. Box 2384
Princeton, N.J. 08543

M & A EDITIONS
Rt. 5, P.O. Box 332
San Antonio, TX 78211
Tel: (210) 628-1440

MILKWEED EDITIONS
P.O. Box 3226
Minneapolis, MN 55403

MOTHEROOT
P.O. Box 8306
Pittsburg, PA 15218

PAJARITO PUBLICATIONS
P.O. Box 7264
Albuquerque, NM 87104

PLACE OF HERONS PRESS
P.O. Box 1952
Austin, TX 78767

RELÁMPAGO BOOKS PRESS
P.O. Box 43194
Austin, TX 78745

ROUTLEDGE
29 West 35th Street
New York, N.Y. 10001

SOUTH END PRESS
116 Saint Botolph St.
Boston, MA 02115

THIRD WOMAN PRESS
Chicano Studies
Dwinelle Hall 3404
University of California
Berkeley, Ca 94720

TOLTECAS EN AZTLÁN
Centro Cultural de la Raza
P.O. Box 8251
San Diego, CA 92102

TONATIUH-QUINTO SOL INTERNATIONAL
Box 9275
Berkeley, CA 94709
(510) 655-8036

UNIVERSITY OF MASSACHUSETTS PRESS
Amherst, MA 01002

UNIVERSITY OF PITTSBURGH PRESS
Pittsburg, PA 15260

WEST END PRESS
P.O.Box 27334
Alquerque, NM 87125

WHITE PINE PRESS
10 Village Square
Fredonia, NY 14063
Tel/FAX (716) 672-5743

Translators, Artists and Critic

Translators

Suzanne Jill Levine is a prolific translator of Latin American writing, including works by Manuel Puig, Carlos Fuentes, José Donoso and others. She and Eliot Weinberger did the translations of Cecilia Vicuña's *Unravelling Words & the Weaving of Water* (1992) in close collaboration with the author. Her exploration of her art form, *The Subversive Scribe: Translating Latin American Fiction*, was recently published by Graywolf Press. She is a professor at the University of California at Santa Barbara.

Naomi Lindstrom is a professor of Spanish and Portuguese, and Director of Publications at the Institute for Latin American Studies of the University of Texas at Austin. Her translations include *The Seven Madmen* by Roberto Arlt and Marjorie Agosín's *Women of Smoke* and *Hogueras/Bonfires*. Her literary criticism includes *Women's Voice in Latin American Literature* (1989) and *Twentieth-Century Spanish American Fiction* (1994).

Catherine Rodríguez-Nieto has translated three volumes of poetry: *Fireflight: Three Latin American Poets* (1976), Lucha Corpi's *Palabras de mediodía/Noon Words* (1980) and *Variaciones sobre una tempestad/Variations on a Storm* (1990). Her translations have appeared in many literary magazines and anthologies, and in educational texts from major publishers. She and her husband, Alcides, own and operate In Other Words...Inc., a translation and editing service in Oakland, California.

Eliot Weinberger is the author of two collections of essays, *Works on Paper* and *Outside Stories*, both published by New Directions. Among his translations are *Collected Poems of Octavio Paz 1957–1987*, Jorge Luis Borges' *Seven Nights*, and Vicente Huidobro's *Altazar*, which was published in Graywolf's *Palabra Sur* series. With Suzanne Jill Levine, he translated Cecilia Vicuña's *Unravelling Words & the Weaving of Water* (1992), in close collaboration with the author.

Artists

Leslie Nemour, an artist from San Diego, California, finds inspiration for her visual narratives in the folkloric Latino *dichos*, and relates *milagro* charms to different life situations. Her work has been exhibited in several San Diego one-person shows, including "Antojitos y Antojados," "Cuerpos y Almas/Bodies and Souls," and "Daily Miracles/Milagros Diarios." Among the many group shows in which her work has appeared are "Espectro de Chicano," "Calabasas y Calaveras: Día de los Muertos 1993," and "Contemporary Visions of the Virgen de Guadalupe."

Mark Piñón, a free-lance artist since 1984, is the art director for *The Americas Review*. For ten years, he has been the main graphic designer-illustrator for the covers published by Arte Público Press, many of which have received awards for art design. Born in Houston, Piñón is a graduate of the Art Institute of Houston. Presently, he is also designing covers for CD records.

Critic

Jean Franco is one of the foremost critics of Latin American literature. The author of numerous studies including *The Modern Culture of Latin America: Society and the Artist*; *César Vallejo: The Dialectics of Poetry and Silence*; and *Plotting Women: Gender and Representations in Mexico*. She is the director of the Center for Latin American Studies at Columbia University.

Permissions

The following list includes previously copyrighted and previously published works. All the works in this volume appear with the kind permission of the authors and/or presses.

Part One—Poetry

Teresa Palomo Acosta: "My Mother Pieced Quilts," "I Should Be Trying to Start Some New Begonia Plants," "For Matisse," and "Untitled." Reprinted from *Passing Time*. Copyright @ 1984 by the author. "Museum Piece." Copyright @ 1992 by the author. Reprinted from *Descant* (Texas Christian University) XXXII: 2 (1992): 46.

Majorie Agosín: "Familiares en la pieza oscura/Family Members in the Dark Room," "Ritual de mis senos/Ritual of My Breasts," "Los zapatos rojos/The Red Shoes." Reprinted with permission from the publisher of *Hogueras/Bonfires* (Bilingual Press, 1990). Translations into English reprinted with permission from Naomi Lindstrom. "Mis pies/My Feet," "La mesa de billar en New Bedford, Mass./The Pool Table in New Bedford, Mass.," and "Estados Unidos/United States." Reprinted with permission from the publisher of *Woman of Her Word: Hispanic Women Write*, Evangelina Vigil-Piñón, ed. (Arte Público Press, 1983). Translations into English reprinted with permission from Naomi Lindstrom.

Rosemary Catacalos: "Katakalos," "Keeping the Vigil," and "A Vision of La Llorona." Reprinted with permission from the author. Copyright @ 1984 by the author. First printed in *Again for the First Time* (Santa Fe: Tooth of Time Books, 1984). "The History of Abuse, a Language Poem." Reprinted with permission from the author. First printed in *Colorado Review* (Fall/Winter, 1993).

Lorna Dee Cervantes: "For Virginia Chavez" and "Poem for the Young White Man Who Asked Me How I, an Intelligent, Well-Read Person Could Believe in the War Between Races" are reprinted from EMPLUMADA, by Lorna Dee Cervantes, by permission of the University of Pittsburgh Press. © 1981 by Lorna Dee Cervantes. "Beneath the Shadow of the Freeway." Reprinted by permission of the publisher, Latin American Literary Review Press, Volume V, No. 10, 1977, Pittsburgh, Pennsylvania. "Pleiades from the Cables of Genocide." Reprinted with permission from the publisher of *From the Cables of Genocide: Poems on Love and Hunger* (Arte Público Press-University of Houston, 1991). " "Astro-no-mía." Reprinted with permission from the publisher of *Chicana Creativity and Criticism: Forging New Frontiers in American Literature*, María Herrera-Sobek and Helena María Viramontes, eds. (Arte Público Press, 1988).

Lucha Corpi: "Romance negro" (First printed in *San Jose Studies* IV: 1 (1978)), "Marina Madre/Marina Mother," "Marina Virgen/Marina Virgin," "La hija del diablo/The Devil's Daughter," and "Ella (Marina ausente)/She (Marina Distant)." Reprinted with permission from the author. Translations into English reprinted with permission from Catherine Rodríguez-Nieto. First printed in *Noon Words/Palabras de mediodía* (Berkeley: Fuego de Aztlán Publications, 1980). "Dos/Two," "Diecisiete/Seventeen," and "Voces/Voices." Reprinted with permission from the author. Translations into English reprinted with permission from Catherine Rodríguez-Nieto. First printed in *Variaciones sobre una tempestad/Variations on a Storm* (Berkeley: Third Woman Press, 1990).

Verónica Cunningham: "Poet," "A Language of Survival," "Porcupine Love," "Heart Pieces," and "El Beso." Printed with permission from the author.

Angela de Hoyos: "To Walt Whitman"/"A Walt Whitman." Printed with permission from the author. "Arise, Chicano!" Reprinted with permission from the author. First printed in *Arise, Chicano! and Other Poems* (San Antonio: M & A Editions, 1980). "Tonantzin Morena," and "Si amas, perdona—si no amas, olvida...." Reprinted with permission from the author. First printed in *Woman, Woman* (Arte Público Press, 1985). "One Ordinary Morning/Una mañana cualquiera" and "On the Unacceptable/Lo inaceptable." Reprinted with permission from the author. First printed in *Selected Poems/Selecciones* (Corpus Christi: Dezkalzo Press, 1989). Translations into Spanish reprinted with permission from Mireya Robles. "Invention of the Camel." Printed with permission from the author.

Rhina Espaillat: "Snapshots in an Album," "Where Childhood Lives," "Translation," "The Ballad of San Isidro," "You Call Me by Old Names," and "Bodega." Printed with permission from the author.

Sandra María Esteves: "Autobiography of a Nuyorican," "Love Affair with a Welfare Hotel," "Sistas," "Amor Negro," "Gringolandia," "Ocha," and "Religious Instructions for Young Casualties." Reprinted with permission from the publisher of *Bluestown Mockingbird Mambo* (Arte Público Press, 1990). "Raising Eyebrows" and "Poem to My Therapist." Printed with permission from the author.

Lourdes Gil: "A Stranger Came," "Mutation Comes by Water," "Last Port," and "This, My Last Thought." Printed with permission from the author.

Carolina Hospital: "Dear Tía." Reprinted with permission from the publisher of *Cuban American Writers: Los Atrevidos.* (Ediciones Ellas/Linden Lane Press, 1988). "A Visit to West New York." Printed with permission from the author. Reprinted from *The Americas Review* XVIII: 3-4 (1990): 107. "Hell's Kitchen," "On the Last Stretch of the Journey," and "For a Sister Here." Printed with permission from the author.

Iraida Iturralde: "A Fragile Heritage," "The Man Who Saved the Fish," "Rite of Passage," "Over a Baroque Portal: The Meow of the Offspring," "The Obligatory Verse" and "On the Altars of Tikal." Printed with permission from the author.

Natashia López: "Epitaph," "All Body and No Soul," and "For Women Who Need Strength." Printed with permission from the author. "From Between Our Legs." Printed with permission from the author. First printed in *Chicana Lesbians: The Girls Our Mothers Warned Us About*, Carla Trujillo, ed. (Berkeley: Third Woman Press, 1991).

Olga Elena Mattei: "Ms. Bourgeois" and "The Angel of the Millennium (Accident at the Nuclear Plant)." Printed with permission from the author.

Pat Mora: "Mi Madre" and "Curandera." Reprinted with permission from the publisher of *Chants* (Arte Público Press, 1984). "Border." Reprinted with permission from the publisher of *Borders* (Arte Público Press, 1986). "Picturesque: San Cristóbal de las Casas," "Tigua Elder," "The Eye of Texas," "The Young Sor Juana," and "Mothers and Daughters." Reprinted with permission from the publisher of *Comunion* (Arte Público Press, 1991). "Doña Feliciana," "Tornabé," and "La Dulcería." Printed with permission from the author.

Naomi Quiñónez: "Ánima," "La Llorona," "Hesitations," "No Shelter," "El Salvador," and "Good Friday." Reprinted with permission from the publisher of *Sueño de Colibrí/Hummingbird Dream* (Los Angeles: West End Press, 1985).

Nina Serrano: "Antepasados/Ancestors," "Lolita Lebrón," "MultiMedia Witch," "Woman Pirate," and "International Woman's Day." Reprinted with permission from the author. First printed in *Heart Songs* (San Francisco: Editorial Pocho Che, 1980).

Carmen Tafolla: "Allí por la Calle San Luis." Reprinted with permission from Bilingual Press. First published in *Five Poets of Aztlán* (Bilingual Press, 1985). "Right in One Language," "MotherMother," "Nací la hija," "Marked," "Woman-hole," and "In Guatemala." Reprinted with the permission from the author and from the publisher of *Sonnets to Human Beings and Other Selected Works* (Santa Monica: Lalo Press, 1993).

Luz María Umpierre: "To a Beautiful Illusion," "For Ellen," and "Elliot's Sunset." Reprinted with permission from the author. First printed in a slightly different version in Spanish and English in *The Americas Review* XIX: 3-4 (1991): 41-42, 44, 48-50. Assistance with English versions from Patsy Boyer and Ellen Stekert.

Gloria Vando: "Divorce," "Latchkey Kid," "At My Father's Funeral," "Cry Uncle," "Legend of the Flamboyán," "Commonwealth, Common Poverty," and "Faith." Reprinted with the permission from the publisher of *Promesas: Geography of the Impossible* (Arte Público Press, 1993).

Anita Vélez-Mitchell: "Abril/April," "Junio/June," "Octubre/October," and "Diciembre/December." Reprinted with permission from the author. First printed in *Primavida: Calendario de Amor* (Río Piedras, Puerto Rico: Ediciones Mairena, 1984). Translations by the author. These poems first appeared in *The Institute of Culture Journal of Puerto Rico.*

Cecilia Vicuña: "Entering," "Poncho: Ritual Dress," "Origins of Weaving," "Precarious," and "De *Palabrarmas*/From *Palabrarmas*" copyright 1992 by Cecilia Vicuña, translated by Eliot Weinberger and Suzanne Jill Levine, Edited by Eliot Weinberger. Reprinted from *Unravelling Words & the Weaving of Water* with the permission of Graywolf Press, Saint Paul.

Evangelina Vigil-Piñón: "El Mercado de San Antonio Where the Tourists Trot." Reprinted with permission from the publisher of *Thirty an' Seen a Lot* (Arte Público Press, 1985). "Daily Progress." Reprinted with permission from the publisher of *The Computer Is Down* (Arte Público Press, 1987). "Equinox." Reprinted with permission from the publisher of *Chicana Creativity and Criticism: Charting New Frontiers in American Literature*, María Herrera-Sobek and Helena María Viramontes, eds. (Arte Público Press, 1988). "Legacy" and "Omniscience." Printed with permission from the author.

Alma Luz Villanueva: "An Act of Creation," "Trust," and "Indian Summer Ritual." Printed with permission from the author.

Marie Elise Wheatwind: "Abortion" and "Perverted Villanelle." Printed with permission from the author. First printed in *Chicana Lesbians: The Girls Our Mothers Warned Us About*, Carla Trujillo, ed. (Berkeley: Third Woman Press, 1991).

Bernice Zamora: "Above Aguilar," "Shade," "Summer's Rage," "Open Gate," "Peatmoss," "Original Seeding," "Piles of Sublime," "A Willing Abdication," and "Our Instructions." Printed with permission from the author.

Part Two—Essay

Gloria Anzaldúa: "La Consciencia de la Mestiza/Towards a New Consciousness." From *Borderlands/La Frontera: The New Mestiza* © 1987 by Gloria Anzaldúa. Reprinted with the permission from Aunt Lute Books, (415) 826-1300.

Roberta Fernández: "(Re)vision of an American Journey." Printed with the permission of the author. First printed in *Without Discovery: A Native Response to Columbus*, Ray González, ed. (Seattle: Broken Moon Press, 1992).

Cherríe Moraga: "Art in América con Acento." Reprinted with the permission of the publisher of *The Last Generation* (Boston: South End Press, 1993).

Judith Ortiz Cofer: "Silent Dancing." Reprinted with the permission of the publisher of *Silent Dancing: A Partial Remembrance of a Puerto Rican Childhood* (Arte Público Press, 1990).

Part Three—Fiction

Elena Castedo: Chapter Nineteen from *Paradise*. Reprinted with the permission of the publisher of *Paradise* (New York: Grove/Atlantic, Inc., 1990).

Lucha Corpi: Chapter Two from *Eulogy for a Brown Angel*. Reprinted with the permission of the publisher of *Eulogy for a Brown Angel* (Arte Público Press, 1992).

Beatriz de la Garza: "Margarita." Reprinted with permission of the publisher of *The Candy Vendor's Boy and Other Stories* (Arte Público Press, 1994).

Margarita Engle: "Buenaventura and the Fifteen Sisters" and "Cimarrón." Printed with permission from the author.

Paula María Espinosa: "Three Day Flight." Printed with permission from the author.

Roberta Fernández: "Zulema." Reprinted with the permission of the publisher of *Intaglio: A Novel in Six Stories* (Arte Público Press, 1990).

Linda Feyder: "Marta del Angel." Printed with permission from the author. First published in *The Americas Review* 19.3 (1991):29-33.

Alicia Gaspar de Alba: "Cimarrona." Reprinted with the permission of the publisher of *The Mystery of Survival and Other Stories* (Tempe, Az: Bilingual Press, 1993).

Nora Glickman: "A Day in New York." Printed with the permission of the author.

Aurora Levins Morales: "A Remedy for Heartburn." Printed with the permission of the author. First published in *Ms Magazine*.

Graciela Limón: Chapters I and II from *In Search of Bernabé*. Reprinted with the permission of the publisher of *In Search of Bernabé* (Arte Público Press, 1993).

Nicholasa Mohr: "Happy Birthday." Reprinted with the permission of the publisher of *Rituals of Survival: A Woman's Portfolio* (Arte Público Press, 1985).

Judith Ortiz Cofer: "Monologue of the Spanish Gentleman." Printed with the permission of the author. First published in *The Americas Review* XX:2 (Summer, 1992): 31-35.

Mary Helen Ponce: "Green? Or Red?" Printed with the permission of the author.

Estela Portillo Trambley: "The Burning." Reprinted with the permission of the publisher of *Rain of Scorpions and Other Stories* (Tempe, Az: Bilingual Press, 1993).

Bessy Reyna: "And This Blue Surroundind Me Again." Printed with the permission of the author.

Helena María Viramontes: "Growing" and "The Moths." Reprinted with the permission of the publisher of *The Moths and Other Stories* (Arte Público Press, 1985).

Part Four—Drama

Dolores Prida: "Beautiful Señoritas." Reprinted with the permission of the publisher of *Beautiful Señoritas and Other Plays* (Arte Público Press, 1991).